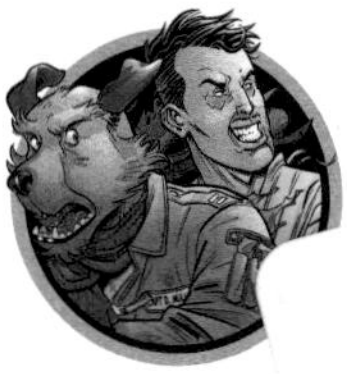

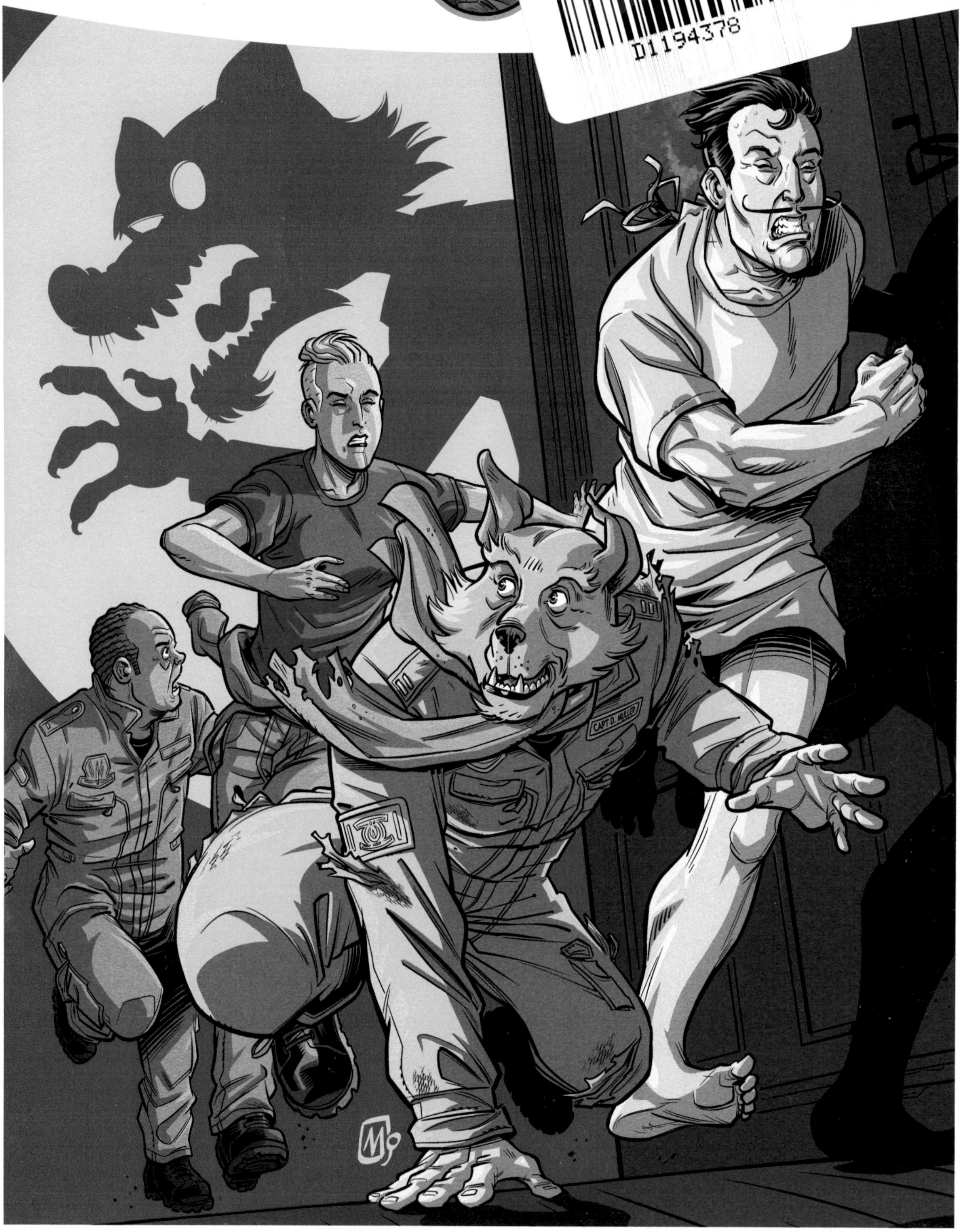
CAPT. D. MULLER

DASTARDLY & MUTTLEY

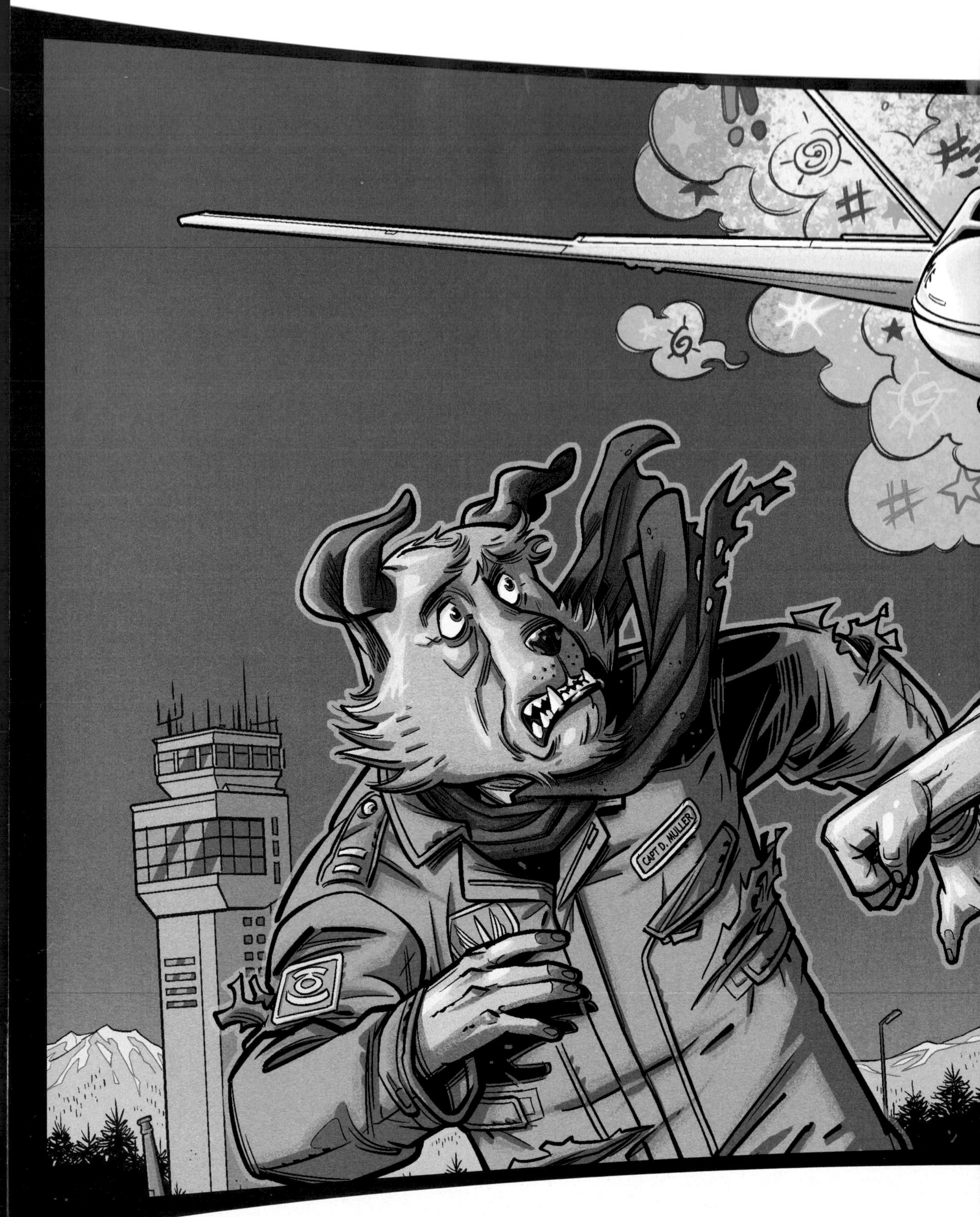
CAPT D. MULLER

DASTARDLY & MUTTLEY

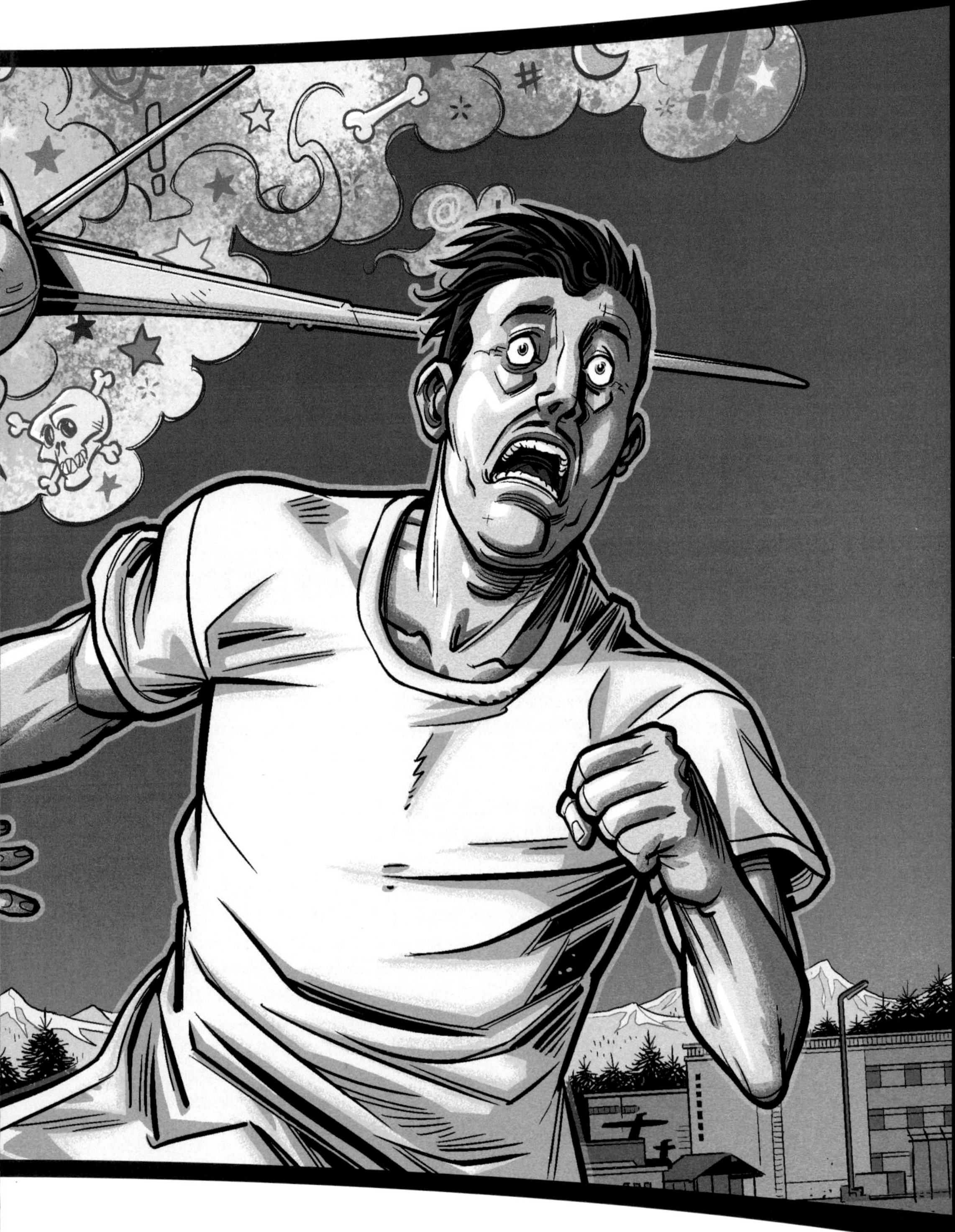

GARTH ENNIS writer
MAURICET artist
JOHN KALISZ colorist
ROB STEEN letterer
collection and original series cover art by **MAURICET**

MARIE JAVINS Editor – Original Series
BRITTANY HOLZHERR Associate Editor – Original Series DIEGO LOPEZ Assistant Editor – Original Series
JEB WOODARD Group Editor – Collected Editions SCOTT NYBAKKEN Editor – Collected Edition
STEVE COOK Design Director – Books DAMIAN RYLAND Publication Design

BOB HARRAS Senior VP – Editor-in-Chief, DC Comics
PAT McCALLUM Executive Editor, DC Comics

DIANE NELSON President DAN DiDIO Publisher JIM LEE Publisher GEOFF JOHNS President & Chief Creative Officer
AMIT DESAI Executive VP – Business & Marketing Strategy, Direct to Consumer & Global Franchise Management
SAM ADES Senior VP & General Manager, Digital Services BOBBIE CHASE VP & Executive Editor, Young Reader & Talent Development
MARK CHIARELLO Senior VP – Art, Design & Collected Editions JOHN CUNNINGHAM Senior VP – Sales & Trade Marketing
ANNE DePIES Senior VP – Business Strategy, Finance & Administration DON FALLETTI VP – Manufacturing Operations
LAWRENCE GANEM VP – Editorial Administration & Talent Relations ALISON GILL Senior VP – Manufacturing & Operations
HANK KANALZ Senior VP – Editorial Strategy & Administration JAY KOGAN VP – Legal Affairs JACK MAHAN VP – Business Affairs
NICK J. NAPOLITANO VP – Manufacturing Administration EDDIE SCANNELL VP – Consumer Marketing
COURTNEY SIMMONS Senior VP – Publicity & Communications JIM (SKI) SOKOLOWSKI VP – Comic Book Specialty Sales & Trade Marketing
NANCY SPEARS VP – Mass, Book, Digital Sales & Trade Marketing MICHELE R. WELLS VP – Content Strategy

DASTARDLY & MUTTLEY

Published by DC Comics. Compilation and all new material Copyright © 2018 Hanna-Barbera. All Rights Reserved. Originally published in single magazine form in DASTARDLY & MUTTLEY 1-6.
Copyright © 2017, 2018 Hanna-Barbera. All Rights Reserved. All characters, their distinctive likenesses and related elements featured in this publication are trademarks of Hanna-Barbera.
The stories, characters and incidents featured in this publication are entirely fictional. DC Comics does not read or accept unsolicited submissions of ideas, stories or artwork.

DC LOGO © & ™ DC Comics.

DC Comics, 2900 West Alameda Ave., Burbank, CA 91505. Printed by LSC Communications, Kendallville, IN, USA. 4/6/18. First Printing. ISBN: 978-1-4012-7461-0

Library of Congress Cataloging-in-Publication Data is available.

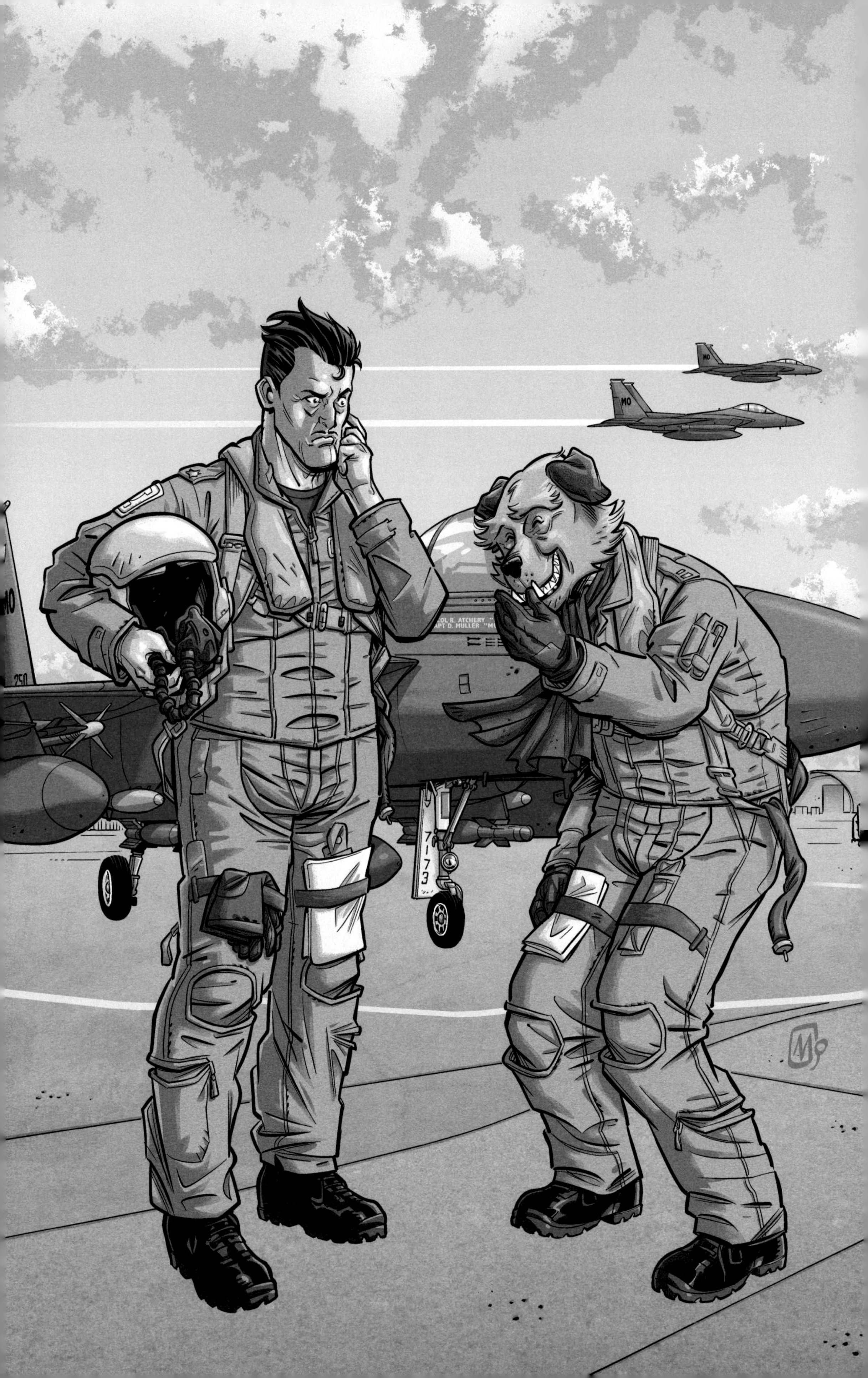
MO
MO
R. ATCHERY
D. MULLER
7-173

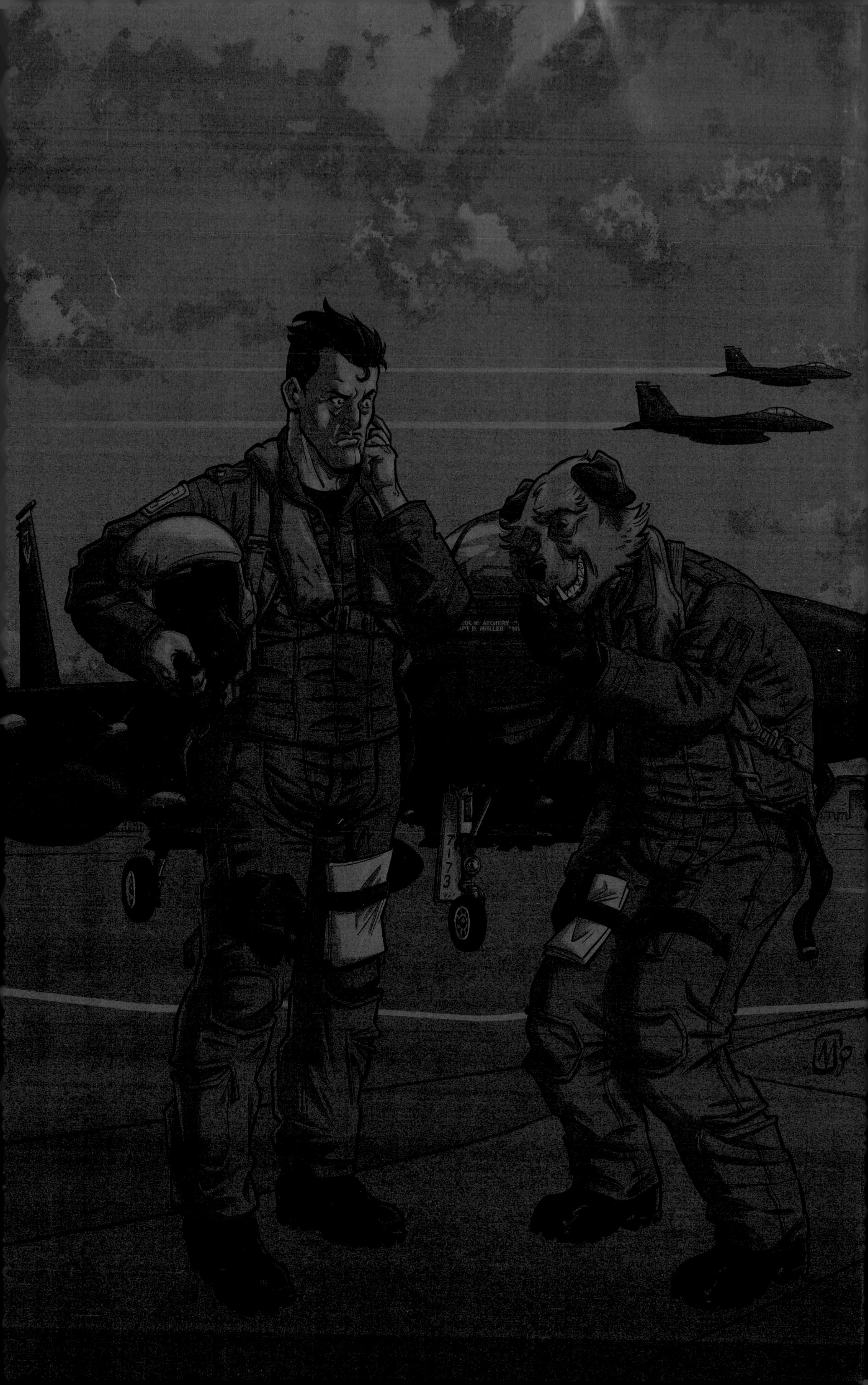

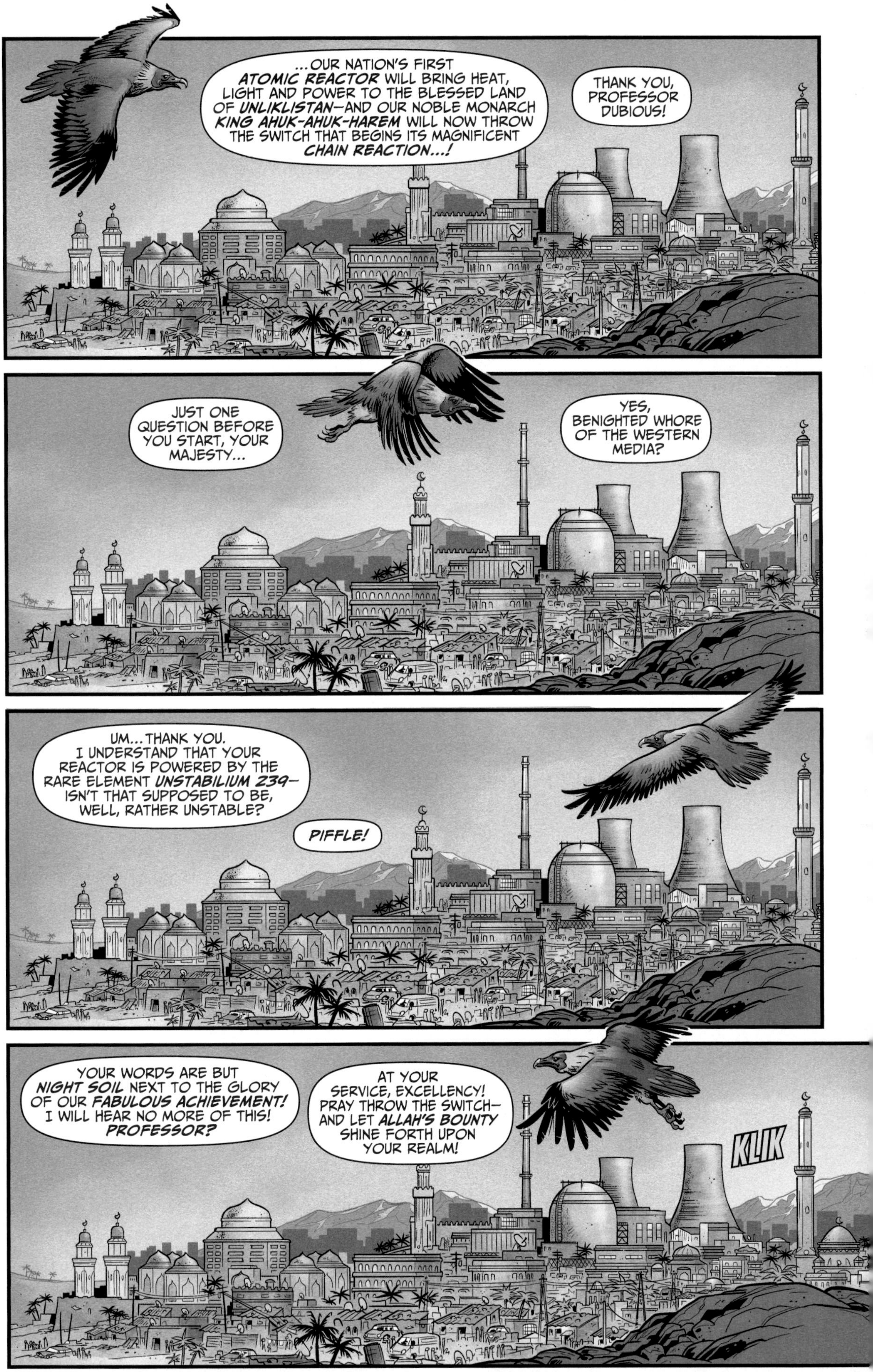
...OUR NATION'S FIRST ATOMIC REACTOR WILL BRING HEAT, LIGHT AND POWER TO THE BLESSED LAND OF UNLIKLISTAN—AND OUR NOBLE MONARCH KING AHUK-AHUK-HAREM WILL NOW THROW THE SWITCH THAT BEGINS ITS MAGNIFICENT CHAIN REACTION...!
THANK YOU, PROFESSOR DUBIOUS!
JUST ONE QUESTION BEFORE YOU START, YOUR MAJESTY...
YES, BENIGHTED WHORE OF THE WESTERN MEDIA?
UM...THANK YOU. I UNDERSTAND THAT YOUR REACTOR IS POWERED BY THE RARE ELEMENT UNSTABILIUM 239—ISN'T THAT SUPPOSED TO BE, WELL, RATHER UNSTABLE?
PIFFLE!
YOUR WORDS ARE BUT NIGHT SOIL NEXT TO THE GLORY OF OUR FABULOUS ACHIEVEMENT! I WILL HEAR NO MORE OF THIS! PROFESSOR?
AT YOUR SERVICE, EXCELLENCY! PRAY THROW THE SWITCH—AND LET ALLAH'S BOUNTY SHINE FORTH UPON YOUR REALM!
KLIK

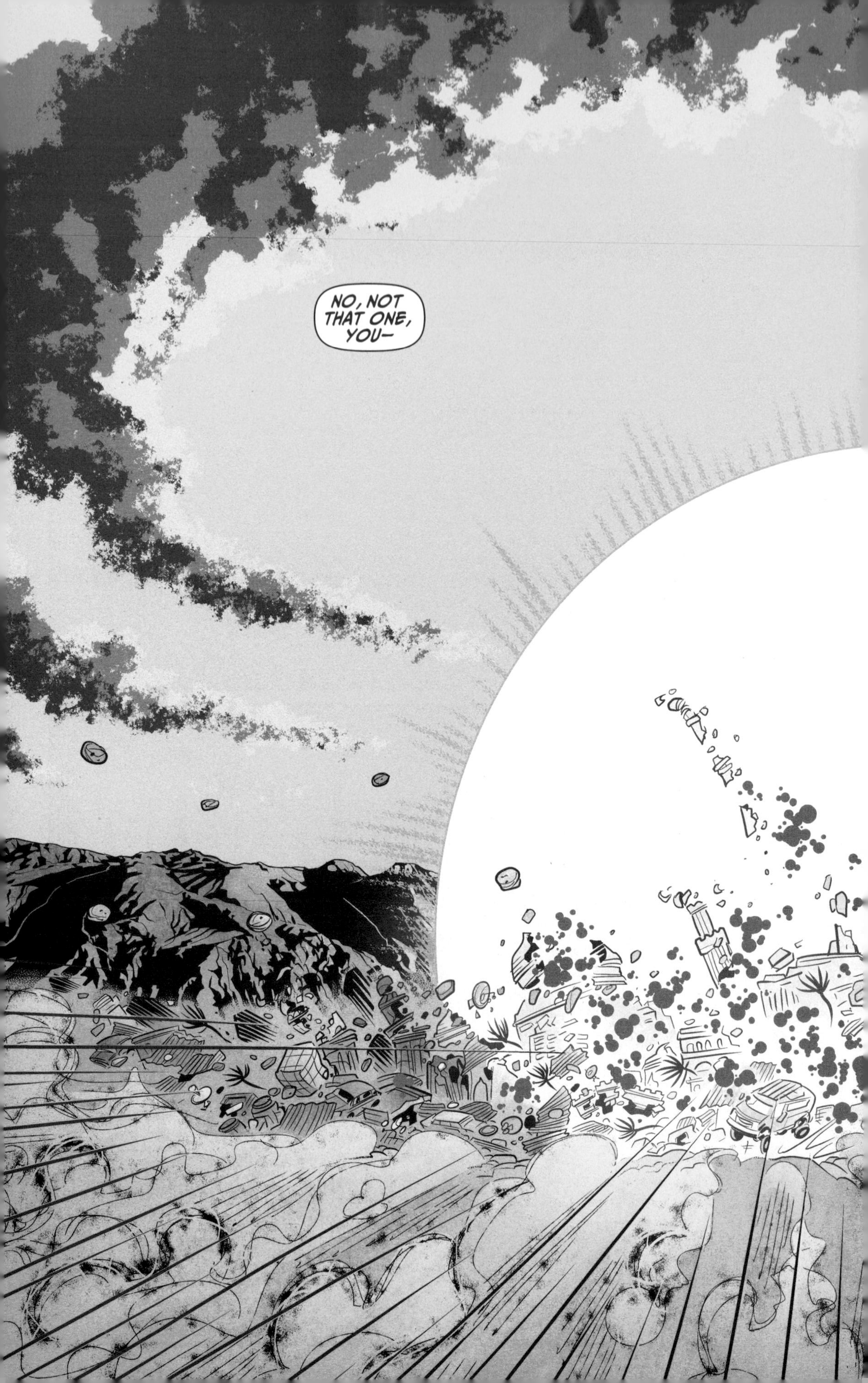
NO, NOT THAT ONE, YOU—

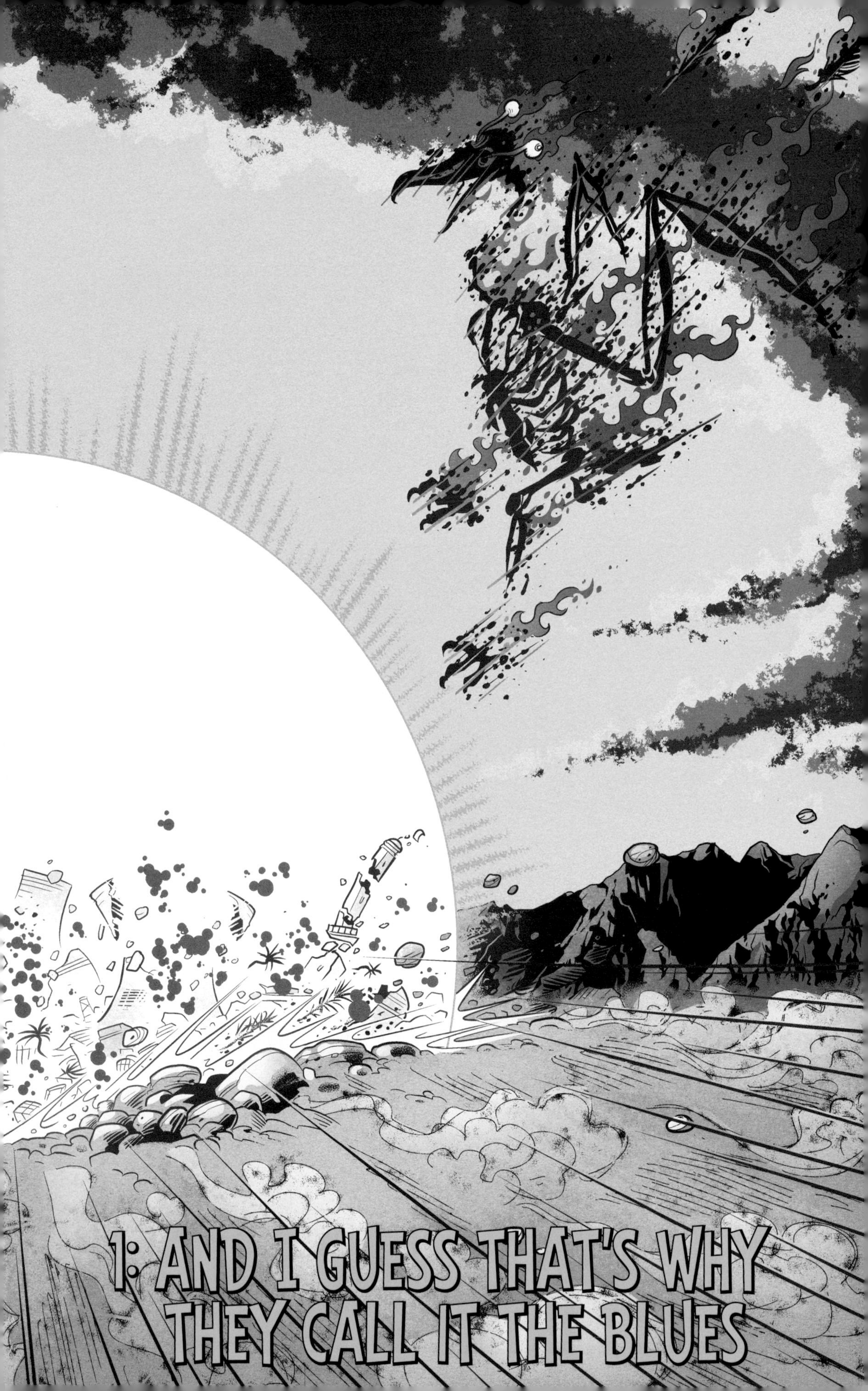
1: AND I GUESS THAT'S WHY
THEY CALL IT THE BLUES

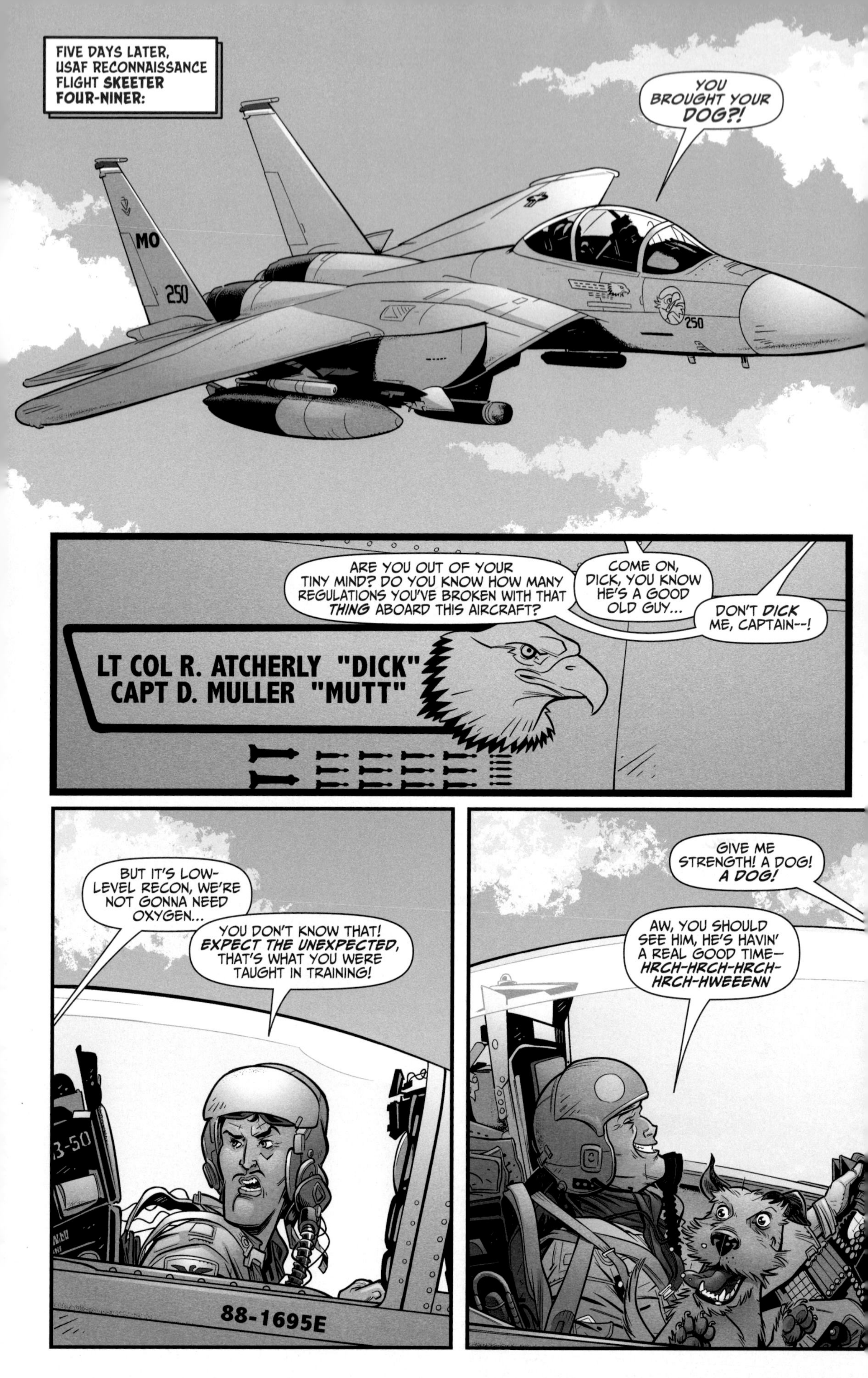
FIVE DAYS LATER, USAF RECONNAISSANCE FLIGHT SKEETER FOUR-NINER:
YOU BROUGHT YOUR DOG?!
MO
250
250
ARE YOU OUT OF YOUR TINY MIND? DO YOU KNOW HOW MANY REGULATIONS YOU'VE BROKEN WITH THAT THING ABOARD THIS AIRCRAFT?
COME ON, DICK, YOU KNOW HE'S A GOOD OLD GUY...
DON'T DICK ME, CAPTAIN--!
LT COL R. ATCHERLY "DICK"
CAPT D. MULLER "MUTT"
BUT IT'S LOW-LEVEL RECON, WE'RE NOT GONNA NEED OXYGEN...
YOU DON'T KNOW THAT! EXPECT THE UNEXPECTED, THAT'S WHAT YOU WERE TAUGHT IN TRAINING!
88-1695E
GIVE ME STRENGTH! A DOG! A DOG!
AW, YOU SHOULD SEE HIM, HE'S HAVIN' A REAL GOOD TIME— HRCH-HRCH-HRCH-HRCH-HWEEENN

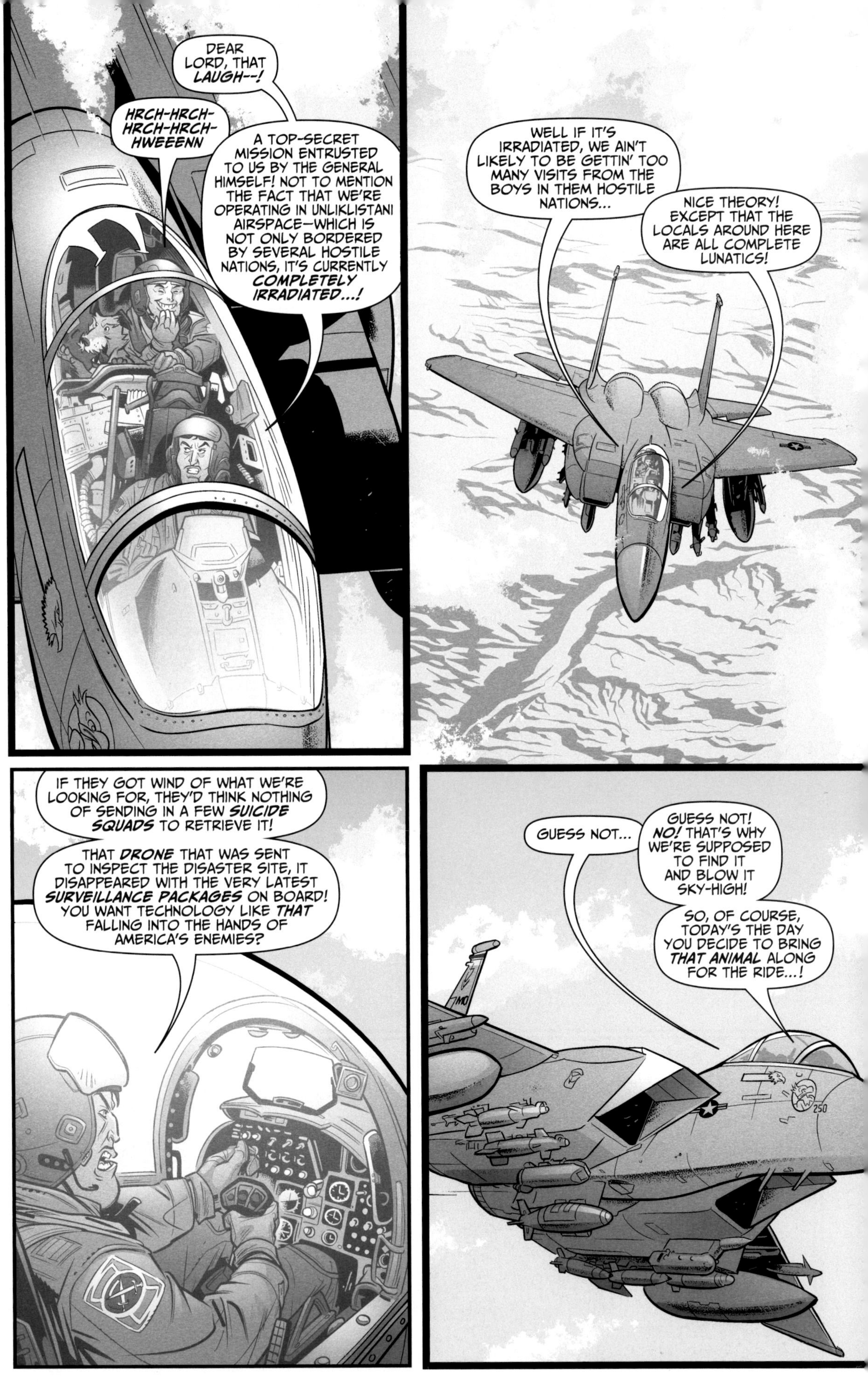
DEAR LORD, THAT LAUGH--!
HRCH-HRCH-HRCH-HRCH-HWEEENN
A TOP-SECRET MISSION ENTRUSTED TO US BY THE GENERAL HIMSELF! NOT TO MENTION THE FACT THAT WE'RE OPERATING IN UNLIKLISTANI AIRSPACE—WHICH IS NOT ONLY BORDERED BY SEVERAL HOSTILE NATIONS, IT'S CURRENTLY COMPLETELY IRRADIATED...!
WELL IF IT'S IRRADIATED, WE AIN'T LIKELY TO BE GETTIN' TOO MANY VISITS FROM THE BOYS IN THEM HOSTILE NATIONS...
NICE THEORY! EXCEPT THAT THE LOCALS AROUND HERE ARE ALL COMPLETE LUNATICS!
IF THEY GOT WIND OF WHAT WE'RE LOOKING FOR, THEY'D THINK NOTHING OF SENDING IN A FEW SUICIDE SQUADS TO RETRIEVE IT!
THAT DRONE THAT WAS SENT TO INSPECT THE DISASTER SITE, IT DISAPPEARED WITH THE VERY LATEST SURVEILLANCE PACKAGES ON BOARD! YOU WANT TECHNOLOGY LIKE THAT FALLING INTO THE HANDS OF AMERICA'S ENEMIES?
GUESS NOT...
GUESS NOT! NO! THAT'S WHY WE'RE SUPPOSED TO FIND IT AND BLOW IT SKY-HIGH!
SO, OF COURSE, TODAY'S THE DAY YOU DECIDE TO BRING THAT ANIMAL ALONG FOR THE RIDE...!
250

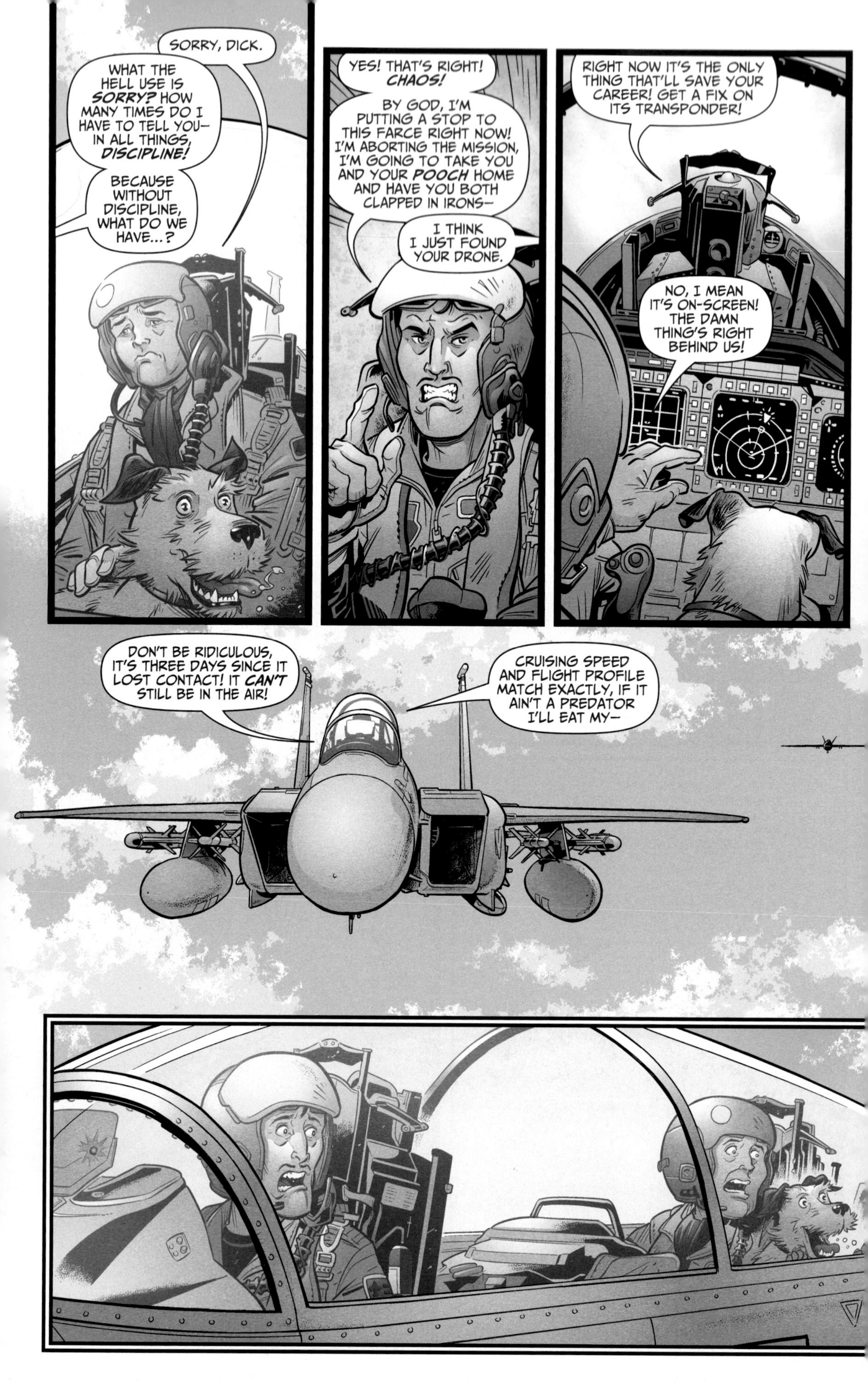
SORRY, DICK.
WHAT THE HELL USE IS SORRY? HOW MANY TIMES DO I HAVE TO TELL YOU— IN ALL THINGS, DISCIPLINE!
BECAUSE WITHOUT DISCIPLINE, WHAT DO WE HAVE...?
YES! THAT'S RIGHT! CHAOS!
BY GOD, I'M PUTTING A STOP TO THIS FARCE RIGHT NOW! I'M ABORTING THE MISSION, I'M GOING TO TAKE YOU AND YOUR POOCH HOME AND HAVE YOU BOTH CLAPPED IN IRONS—
I THINK I JUST FOUND YOUR DRONE.
RIGHT NOW IT'S THE ONLY THING THAT'LL SAVE YOUR CAREER! GET A FIX ON ITS TRANSPONDER!
NO, I MEAN IT'S ON-SCREEN! THE DAMN THING'S RIGHT BEHIND US!
DON'T BE RIDICULOUS, IT'S THREE DAYS SINCE IT LOST CONTACT! IT CAN'T STILL BE IN THE AIR!
CRUISING SPEED AND FLIGHT PROFILE MATCH EXACTLY, IF IT AIN'T A PREDATOR I'LL EAT MY—

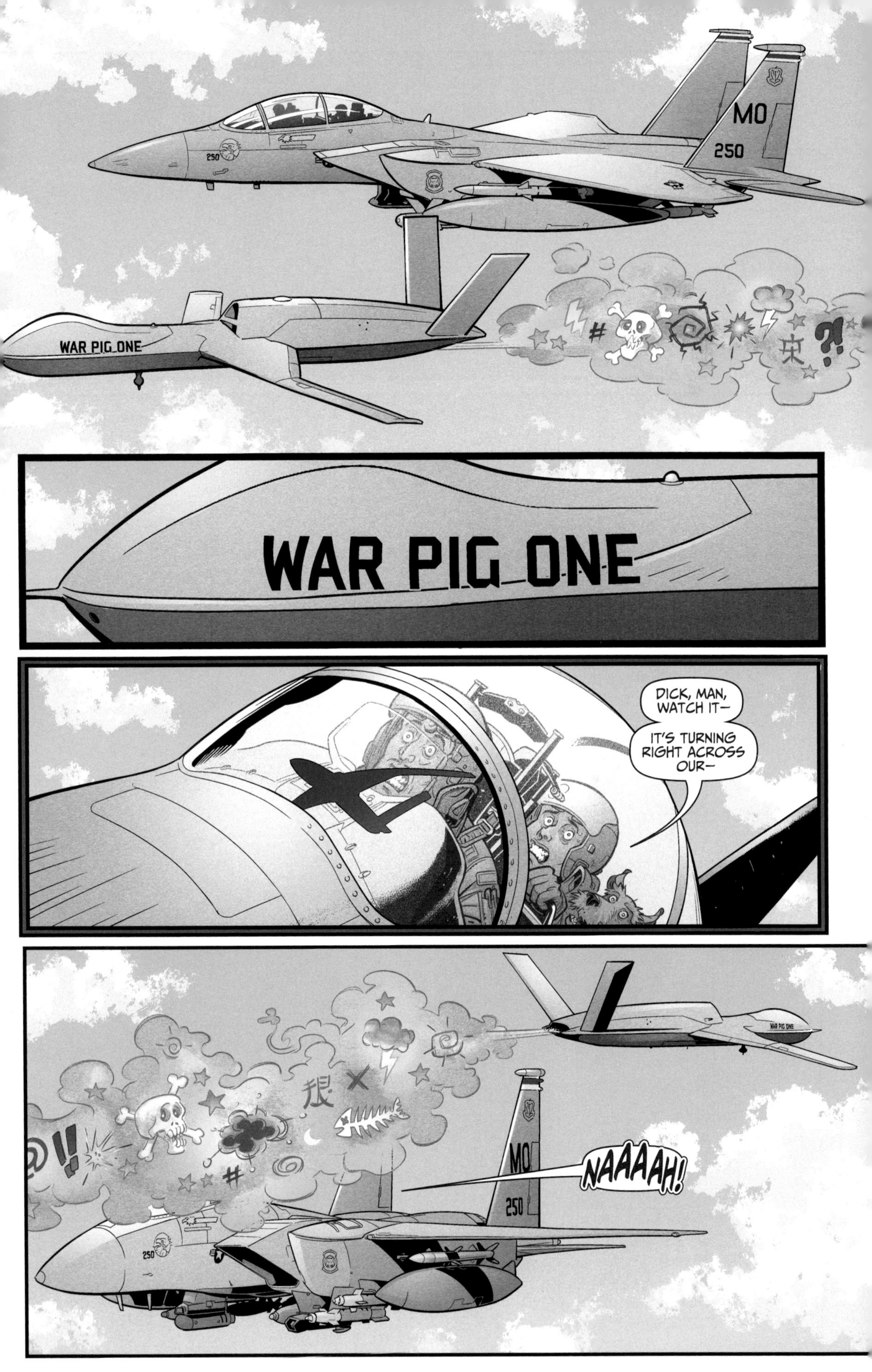
MO
250
WAR PIG ONE
WAR PIG ONE
DICK, MAN, WATCH IT—
IT'S TURNING RIGHT ACROSS OUR—
NAAAAH!

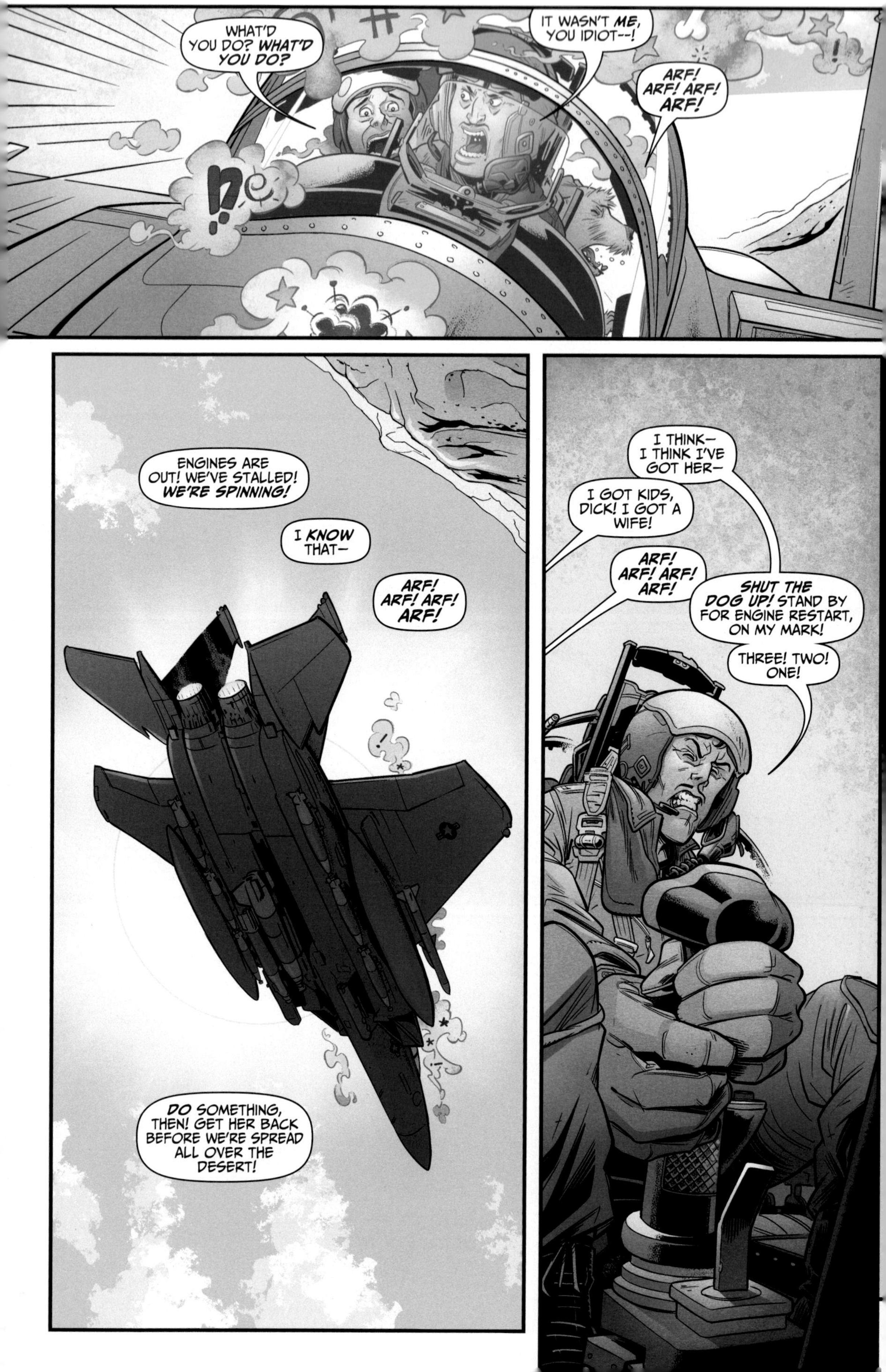
WHAT'D YOU DO? WHAT'D YOU DO?
IT WASN'T ME, YOU IDIOT--!
ARF! ARF! ARF! ARF!
ENGINES ARE OUT! WE'VE STALLED! WE'RE SPINNING!
I KNOW THAT—
ARF! ARF! ARF! ARF!
DO SOMETHING, THEN! GET HER BACK BEFORE WE'RE SPREAD ALL OVER THE DESERT!
I THINK— I THINK I'VE GOT HER—
I GOT KIDS, DICK! I GOT A WIFE!
ARF! ARF! ARF! ARF!
SHUT THE DOG UP! STAND BY FOR ENGINE RESTART, ON MY MARK!
THREE! TWO! ONE!

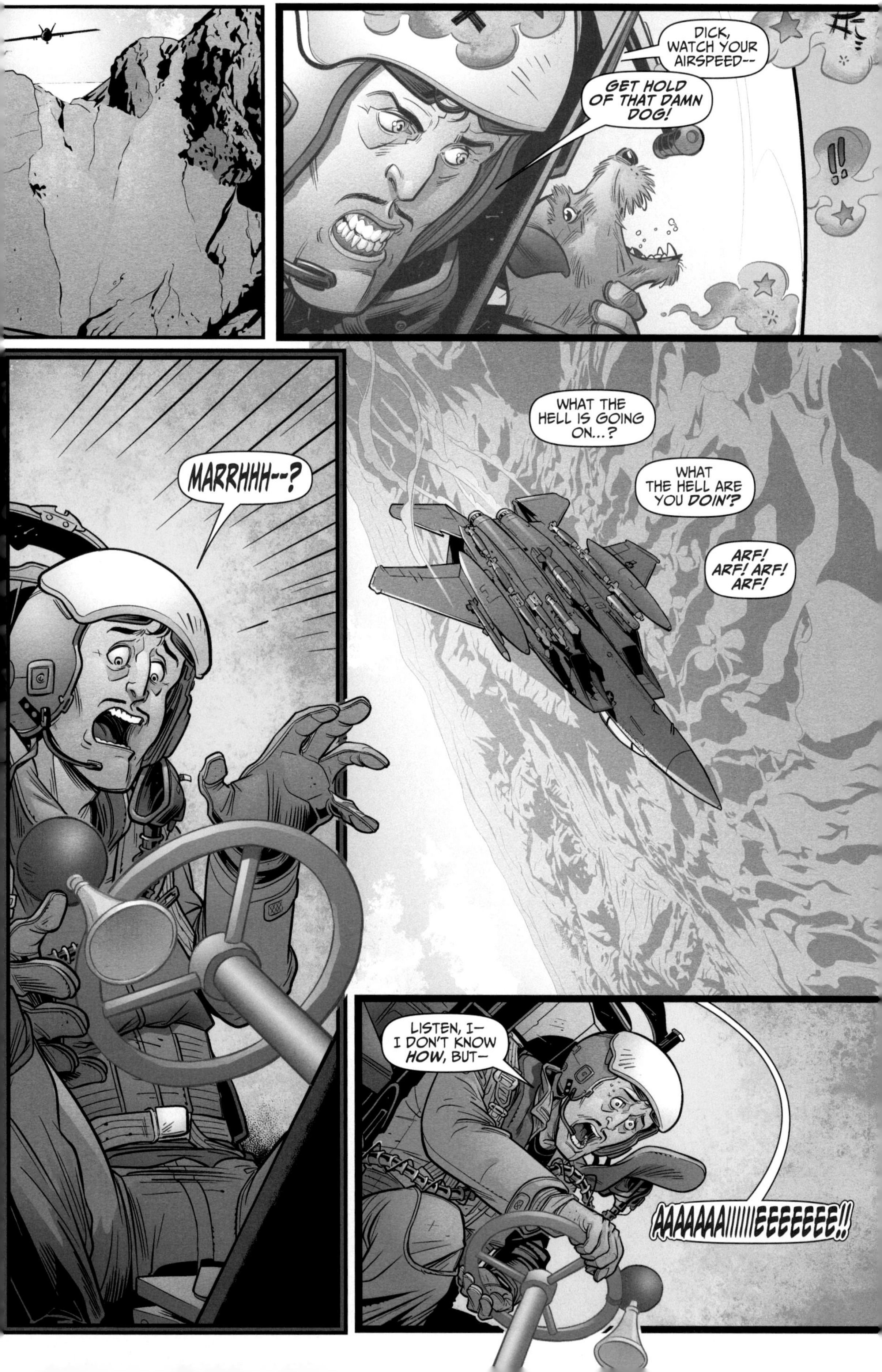
DICK, WATCH YOUR AIRSPEED--
GET HOLD OF THAT DAMN DOG!
MARRHHH--?
WHAT THE HELL IS GOING ON...?
WHAT THE HELL ARE YOU DOIN'?
ARF! ARF! ARF! ARF!
LISTEN, I— I DON'T KNOW HOW, BUT—
AAAAAAIIIIIIEEEEEEE!!

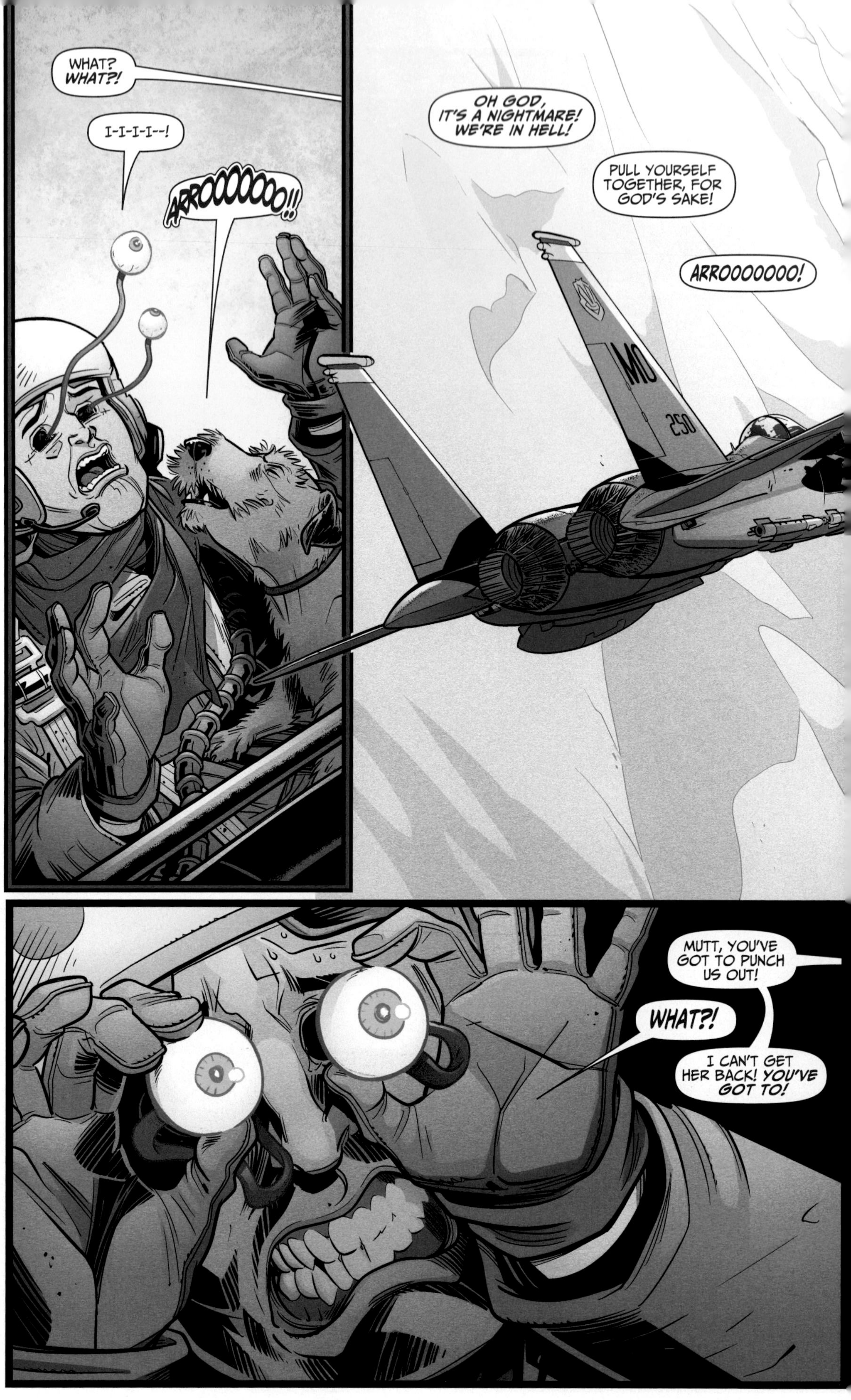
WHAT? WHAT?!
I-I-I-I--!
ARROOOOOOO!!
OH GOD, IT'S A NIGHTMARE! WE'RE IN HELL!
PULL YOURSELF TOGETHER, FOR GOD'S SAKE!
ARROOOOOOO!
MO
250
MUTT, YOU'VE GOT TO PUNCH US OUT!
WHAT?!
I CAN'T GET HER BACK! YOU'VE GOT TO!

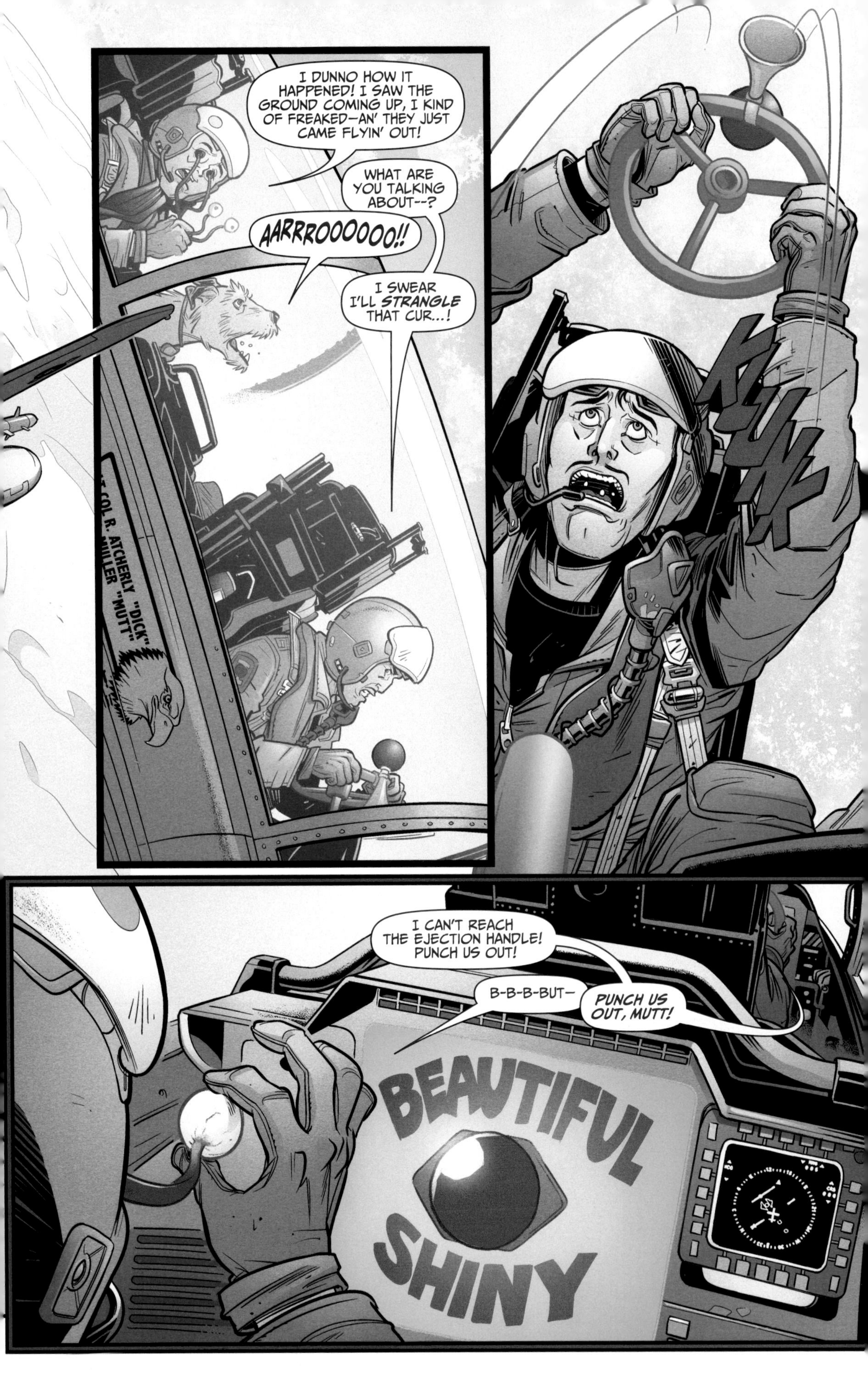
I DUNNO HOW IT HAPPENED! I SAW THE GROUND COMING UP, I KIND OF FREAKED—AN' THEY JUST CAME FLYIN' OUT!
WHAT ARE YOU TALKING ABOUT--?
AARROOOOOO!!
I SWEAR I'LL *STRANGLE* THAT CUR...!
KLUNK
I CAN'T REACH THE EJECTION HANDLE! PUNCH US OUT!
B-B-B-BUT—
PUNCH US OUT, MUTT!
BEAUTIFUL SHINY

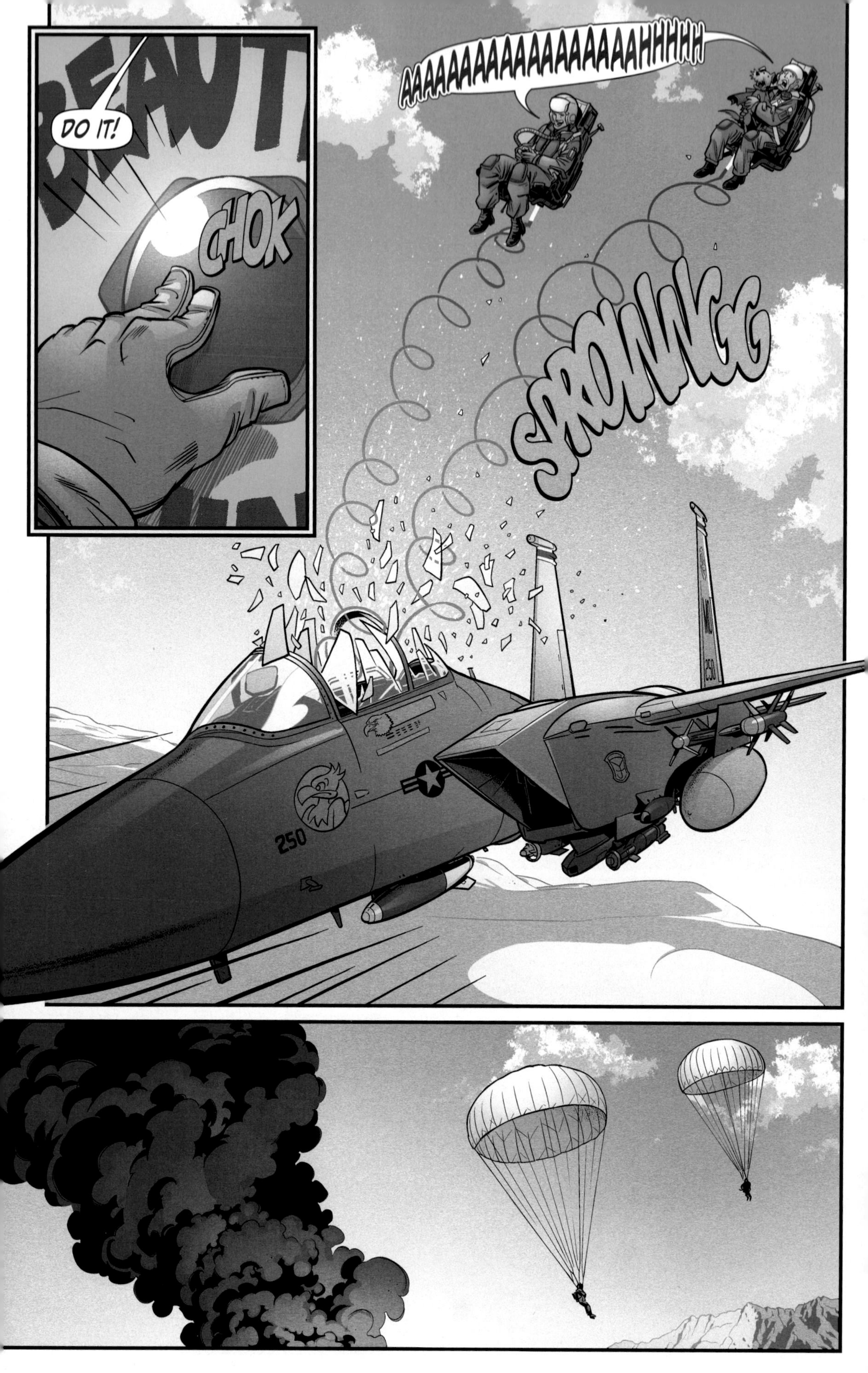
DO IT!
CHOK
AAAAAAAAAAAAAAAAHHHHH
SPRONNGG

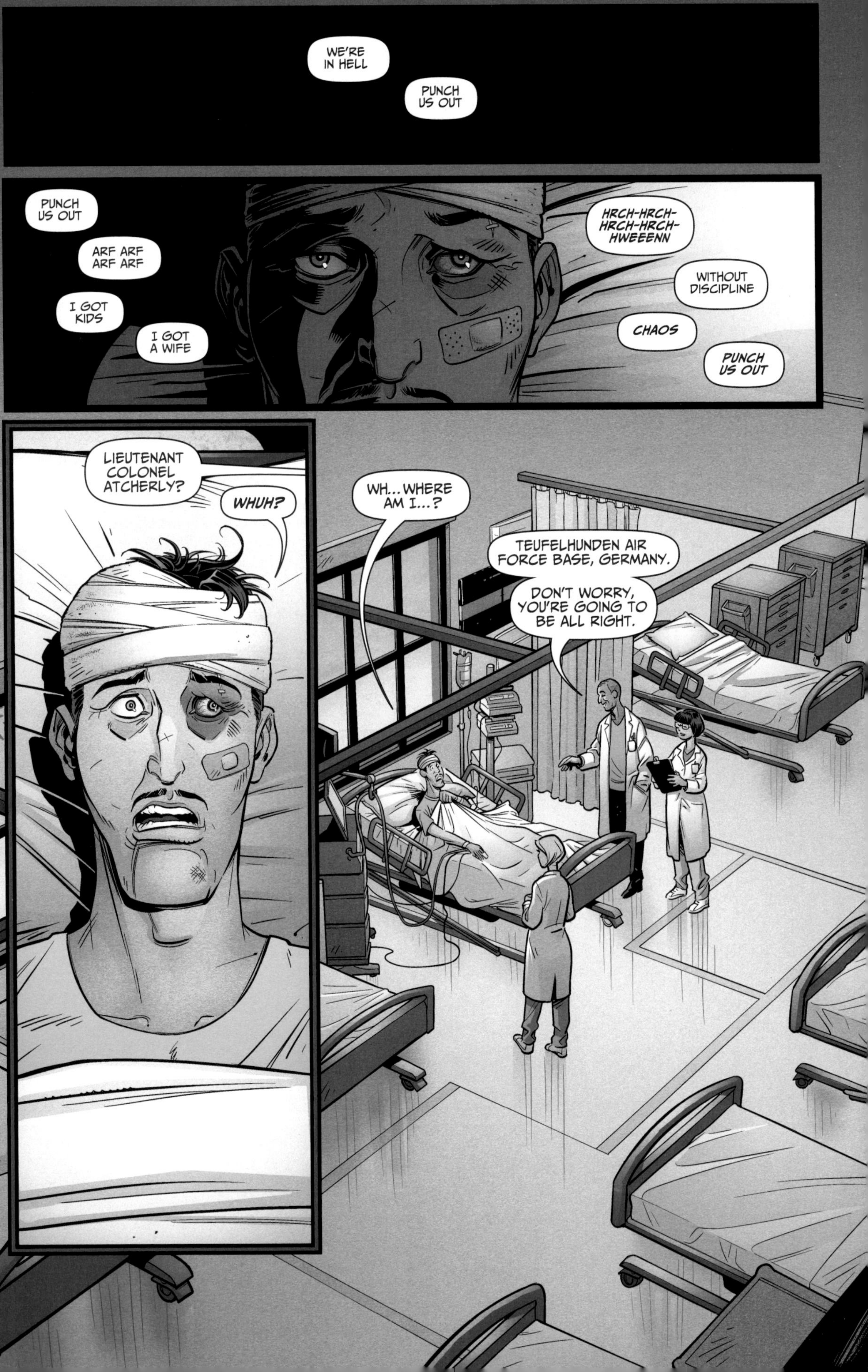
WE'RE IN HELL
PUNCH US OUT
PUNCH US OUT
ARF ARF ARF ARF
I GOT KIDS
I GOT A WIFE
HRCH-HRCH-HRCH-HRCH-HWEEENN
WITHOUT DISCIPLINE
CHAOS
PUNCH US OUT
LIEUTENANT COLONEL ATCHERLY?
WHUH?
WH...WHERE AM I...?
TEUFELHUNDEN AIR FORCE BASE, GERMANY.
DON'T WORRY, YOU'RE GOING TO BE ALL RIGHT.

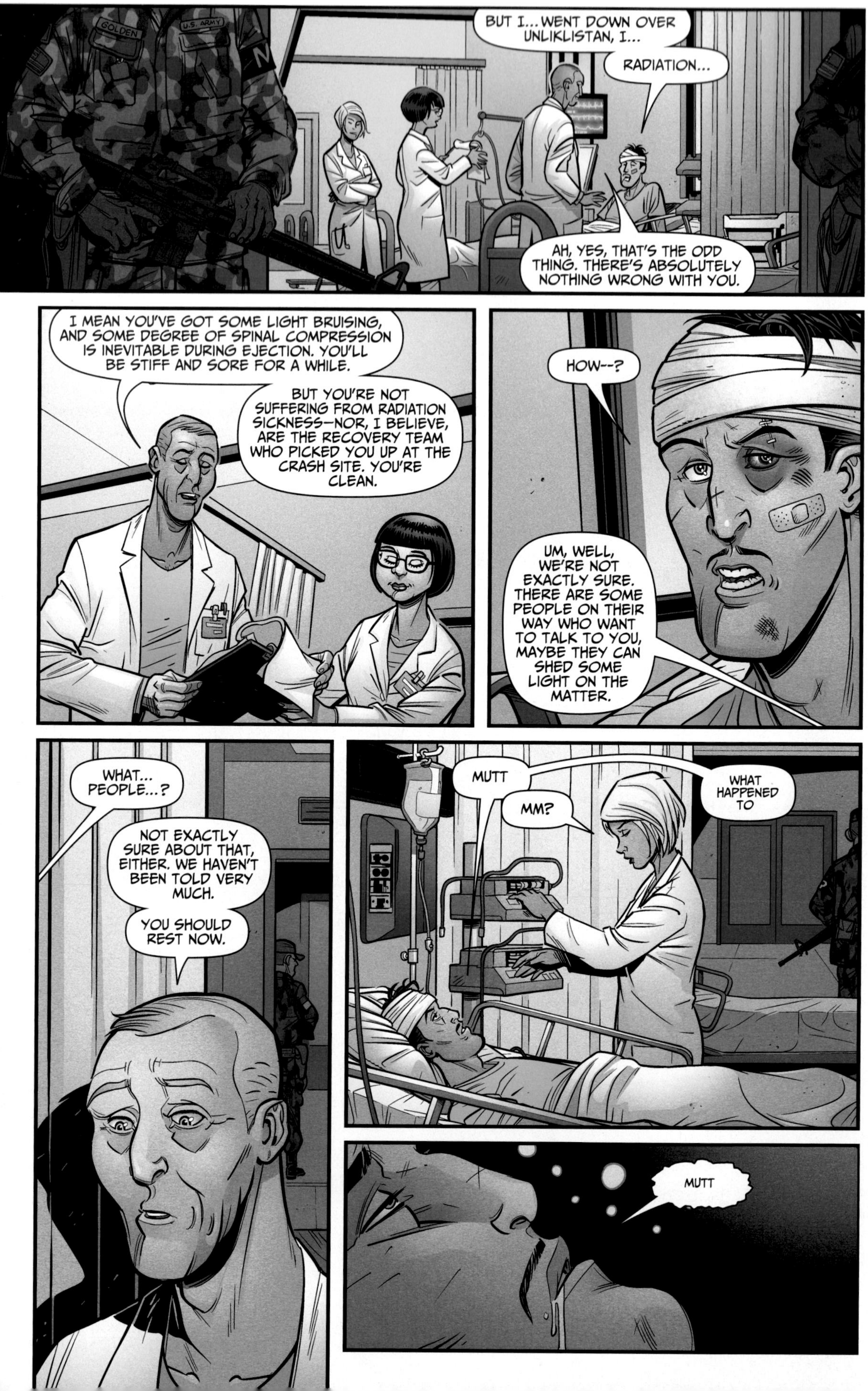
GOLDEN
U.S. ARMY
BUT I...WENT DOWN OVER UNLIKLISTAN, I...
RADIATION...
AH, YES, THAT'S THE ODD THING. THERE'S ABSOLUTELY NOTHING WRONG WITH YOU.
I MEAN YOU'VE GOT SOME LIGHT BRUISING, AND SOME DEGREE OF SPINAL COMPRESSION IS INEVITABLE DURING EJECTION. YOU'LL BE STIFF AND SORE FOR A WHILE.
BUT YOU'RE NOT SUFFERING FROM RADIATION SICKNESS--NOR, I BELIEVE, ARE THE RECOVERY TEAM WHO PICKED YOU UP AT THE CRASH SITE. YOU'RE CLEAN.
HOW--?
UM, WELL, WE'RE NOT EXACTLY SURE. THERE ARE SOME PEOPLE ON THEIR WAY WHO WANT TO TALK TO YOU, MAYBE THEY CAN SHED SOME LIGHT ON THE MATTER.
WHAT... PEOPLE...?
NOT EXACTLY SURE ABOUT THAT, EITHER. WE HAVEN'T BEEN TOLD VERY MUCH.
YOU SHOULD REST NOW.
WHAT HAPPENED TO
MM?
MUTT
MUTT

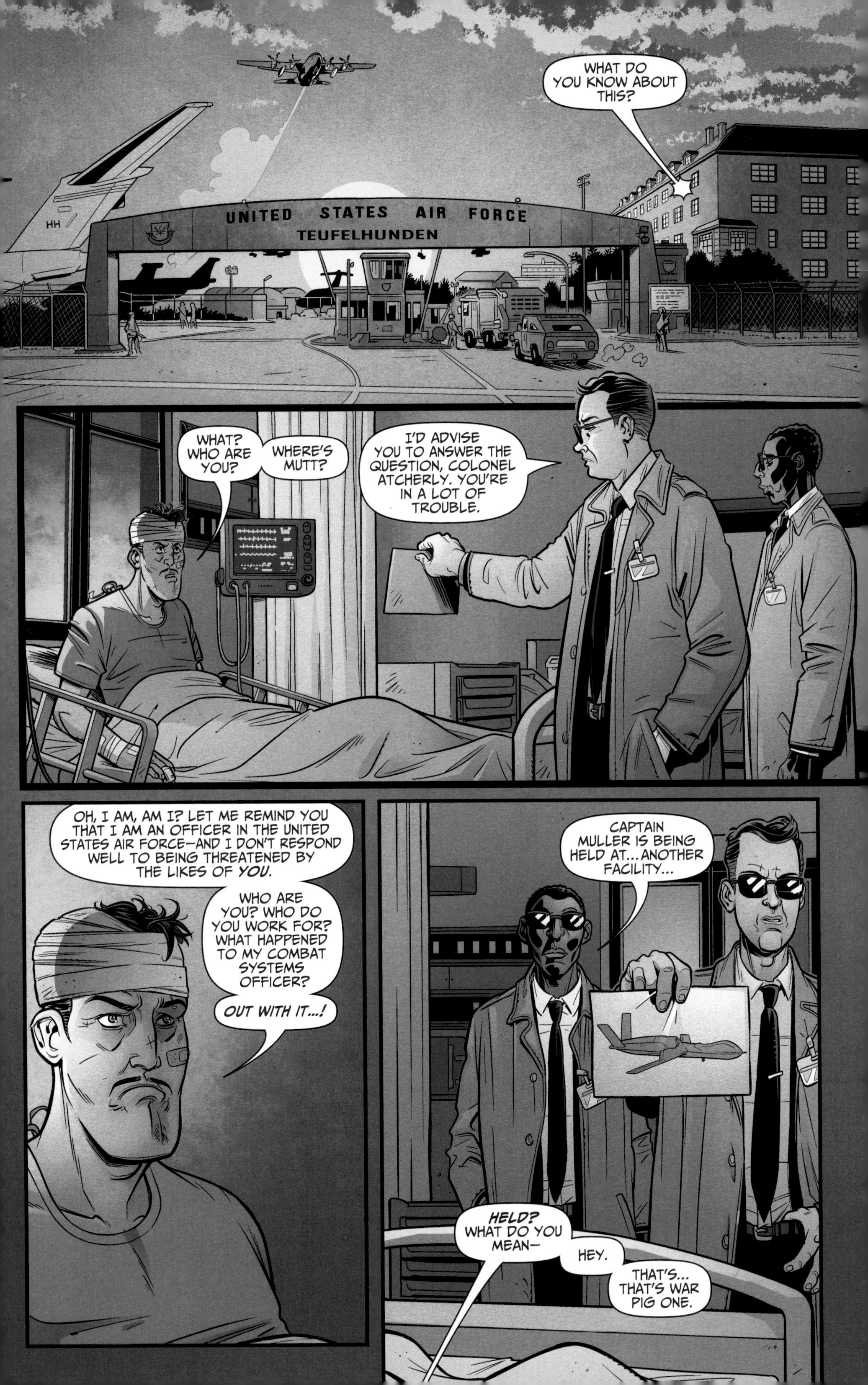
WHAT DO YOU KNOW ABOUT THIS?
UNITED STATES AIR FORCE
TEUFELHUNDEN
WHAT? WHO ARE YOU?
WHERE'S MUTT?
I'D ADVISE YOU TO ANSWER THE QUESTION, COLONEL ATCHERLY. YOU'RE IN A LOT OF TROUBLE.
OH, I AM, AM I? LET ME REMIND YOU THAT I AM AN OFFICER IN THE UNITED STATES AIR FORCE—AND I DON'T RESPOND WELL TO BEING THREATENED BY THE LIKES OF *YOU*.
WHO ARE YOU? WHO DO YOU WORK FOR? WHAT HAPPENED TO MY COMBAT SYSTEMS OFFICER?
OUT WITH IT...!
CAPTAIN MULLER IS BEING HELD AT...ANOTHER FACILITY...
HELD? WHAT DO YOU MEAN—
HEY.
THAT'S... THAT'S WAR PIG ONE.

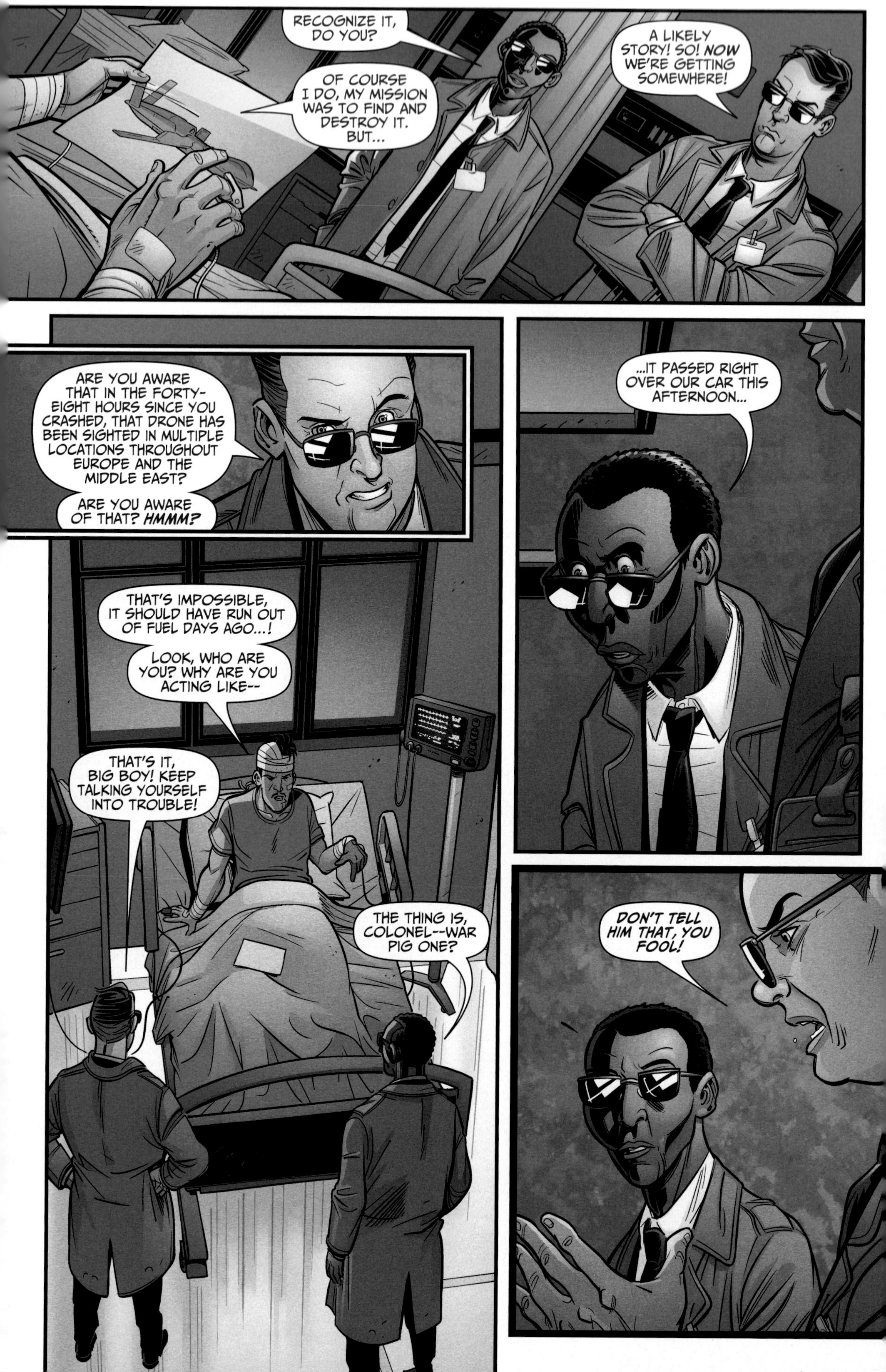
RECOGNIZE IT, DO YOU?
OF COURSE I DO, MY MISSION WAS TO FIND AND DESTROY IT. BUT...
A LIKELY STORY! SO! NOW WE'RE GETTING SOMEWHERE!
ARE YOU AWARE THAT IN THE FORTY-EIGHT HOURS SINCE YOU CRASHED, THAT DRONE HAS BEEN SIGHTED IN MULTIPLE LOCATIONS THROUGHOUT EUROPE AND THE MIDDLE EAST?
ARE YOU AWARE OF THAT? HMMM?
THAT'S IMPOSSIBLE, IT SHOULD HAVE RUN OUT OF FUEL DAYS AGO...!
LOOK, WHO ARE YOU? WHY ARE YOU ACTING LIKE--
THAT'S IT, BIG BOY! KEEP TALKING YOURSELF INTO TROUBLE!
THE THING IS, COLONEL--WAR PIG ONE?
...IT PASSED RIGHT OVER OUR CAR THIS AFTERNOON...
DON'T TELL HIM THAT, YOU FOOL!

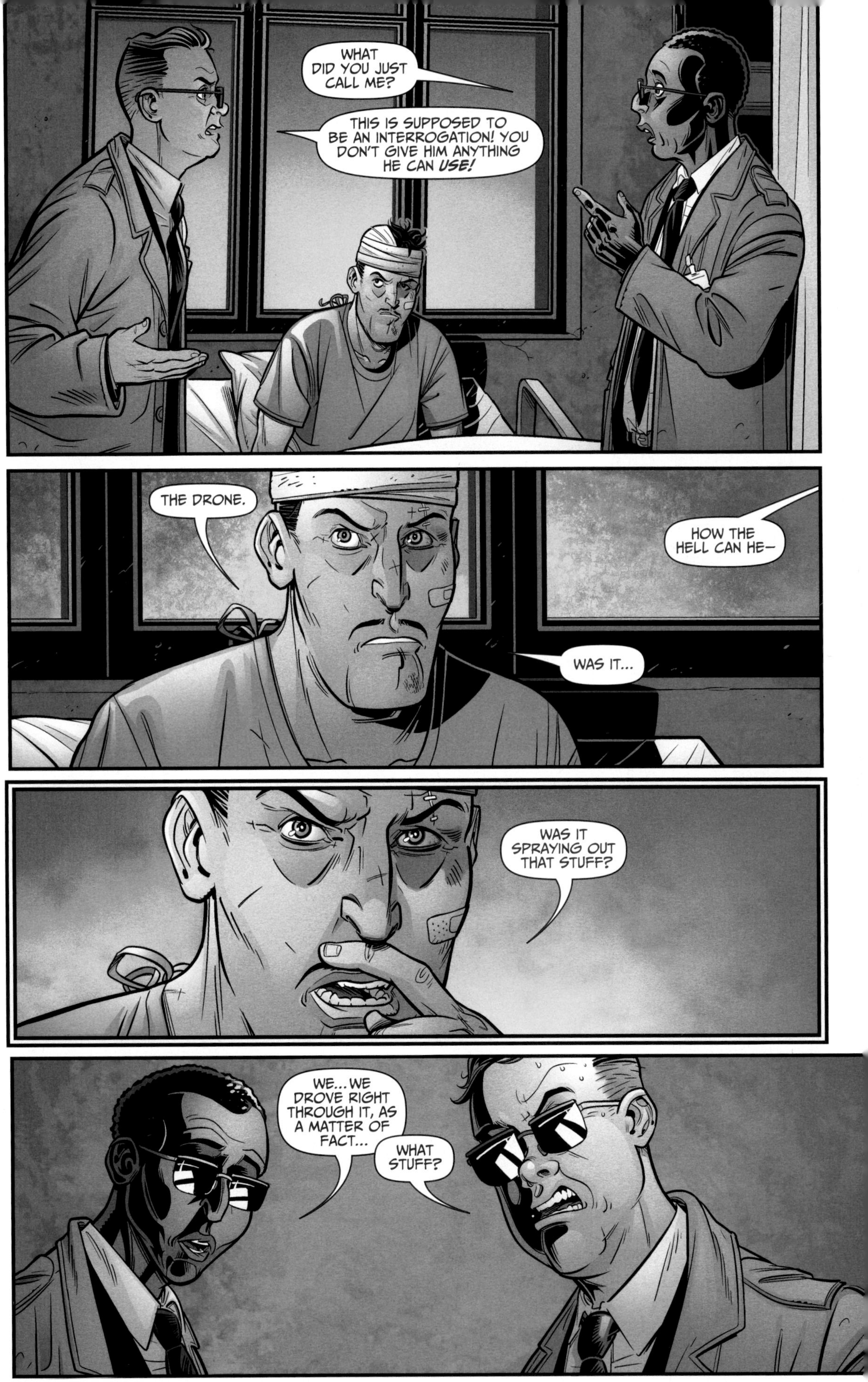
WHAT DID YOU JUST CALL ME?
THIS IS SUPPOSED TO BE AN INTERROGATION! YOU DON'T GIVE HIM ANYTHING HE CAN *USE!*
THE DRONE.
HOW THE HELL CAN HE—
WAS IT...
WAS IT SPRAYING OUT THAT STUFF?
WE...WE DROVE RIGHT THROUGH IT, AS A MATTER OF FACT...
WHAT STUFF?

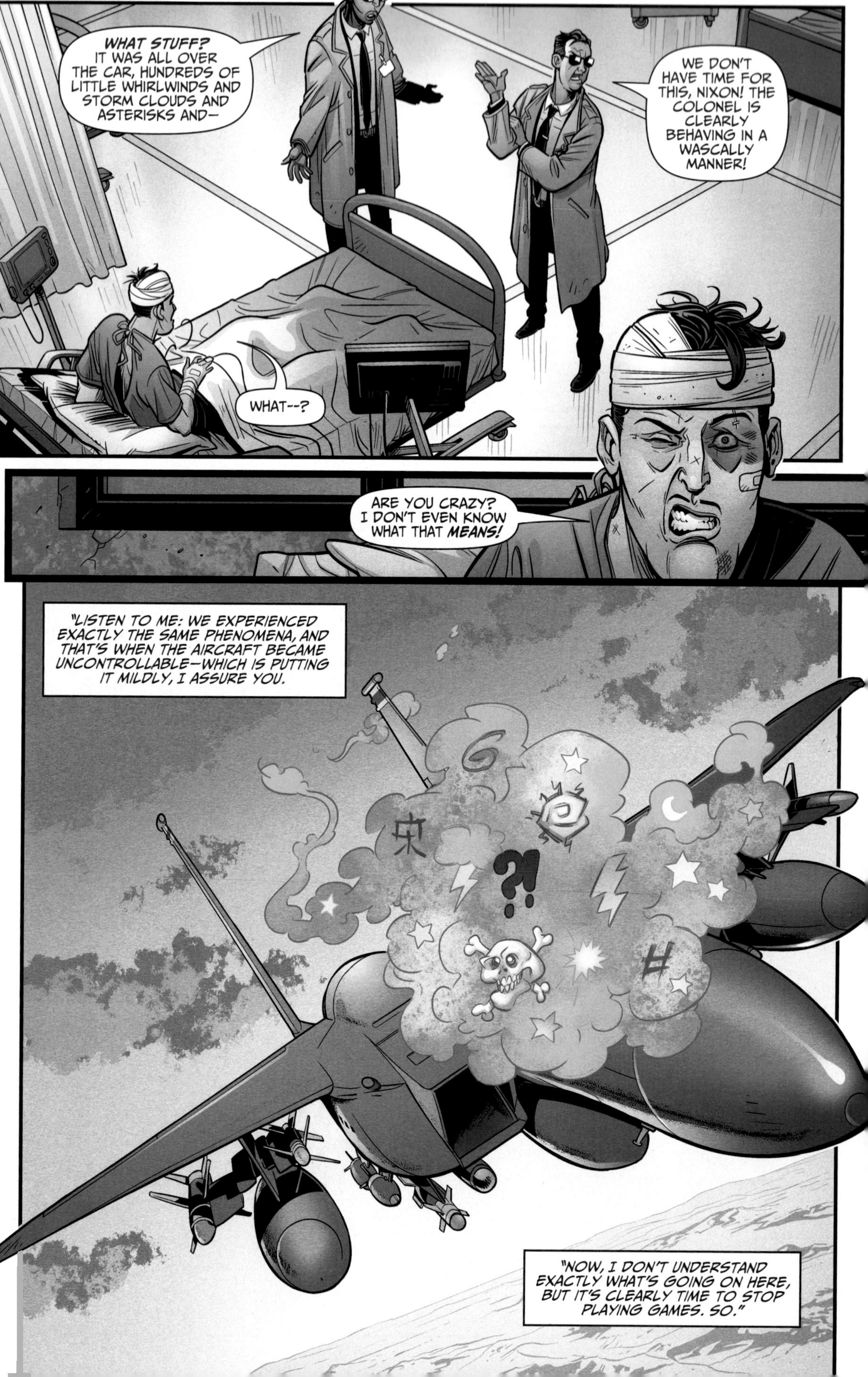
WHAT STUFF? IT WAS ALL OVER THE CAR, HUNDREDS OF LITTLE WHIRLWINDS AND STORM CLOUDS AND ASTERISKS AND—
WE DON'T HAVE TIME FOR THIS, NIXON! THE COLONEL IS CLEARLY BEHAVING IN A WASCALLY MANNER!
WHAT--?
ARE YOU CRAZY? I DON'T EVEN KNOW WHAT THAT MEANS!
"LISTEN TO ME: WE EXPERIENCED EXACTLY THE SAME PHENOMENA, AND THAT'S WHEN THE AIRCRAFT BECAME UNCONTROLLABLE—WHICH IS PUTTING IT MILDLY, I ASSURE YOU.
"NOW, I DON'T UNDERSTAND EXACTLY WHAT'S GOING ON HERE, BUT IT'S CLEARLY TIME TO STOP PLAYING GAMES. SO."

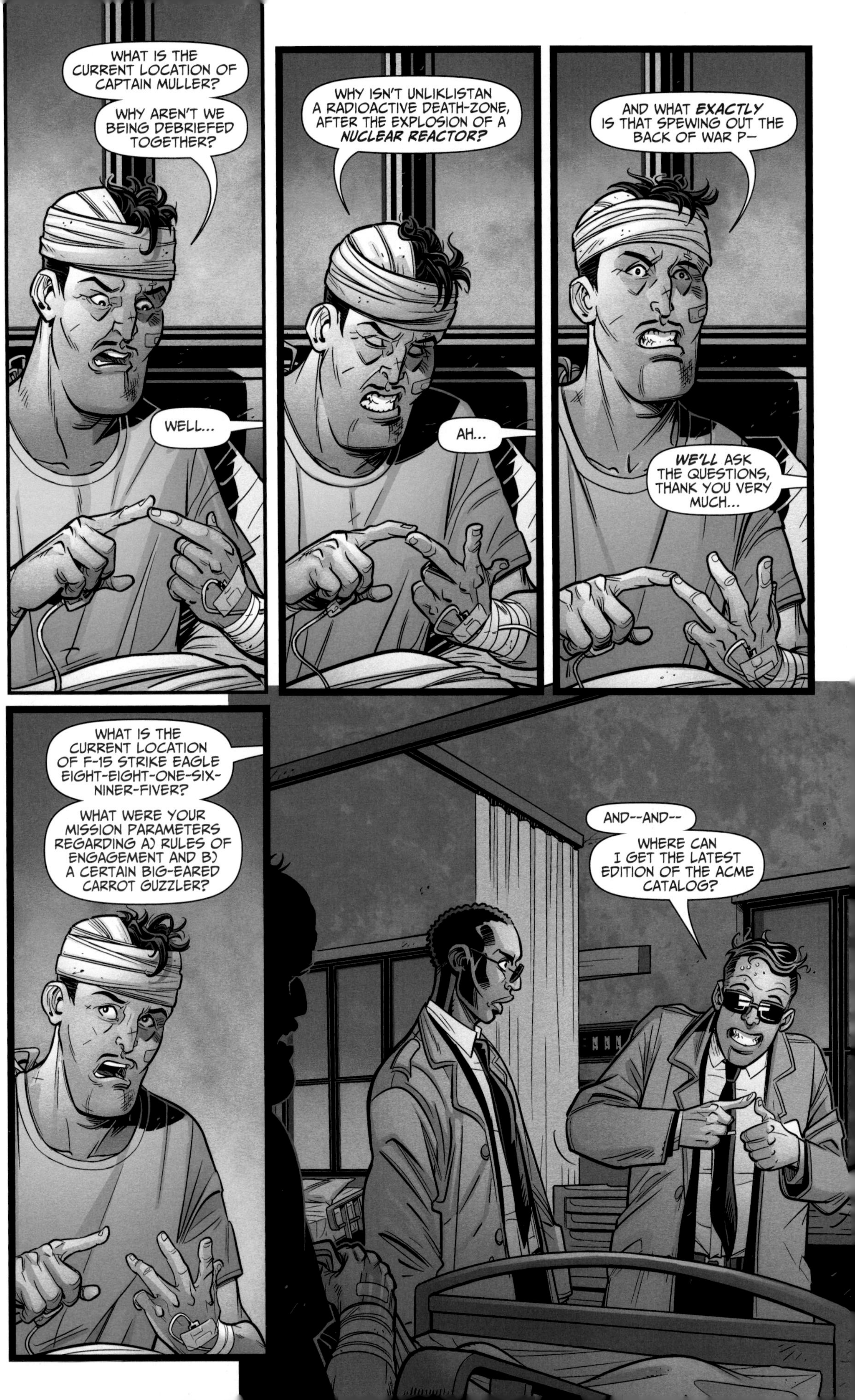
WHAT IS THE CURRENT LOCATION OF CAPTAIN MULLER?
WHY AREN'T WE BEING DEBRIEFED TOGETHER?
WELL...
WHY ISN'T UNLIKLISTAN A RADIOACTIVE DEATH-ZONE, AFTER THE EXPLOSION OF A NUCLEAR REACTOR?
AH...
AND WHAT EXACTLY IS THAT SPEWING OUT THE BACK OF WAR P—
WE'LL ASK THE QUESTIONS, THANK YOU VERY MUCH...
WHAT IS THE CURRENT LOCATION OF F-15 STRIKE EAGLE EIGHT-EIGHT-ONE-SIX-NINER-FIVER?
WHAT WERE YOUR MISSION PARAMETERS REGARDING A) RULES OF ENGAGEMENT AND B) A CERTAIN BIG-EARED CARROT GUZZLER?
AND--AND--
WHERE CAN I GET THE LATEST EDITION OF THE ACME CATALOG?

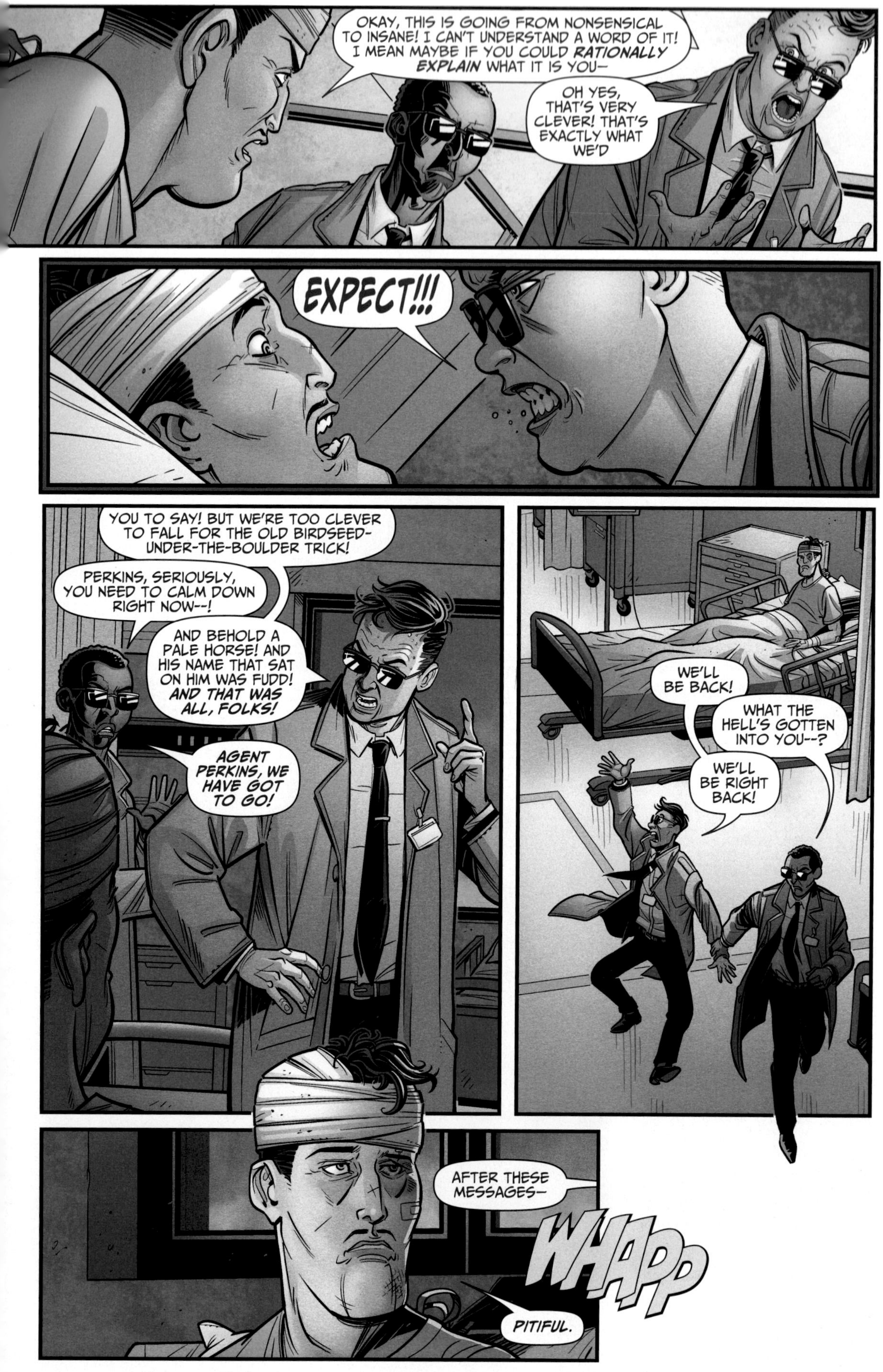
OKAY, THIS IS GOING FROM NONSENSICAL TO INSANE! I CAN'T UNDERSTAND A WORD OF IT! I MEAN MAYBE IF YOU COULD RATIONALLY EXPLAIN WHAT IT IS YOU–
OH YES, THAT'S VERY CLEVER! THAT'S EXACTLY WHAT WE'D
EXPECT!!!
YOU TO SAY! BUT WE'RE TOO CLEVER TO FALL FOR THE OLD BIRDSEED-UNDER-THE-BOULDER TRICK!
PERKINS, SERIOUSLY, YOU NEED TO CALM DOWN RIGHT NOW--!
AND BEHOLD A PALE HORSE! AND HIS NAME THAT SAT ON HIM WAS FUDD! AND THAT WAS ALL, FOLKS!
AGENT PERKINS, WE HAVE GOT TO GO!
WE'LL BE BACK!
WHAT THE HELL'S GOTTEN INTO YOU--?
WE'LL BE RIGHT BACK!
AFTER THESE MESSAGES–
WHAPP
PITIFUL.

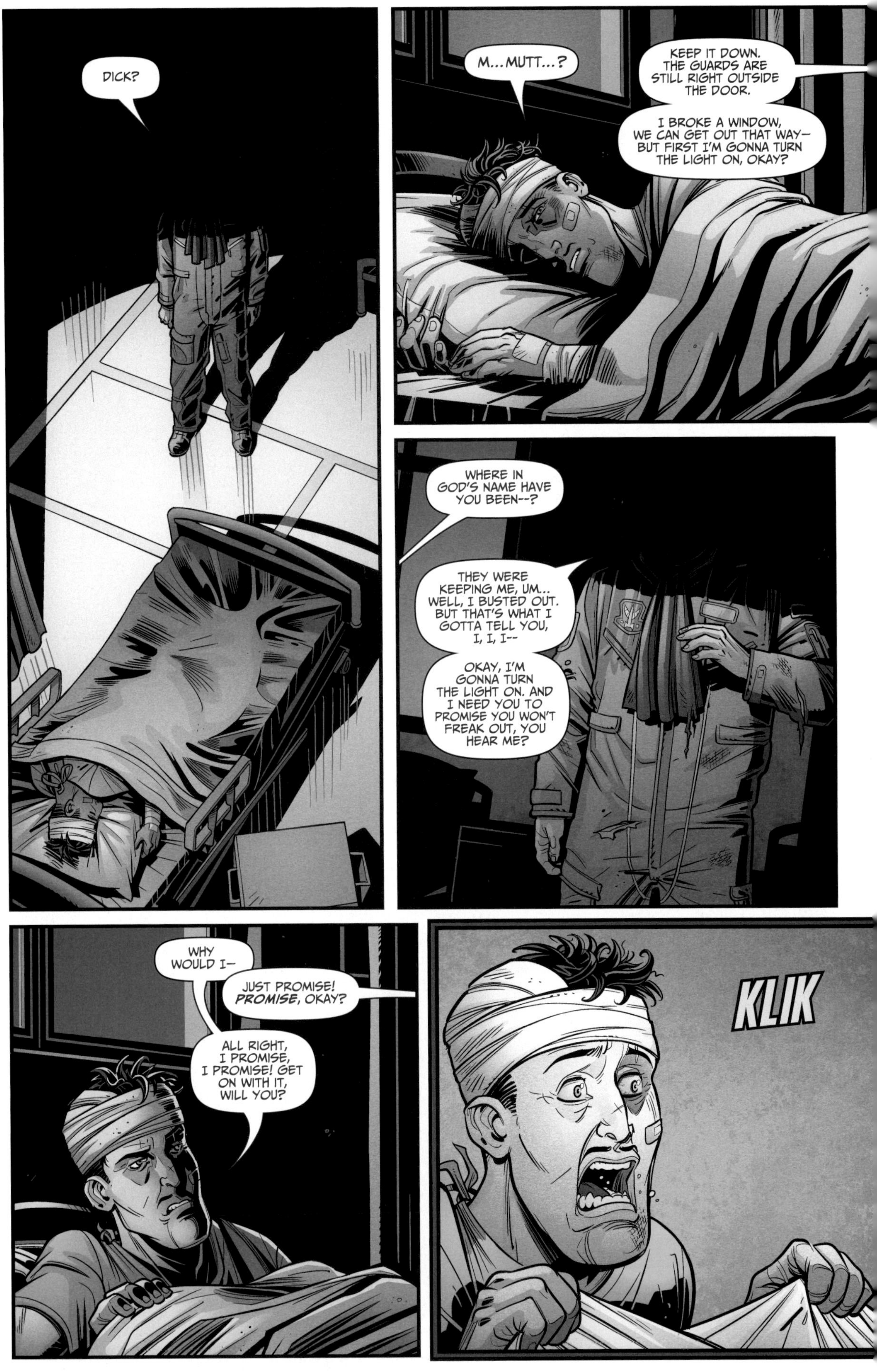
DICK?
M...MUTT...?
KEEP IT DOWN. THE GUARDS ARE STILL RIGHT OUTSIDE THE DOOR.
I BROKE A WINDOW, WE CAN GET OUT THAT WAY— BUT FIRST I'M GONNA TURN THE LIGHT ON, OKAY?
WHERE IN GOD'S NAME HAVE YOU BEEN--?
THEY WERE KEEPING ME, UM... WELL, I BUSTED OUT. BUT THAT'S WHAT I GOTTA TELL YOU, I, I, I--
OKAY, I'M GONNA TURN THE LIGHT ON. AND I NEED YOU TO PROMISE YOU WON'T FREAK OUT, YOU HEAR ME?
WHY WOULD I—
JUST PROMISE! *PROMISE*, OKAY?
ALL RIGHT, I PROMISE, I PROMISE! GET ON WITH IT, WILL YOU?
KLIK

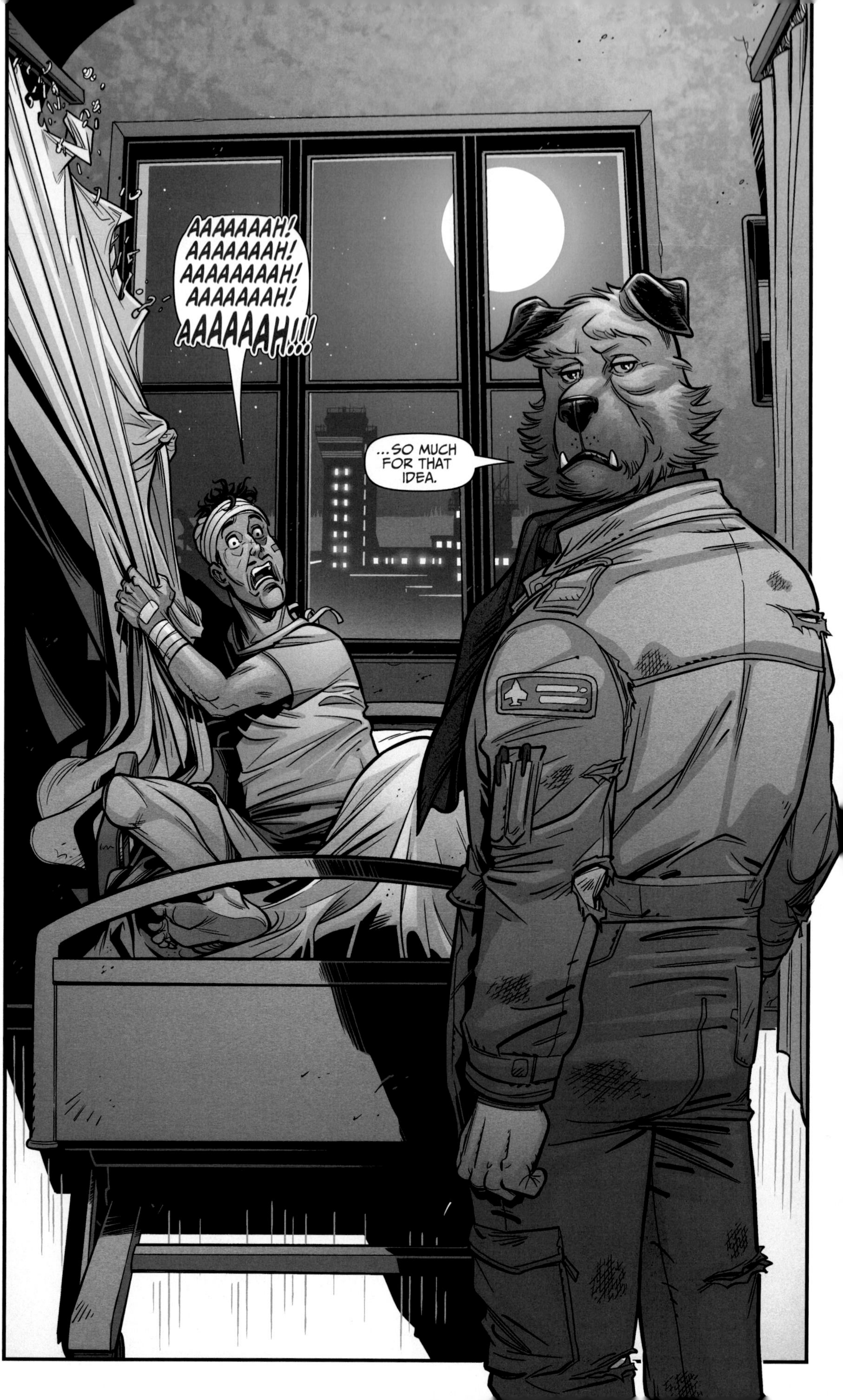
AAAAAAAH! AAAAAAAAH! AAAAAAAAAH! AAAAAAAAH! AAAAAAAH!!!!
...SO MUCH FOR THAT IDEA.

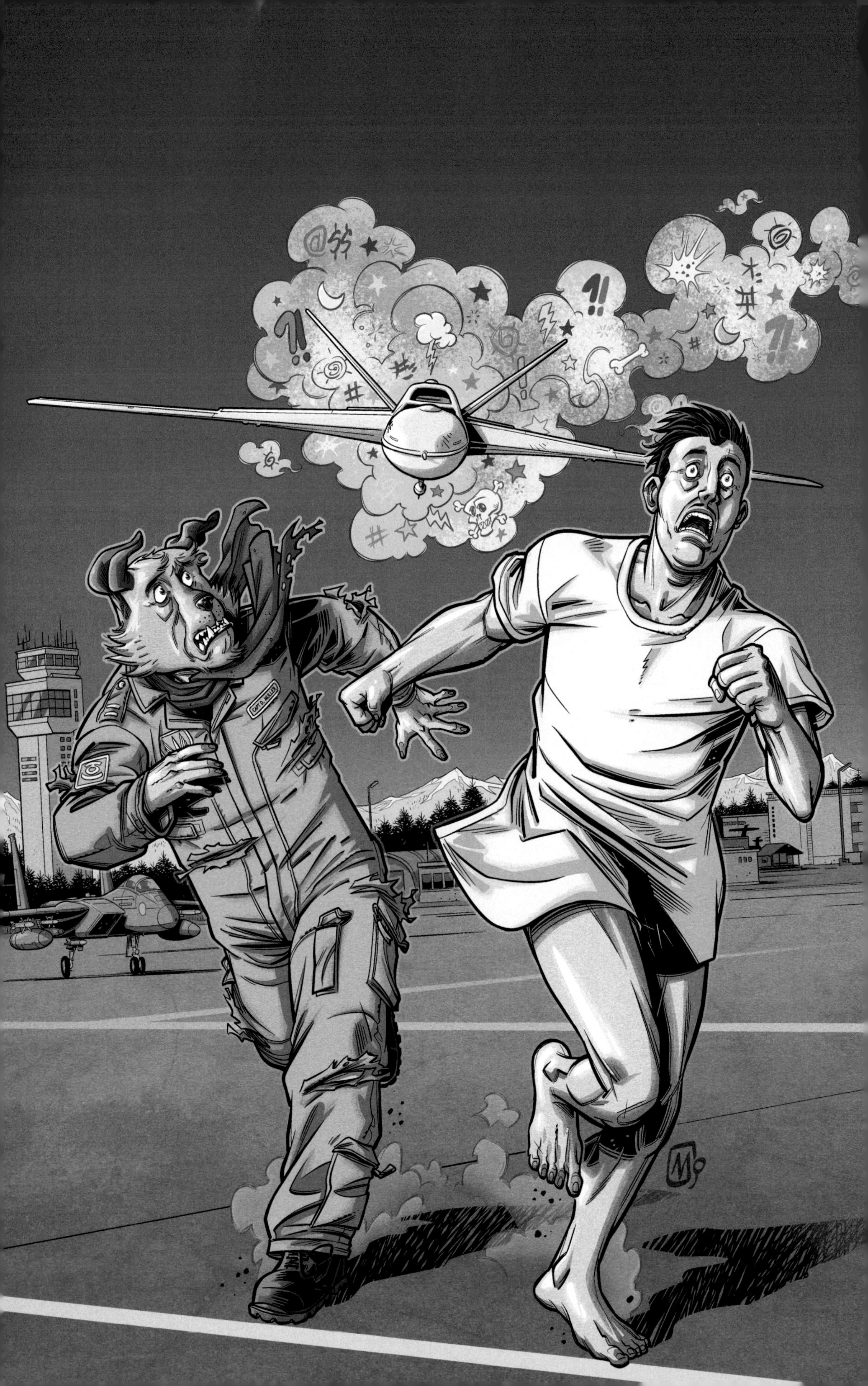
CAPT D. MULLER

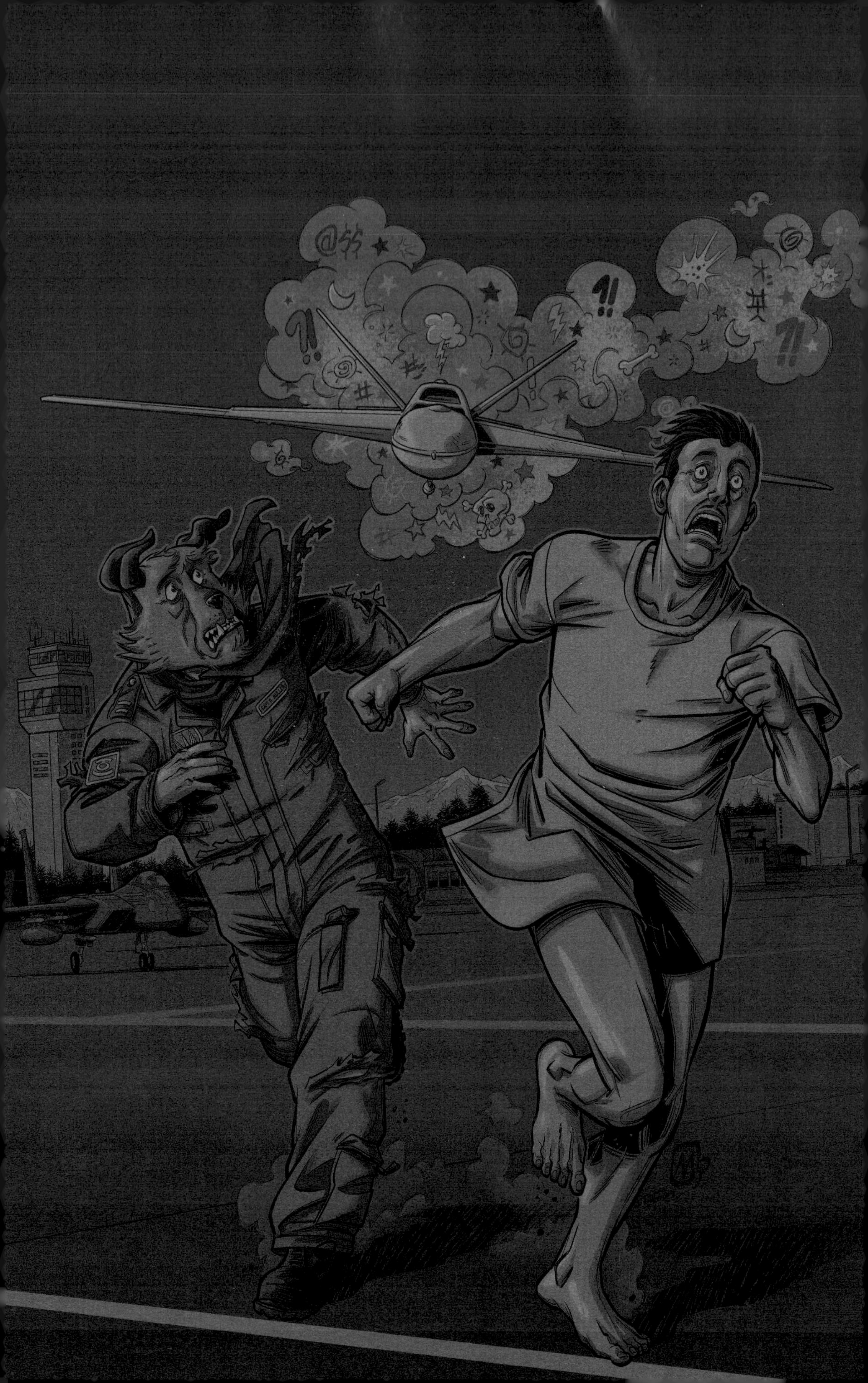

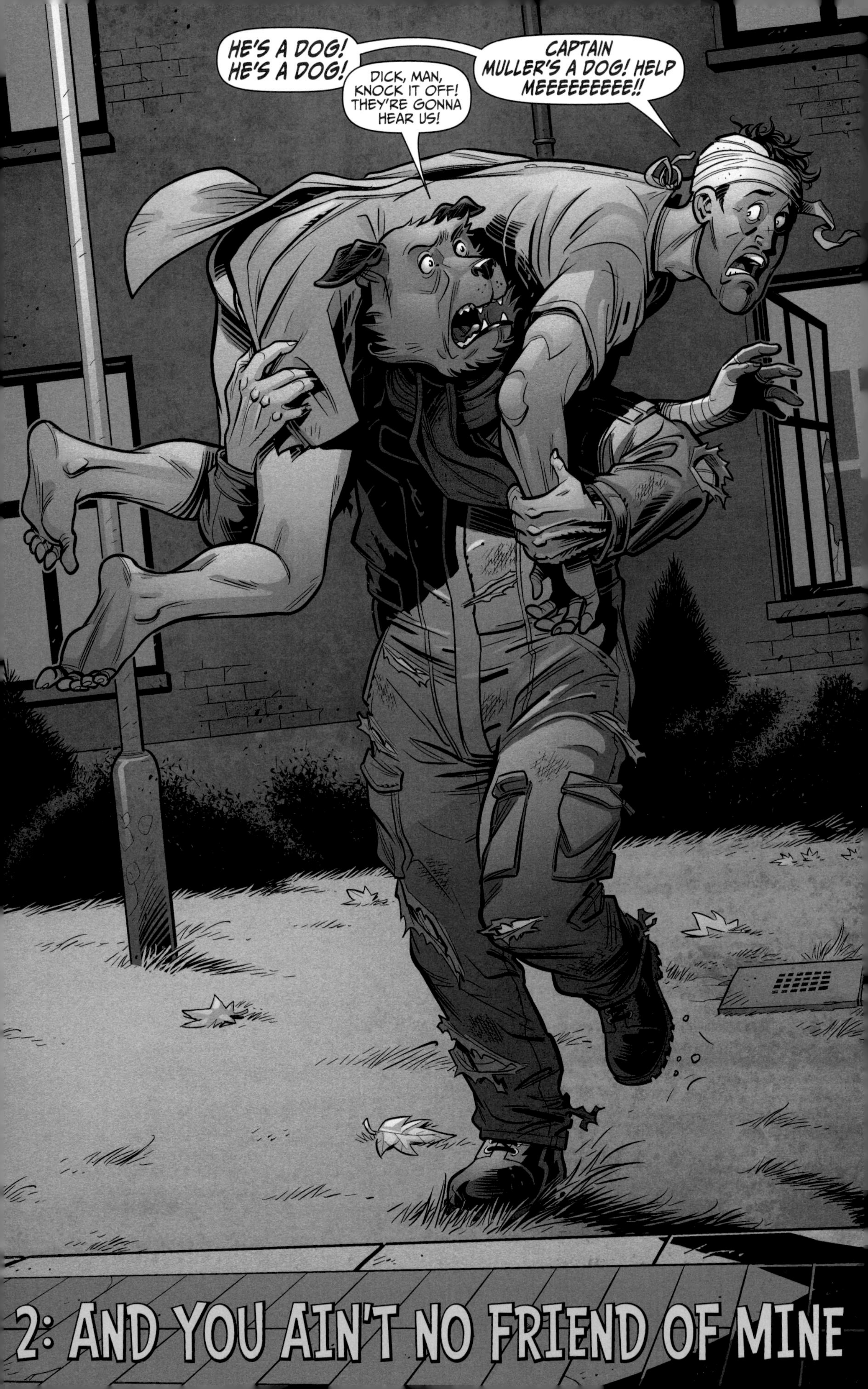
HE'S A DOG! HE'S A DOG!
DICK, MAN, KNOCK IT OFF! THEY'RE GONNA HEAR US!
CAPTAIN MULLER'S A DOG! HELP MEEEEEEEEE!!
2: AND YOU AIN'T NO FRIEND OF MINE

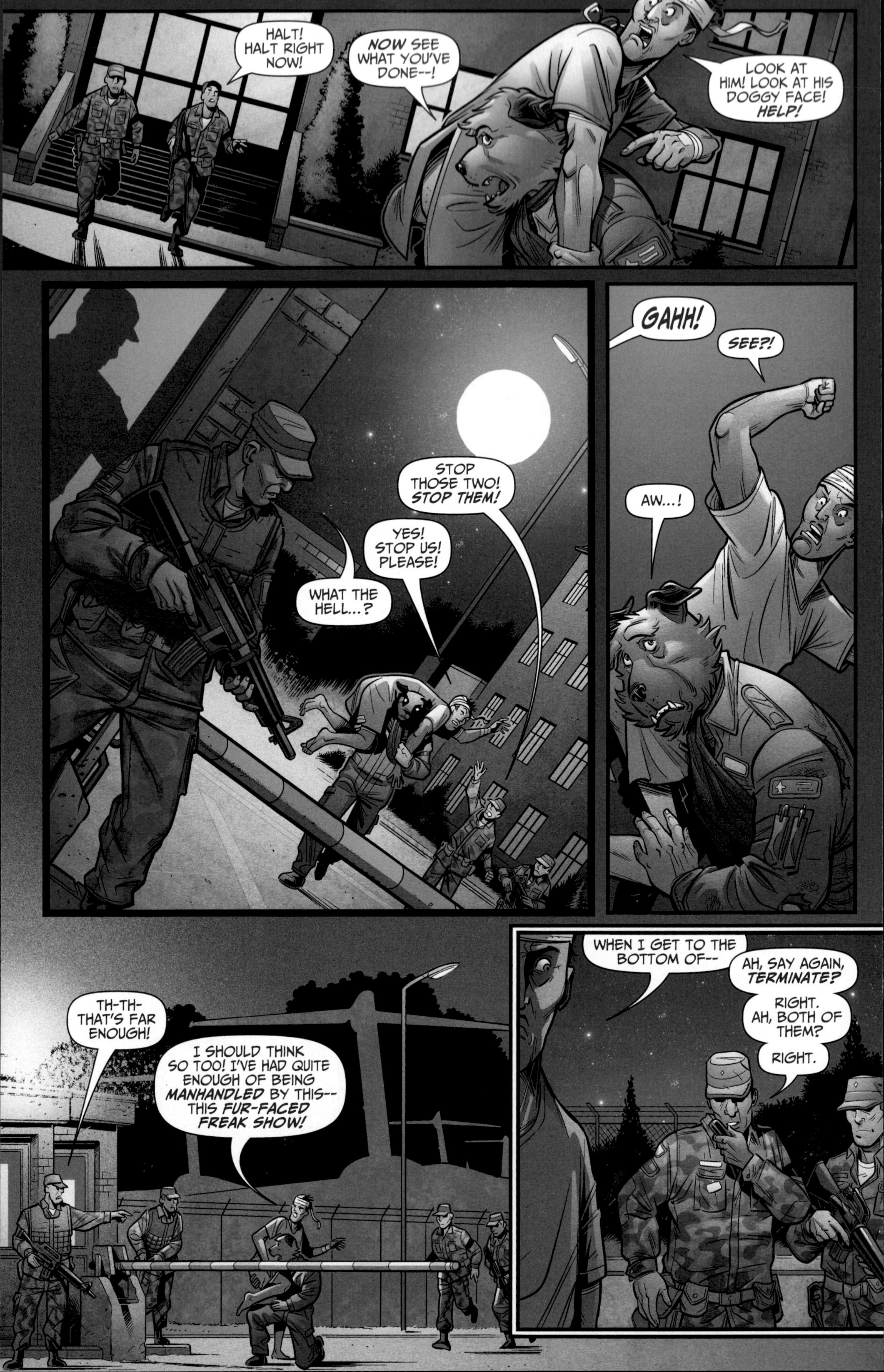

HALT! HALT RIGHT NOW!
NOW SEE WHAT YOU'VE DONE--!
LOOK AT HIM! LOOK AT HIS DOGGY FACE! HELP!
STOP THOSE TWO! STOP THEM!
YES! STOP US! PLEASE!
WHAT THE HELL...?
GAHH!
SEE?!
AW...!
TH-TH-THAT'S FAR ENOUGH!
I SHOULD THINK SO TOO! I'VE HAD QUITE ENOUGH OF BEING MANHANDLED BY THIS-- THIS FUR-FACED FREAK SHOW!
WHEN I GET TO THE BOTTOM OF--
AH, SAY AGAIN, TERMINATE?
RIGHT. AH, BOTH OF THEM?
RIGHT.

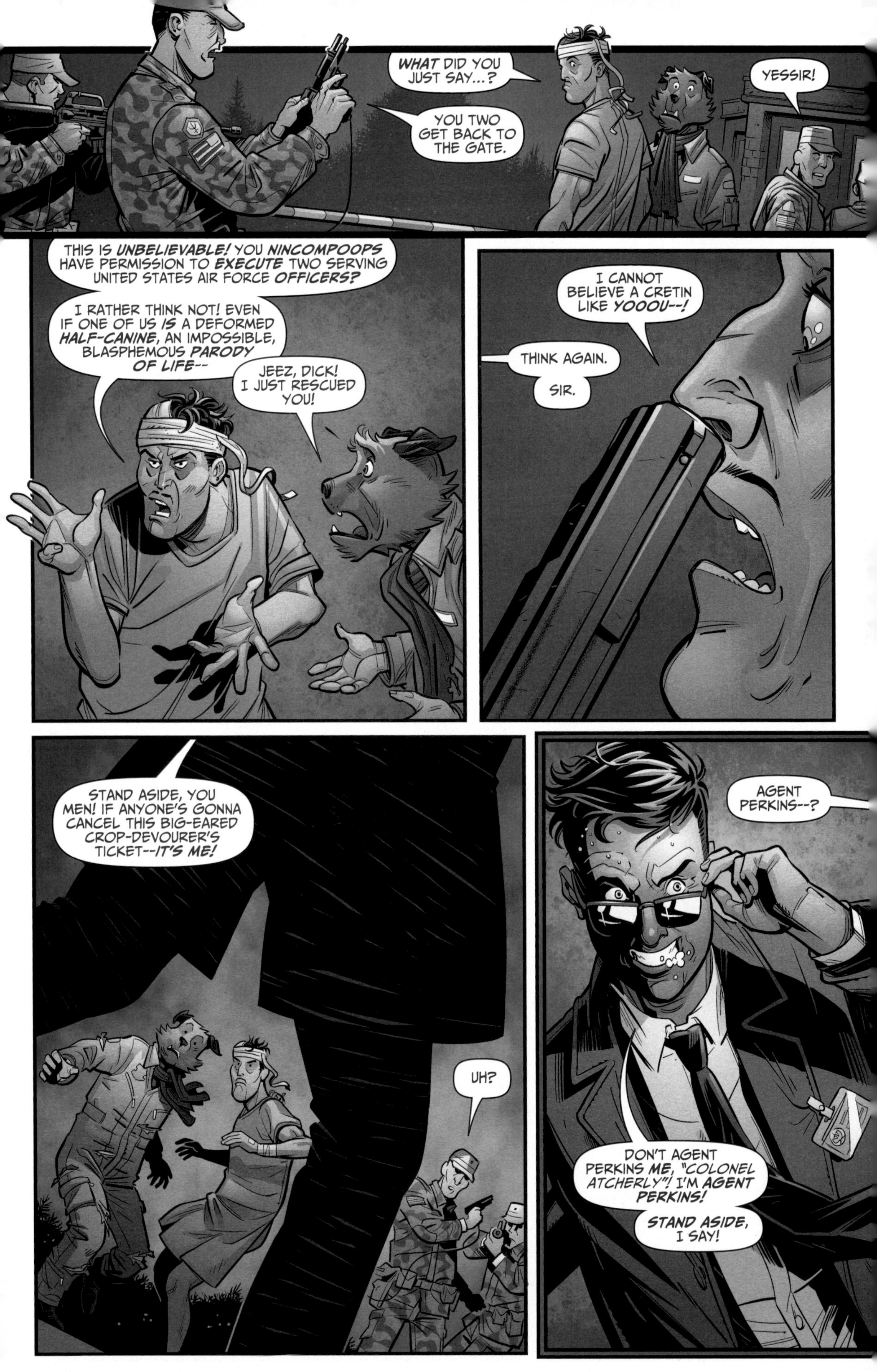
WHAT DID YOU JUST SAY...?
YOU TWO GET BACK TO THE GATE.
YESSIR!
THIS IS UNBELIEVABLE! YOU NINCOMPOOPS HAVE PERMISSION TO EXECUTE TWO SERVING UNITED STATES AIR FORCE OFFICERS?
I RATHER THINK NOT! EVEN IF ONE OF US IS A DEFORMED HALF-CANINE, AN IMPOSSIBLE, BLASPHEMOUS PARODY OF LIFE--
JEEZ, DICK! I JUST RESCUED YOU!
I CANNOT BELIEVE A CRETIN LIKE YOOOU--!
THINK AGAIN.
SIR.
STAND ASIDE, YOU MEN! IF ANYONE'S GONNA CANCEL THIS BIG-EARED CROP-DEVOURER'S TICKET--IT'S ME!
UH?
AGENT PERKINS--?
DON'T AGENT PERKINS ME, "COLONEL ATCHERLY"! I'M AGENT PERKINS!
STAND ASIDE, I SAY!

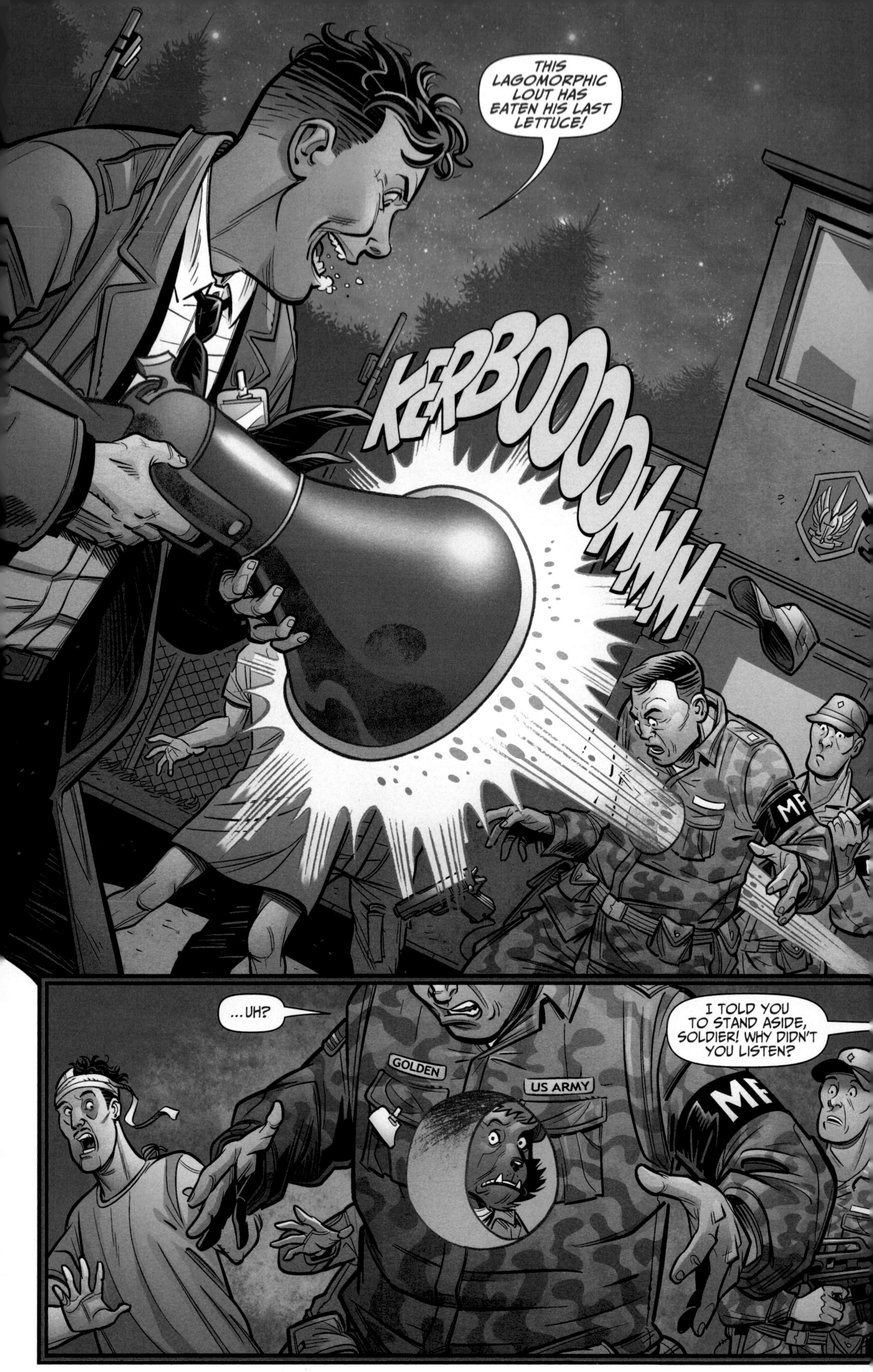
THIS LAGOMORPHIC LOUT HAS EATEN HIS LAST LETTUCE!
KERBOOOOMMM
...UH?
I TOLD YOU TO STAND ASIDE, SOLDIER! WHY DIDN'T YOU LISTEN?
GOLDEN
US ARMY
MP

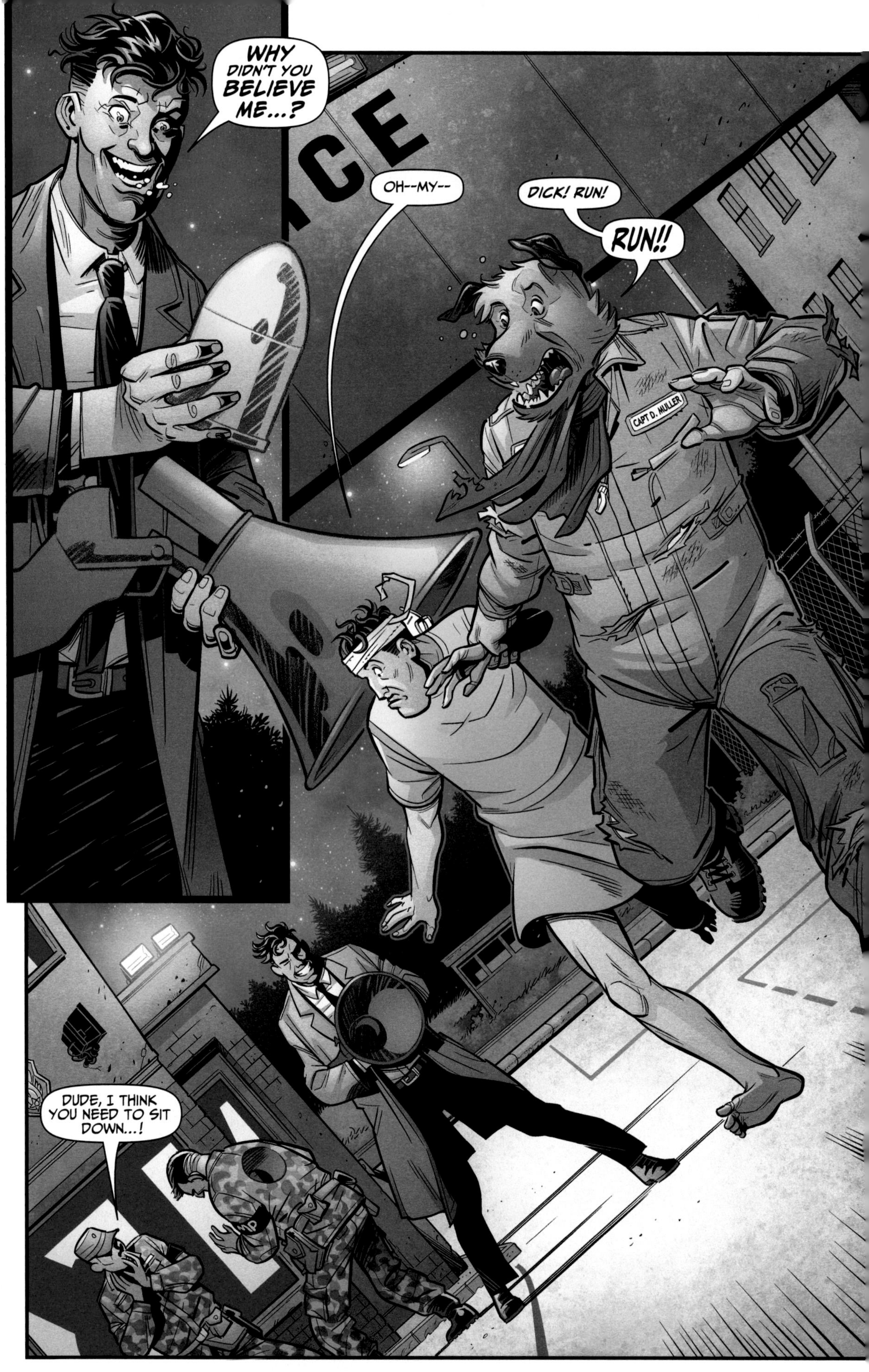
WHY DIDN'T YOU BELIEVE ME...?
OH--MY--
DICK! RUN!
RUN!!
CAPT D. MULLER
DUDE, I THINK YOU NEED TO SIT DOWN...!

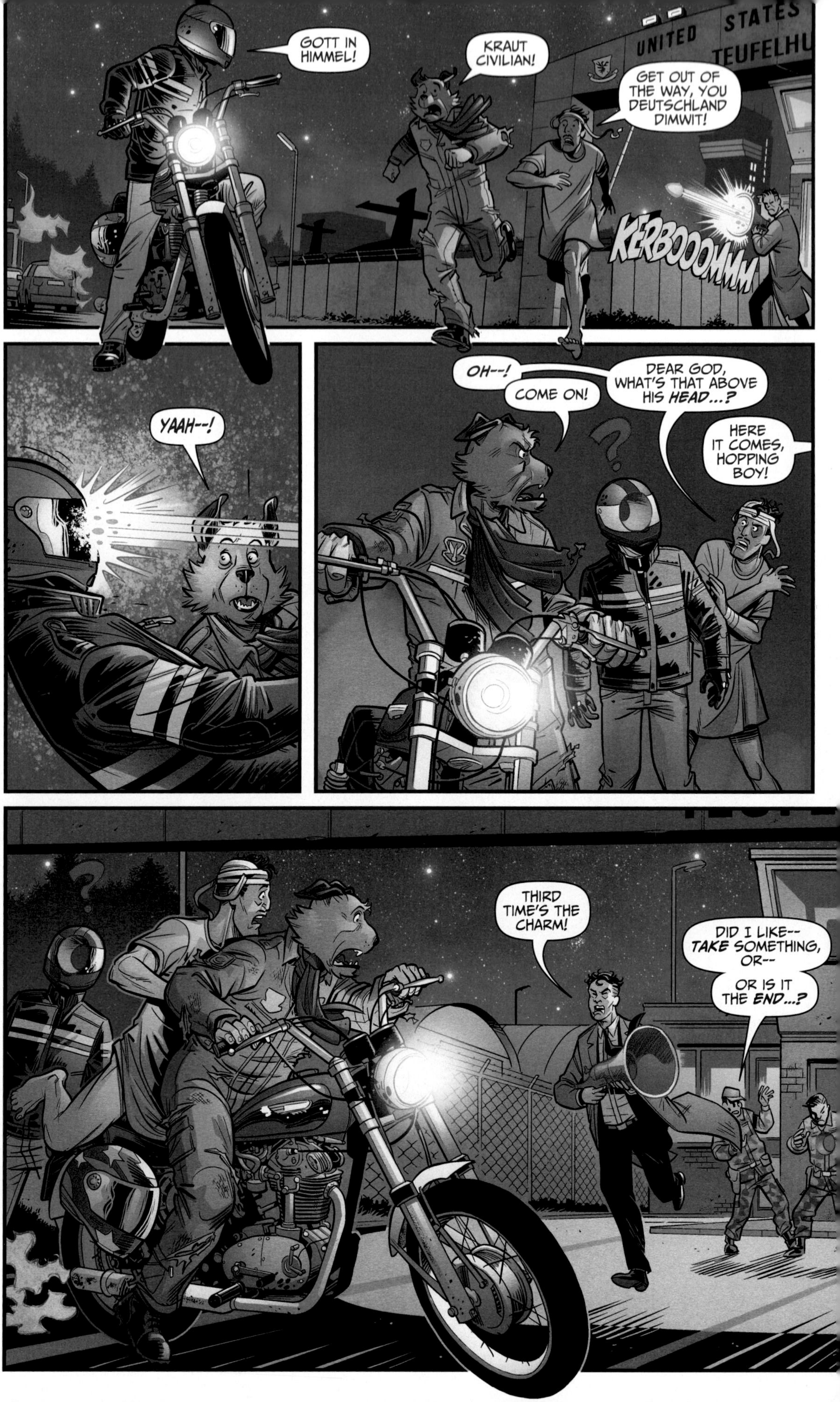
UNITED STATES
TEUFELHU
GOTT IN HIMMEL!
KRAUT CIVILIAN!
GET OUT OF THE WAY, YOU DEUTSCHLAND DIMWIT!
KERBOOOMMM
YAAH--!
OH--!
COME ON!
DEAR GOD, WHAT'S THAT ABOVE HIS HEAD...?
HERE IT COMES, HOPPING BOY!
THIRD TIME'S THE CHARM!
DID I LIKE-- TAKE SOMETHING, OR--
OR IS IT THE END...?

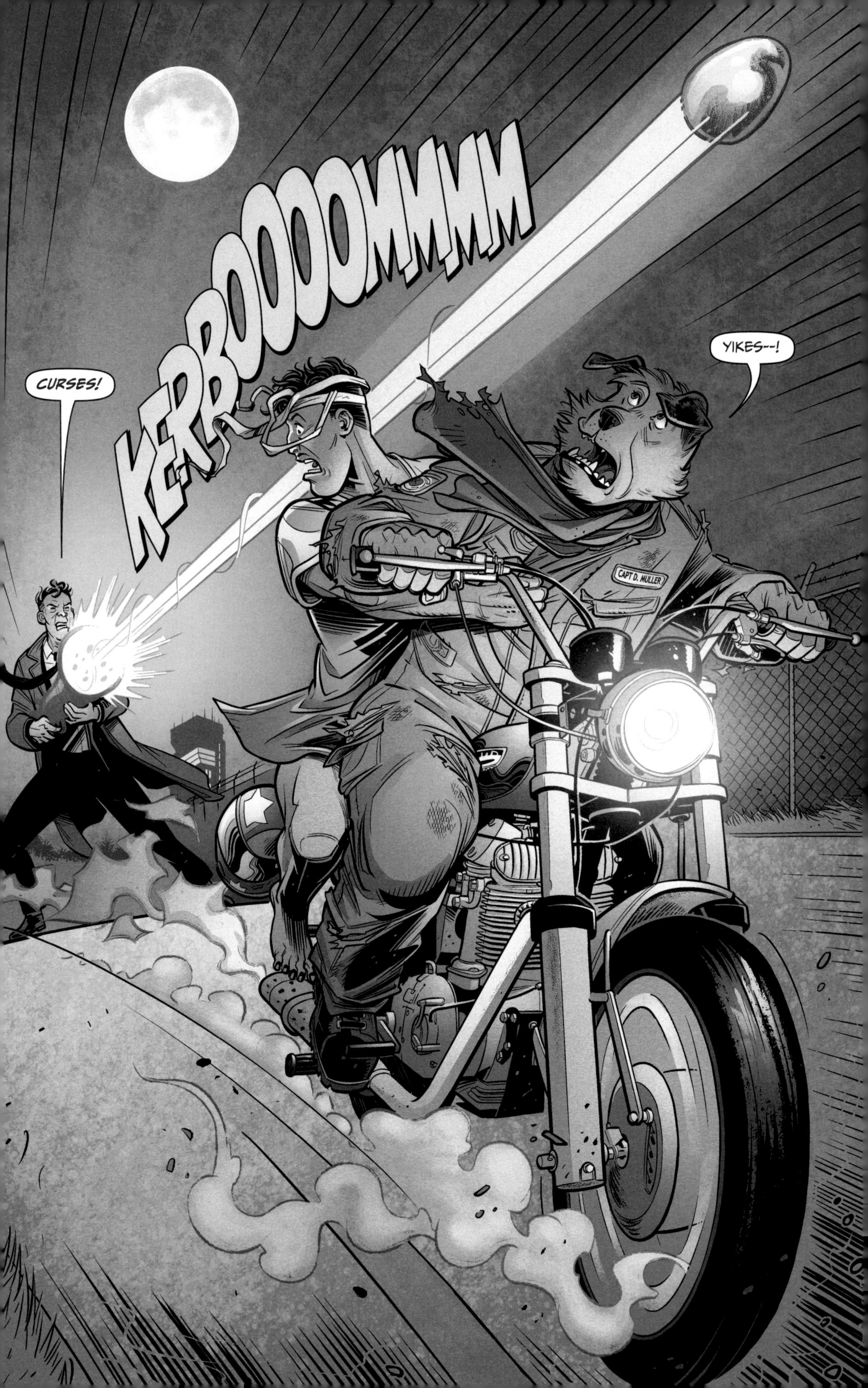
KERBOOOOMMMM
CURSES!
YIKES--!
CAPT D. MULLER

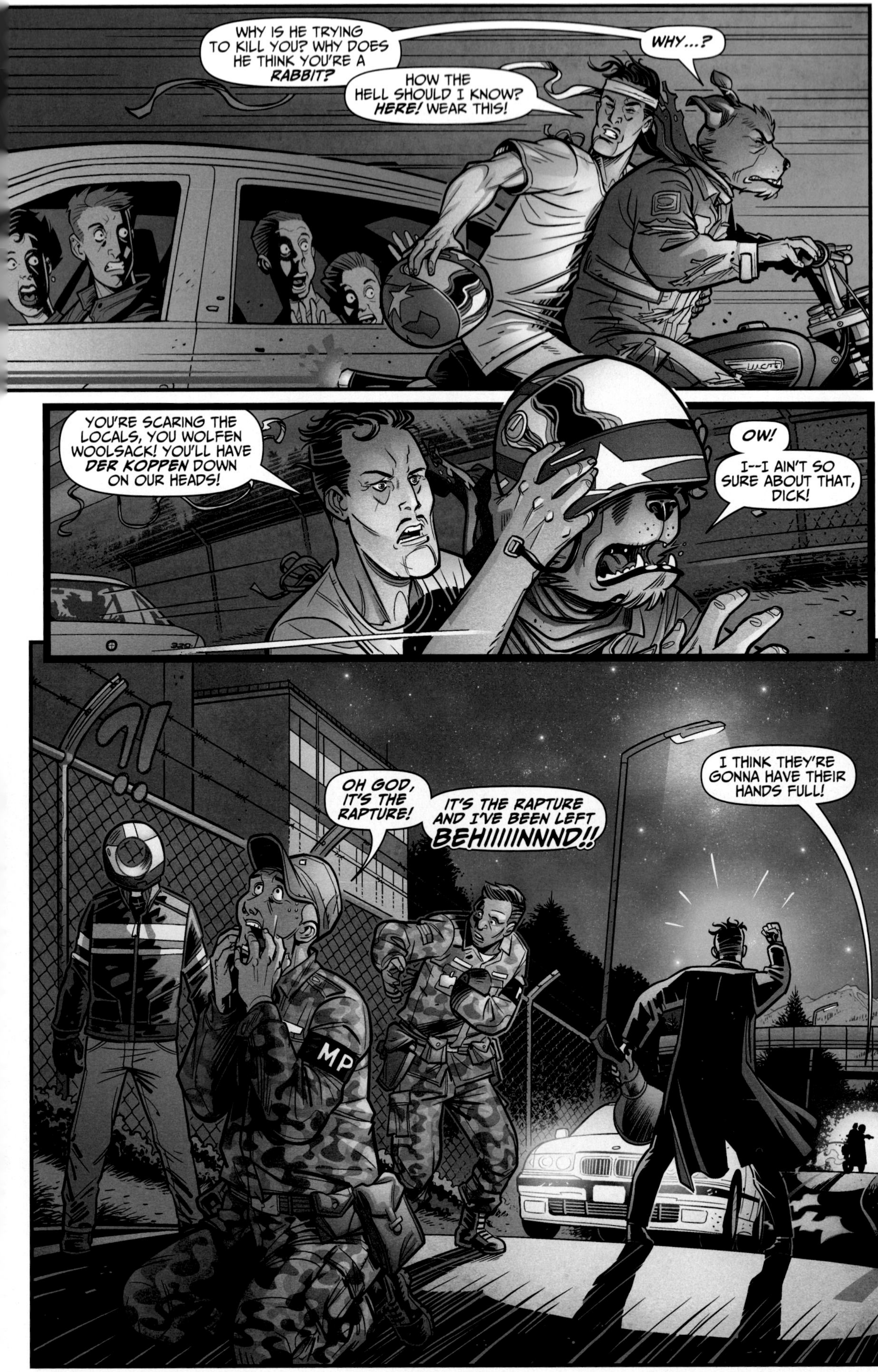
WHY IS HE TRYING TO KILL YOU? WHY DOES HE THINK YOU'RE A RABBIT?
WHY...?
HOW THE HELL SHOULD I KNOW? HERE! WEAR THIS!
YOU'RE SCARING THE LOCALS, YOU WOLFEN WOOLSACK! YOU'LL HAVE DER KOPPEN DOWN ON OUR HEADS!
OW!
I--I AIN'T SO SURE ABOUT THAT, DICK!
OH GOD, IT'S THE RAPTURE!
IT'S THE RAPTURE AND I'VE BEEN LEFT BEHIIIIIINNND!!
I THINK THEY'RE GONNA HAVE THEIR HANDS FULL!
MP

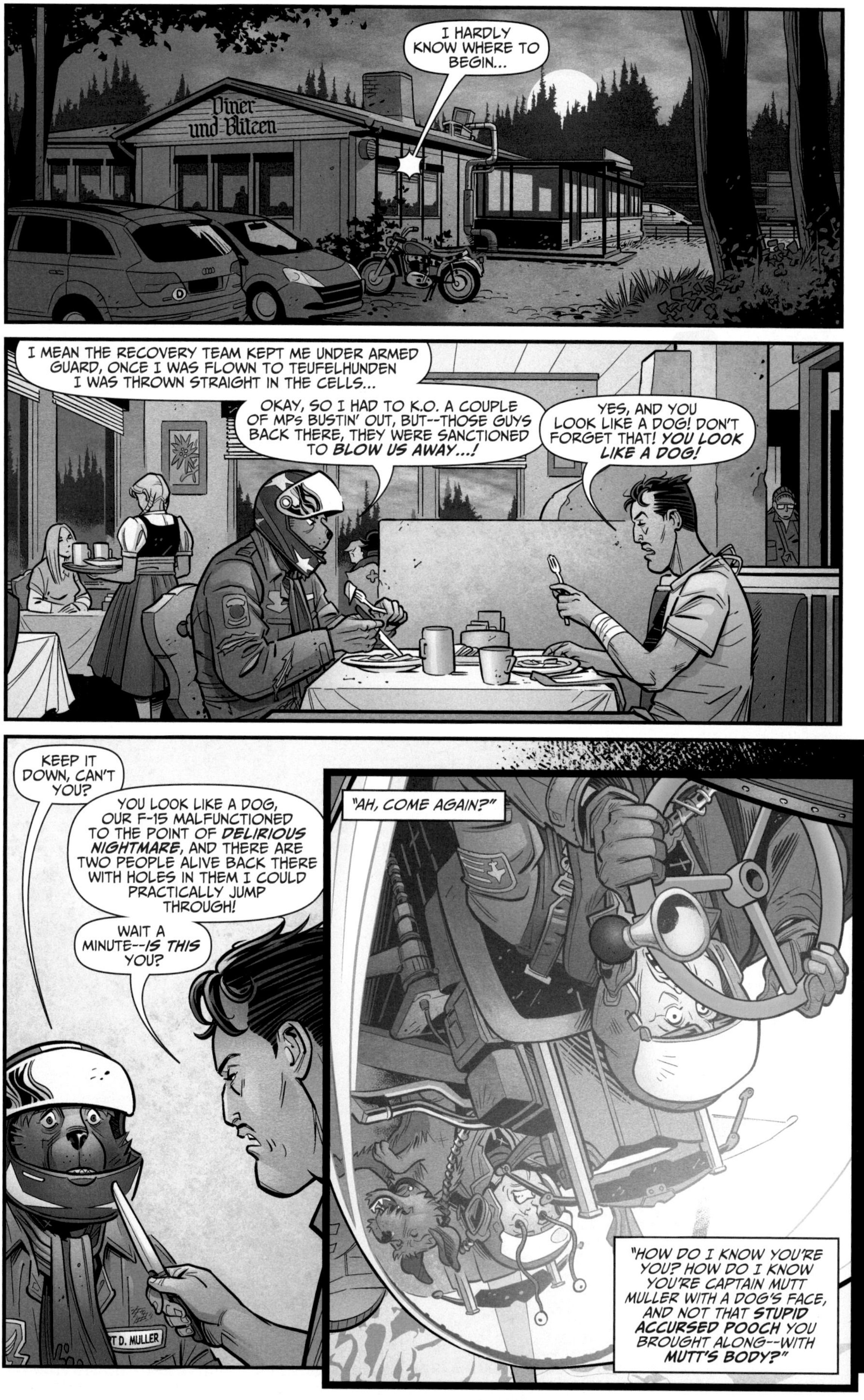
I HARDLY KNOW WHERE TO BEGIN...
Diner und-Blitzen
I MEAN THE RECOVERY TEAM KEPT ME UNDER ARMED GUARD, ONCE I WAS FLOWN TO TEUFELHUNDEN I WAS THROWN STRAIGHT IN THE CELLS...
OKAY, SO I HAD TO K.O. A COUPLE OF MPs BUSTIN' OUT, BUT--THOSE GUYS BACK THERE, THEY WERE SANCTIONED TO BLOW US AWAY...!
YES, AND YOU LOOK LIKE A DOG! DON'T FORGET THAT! YOU LOOK LIKE A DOG!
KEEP IT DOWN, CAN'T YOU?
YOU LOOK LIKE A DOG, OUR F-15 MALFUNCTIONED TO THE POINT OF DELIRIOUS NIGHTMARE, AND THERE ARE TWO PEOPLE ALIVE BACK THERE WITH HOLES IN THEM I COULD PRACTICALLY JUMP THROUGH!
WAIT A MINUTE--IS THIS YOU?
T D. MULLER
"AH, COME AGAIN?"
"HOW DO I KNOW YOU'RE YOU? HOW DO I KNOW YOU'RE CAPTAIN MUTT MULLER WITH A DOG'S FACE, AND NOT THAT STUPID ACCURSED POOCH YOU BROUGHT ALONG--WITH MUTT'S BODY?"

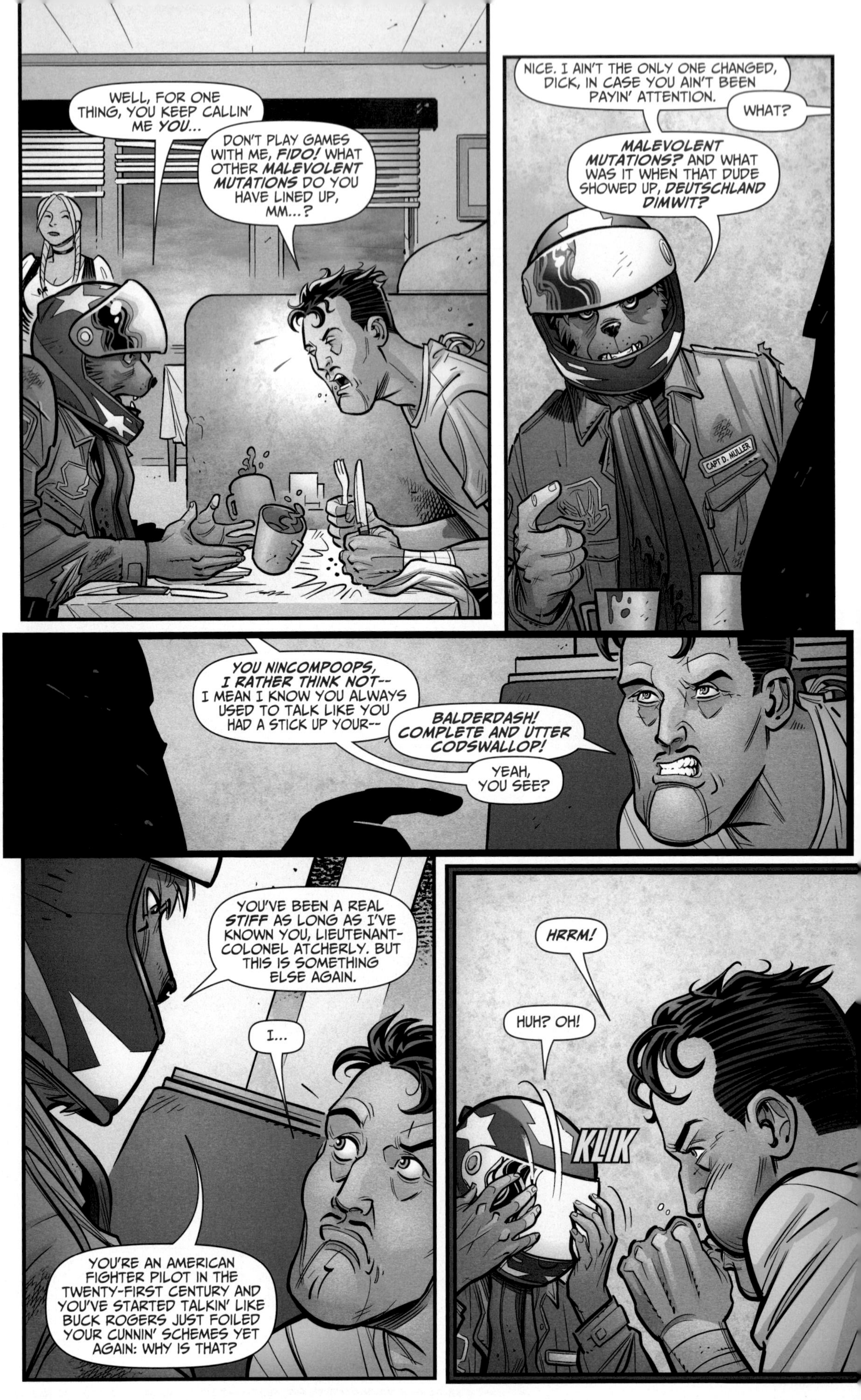
WELL, FOR ONE THING, YOU KEEP CALLIN' ME YOU...
DON'T PLAY GAMES WITH ME, FIDO! WHAT OTHER MALEVOLENT MUTATIONS DO YOU HAVE LINED UP, MM...?
NICE. I AIN'T THE ONLY ONE CHANGED, DICK, IN CASE YOU AIN'T BEEN PAYIN' ATTENTION.
WHAT?
MALEVOLENT MUTATIONS? AND WHAT WAS IT WHEN THAT DUDE SHOWED UP, DEUTSCHLAND DIMWIT?
CAPT D. MULLER
YOU NINCOMPOOPS, I RATHER THINK NOT-- I MEAN I KNOW YOU ALWAYS USED TO TALK LIKE YOU HAD A STICK UP YOUR--
BALDERDASH! COMPLETE AND UTTER CODSWALLOP!
YEAH, YOU SEE?
YOU'VE BEEN A REAL STIFF AS LONG AS I'VE KNOWN YOU, LIEUTENANT-COLONEL ATCHERLY. BUT THIS IS SOMETHING ELSE AGAIN.
I...
YOU'RE AN AMERICAN FIGHTER PILOT IN THE TWENTY-FIRST CENTURY AND YOU'VE STARTED TALKIN' LIKE BUCK ROGERS JUST FOILED YOUR CUNNIN' SCHEMES YET AGAIN: WHY IS THAT?
HRRM!
HUH? OH!
KLIK

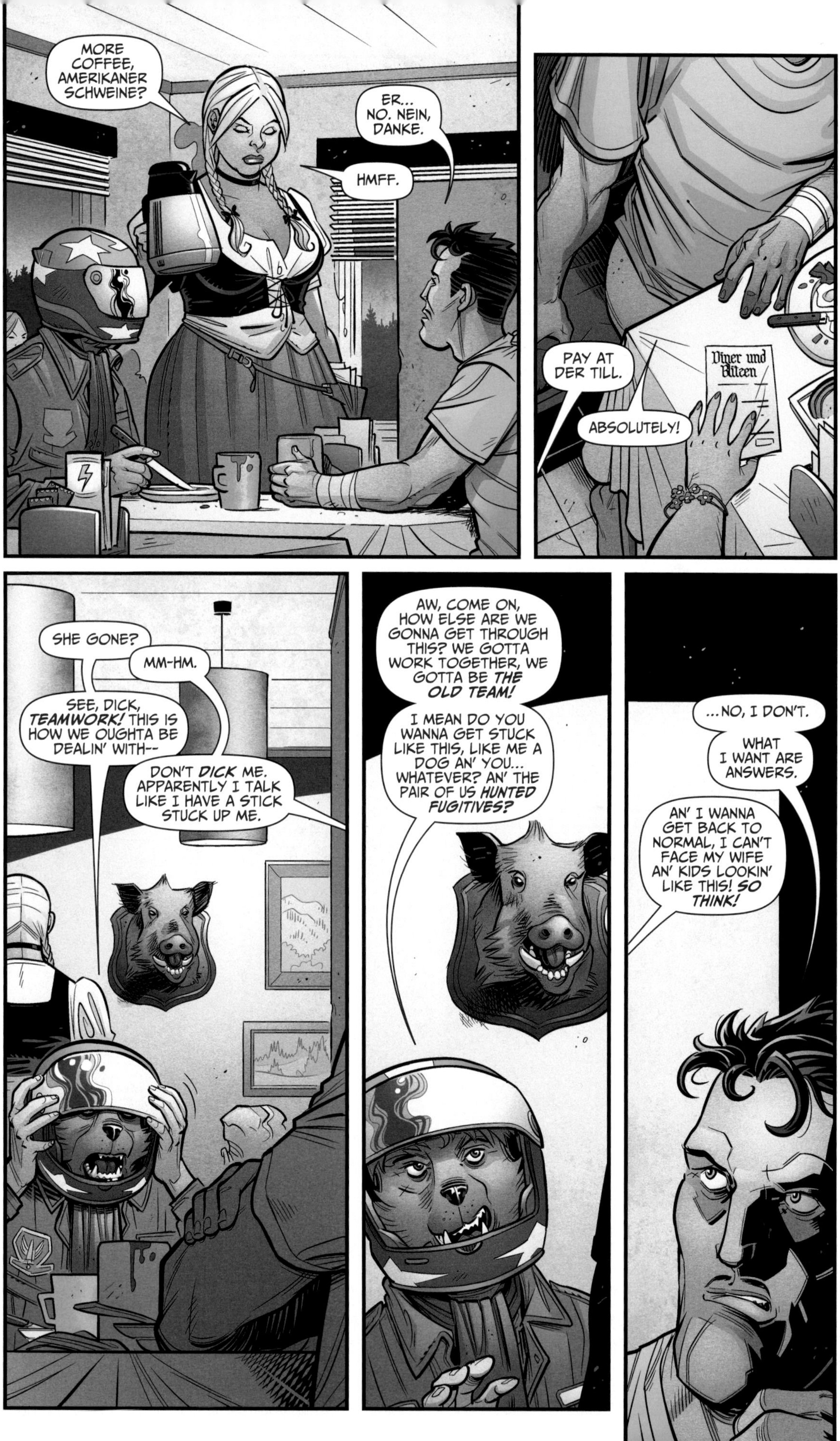
MORE COFFEE, AMERIKANER SCHWEINE?
ER... NO. NEIN, DANKE.
HMFF.
Diner und Bitten
PAY AT DER TILL.
ABSOLUTELY!
SHE GONE?
MM-HM.
SEE, DICK, TEAMWORK! THIS IS HOW WE OUGHTA BE DEALIN' WITH--
DON'T DICK ME. APPARENTLY I TALK LIKE I HAVE A STICK STUCK UP ME.
AW, COME ON, HOW ELSE ARE WE GONNA GET THROUGH THIS? WE GOTTA WORK TOGETHER, WE GOTTA BE THE OLD TEAM!
I MEAN DO YOU WANNA GET STUCK LIKE THIS, LIKE ME A DOG AN' YOU... WHATEVER? AN' THE PAIR OF US HUNTED FUGITIVES?
...NO, I DON'T.
WHAT I WANT ARE ANSWERS.
AN' I WANNA GET BACK TO NORMAL, I CAN'T FACE MY WIFE AN' KIDS LOOKIN' LIKE THIS! SO THINK!

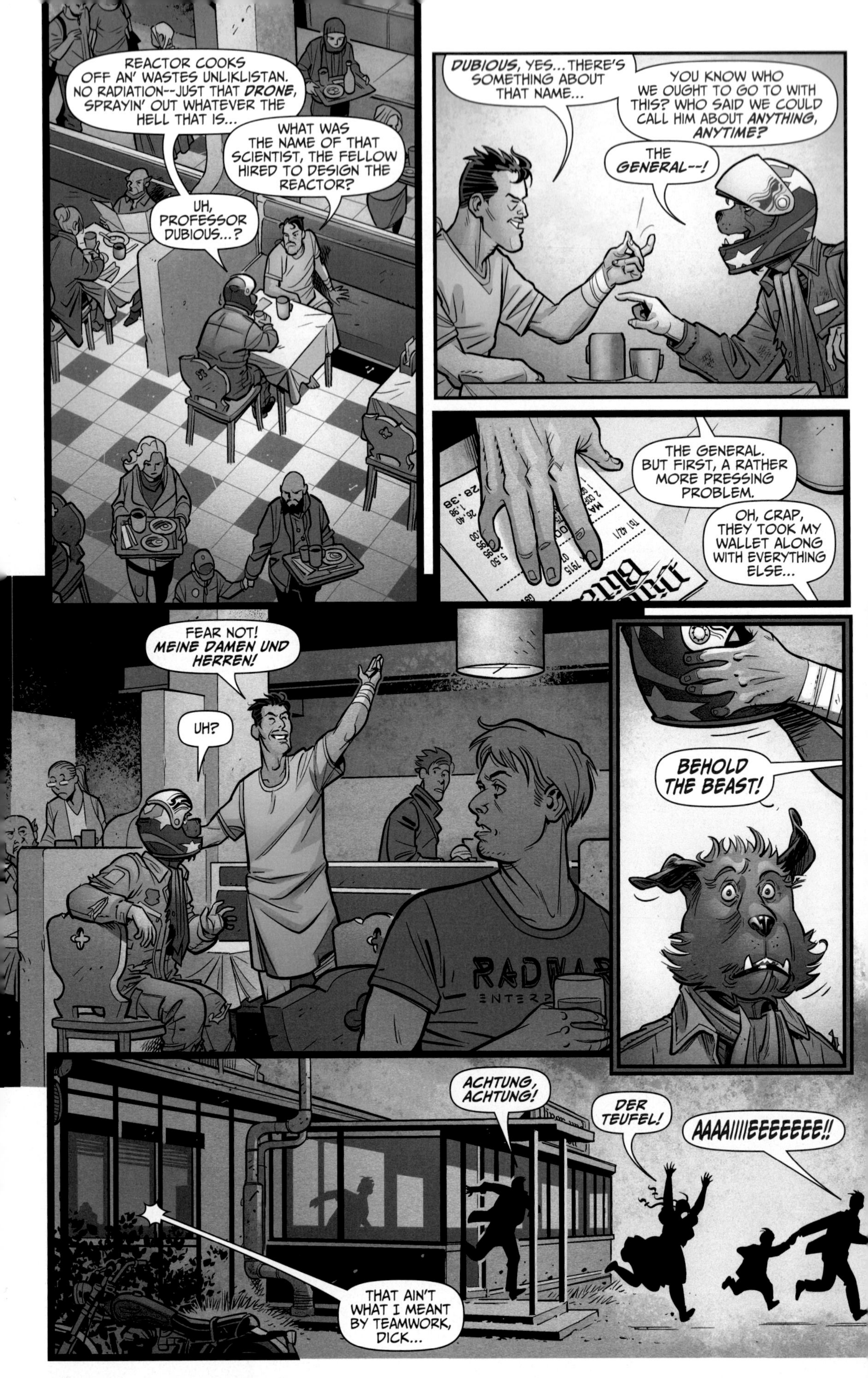
REACTOR COOKS OFF AN' WASTES UNLIKLISTAN. NO RADIATION--JUST THAT *DRONE*, SPRAYIN' OUT WHATEVER THE HELL THAT IS...
WHAT WAS THE NAME OF THAT SCIENTIST, THE FELLOW HIRED TO DESIGN THE REACTOR?
UH, PROFESSOR DUBIOUS...?
DUBIOUS, YES... THERE'S SOMETHING ABOUT THAT NAME...
YOU KNOW WHO WE OUGHT TO GO TO WITH THIS? WHO SAID WE COULD CALL HIM ABOUT *ANYTHING, ANYTIME?*
THE *GENERAL--!*
THE GENERAL. BUT FIRST, A RATHER MORE PRESSING PROBLEM.
OH, CRAP, THEY TOOK MY WALLET ALONG WITH EVERYTHING ELSE...
FEAR NOT! *MEINE DAMEN UND HERREN!*
UH?
BEHOLD THE BEAST!
ACHTUNG, ACHTUNG!
DER TEUFEL!
AAAIIIIEEEEEEE!!
THAT AIN'T WHAT I MEANT BY TEAMWORK, DICK...

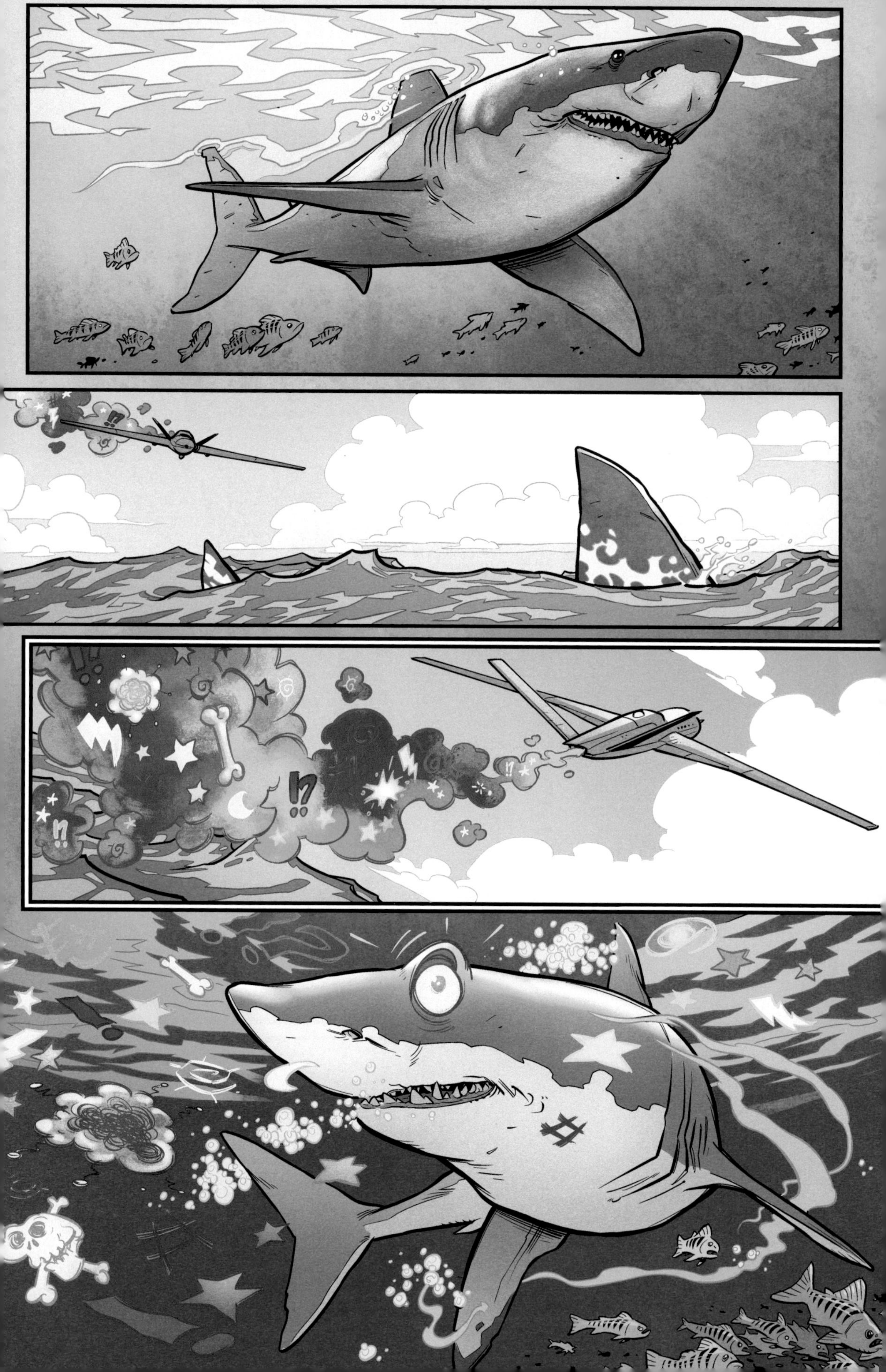

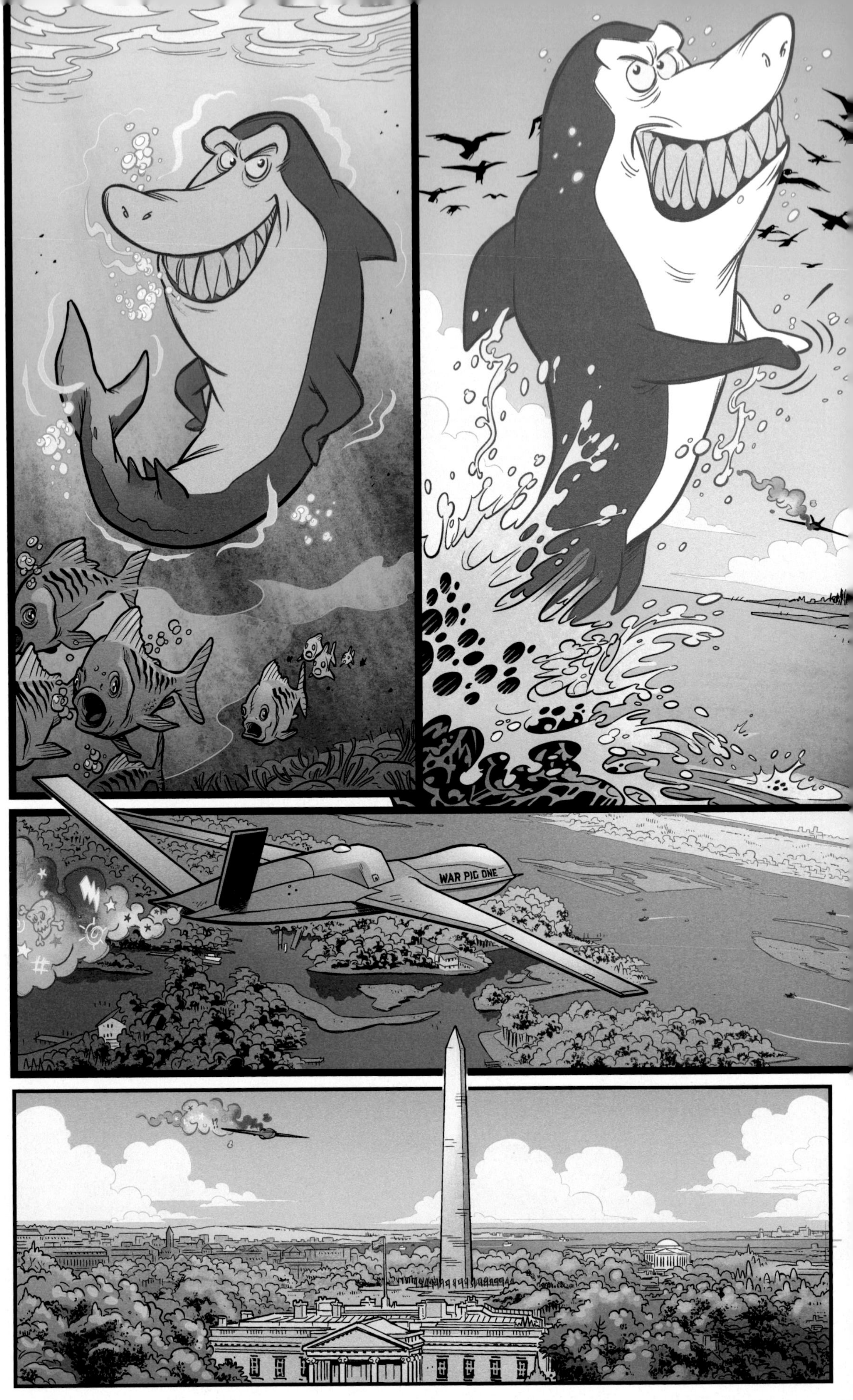
WAR PIG ONE

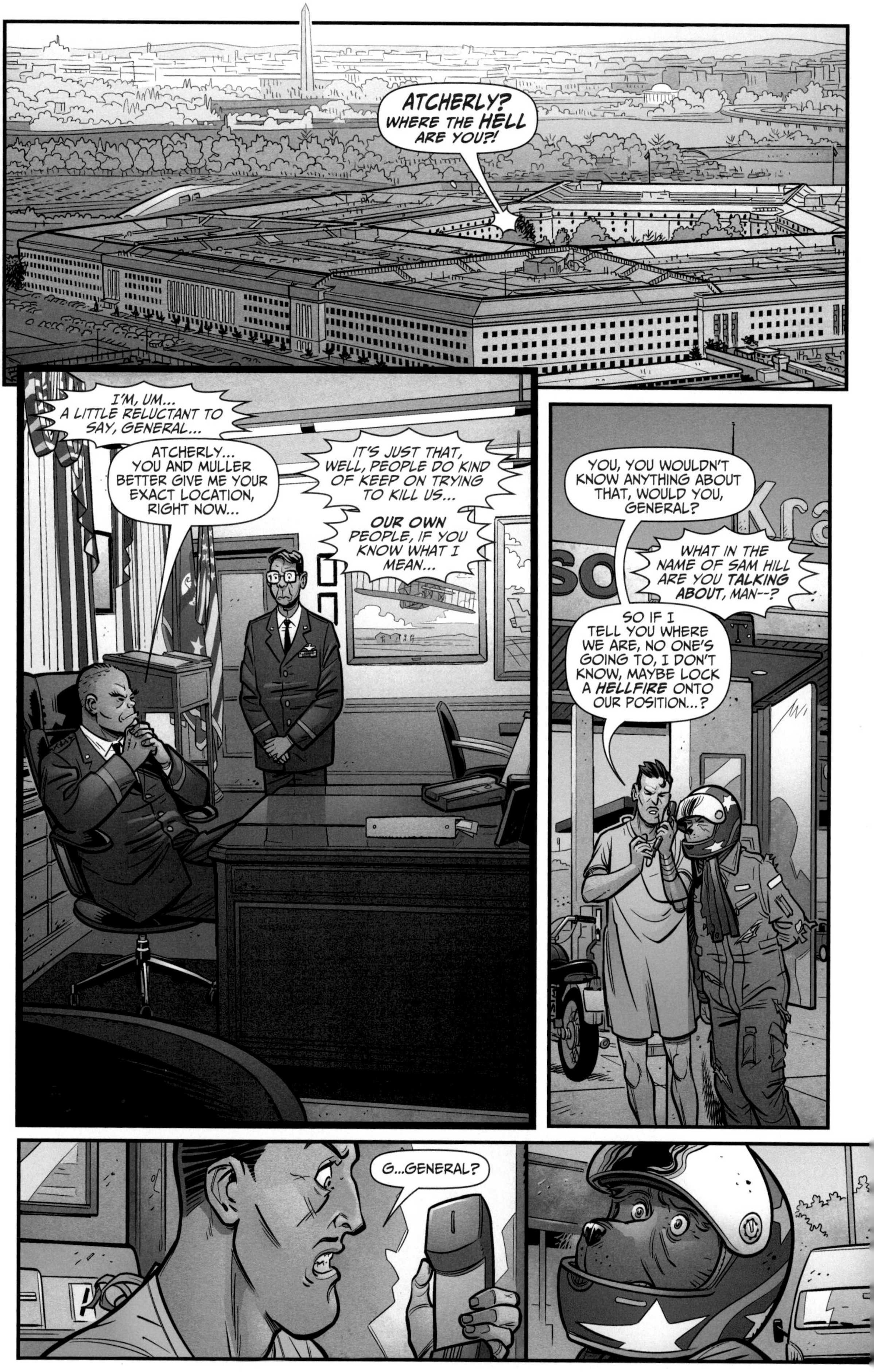
ATCHERLY? WHERE THE HELL ARE YOU?!
I'M, UM... A LITTLE RELUCTANT TO SAY, GENERAL...
ATCHERLY... YOU AND MULLER BETTER GIVE ME YOUR EXACT LOCATION, RIGHT NOW...
IT'S JUST THAT, WELL, PEOPLE DO KIND OF KEEP ON TRYING TO KILL US...
OUR OWN PEOPLE, IF YOU KNOW WHAT I MEAN...
YOU, YOU WOULDN'T KNOW ANYTHING ABOUT THAT, WOULD YOU, GENERAL?
WHAT IN THE NAME OF SAM HILL ARE YOU TALKING ABOUT, MAN--?
SO IF I TELL YOU WHERE WE ARE, NO ONE'S GOING TO, I DON'T KNOW, MAYBE LOCK A HELLFIRE ONTO OUR POSITION...?
G...GENERAL?

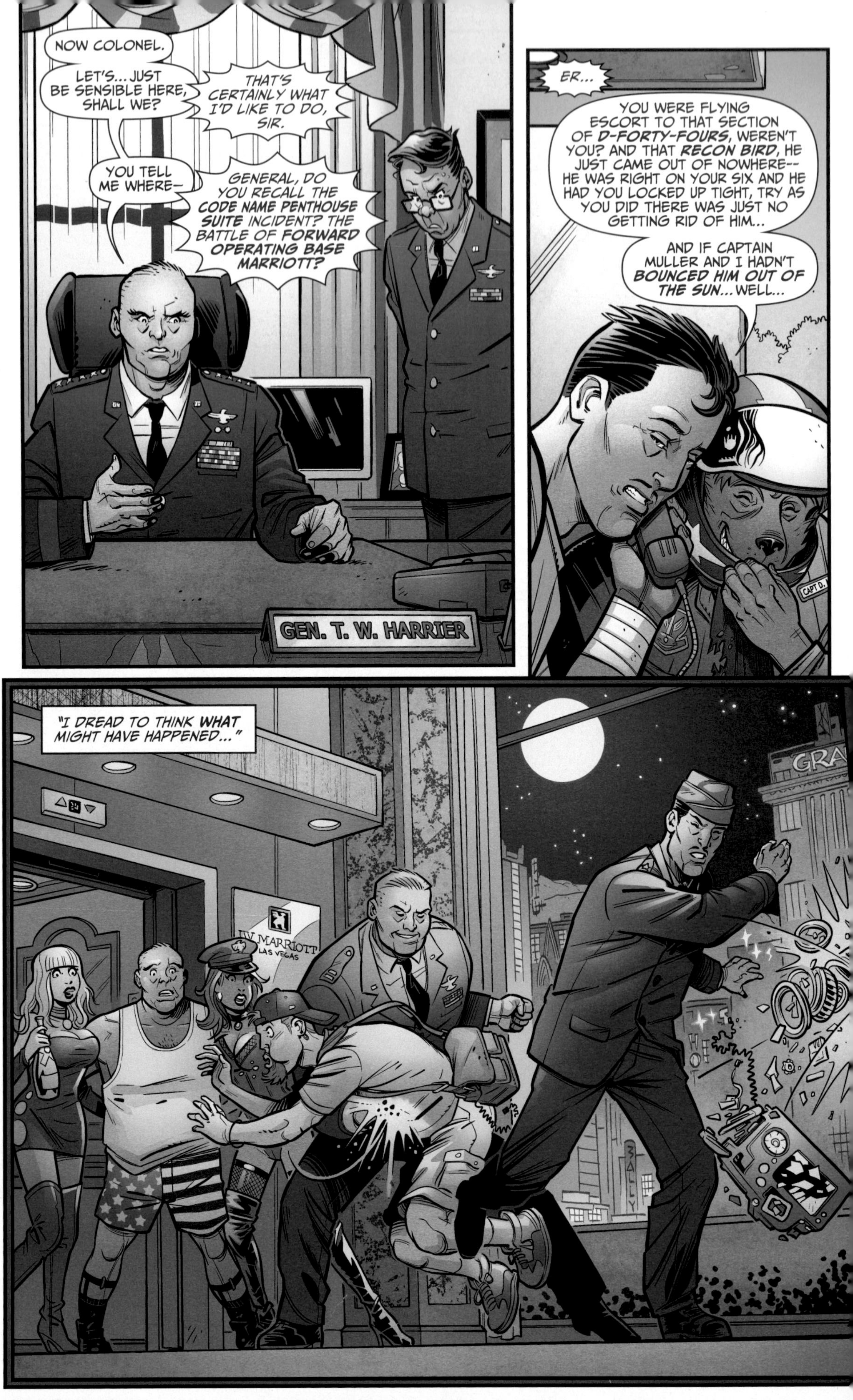
NOW COLONEL.
LET'S... JUST BE SENSIBLE HERE, SHALL WE?
THAT'S CERTAINLY WHAT I'D LIKE TO DO, SIR.
YOU TELL ME WHERE—
GENERAL, DO YOU RECALL THE CODE NAME PENTHOUSE SUITE INCIDENT? THE BATTLE OF FORWARD OPERATING BASE MARRIOTT?
GEN. T. W. HARRIER
ER...
YOU WERE FLYING ESCORT TO THAT SECTION OF D-FORTY-FOURS, WEREN'T YOU? AND THAT RECON BIRD, HE JUST CAME OUT OF NOWHERE-- HE WAS RIGHT ON YOUR SIX AND HE HAD YOU LOCKED UP TIGHT, TRY AS YOU DID THERE WAS JUST NO GETTING RID OF HIM...
AND IF CAPTAIN MULLER AND I HADN'T BOUNCED HIM OUT OF THE SUN... WELL...
"I DREAD TO THINK WHAT MIGHT HAVE HAPPENED..."
JW MARRIOTT LAS VEGAS

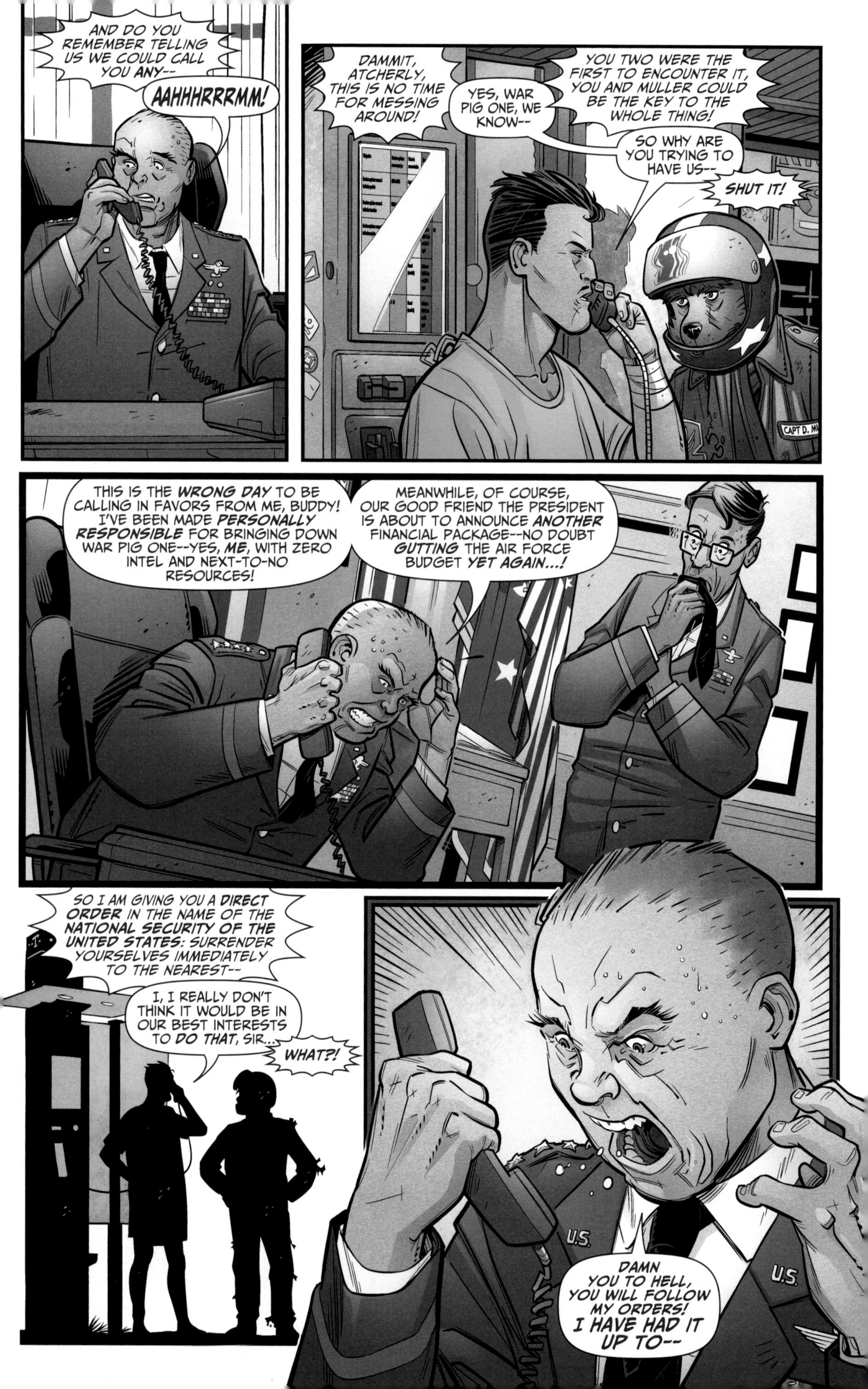
AND DO YOU REMEMBER TELLING US WE COULD CALL YOU ANY--
AAHHHRRRMM!
DAMMIT, ATCHERLY, THIS IS NO TIME FOR MESSING AROUND!
YES, WAR PIG ONE, WE KNOW--
YOU TWO WERE THE FIRST TO ENCOUNTER IT, YOU AND MULLER COULD BE THE KEY TO THE WHOLE THING!
SO WHY ARE YOU TRYING TO HAVE US--
SHUT IT!
CAPT D. MU
THIS IS THE WRONG DAY TO BE CALLING IN FAVORS FROM ME, BUDDY! I'VE BEEN MADE PERSONALLY RESPONSIBLE FOR BRINGING DOWN WAR PIG ONE--YES, ME, WITH ZERO INTEL AND NEXT-TO-NO RESOURCES!
MEANWHILE, OF COURSE, OUR GOOD FRIEND THE PRESIDENT IS ABOUT TO ANNOUNCE ANOTHER FINANCIAL PACKAGE--NO DOUBT GUTTING THE AIR FORCE BUDGET YET AGAIN...!
SO I AM GIVING YOU A DIRECT ORDER IN THE NAME OF THE NATIONAL SECURITY OF THE UNITED STATES: SURRENDER YOURSELVES IMMEDIATELY TO THE NEAREST--
I, I REALLY DON'T THINK IT WOULD BE IN OUR BEST INTERESTS TO DO THAT, SIR...
WHAT?!
U.S.
U.S.
DAMN YOU TO HELL, YOU WILL FOLLOW MY ORDERS! I HAVE HAD IT UP TO--

HERE!

POW

UNHH!

ER... GENERAL?

I'M JUST GONNA HANG UP NOW, SIR.

OLP

KLK

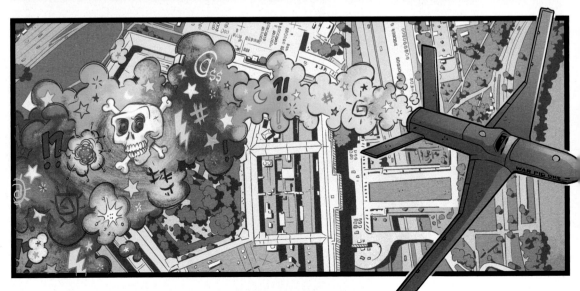

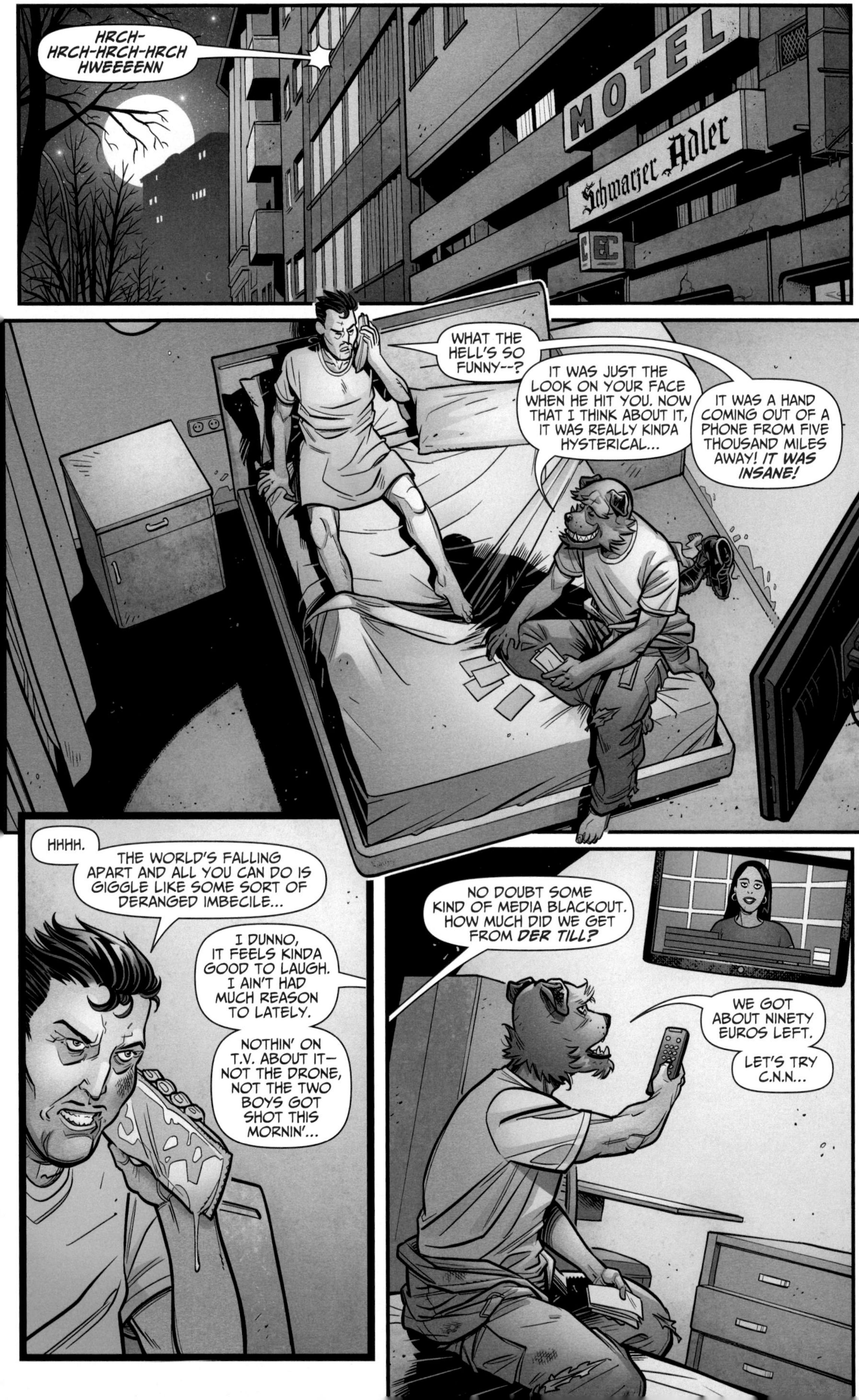
HRCH-HRCH-HRCH-HRCH HWEEEENN
MOTEL
Schwarzer Adler
WHAT THE HELL'S SO FUNNY--?
IT WAS JUST THE LOOK ON YOUR FACE WHEN HE HIT YOU. NOW THAT I THINK ABOUT IT, IT WAS REALLY KINDA HYSTERICAL...
IT WAS A HAND COMING OUT OF A PHONE FROM FIVE THOUSAND MILES AWAY! IT WAS INSANE!
HHHH.
THE WORLD'S FALLING APART AND ALL YOU CAN DO IS GIGGLE LIKE SOME SORT OF DERANGED IMBECILE...
I DUNNO, IT FEELS KINDA GOOD TO LAUGH. I AIN'T HAD MUCH REASON TO LATELY.
NOTHIN' ON T.V. ABOUT IT-- NOT THE DRONE, NOT THE TWO BOYS GOT SHOT THIS MORNIN'...
NO DOUBT SOME KIND OF MEDIA BLACKOUT. HOW MUCH DID WE GET FROM DER TILL?
WE GOT ABOUT NINETY EUROS LEFT.
LET'S TRY C.N.N...

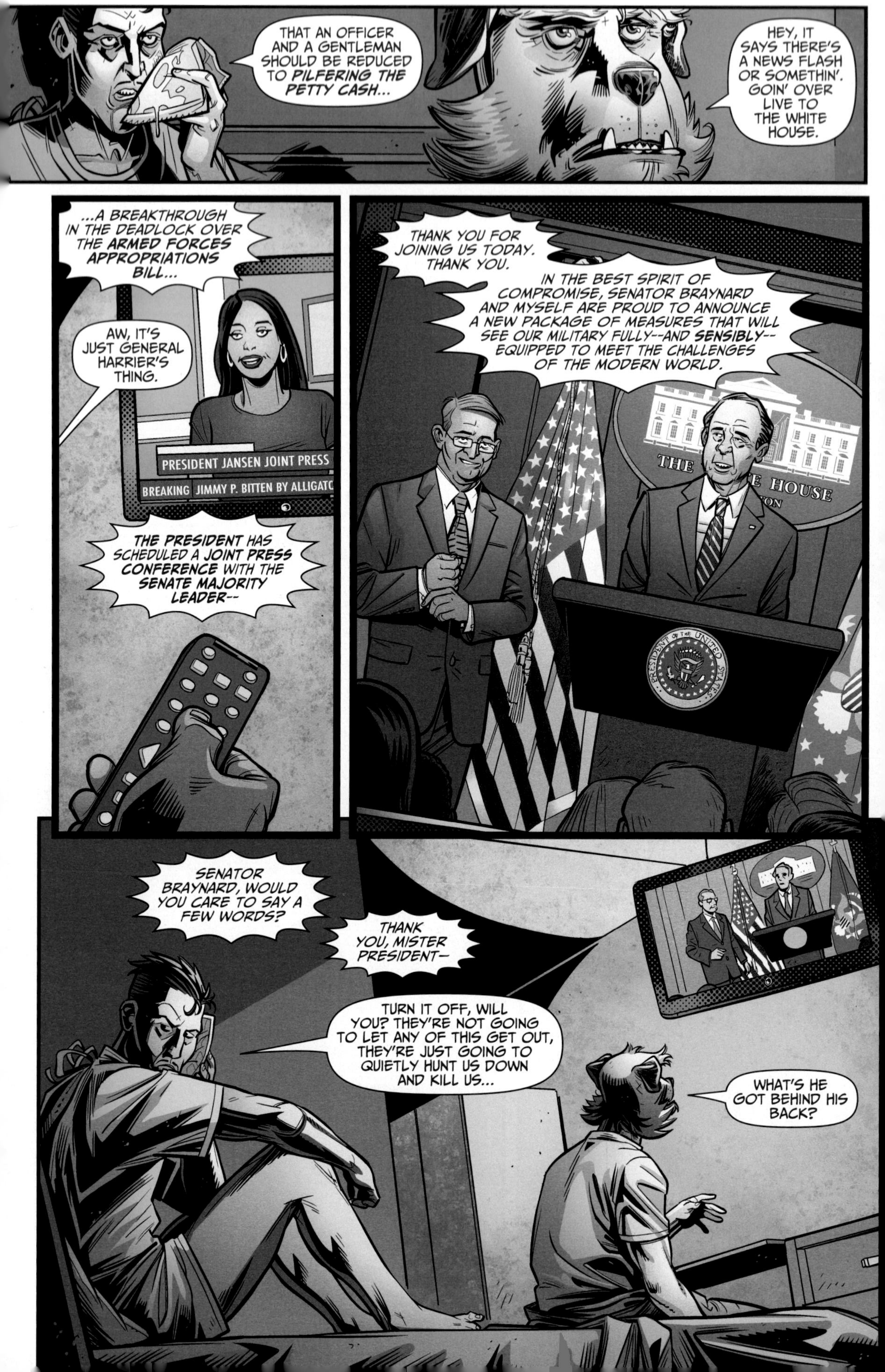
THAT AN OFFICER AND A GENTLEMAN SHOULD BE REDUCED TO PILFERING THE PETTY CASH...
HEY, IT SAYS THERE'S A NEWS FLASH OR SOMETHIN'. GOIN' OVER LIVE TO THE WHITE HOUSE.
...A BREAKTHROUGH IN THE DEADLOCK OVER THE ARMED FORCES APPROPRIATIONS BILL...
AW, IT'S JUST GENERAL HARRIER'S THING.
PRESIDENT JANSEN JOINT PRESS
BREAKING JIMMY P. BITTEN BY ALLIGATO
THE PRESIDENT HAS SCHEDULED A JOINT PRESS CONFERENCE WITH THE SENATE MAJORITY LEADER--
THANK YOU FOR JOINING US TODAY. THANK YOU.
IN THE BEST SPIRIT OF COMPROMISE, SENATOR BRAYNARD AND MYSELF ARE PROUD TO ANNOUNCE A NEW PACKAGE OF MEASURES THAT WILL SEE OUR MILITARY FULLY--AND SENSIBLY--EQUIPPED TO MEET THE CHALLENGES OF THE MODERN WORLD.
SENATOR BRAYNARD, WOULD YOU CARE TO SAY A FEW WORDS?
THANK YOU, MISTER PRESIDENT—
TURN IT OFF, WILL YOU? THEY'RE NOT GOING TO LET ANY OF THIS GET OUT, THEY'RE JUST GOING TO QUIETLY HUNT US DOWN AND KILL US...
WHAT'S HE GOT BEHIND HIS BACK?

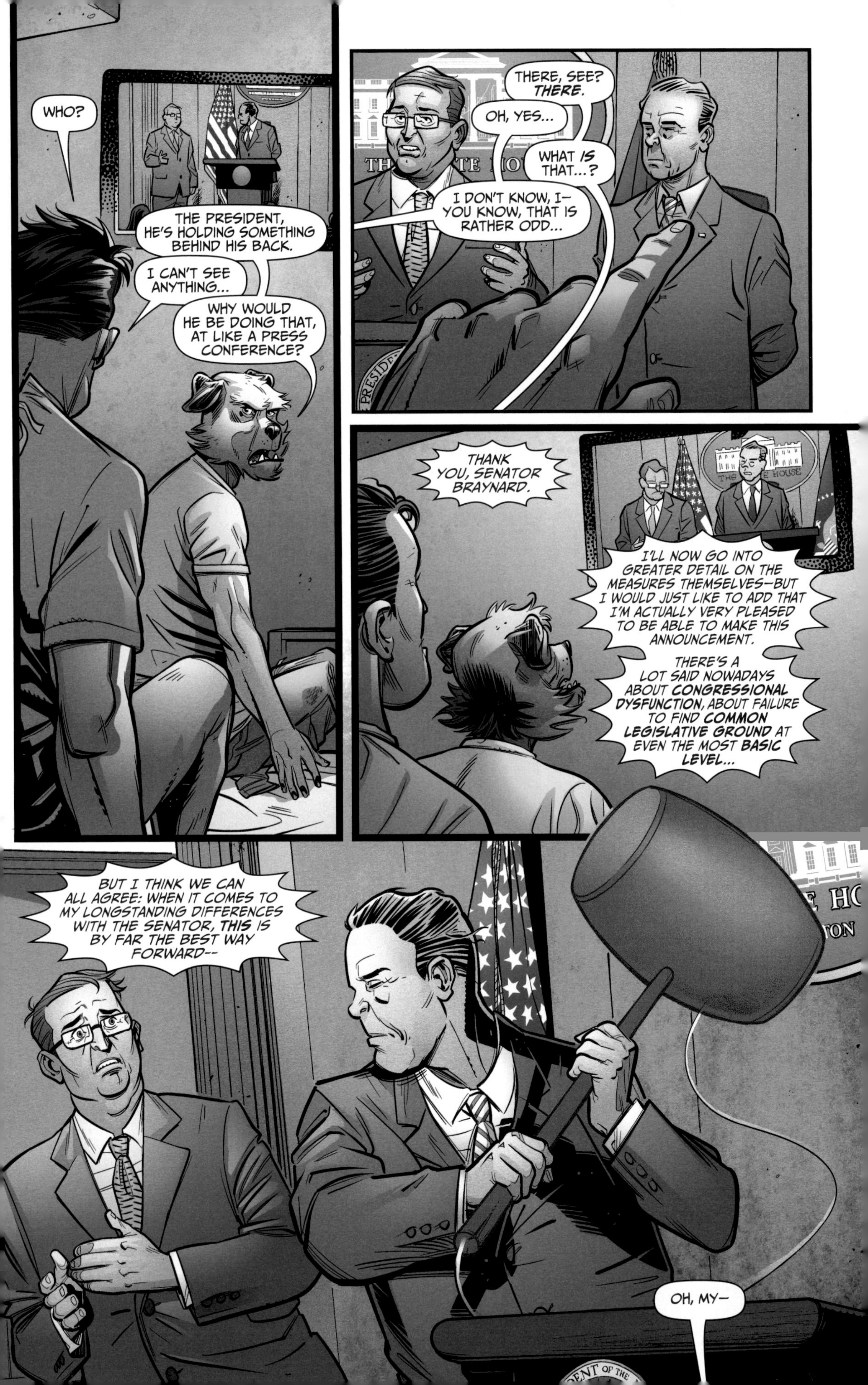
WHO?
THE PRESIDENT, HE'S HOLDING SOMETHING BEHIND HIS BACK.
I CAN'T SEE ANYTHING...
WHY WOULD HE BE DOING THAT, AT LIKE A PRESS CONFERENCE?
THERE, SEE? THERE.
OH, YES...
WHAT IS THAT...?
I DON'T KNOW, I- YOU KNOW, THAT IS RATHER ODD...
THANK YOU, SENATOR BRAYNARD.
I'LL NOW GO INTO GREATER DETAIL ON THE MEASURES THEMSELVES—BUT I WOULD JUST LIKE TO ADD THAT I'M ACTUALLY VERY PLEASED TO BE ABLE TO MAKE THIS ANNOUNCEMENT.
THERE'S A LOT SAID NOWADAYS ABOUT CONGRESSIONAL DYSFUNCTION, ABOUT FAILURE TO FIND COMMON LEGISLATIVE GROUND AT EVEN THE MOST BASIC LEVEL...
BUT I THINK WE CAN ALL AGREE: WHEN IT COMES TO MY LONGSTANDING DIFFERENCES WITH THE SENATOR, THIS IS BY FAR THE BEST WAY FORWARD--
OH, MY—

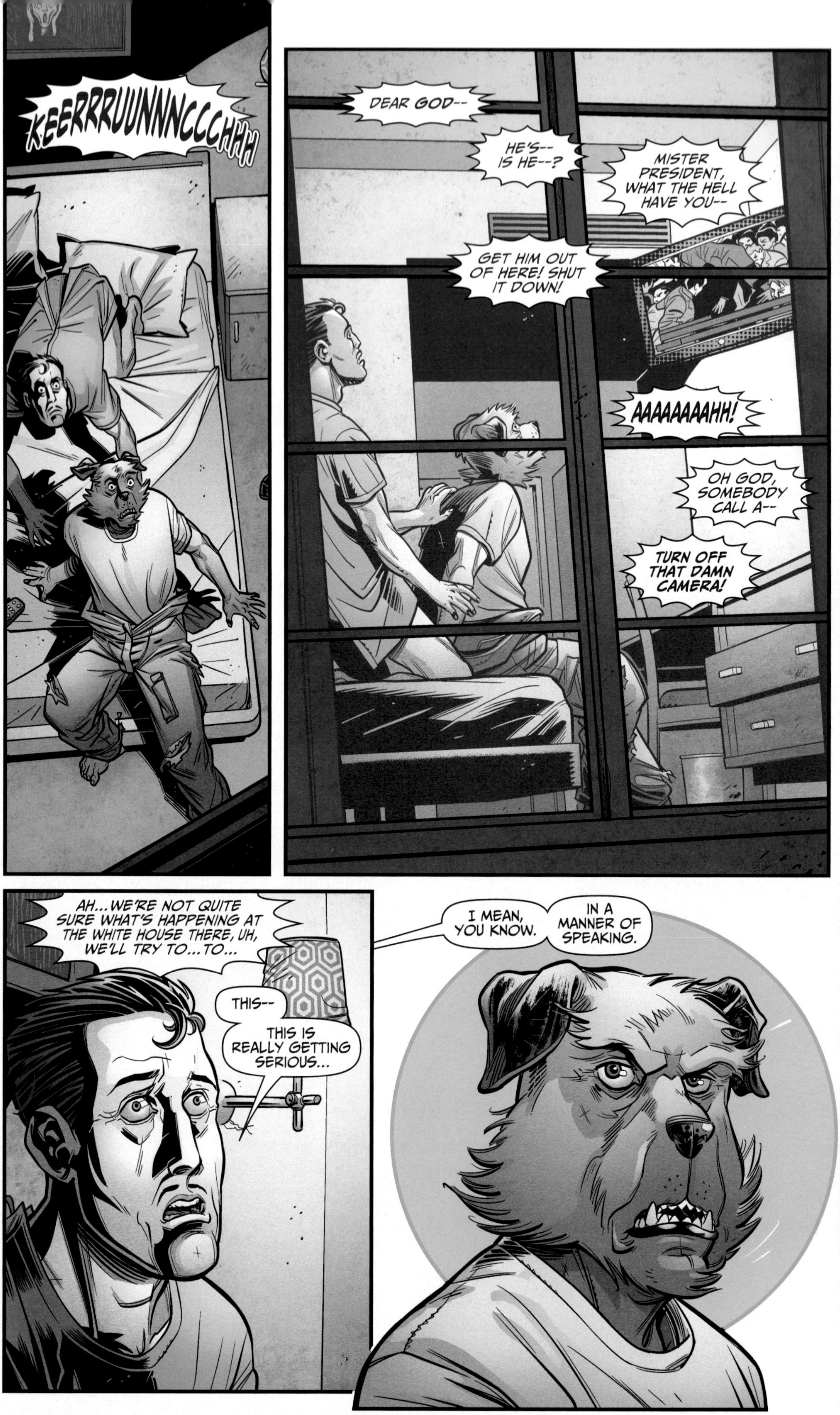
KEERRRUUNNNCCCHHH
DEAR GOD--
HE'S-- IS HE--?
MISTER PRESIDENT, WHAT THE HELL HAVE YOU--
GET HIM OUT OF HERE! SHUT IT DOWN!
AAAAAAAAHH!
OH GOD, SOMEBODY CALL A--
TURN OFF THAT DAMN CAMERA!
AH...WE'RE NOT QUITE SURE WHAT'S HAPPENING AT THE WHITE HOUSE THERE, UH, WE'LL TRY TO...TO...
THIS--
THIS IS REALLY GETTING SERIOUS...
I MEAN, YOU KNOW.
IN A MANNER OF SPEAKING.

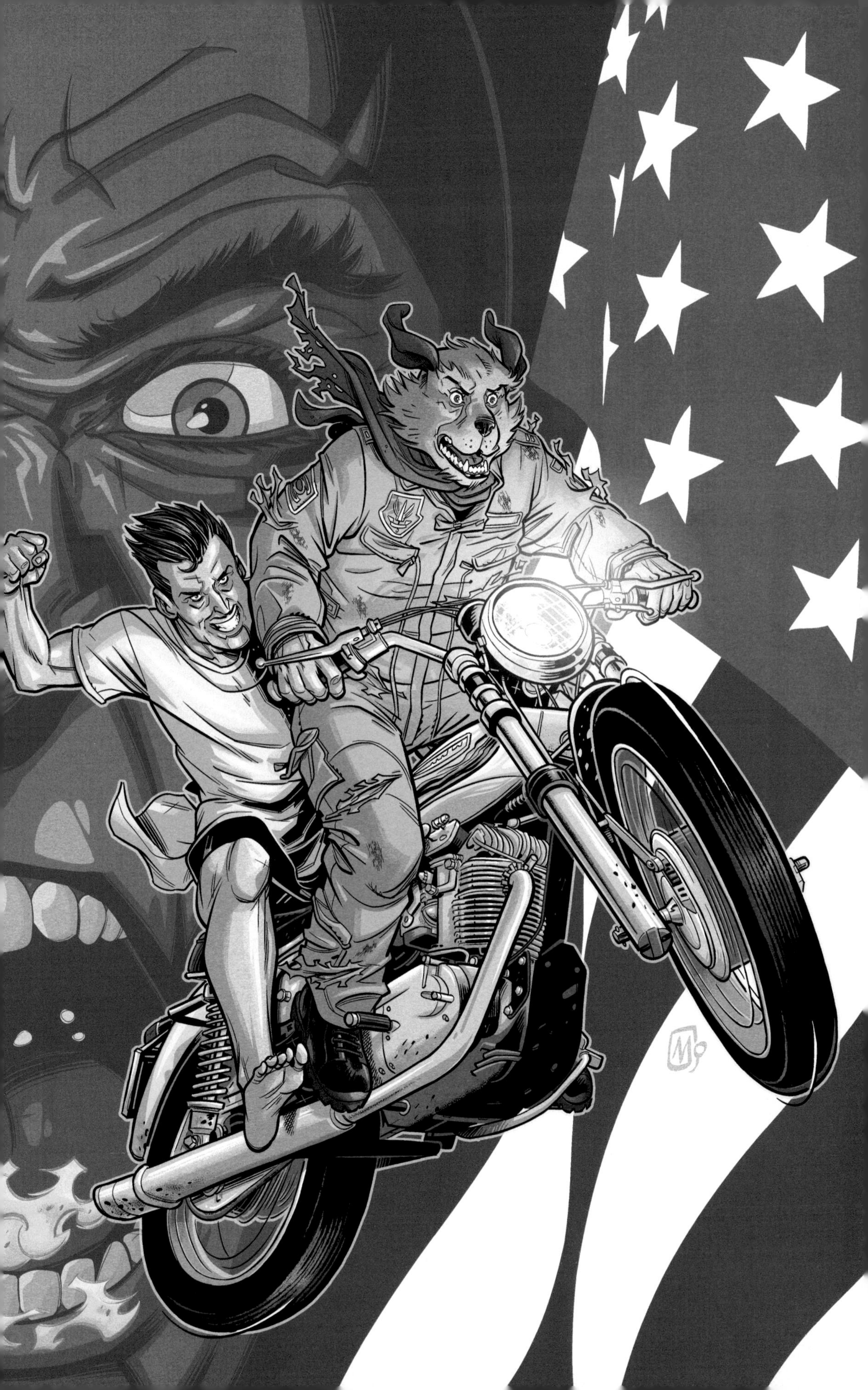

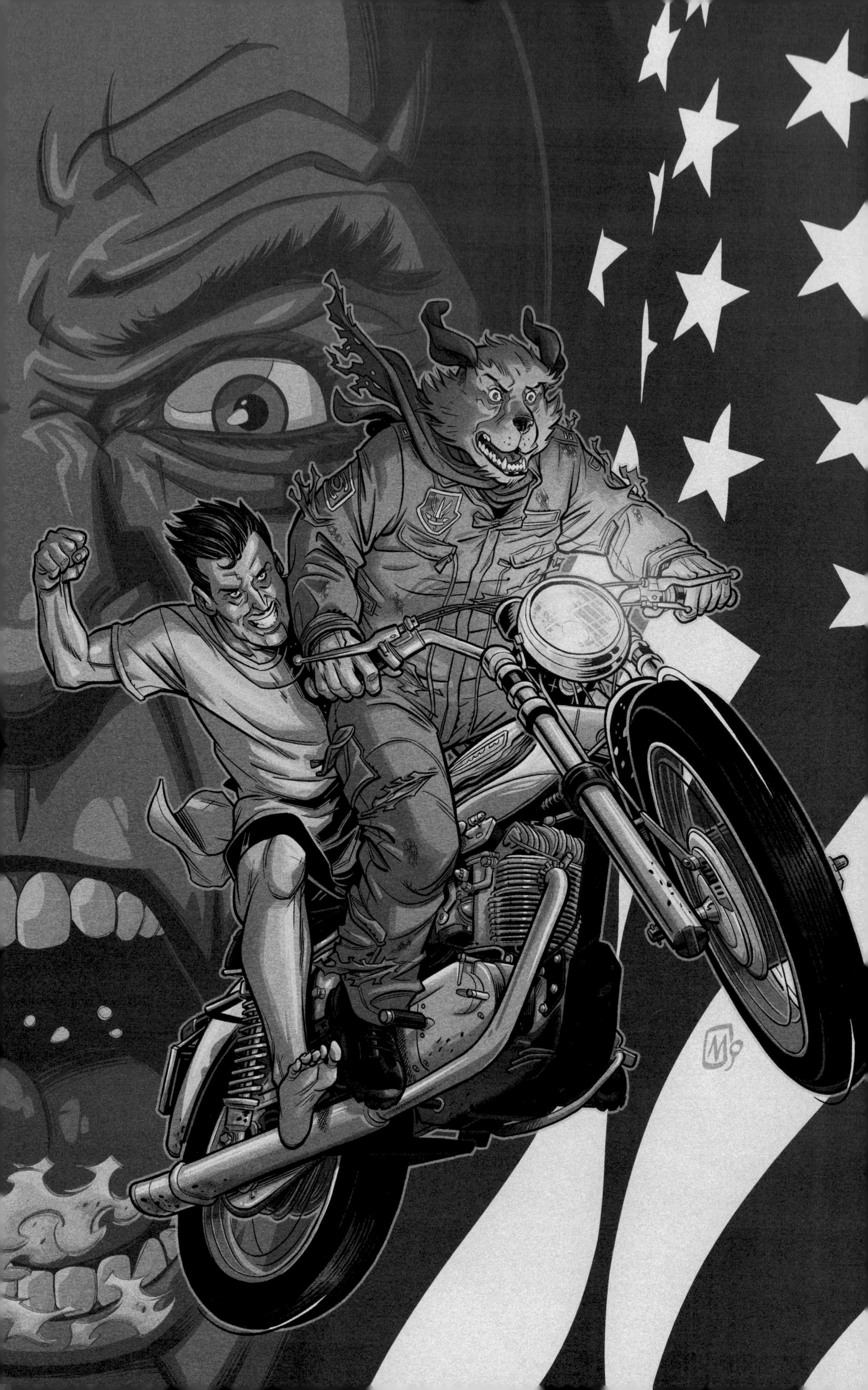

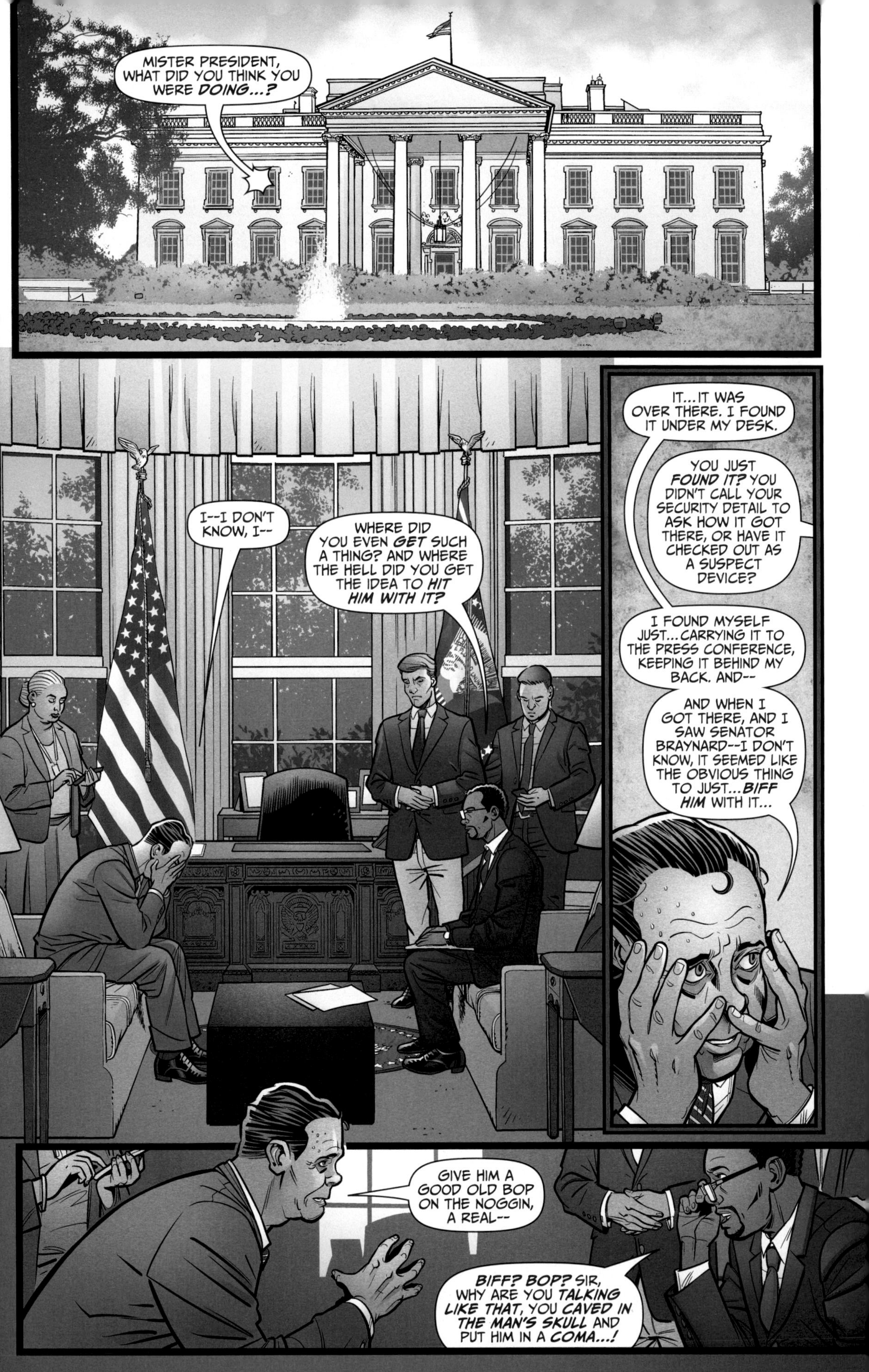
MISTER PRESIDENT, WHAT DID YOU THINK YOU WERE DOING...?
I--I DON'T KNOW, I--
WHERE DID YOU EVEN GET SUCH A THING? AND WHERE THE HELL DID YOU GET THE IDEA TO HIT HIM WITH IT?
IT...IT WAS OVER THERE. I FOUND IT UNDER MY DESK.
YOU JUST FOUND IT? YOU DIDN'T CALL YOUR SECURITY DETAIL TO ASK HOW IT GOT THERE, OR HAVE IT CHECKED OUT AS A SUSPECT DEVICE?
I FOUND MYSELF JUST...CARRYING IT TO THE PRESS CONFERENCE, KEEPING IT BEHIND MY BACK. AND--
AND WHEN I GOT THERE, AND I SAW SENATOR BRAYNARD--I DON'T KNOW, IT SEEMED LIKE THE OBVIOUS THING TO JUST...BIFF HIM WITH IT...
GIVE HIM A GOOD OLD BOP ON THE NOGGIN, A REAL--
BIFF? BOP? SIR, WHY ARE YOU TALKING LIKE THAT, YOU CAVED IN THE MAN'S SKULL AND PUT HIM IN A COMA...!

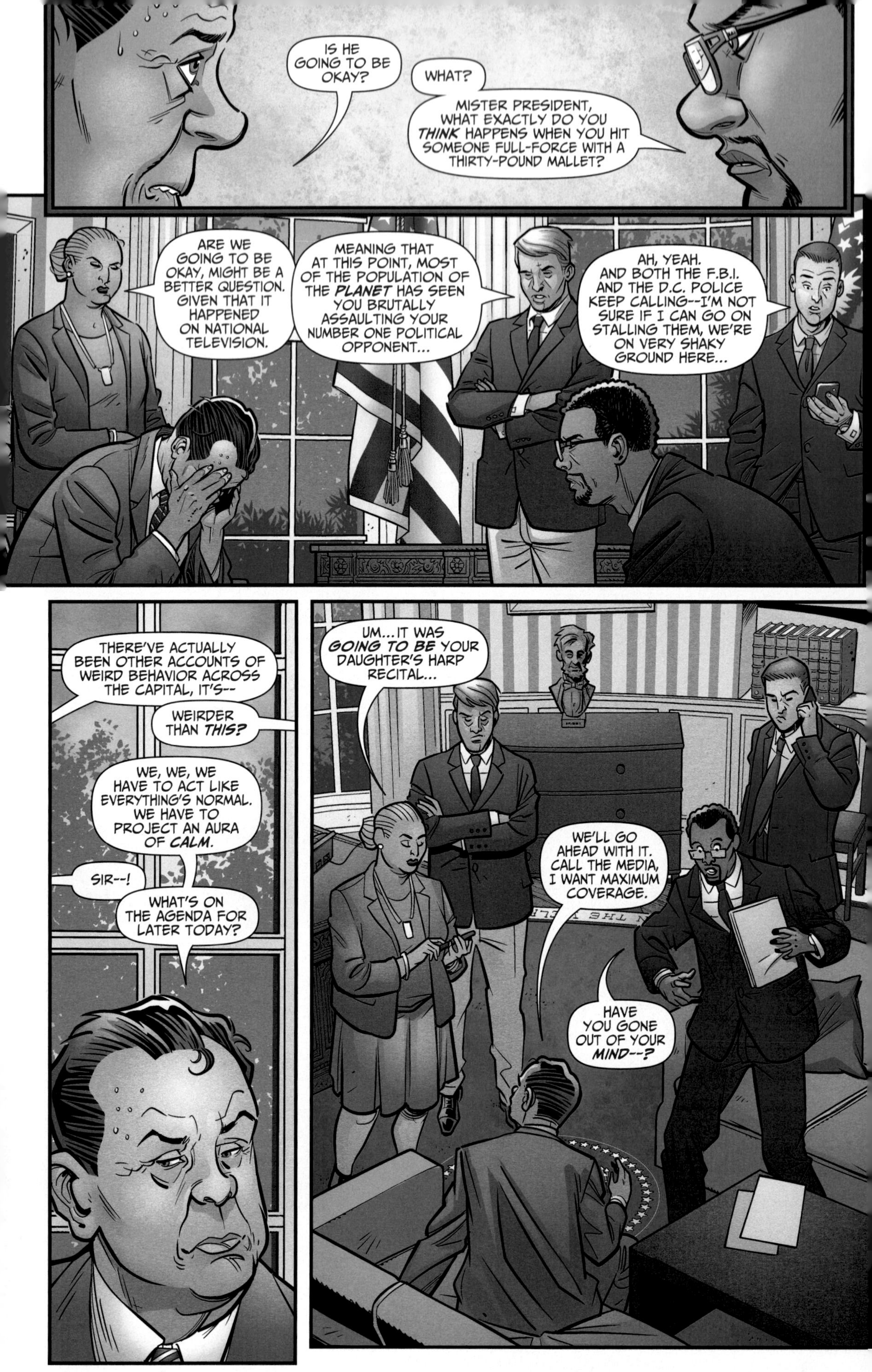
IS HE GOING TO BE OKAY?
WHAT?
MISTER PRESIDENT, WHAT EXACTLY DO YOU *THINK* HAPPENS WHEN YOU HIT SOMEONE FULL-FORCE WITH A THIRTY-POUND MALLET?
ARE WE GOING TO BE OKAY, MIGHT BE A BETTER QUESTION. GIVEN THAT IT HAPPENED ON NATIONAL TELEVISION.
MEANING THAT AT THIS POINT, MOST OF THE POPULATION OF THE *PLANET* HAS SEEN YOU BRUTALLY ASSAULTING YOUR NUMBER ONE POLITICAL OPPONENT...
AH, YEAH. AND BOTH THE F.B.I. AND THE D.C. POLICE KEEP CALLING--I'M NOT SURE IF I CAN GO ON STALLING THEM, WE'RE ON VERY SHAKY GROUND HERE...
THERE'VE ACTUALLY BEEN OTHER ACCOUNTS OF WEIRD BEHAVIOR ACROSS THE CAPITAL, IT'S--
WEIRDER THAN *THIS?*
WE, WE, WE HAVE TO ACT LIKE EVERYTHING'S NORMAL. WE HAVE TO PROJECT AN AURA OF *CALM*.
SIR--!
WHAT'S ON THE AGENDA FOR LATER TODAY?
UM...IT WAS *GOING TO BE* YOUR DAUGHTER'S HARP RECITAL...
WE'LL GO AHEAD WITH IT. CALL THE MEDIA, I WANT MAXIMUM COVERAGE.
HAVE YOU GONE OUT OF YOUR *MIND--?*

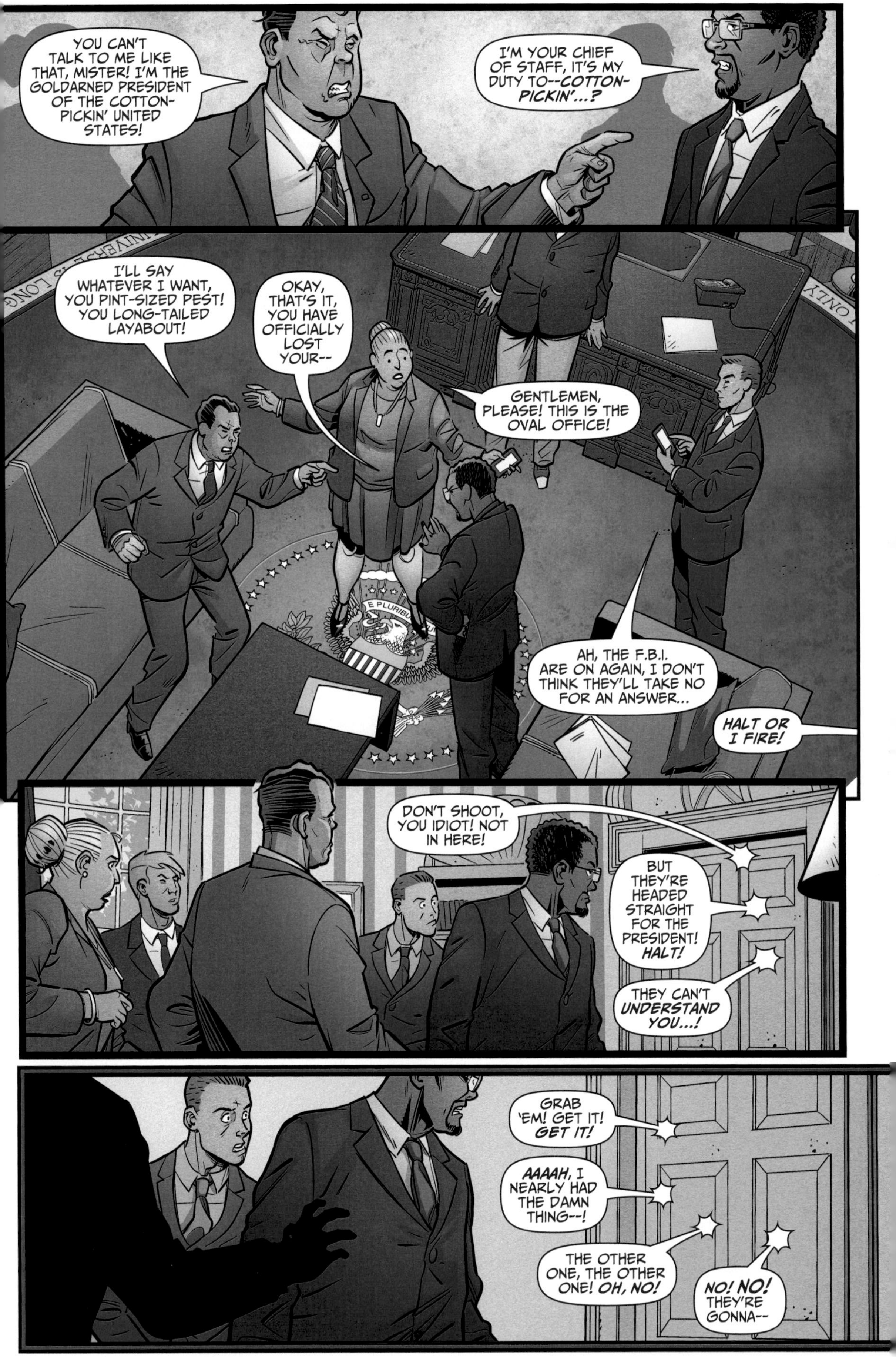
YOU CAN'T TALK TO ME LIKE THAT, MISTER! I'M THE GOLDARNED PRESIDENT OF THE COTTON-PICKIN' UNITED STATES!
I'M YOUR CHIEF OF STAFF, IT'S MY DUTY TO--*COTTON-PICKIN'...?*
I'LL SAY WHATEVER I WANT, YOU PINT-SIZED PEST! YOU LONG-TAILED LAYABOUT!
OKAY, THAT'S IT, YOU HAVE OFFICIALLY LOST YOUR--
GENTLEMEN, PLEASE! THIS IS THE OVAL OFFICE!
AH, THE F.B.I. ARE ON AGAIN, I DON'T THINK THEY'LL TAKE NO FOR AN ANSWER...
HALT OR I FIRE!
DON'T SHOOT, YOU IDIOT! NOT IN HERE!
BUT THEY'RE HEADED STRAIGHT FOR THE PRESIDENT! *HALT!*
THEY CAN'T *UNDERSTAND YOU...!*
GRAB 'EM! GET IT! *GET IT!*
AAAAH, I NEARLY HAD THE DAMN THING--!
THE OTHER ONE, THE OTHER ONE! *OH, NO!*
NO! NO! THEY'RE GONNA--

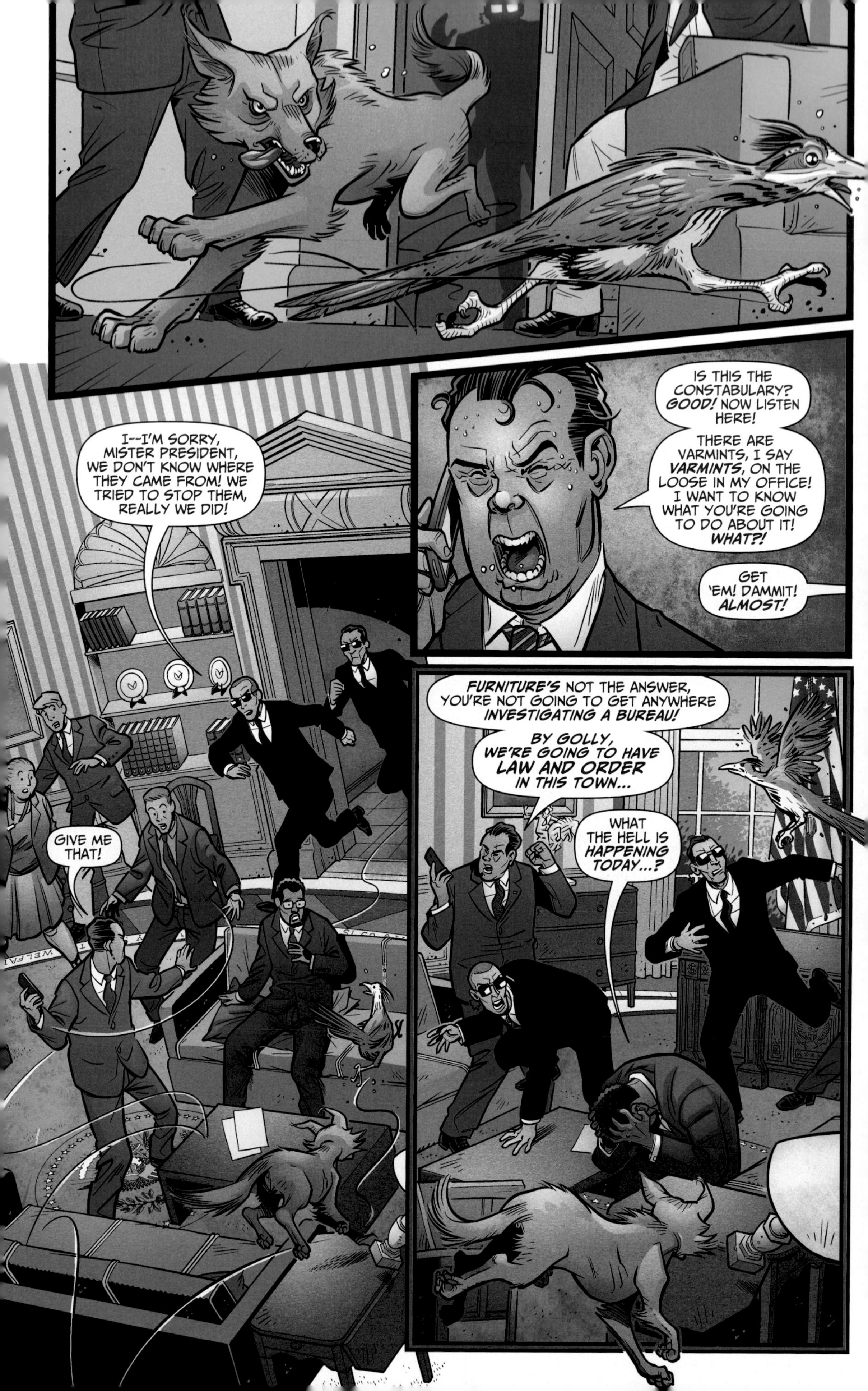
I--I'M SORRY, MISTER PRESIDENT, WE DON'T KNOW WHERE THEY CAME FROM! WE TRIED TO STOP THEM, REALLY WE DID!
IS THIS THE CONSTABULARY? GOOD! NOW LISTEN HERE!
THERE ARE VARMINTS, I SAY VARMINTS, ON THE LOOSE IN MY OFFICE! I WANT TO KNOW WHAT YOU'RE GOING TO DO ABOUT IT! WHAT?!
GET 'EM! DAMMIT! ALMOST!
GIVE ME THAT!
FURNITURE'S NOT THE ANSWER, YOU'RE NOT GOING TO GET ANYWHERE INVESTIGATING A BUREAU!
BY GOLLY, WE'RE GOING TO HAVE LAW AND ORDER IN THIS TOWN...
WHAT THE HELL IS HAPPENING TODAY...?

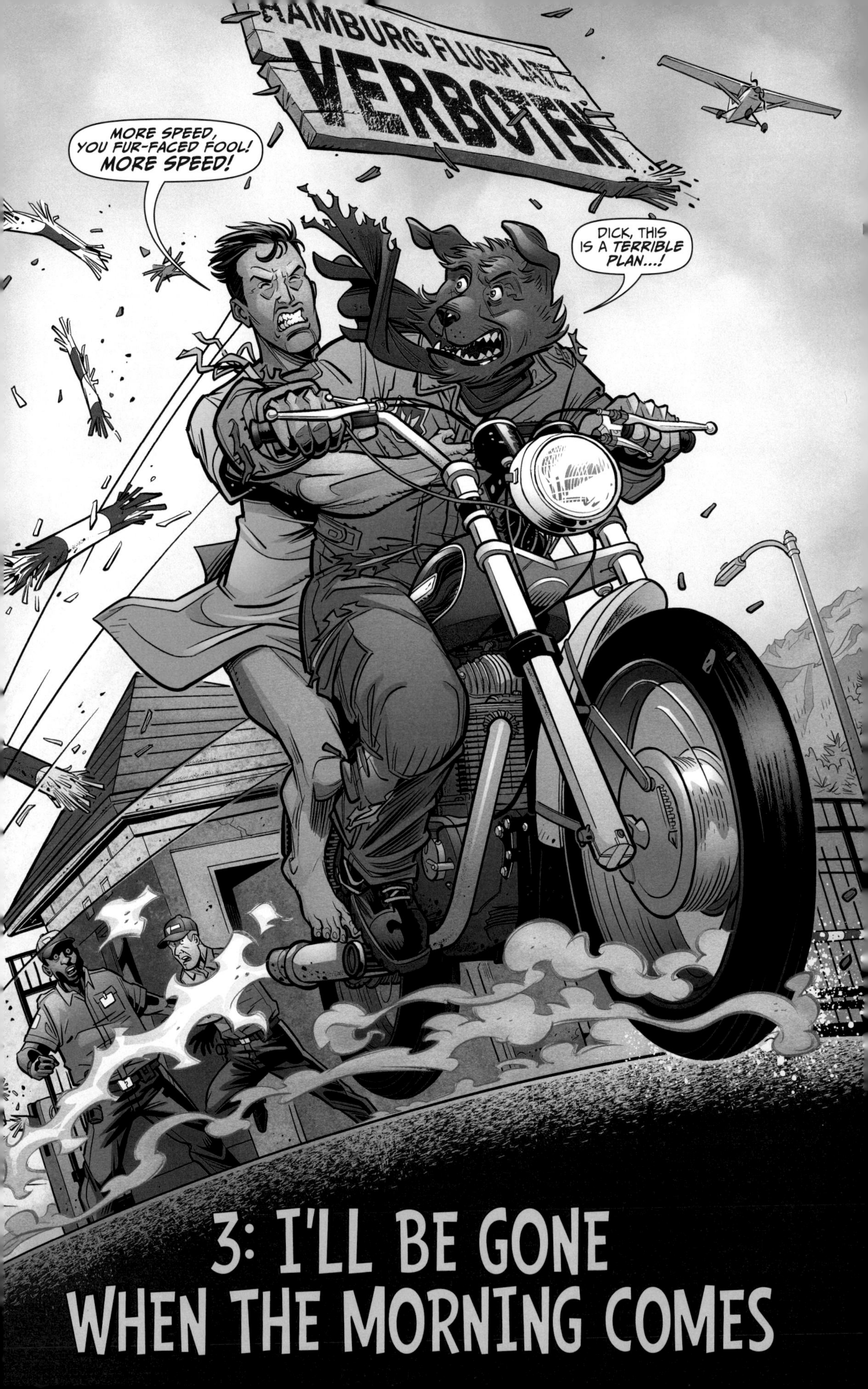
HAMBURG FLUGPLATZ
VERBOTEN
MORE SPEED, YOU FUR-FACED FOOL! MORE SPEED!
DICK, THIS IS A TERRIBLE PLAN...!

3: I'LL BE GONE WHEN THE MORNING COMES

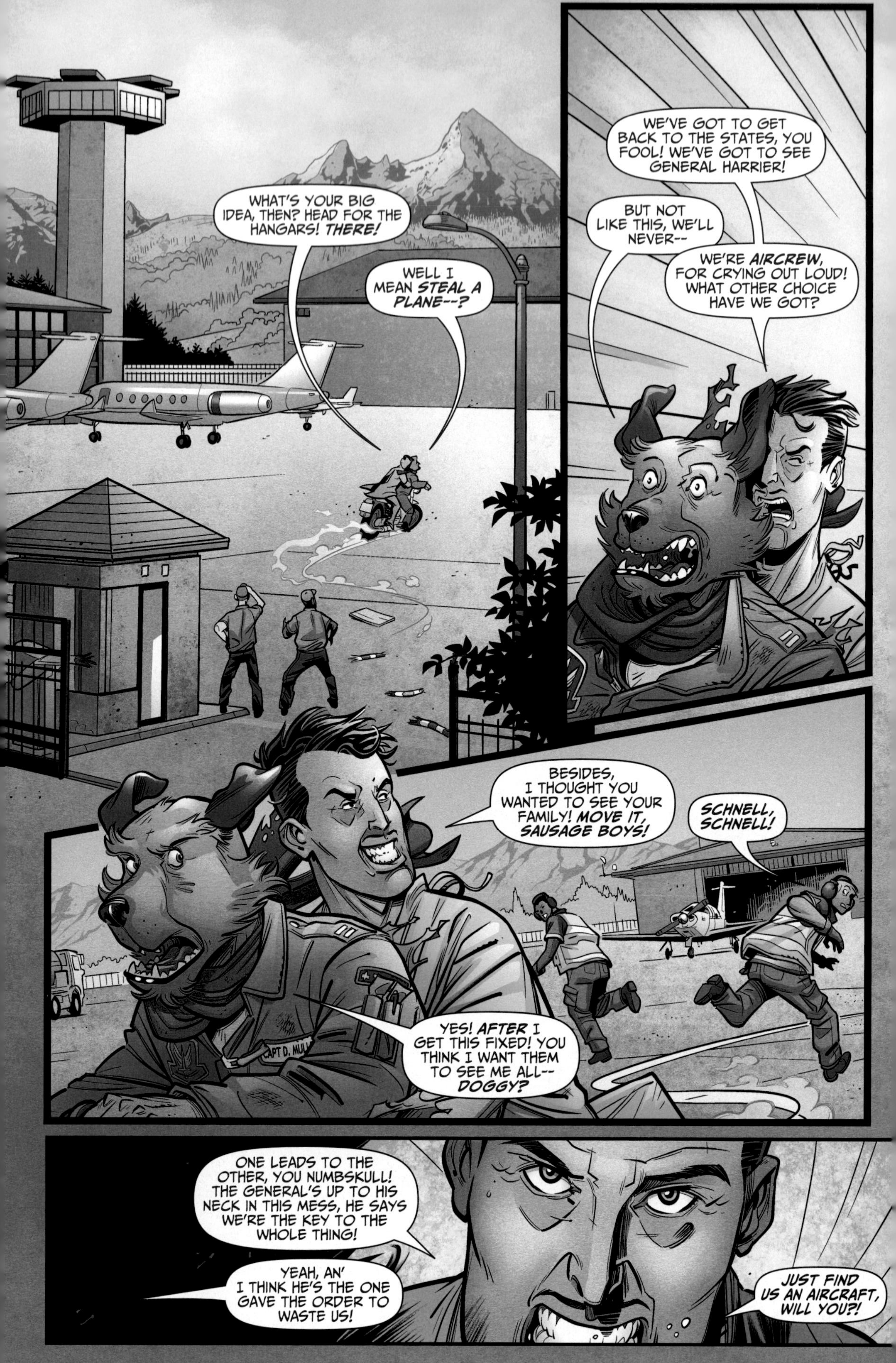
WHAT'S YOUR BIG IDEA, THEN? HEAD FOR THE HANGARS! THERE!
WELL I MEAN STEAL A PLANE--?
WE'VE GOT TO GET BACK TO THE STATES, YOU FOOL! WE'VE GOT TO SEE GENERAL HARRIER!
BUT NOT LIKE THIS, WE'LL NEVER--
WE'RE AIRCREW, FOR CRYING OUT LOUD! WHAT OTHER CHOICE HAVE WE GOT?
BESIDES, I THOUGHT YOU WANTED TO SEE YOUR FAMILY! MOVE IT, SAUSAGE BOYS!
SCHNELL, SCHNELL!
YES! AFTER I GET THIS FIXED! YOU THINK I WANT THEM TO SEE ME ALL-- DOGGY?
CAPT D. MUL
ONE LEADS TO THE OTHER, YOU NUMBSKULL! THE GENERAL'S UP TO HIS NECK IN THIS MESS, HE SAYS WE'RE THE KEY TO THE WHOLE THING!
YEAH, AN' I THINK HE'S THE ONE GAVE THE ORDER TO WASTE US!
JUST FIND US AN AIRCRAFT, WILL YOU?!

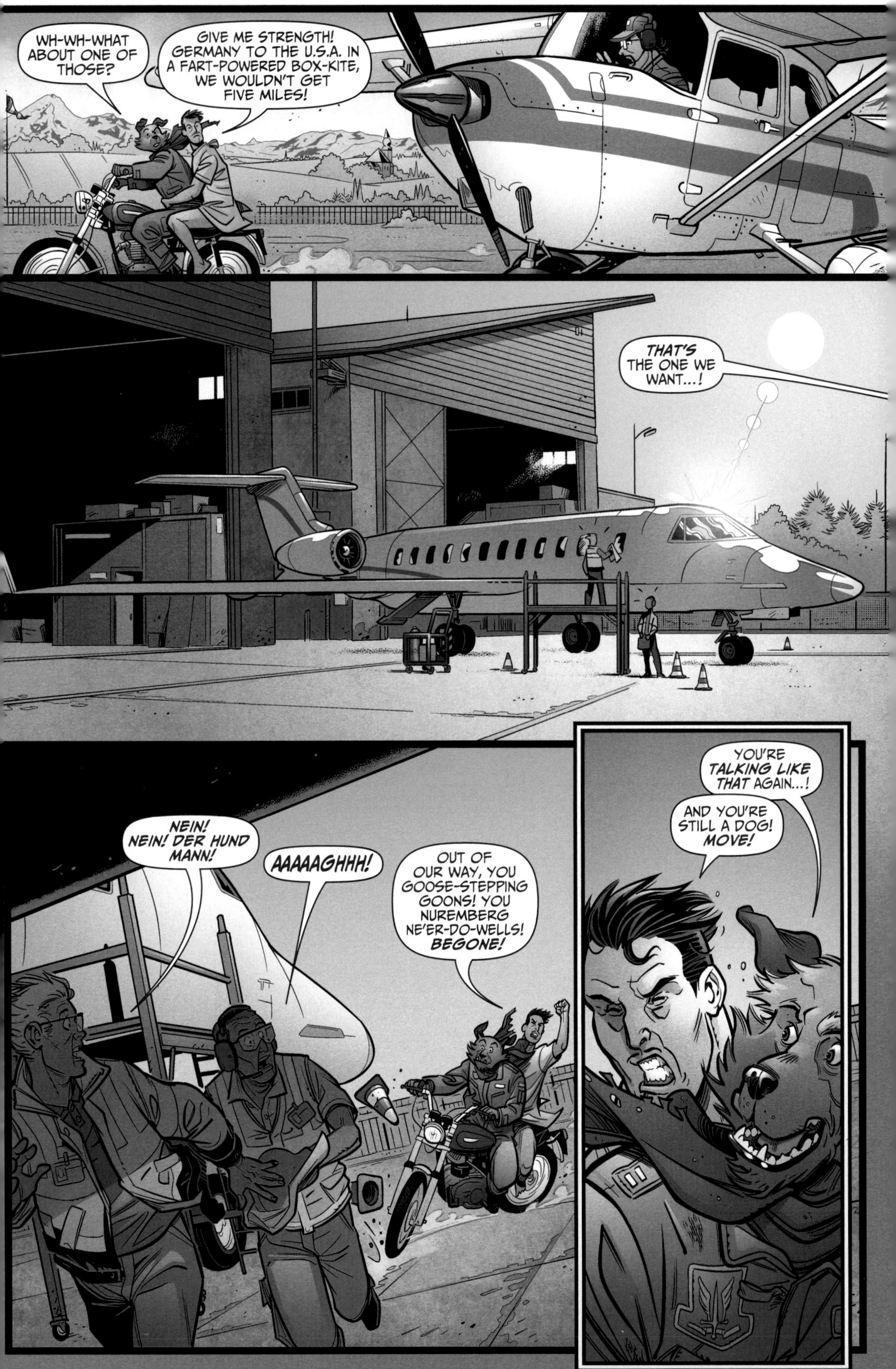
WH-WH-WHAT ABOUT ONE OF THOSE?
GIVE ME STRENGTH! GERMANY TO THE U.S.A. IN A FART-POWERED BOX-KITE, WE WOULDN'T GET FIVE MILES!
THAT'S THE ONE WE WANT...!
NEIN! NEIN! DER HUND MANN!
AAAAAGHHH!
OUT OF OUR WAY, YOU GOOSE-STEPPING GOONS! YOU NUREMBERG NE'ER-DO-WELLS! BEGONE!
YOU'RE TALKING LIKE THAT AGAIN...!
AND YOU'RE STILL A DOG! MOVE!

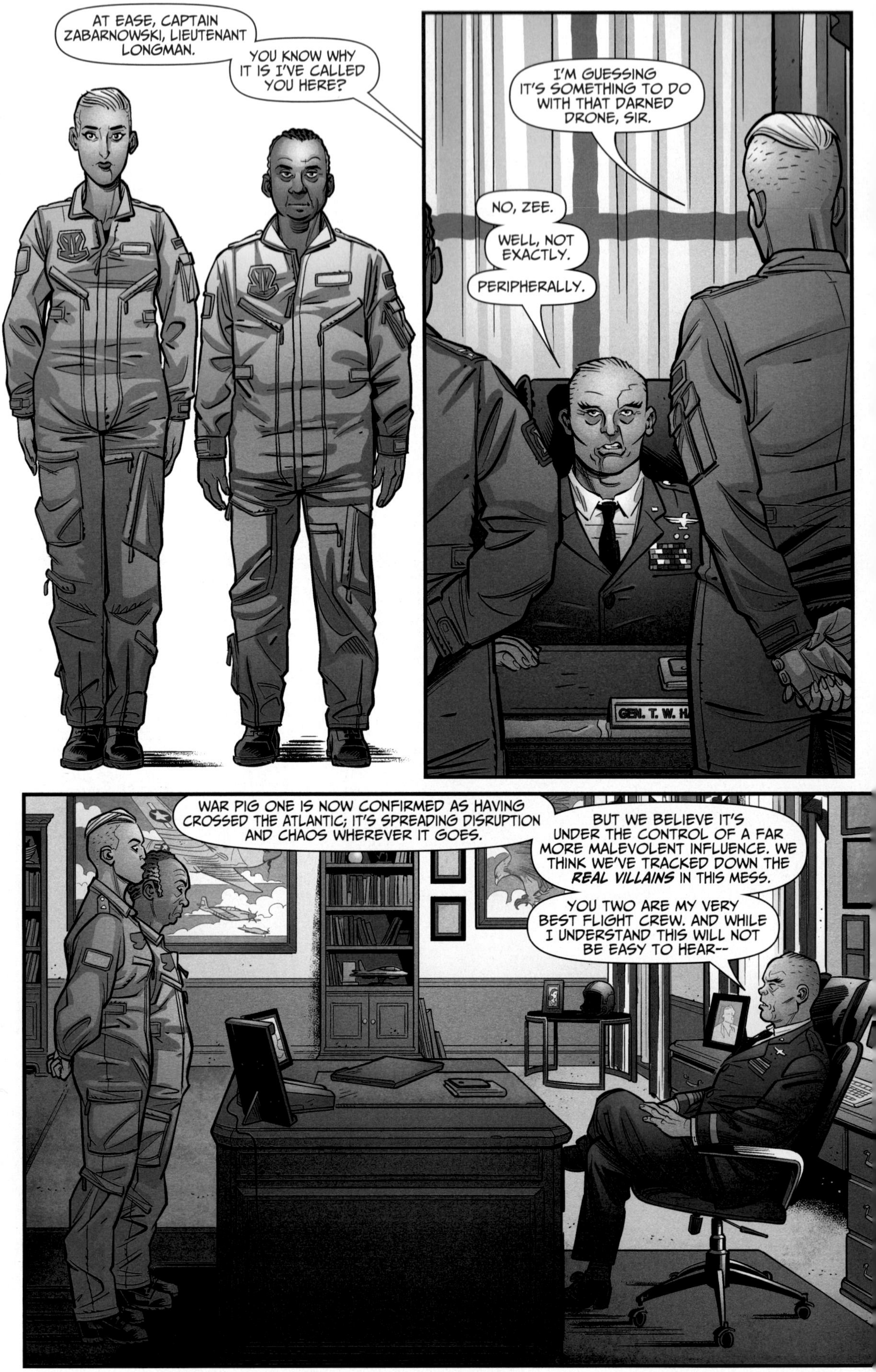
AT EASE, CAPTAIN ZABARNOWSKI, LIEUTENANT LONGMAN.
YOU KNOW WHY IT IS I'VE CALLED YOU HERE?
I'M GUESSING IT'S SOMETHING TO DO WITH THAT DARNED DRONE, SIR.
NO, ZEE.
WELL, NOT EXACTLY.
PERIPHERALLY.
GEN. T. W. H
WAR PIG ONE IS NOW CONFIRMED AS HAVING CROSSED THE ATLANTIC; IT'S SPREADING DISRUPTION AND CHAOS WHEREVER IT GOES.
BUT WE BELIEVE IT'S UNDER THE CONTROL OF A FAR MORE MALEVOLENT INFLUENCE. WE THINK WE'VE TRACKED DOWN THE ***REAL VILLAINS*** IN THIS MESS.
YOU TWO ARE MY VERY BEST FLIGHT CREW. AND WHILE I UNDERSTAND THIS WILL NOT BE EASY TO HEAR--

YOUR TARGETS ARE LIEUTENANT-COLONEL RICHARD ATCHERLY AND CAPTAIN DUDLEY MULLER.

YOUR MISSION IS TO TERMINATE THEM WITH EXTREME PREJUDICE.

DICK AND MUTT--?

SIR, ARE YOU *CERTAIN* ABOUT THIS...?

REGRETFULLY YES, ZEE.

WHEREVER THE DRONE GOES, THEY FOLLOW. AND THEN ALL HELL BREAKS LOOSE.

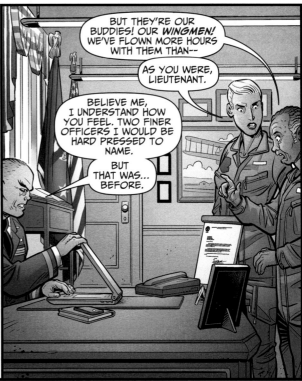

BUT THEY'RE OUR BUDDIES! OUR *WINGMEN!* WE'VE FLOWN MORE HOURS WITH THEM THAN--

AS YOU WERE, LIEUTENANT.

BELIEVE ME, I UNDERSTAND HOW YOU FEEL. TWO FINER OFFICERS I WOULD BE HARD PRESSED TO NAME.

BUT THAT WAS... BEFORE.

TRUST ME WHEN I SAY THAT I DO NOT SHOW YOU THESE LIGHTLY.

GAH!!

GOLDEN

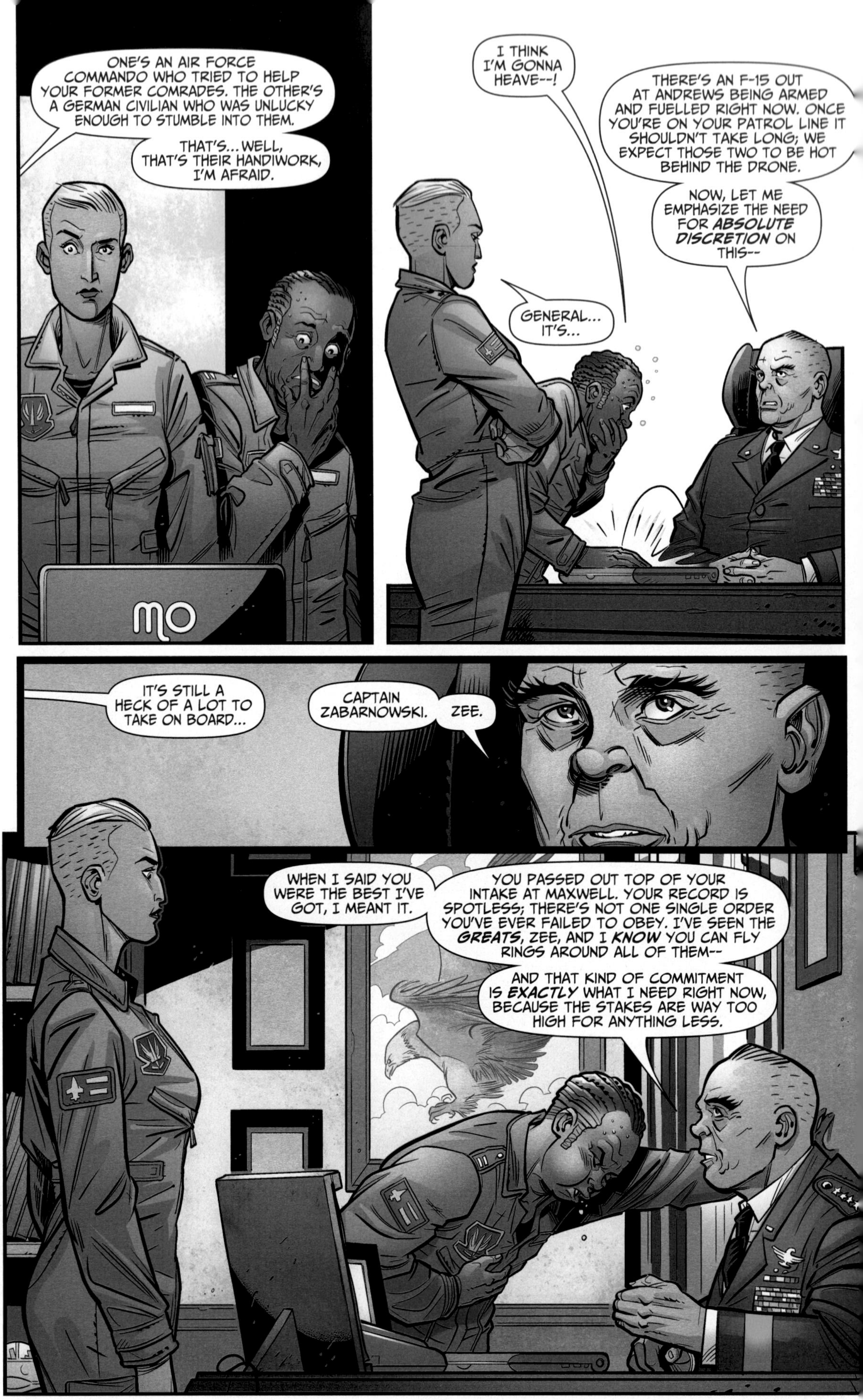
ONE'S AN AIR FORCE COMMANDO WHO TRIED TO HELP YOUR FORMER COMRADES. THE OTHER'S A GERMAN CIVILIAN WHO WAS UNLUCKY ENOUGH TO STUMBLE INTO THEM.
THAT'S...WELL, THAT'S THEIR HANDIWORK, I'M AFRAID.
MO
I THINK I'M GONNA HEAVE--!
THERE'S AN F-15 OUT AT ANDREWS BEING ARMED AND FUELLED RIGHT NOW. ONCE YOU'RE ON YOUR PATROL LINE IT SHOULDN'T TAKE LONG; WE EXPECT THOSE TWO TO BE HOT BEHIND THE DRONE.
NOW, LET ME EMPHASIZE THE NEED FOR ***ABSOLUTE DISCRETION*** ON THIS--
GENERAL... IT'S...
IT'S STILL A HECK OF A LOT TO TAKE ON BOARD...
CAPTAIN ZABARNOWSKI.
ZEE.
WHEN I SAID YOU WERE THE BEST I'VE GOT, I MEANT IT.
YOU PASSED OUT TOP OF YOUR INTAKE AT MAXWELL. YOUR RECORD IS SPOTLESS; THERE'S NOT ONE SINGLE ORDER YOU'VE EVER FAILED TO OBEY. I'VE SEEN THE ***GREATS***, ZEE, AND I ***KNOW*** YOU CAN FLY RINGS AROUND ALL OF THEM--
AND THAT KIND OF COMMITMENT IS ***EXACTLY*** WHAT I NEED RIGHT NOW, BECAUSE THE STAKES ARE WAY TOO HIGH FOR ANYTHING LESS.

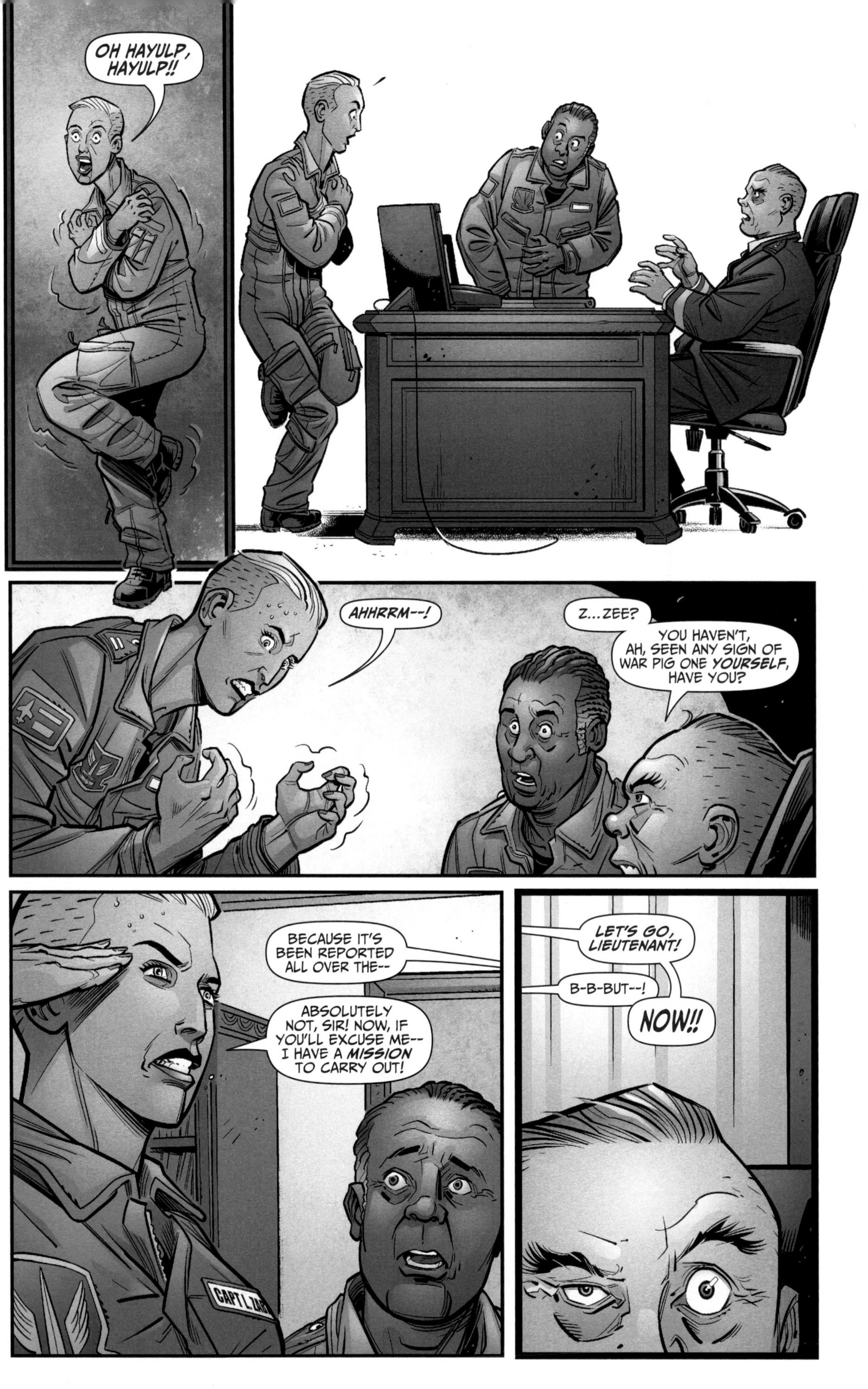
OH HAYULP, HAYULP!!
AHHRRM--!
Z...ZEE?
YOU HAVEN'T, AH, SEEN ANY SIGN OF WAR PIG ONE YOURSELF, HAVE YOU?
BECAUSE IT'S BEEN REPORTED ALL OVER THE--
ABSOLUTELY NOT, SIR! NOW, IF YOU'LL EXCUSE ME-- I HAVE A MISSION TO CARRY OUT!
CAPT. L. ZAB
LET'S GO, LIEUTENANT!
B-B-BUT--!
NOW!!

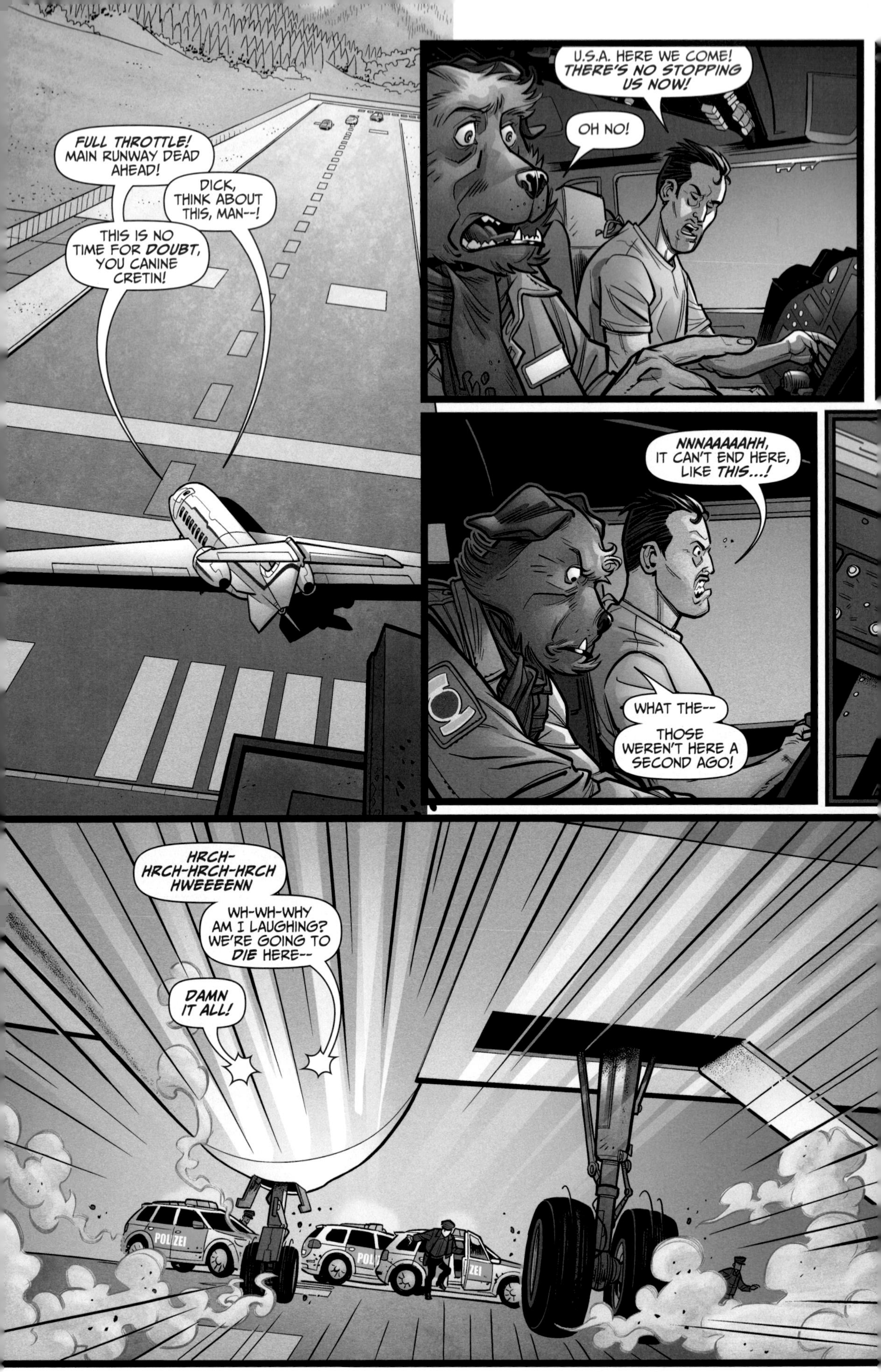
FULL THROTTLE! MAIN RUNWAY DEAD AHEAD!
DICK, THINK ABOUT THIS, MAN--!
THIS IS NO TIME FOR DOUBT, YOU CANINE CRETIN!
U.S.A. HERE WE COME! THERE'S NO STOPPING US NOW!
OH NO!
NNNAAAAAHH, IT CAN'T END HERE, LIKE THIS...!
WHAT THE--
THOSE WEREN'T HERE A SECOND AGO!
HRCH-HRCH-HRCH-HRCH HWEEEENN
WH-WH-WHY AM I LAUGHING? WE'RE GOING TO DIE HERE--
DAMN IT ALL!
POLIZEI
POLI
ZEI

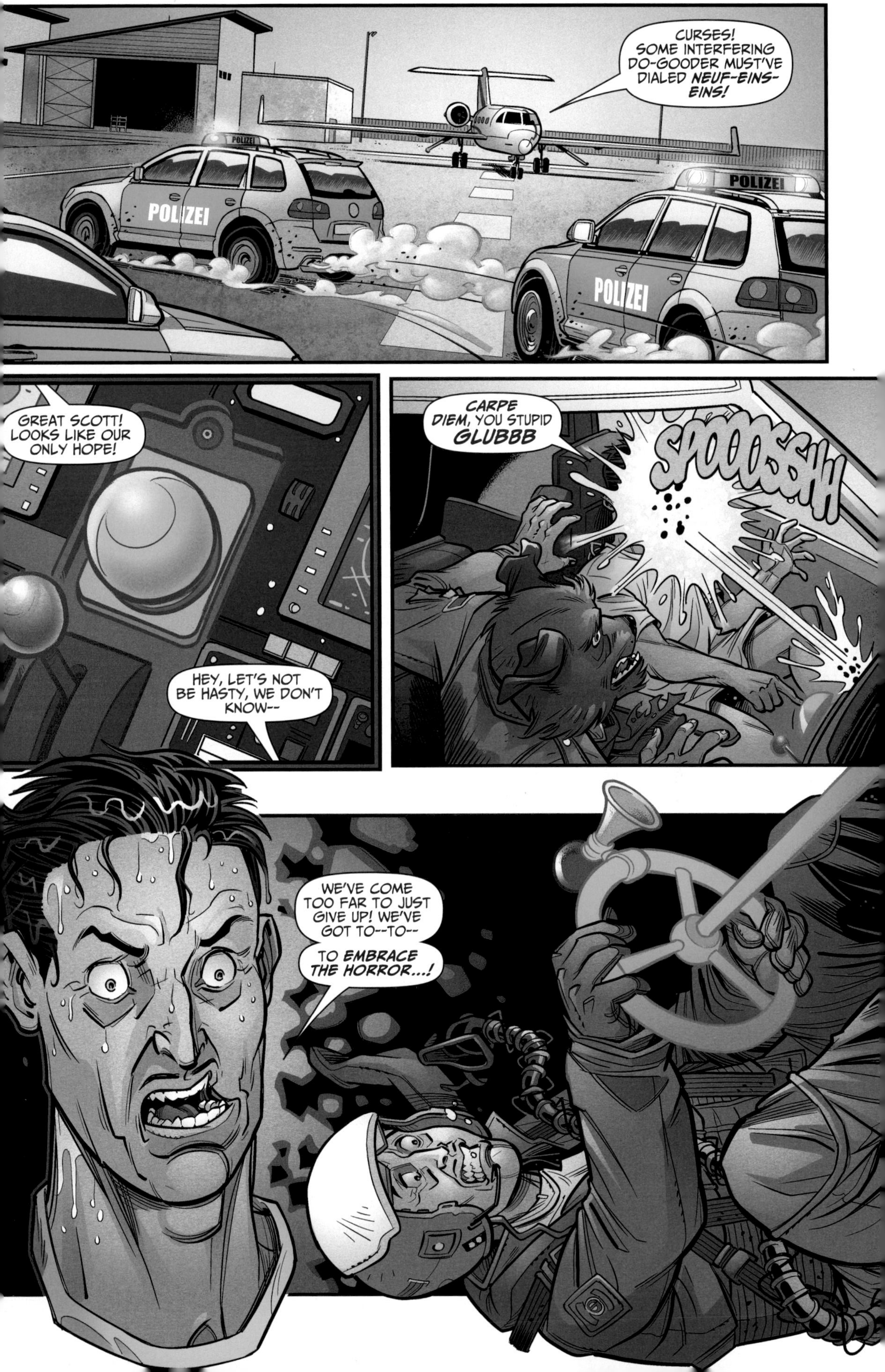

CURSES! SOME INTERFERING DO-GOODER MUST'VE DIALED *NEUF-EINS-EINS!*
POLIZEI
POLIZEI
POLIZEI
POLIZEI
GREAT SCOTT! LOOKS LIKE OUR ONLY HOPE!
HEY, LET'S NOT BE HASTY, WE DON'T KNOW--
CARPE DIEM, YOU STUPID **GLUBBB**
SPOOOSSHH
WE'VE COME TOO FAR TO JUST GIVE UP! WE'VE GOT TO--TO--
TO ***EMBRACE THE HORROR...!***

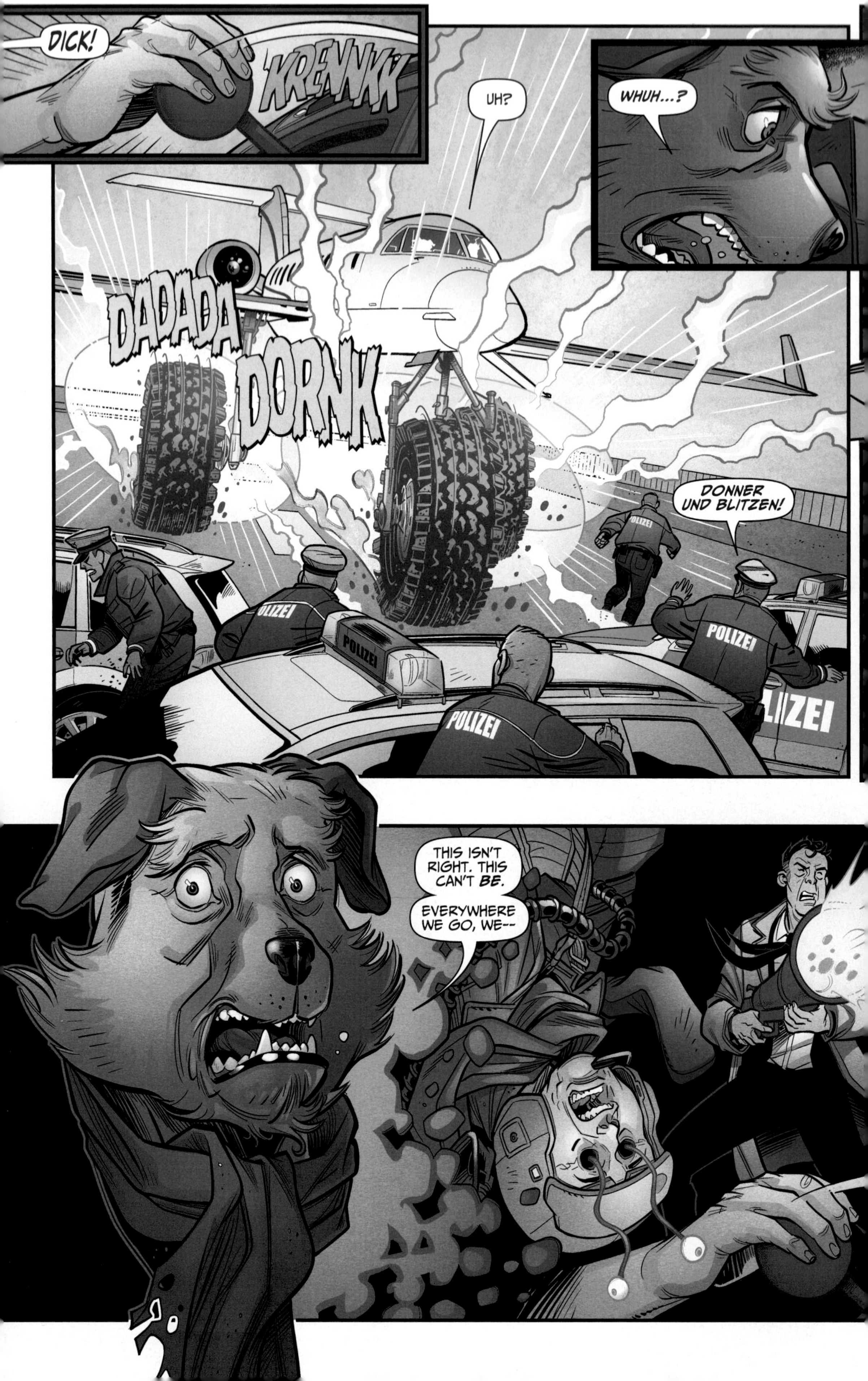
DICK!
KRENNKK
UH?
WHUH...?
DADADA
DORNK
DONNER UND BLITZEN!
POLIZEI
THIS ISN'T RIGHT. THIS CAN'T BE.
EVERYWHERE WE GO, WE--

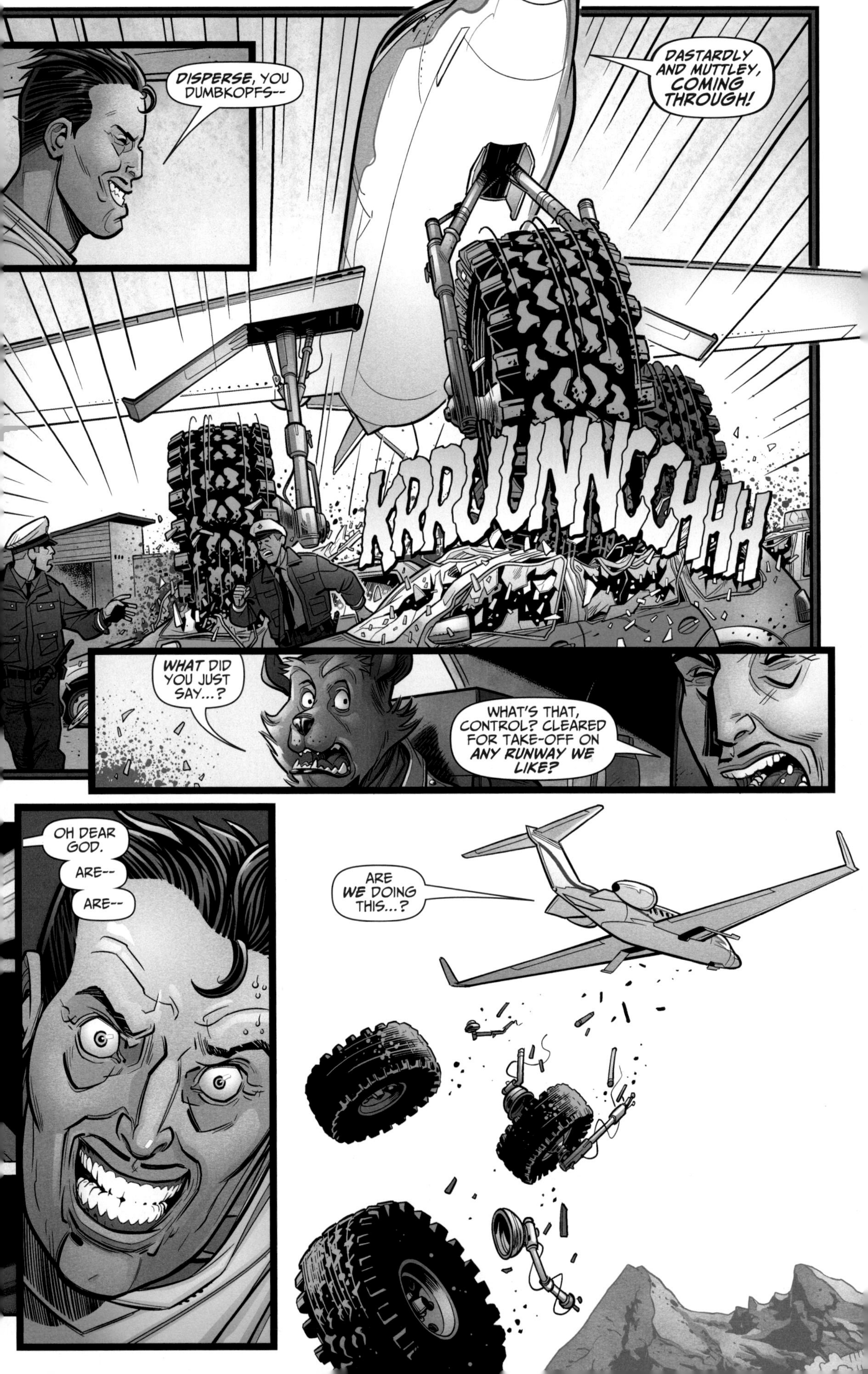

DISPERSE, YOU DUMBKOPFS--
DASTARDLY AND MUTTLEY, COMING THROUGH!
KRRUUNNCHHH
WHAT DID YOU JUST SAY...?
WHAT'S THAT, CONTROL? CLEARED FOR TAKE-OFF ON ANY RUNWAY WE LIKE?
OH DEAR GOD.
ARE--
ARE--
ARE WE DOING THIS...?

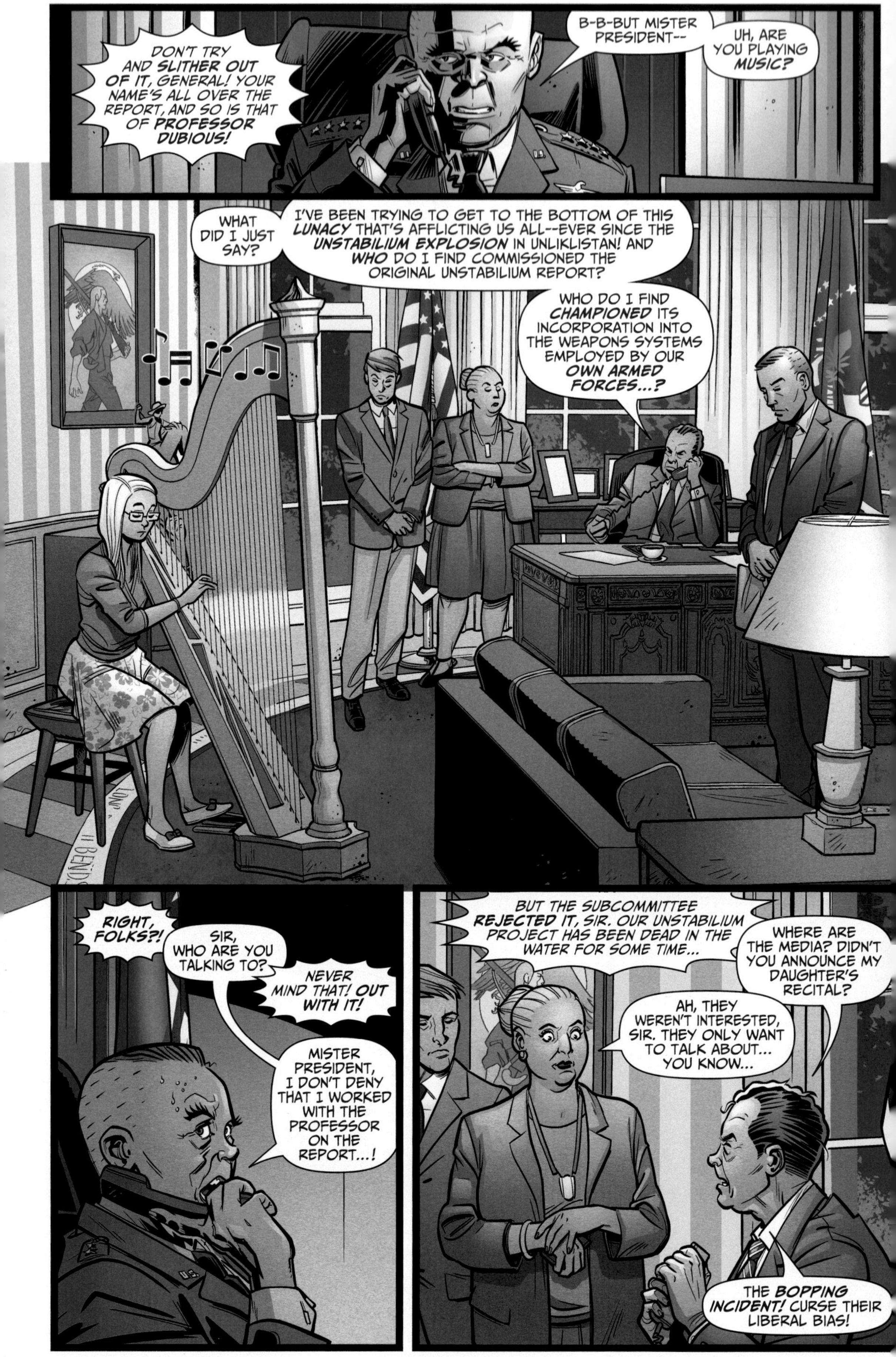
DON'T TRY AND SLITHER OUT OF IT, GENERAL! YOUR NAME'S ALL OVER THE REPORT, AND SO IS THAT OF PROFESSOR DUBIOUS!
B-B-BUT MISTER PRESIDENT--
UH, ARE YOU PLAYING MUSIC?
WHAT DID I JUST SAY?
I'VE BEEN TRYING TO GET TO THE BOTTOM OF THIS LUNACY THAT'S AFFLICTING US ALL--EVER SINCE THE UNSTABILIUM EXPLOSION IN UNLIKLISTAN! AND WHO DO I FIND COMMISSIONED THE ORIGINAL UNSTABILIUM REPORT?
WHO DO I FIND CHAMPIONED ITS INCORPORATION INTO THE WEAPONS SYSTEMS EMPLOYED BY OUR OWN ARMED FORCES...?
RIGHT, FOLKS?!
SIR, WHO ARE YOU TALKING TO?
NEVER MIND THAT! OUT WITH IT!
MISTER PRESIDENT, I DON'T DENY THAT I WORKED WITH THE PROFESSOR ON THE REPORT...!
BUT THE SUBCOMMITTEE REJECTED IT, SIR. OUR UNSTABILIUM PROJECT HAS BEEN DEAD IN THE WATER FOR SOME TIME...
WHERE ARE THE MEDIA? DIDN'T YOU ANNOUNCE MY DAUGHTER'S RECITAL?
AH, THEY WEREN'T INTERESTED, SIR. THEY ONLY WANT TO TALK ABOUT... YOU KNOW...
THE BOPPING INCIDENT! CURSE THEIR LIBERAL BIAS!

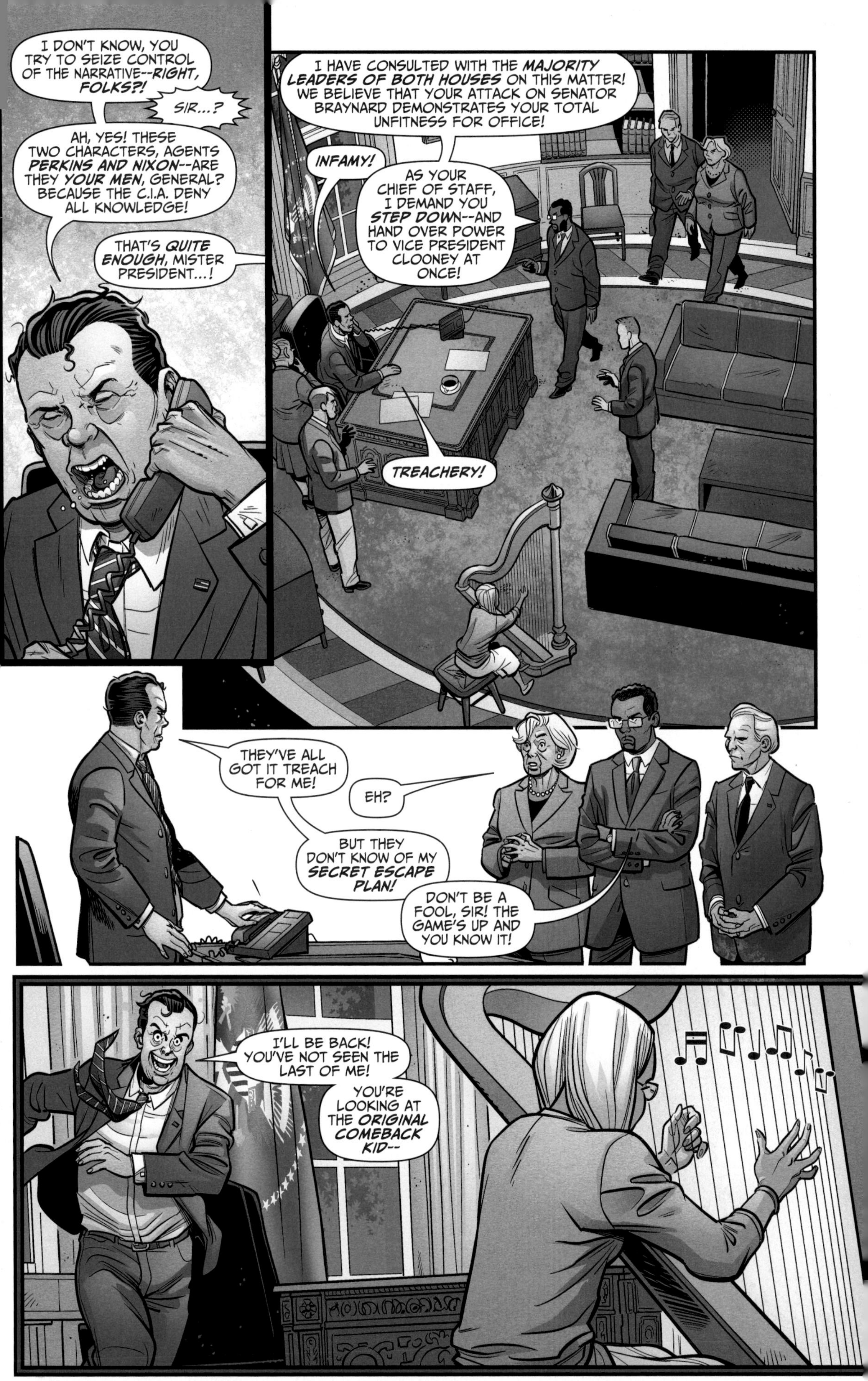
I DON'T KNOW, YOU TRY TO SEIZE CONTROL OF THE NARRATIVE--RIGHT, FOLKS?!
SIR...?
AH, YES! THESE TWO CHARACTERS, AGENTS PERKINS AND NIXON--ARE THEY YOUR MEN, GENERAL? BECAUSE THE C.I.A. DENY ALL KNOWLEDGE!
THAT'S QUITE ENOUGH, MISTER PRESIDENT...!
I HAVE CONSULTED WITH THE MAJORITY LEADERS OF BOTH HOUSES ON THIS MATTER! WE BELIEVE THAT YOUR ATTACK ON SENATOR BRAYNARD DEMONSTRATES YOUR TOTAL UNFITNESS FOR OFFICE!
INFAMY!
AS YOUR CHIEF OF STAFF, I DEMAND YOU STEP DOWN--AND HAND OVER POWER TO VICE PRESIDENT CLOONEY AT ONCE!
TREACHERY!
THEY'VE ALL GOT IT TREACH FOR ME!
EH?
BUT THEY DON'T KNOW OF MY SECRET ESCAPE PLAN!
DON'T BE A FOOL, SIR! THE GAME'S UP AND YOU KNOW IT!
I'LL BE BACK! YOU'VE NOT SEEN THE LAST OF ME!
YOU'RE LOOKING AT THE ORIGINAL COMEBACK KID--

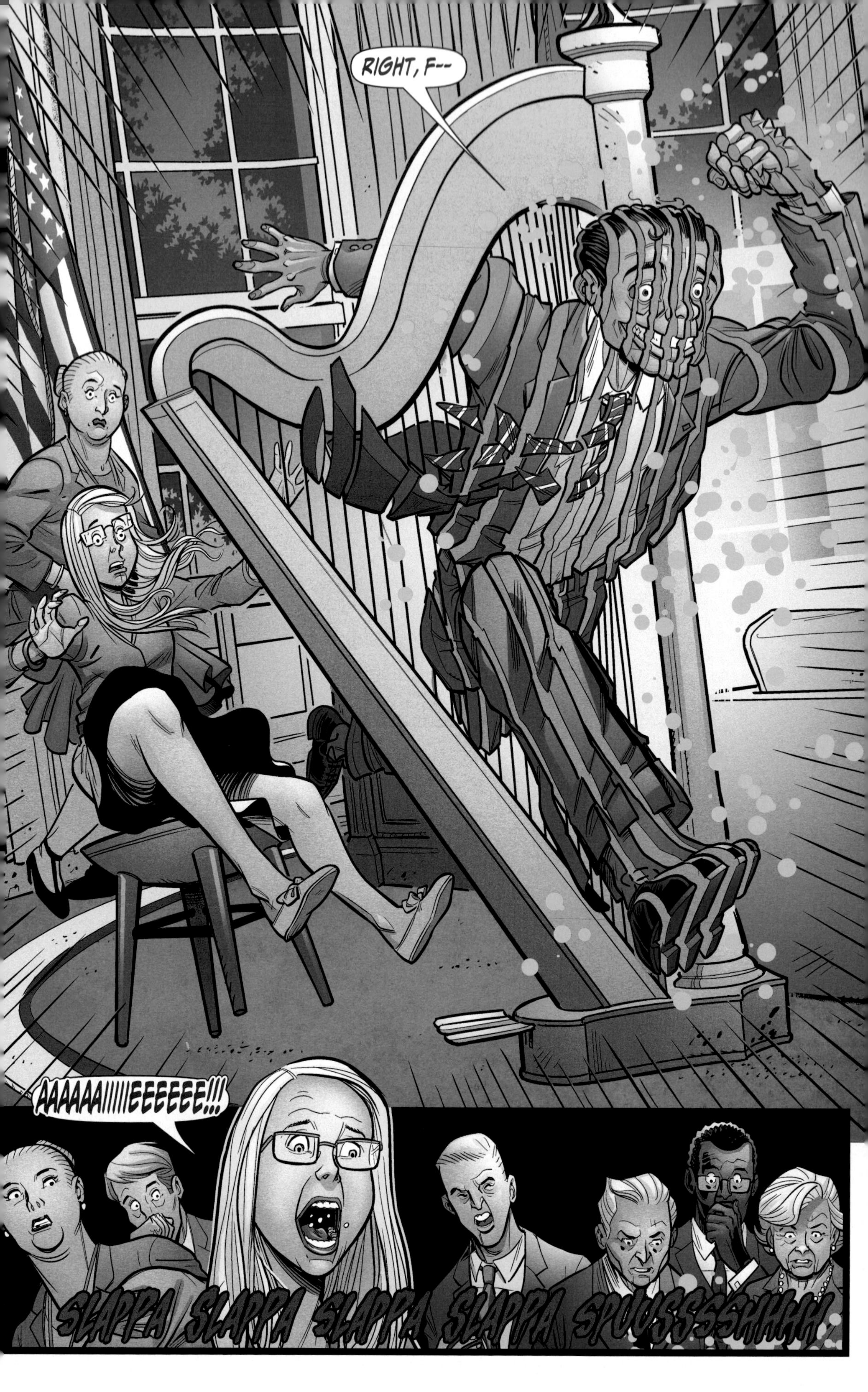

RIGHT, F--
AAAAAAIIIIIIEEEEEE!!!
SLAPPA SLAPPA SLAPPA SLAPPA SPUUSSSSHHHH

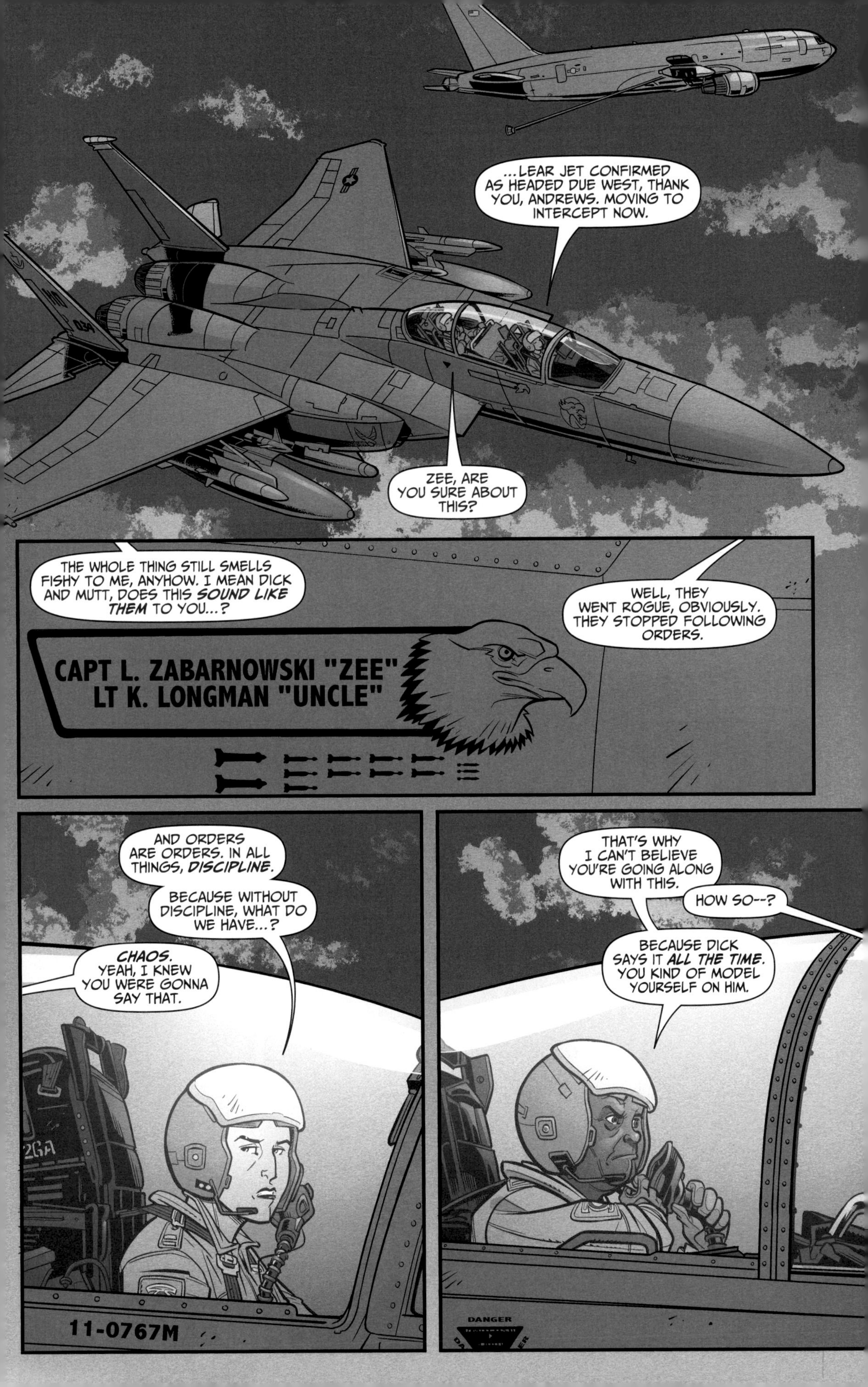
...LEAR JET CONFIRMED AS HEADED DUE WEST, THANK YOU, ANDREWS. MOVING TO INTERCEPT NOW.
ZEE, ARE YOU SURE ABOUT THIS?
THE WHOLE THING STILL SMELLS FISHY TO ME, ANYHOW. I MEAN DICK AND MUTT, DOES THIS *SOUND LIKE THEM* TO YOU...?
WELL, THEY WENT ROGUE, OBVIOUSLY. THEY STOPPED FOLLOWING ORDERS.
CAPT L. ZABARNOWSKI "ZEE"
LT K. LONGMAN "UNCLE"
AND ORDERS ARE ORDERS. IN ALL THINGS, *DISCIPLINE*.
BECAUSE WITHOUT DISCIPLINE, WHAT DO WE HAVE...?
CHAOS. YEAH, I KNEW YOU WERE GONNA SAY THAT.
11-0767M
THAT'S WHY I CAN'T BELIEVE YOU'RE GOING ALONG WITH THIS.
HOW SO--?
BECAUSE DICK SAYS IT *ALL THE TIME*. YOU KIND OF MODEL YOURSELF ON HIM.
DANGER

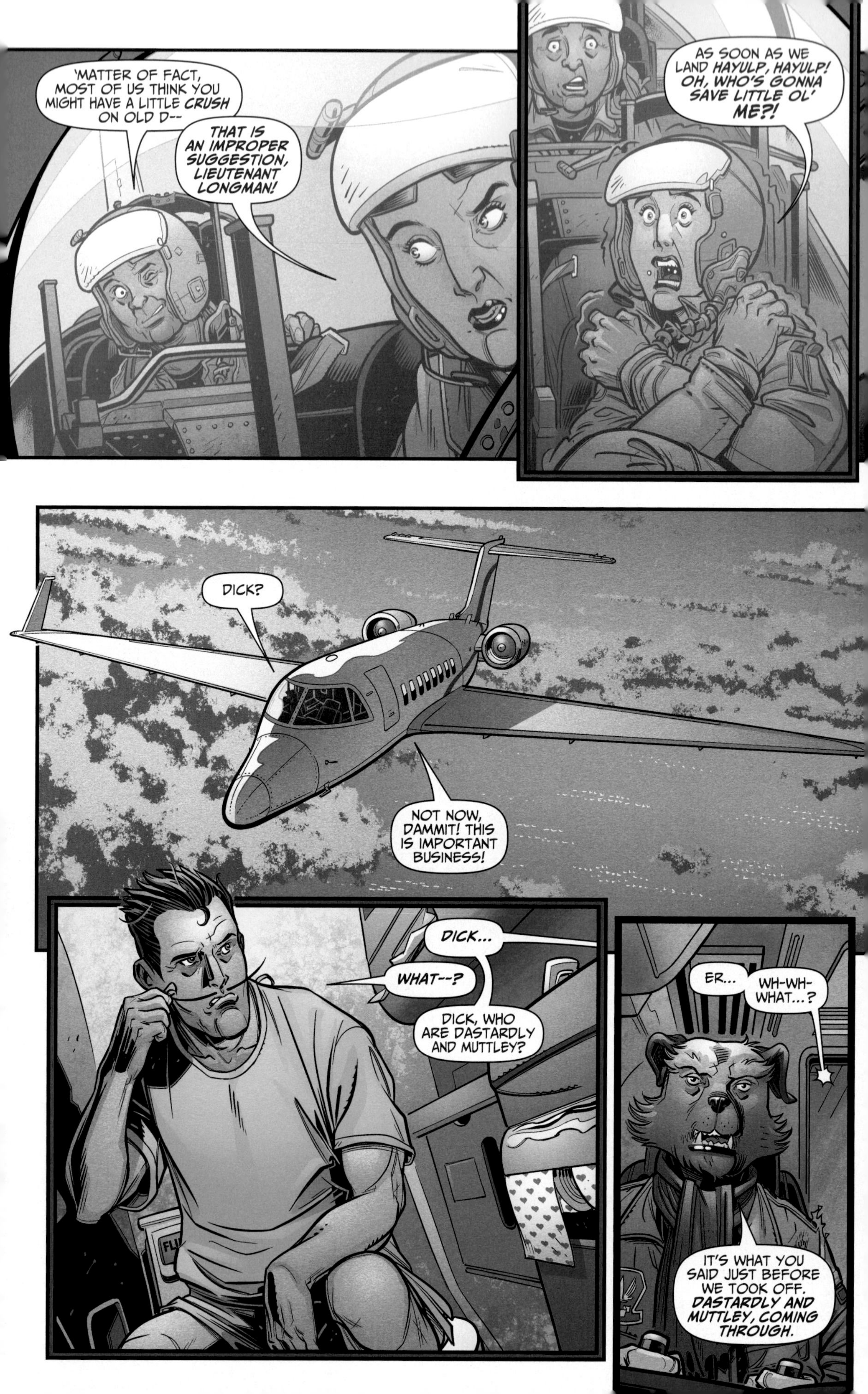
'MATTER OF FACT, MOST OF US THINK YOU MIGHT HAVE A LITTLE CRUSH ON OLD D--
THAT IS AN IMPROPER SUGGESTION, LIEUTENANT LONGMAN!
AS SOON AS WE LAND HAYULP, HAYULP! OH, WHO'S GONNA SAVE LITTLE OL' ME?!
DICK?
NOT NOW, DAMMIT! THIS IS IMPORTANT BUSINESS!
DICK...
WHAT--?
DICK, WHO ARE DASTARDLY AND MUTTLEY?
ER...
WH-WH-WHAT...?
IT'S WHAT YOU SAID JUST BEFORE WE TOOK OFF. DASTARDLY AND MUTTLEY, COMING THROUGH.

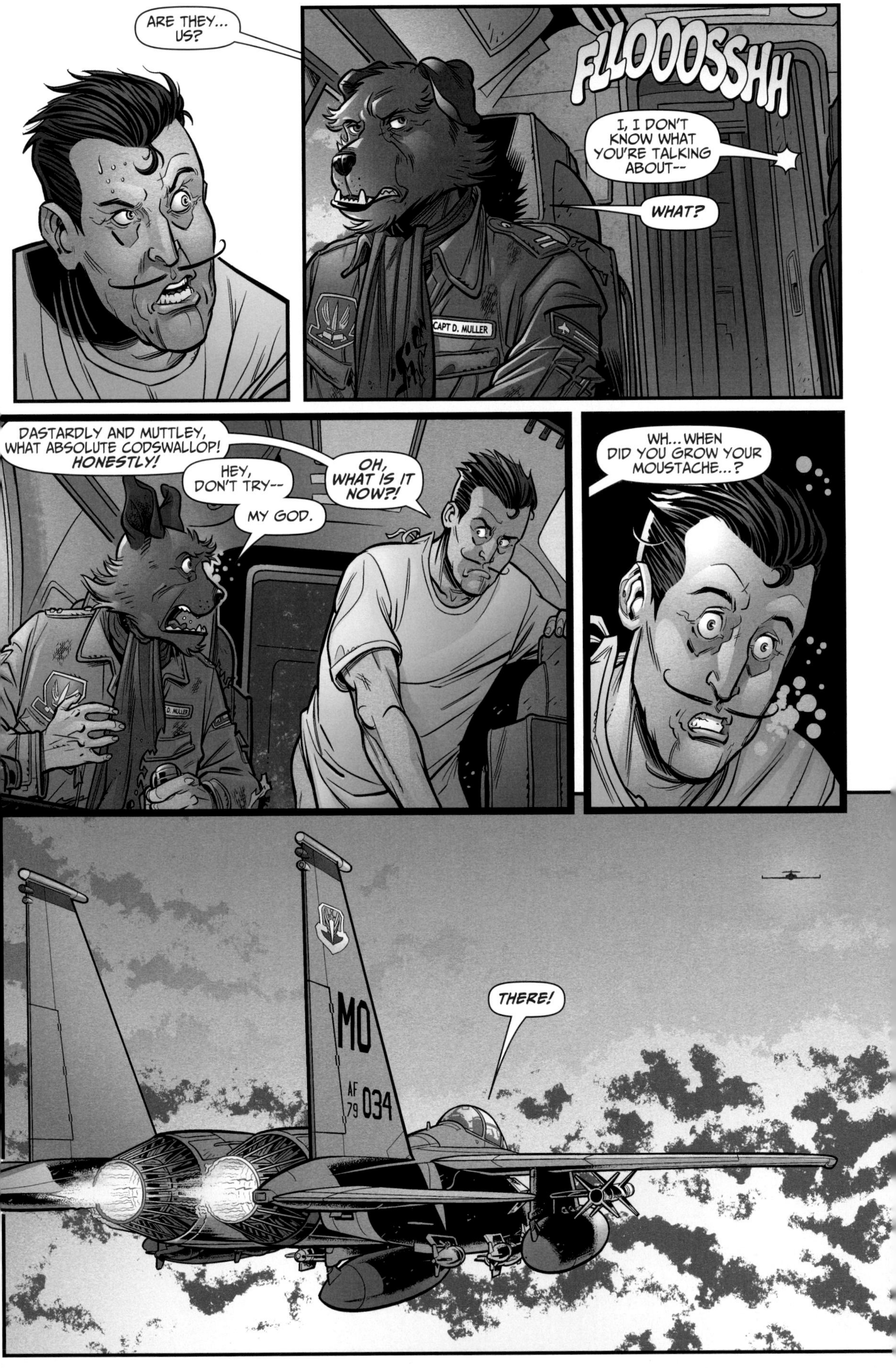
ARE THEY... US?
FLLOOOSSHH
I, I DON'T KNOW WHAT YOU'RE TALKING ABOUT--
WHAT?
CAPT D. MULLER
DASTARDLY AND MUTTLEY, WHAT ABSOLUTE CODSWALLOP! HONESTLY!
HEY, DON'T TRY--
MY GOD.
OH, WHAT IS IT NOW?!
D. MULLER
WH...WHEN DID YOU GROW YOUR MOUSTACHE...?
THERE!
MO
AF 79 034

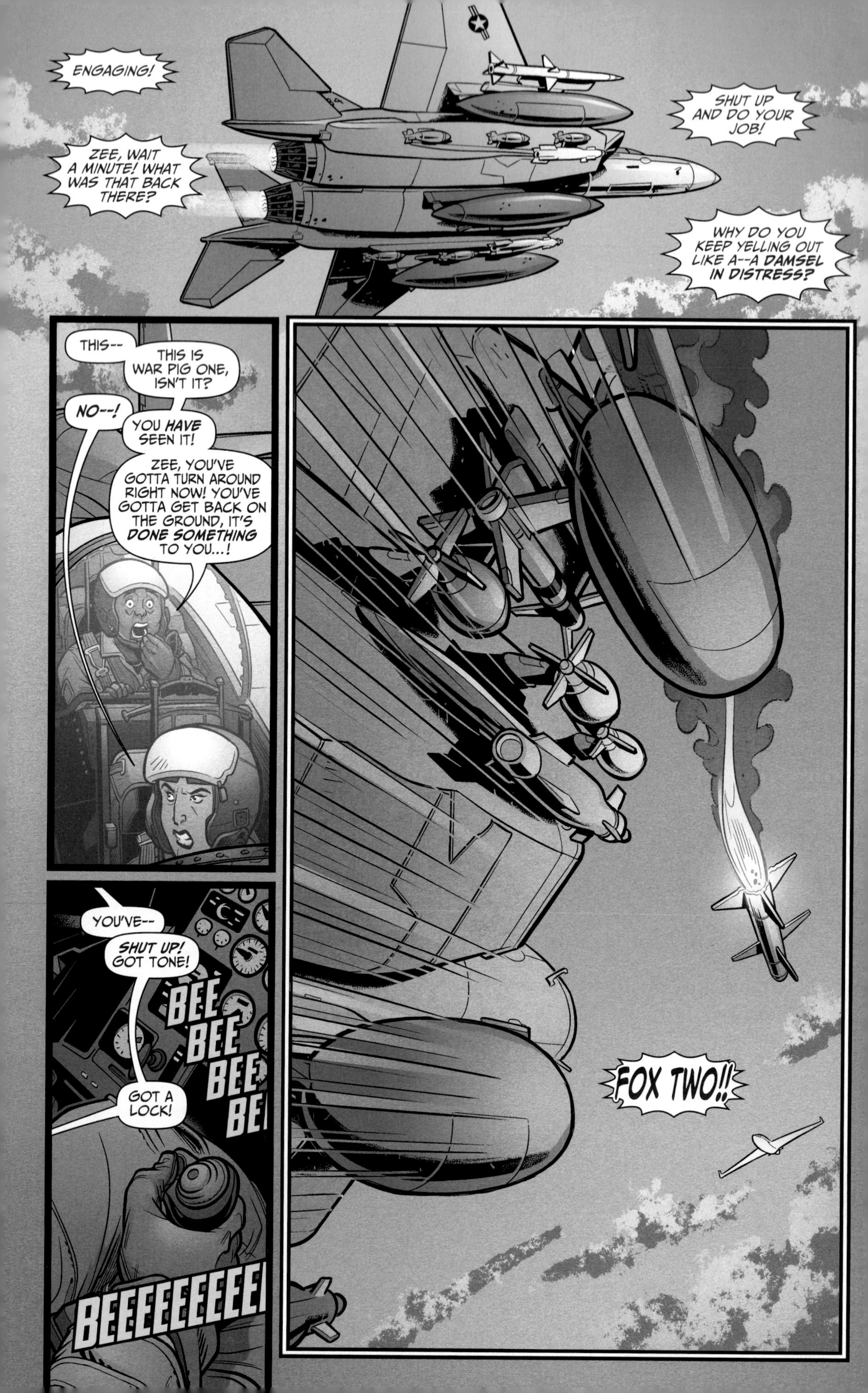
ENGAGING!
ZEE, WAIT A MINUTE! WHAT WAS THAT BACK THERE?
SHUT UP AND DO YOUR JOB!
WHY DO YOU KEEP YELLING OUT LIKE A--A DAMSEL IN DISTRESS?
THIS--
THIS IS WAR PIG ONE, ISN'T IT?
NO--!
YOU HAVE SEEN IT!
ZEE, YOU'VE GOTTA TURN AROUND RIGHT NOW! YOU'VE GOTTA GET BACK ON THE GROUND, IT'S DONE SOMETHING TO YOU...!
YOU'VE--
SHUT UP! GOT TONE!
BEE
BEE
BEE
GOT A LOCK!
BEEEEEEEEEE
FOX TWO!!

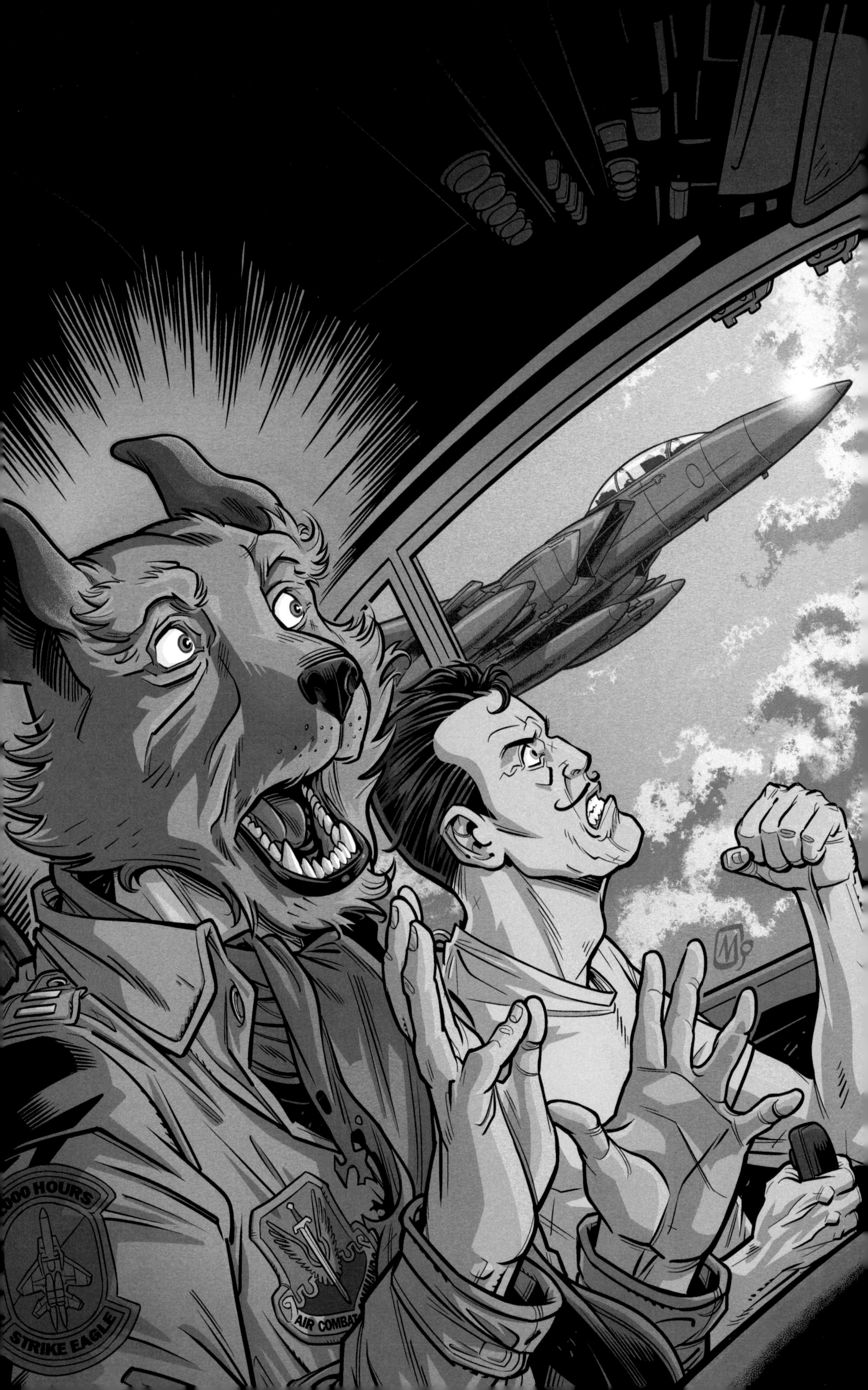
000 HOURS
STRIKE EAGLE
AIR COMBAT

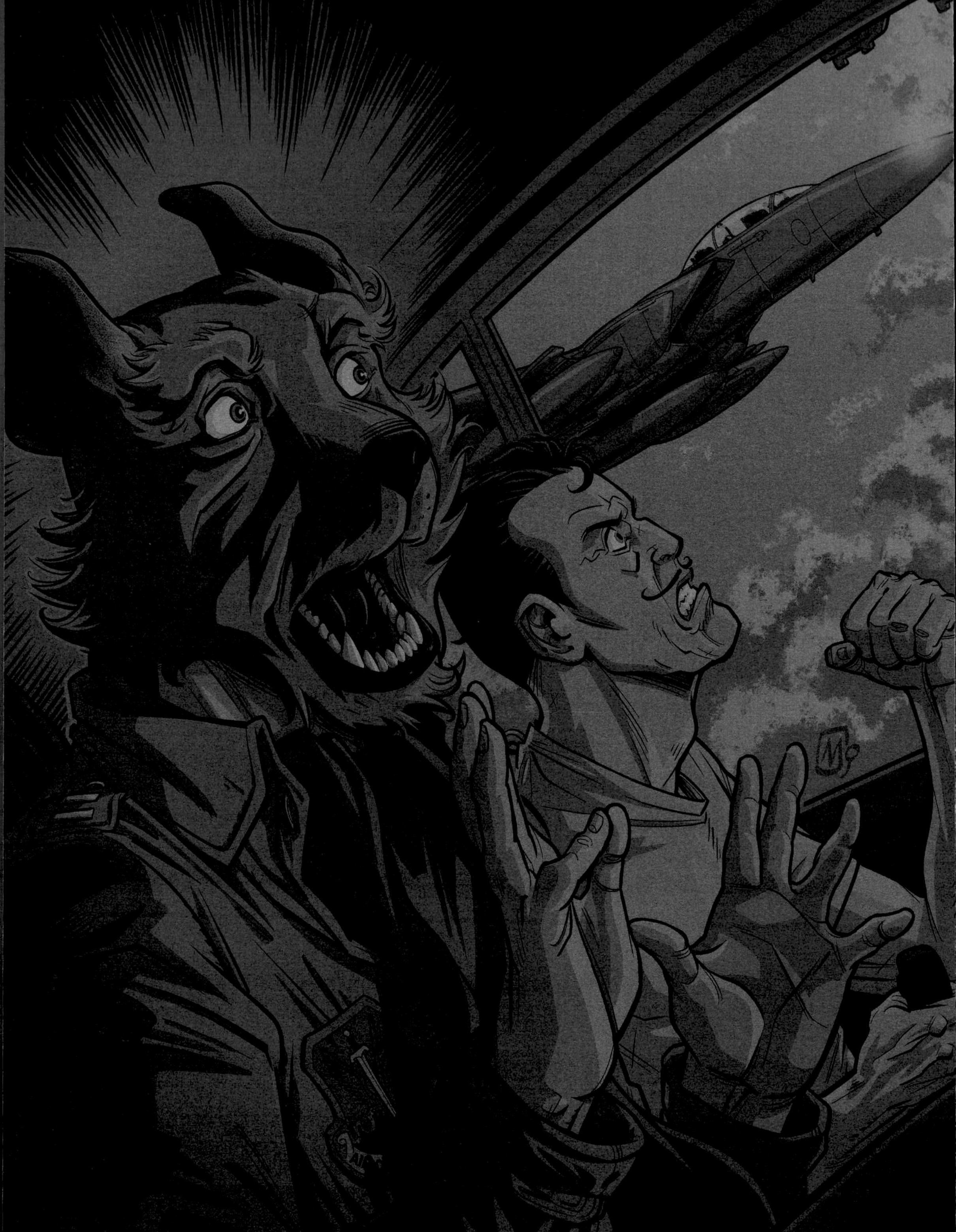

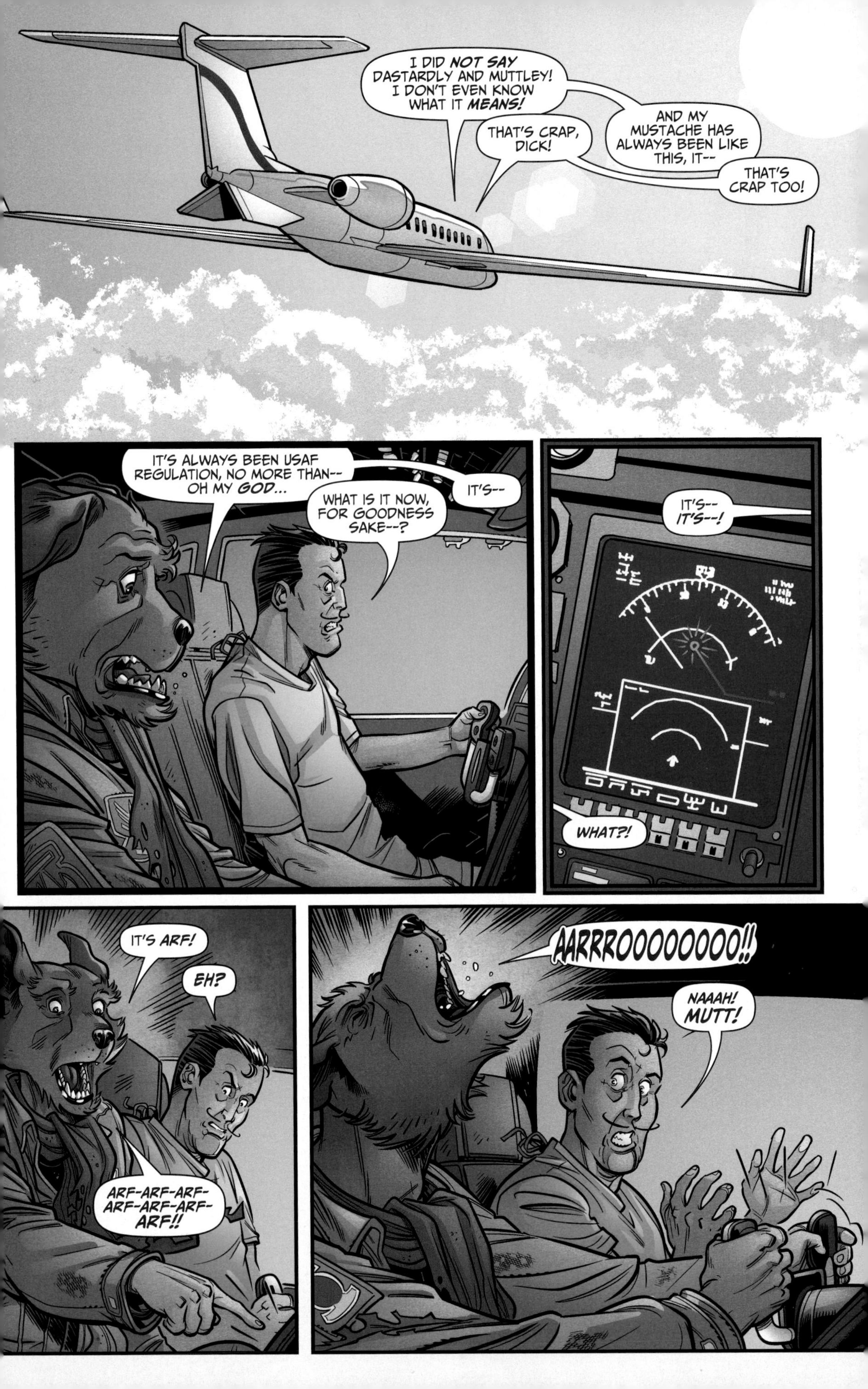
I DID NOT SAY DASTARDLY AND MUTTLEY! I DON'T EVEN KNOW WHAT IT MEANS!
AND MY MUSTACHE HAS ALWAYS BEEN LIKE THIS, IT--
THAT'S CRAP, DICK!
THAT'S CRAP TOO!
IT'S ALWAYS BEEN USAF REGULATION, NO MORE THAN-- OH MY GOD...
WHAT IS IT NOW, FOR GOODNESS SAKE--?
IT'S--
IT'S-- IT'S--!
WHAT?!
IT'S ARF!
EH?
ARF-ARF-ARF-ARF-ARF-ARF-ARF!!
AARRROOOOOOOOO!!
NAAAH! MUTT!

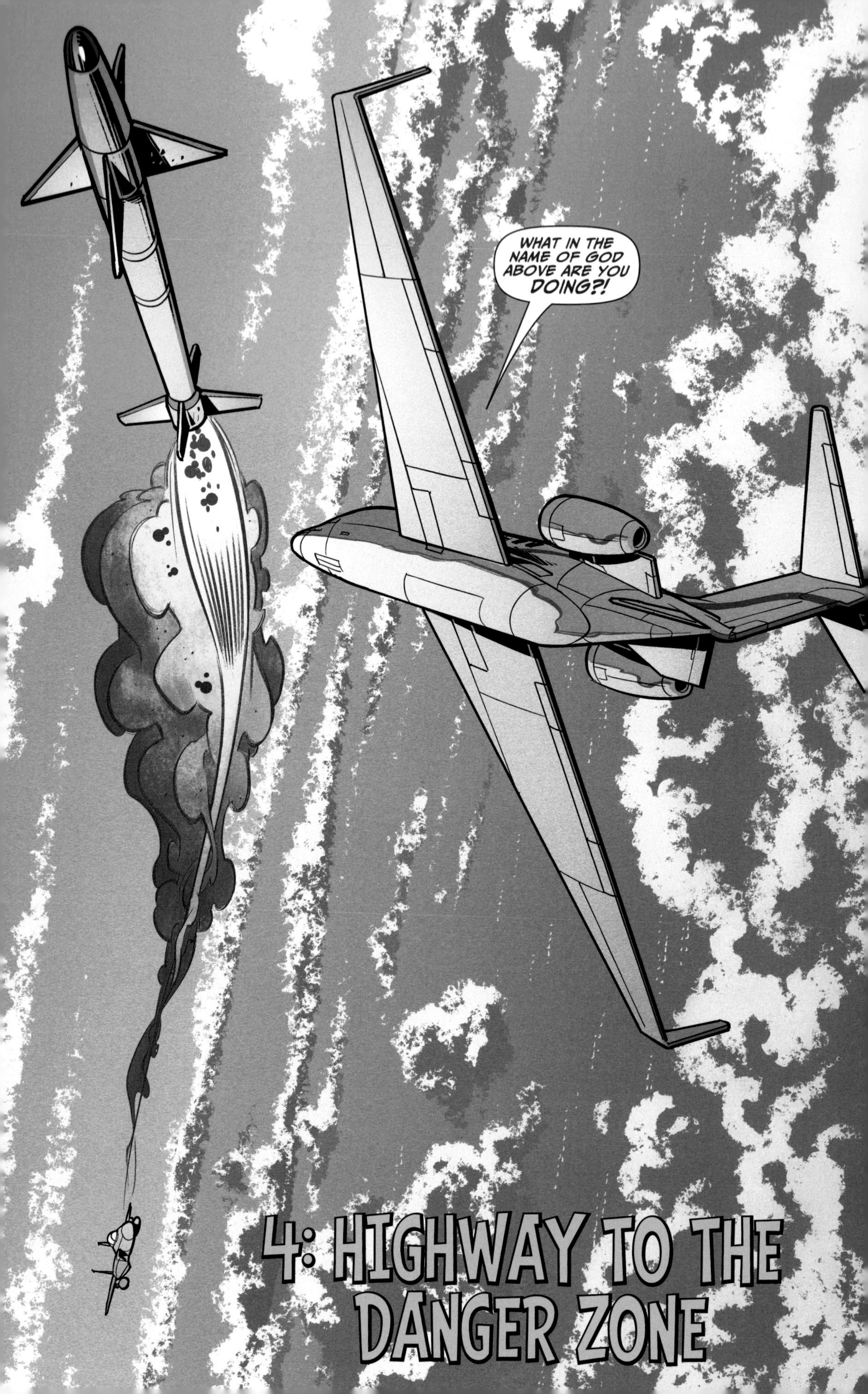
WHAT IN THE NAME OF GOD ABOVE ARE YOU DOING?!
4: HIGHWAY TO THE DANGER ZONE

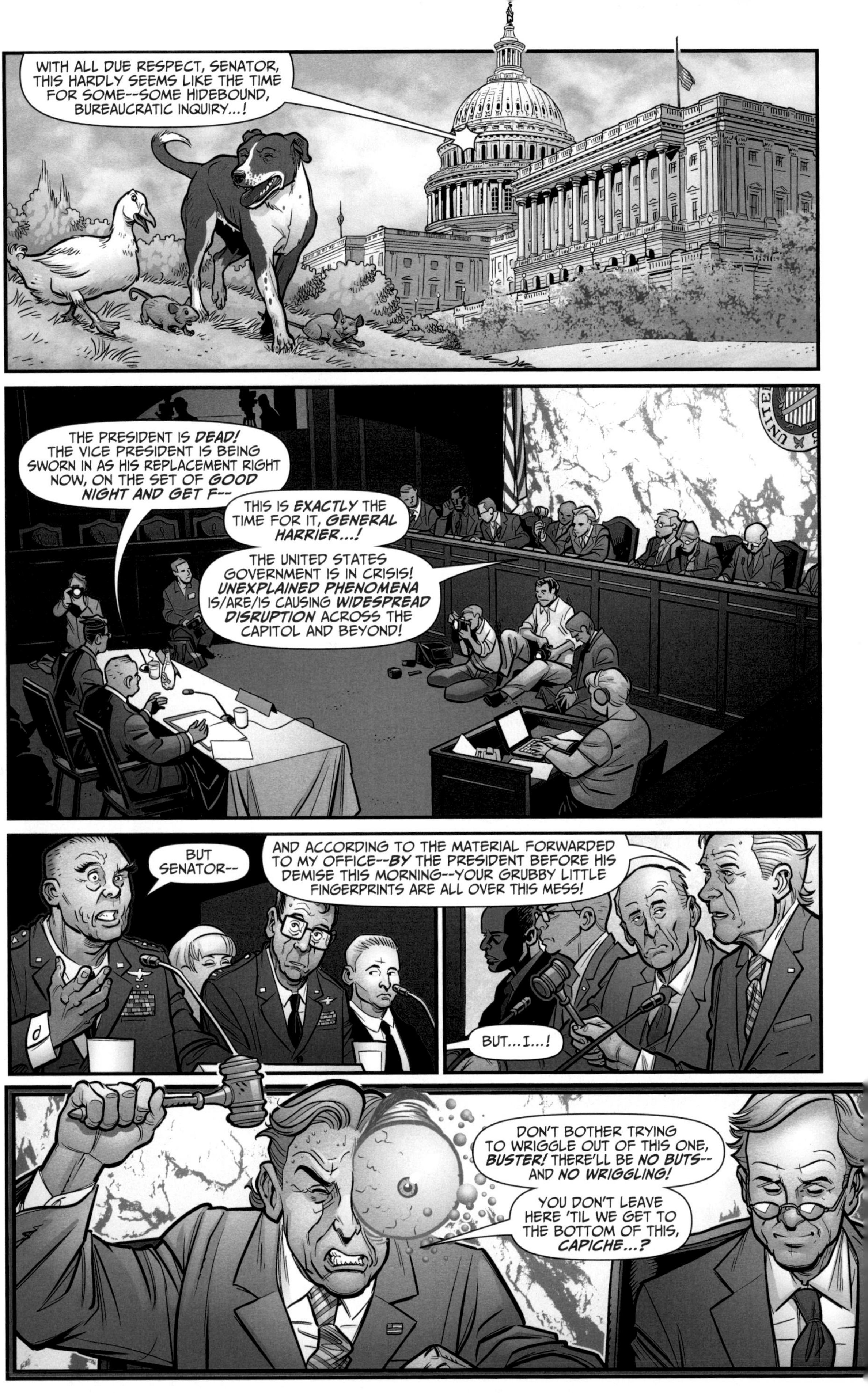

WITH ALL DUE RESPECT, SENATOR, THIS HARDLY SEEMS LIKE THE TIME FOR SOME--SOME HIDEBOUND, BUREAUCRATIC INQUIRY...!
THE PRESIDENT IS DEAD! THE VICE PRESIDENT IS BEING SWORN IN AS HIS REPLACEMENT RIGHT NOW, ON THE SET OF GOOD NIGHT AND GET F--
THIS IS EXACTLY THE TIME FOR IT, GENERAL HARRIER...!
THE UNITED STATES GOVERNMENT IS IN CRISIS! UNEXPLAINED PHENOMENA IS/ARE/IS CAUSING WIDESPREAD DISRUPTION ACROSS THE CAPITOL AND BEYOND!
BUT SENATOR--
AND ACCORDING TO THE MATERIAL FORWARDED TO MY OFFICE--BY THE PRESIDENT BEFORE HIS DEMISE THIS MORNING--YOUR GRUBBY LITTLE FINGERPRINTS ARE ALL OVER THIS MESS!
BUT...I...!
DON'T BOTHER TRYING TO WRIGGLE OUT OF THIS ONE, BUSTER! THERE'LL BE NO BUTS-- AND NO WRIGGLING!
YOU DON'T LEAVE HERE 'TIL WE GET TO THE BOTTOM OF THIS, CAPICHE...?

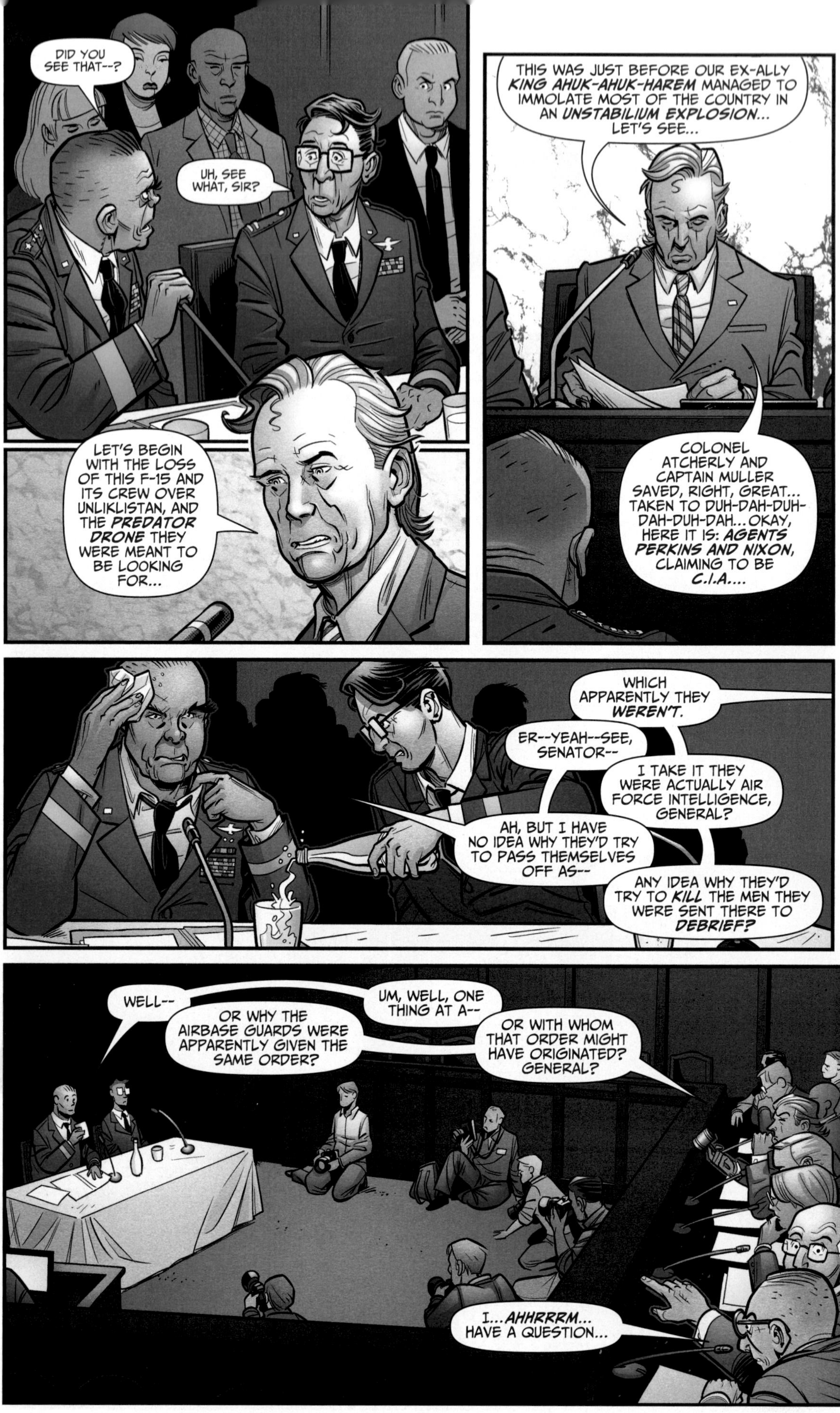
DID YOU SEE THAT--?
UH, SEE WHAT, SIR?
THIS WAS JUST BEFORE OUR EX-ALLY KING AHUK-AHUK-HAREM MANAGED TO IMMOLATE MOST OF THE COUNTRY IN AN UNSTABILIUM EXPLOSION... LET'S SEE...
LET'S BEGIN WITH THE LOSS OF THIS F-15 AND ITS CREW OVER UNLIKLISTAN, AND THE PREDATOR DRONE THEY WERE MEANT TO BE LOOKING FOR...
COLONEL ATCHERLY AND CAPTAIN MULLER SAVED, RIGHT, GREAT... TAKEN TO DUH-DAH-DUH-DAH-DUH-DAH... OKAY, HERE IT IS: AGENTS PERKINS AND NIXON, CLAIMING TO BE C.I.A....
WHICH APPARENTLY THEY WEREN'T.
ER--YEAH--SEE, SENATOR--
I TAKE IT THEY WERE ACTUALLY AIR FORCE INTELLIGENCE, GENERAL?
AH, BUT I HAVE NO IDEA WHY THEY'D TRY TO PASS THEMSELVES OFF AS--
ANY IDEA WHY THEY'D TRY TO KILL THE MEN THEY WERE SENT THERE TO DEBRIEF?
WELL--
UM, WELL, ONE THING AT A--
OR WHY THE AIRBASE GUARDS WERE APPARENTLY GIVEN THE SAME ORDER?
OR WITH WHOM THAT ORDER MIGHT HAVE ORIGINATED? GENERAL?
I...AHHRRRM... HAVE A QUESTION...

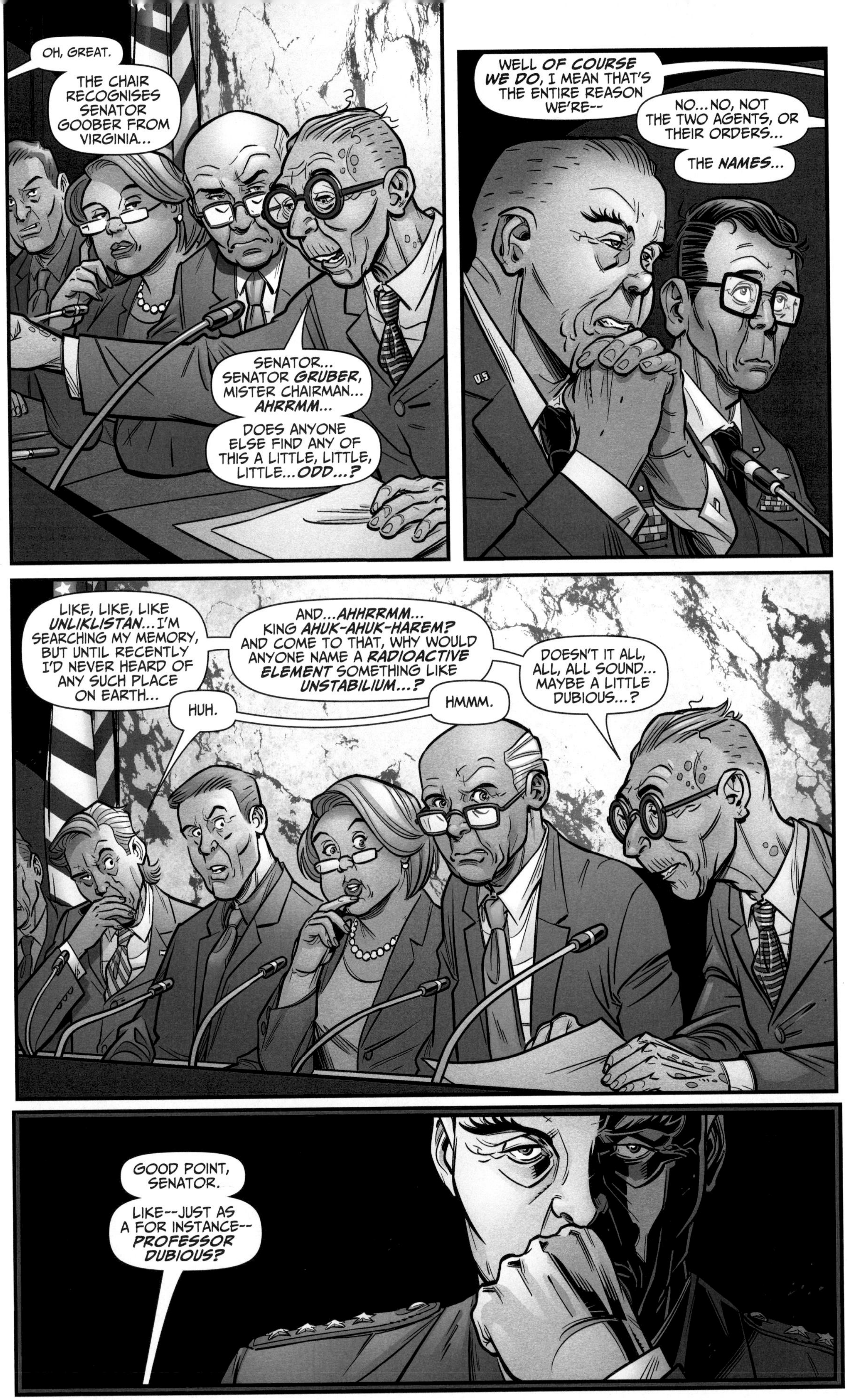
OH, GREAT.
THE CHAIR RECOGNISES SENATOR GOOBER FROM VIRGINIA...
SENATOR... SENATOR GRUBER, MISTER CHAIRMAN... AHRRMM...
DOES ANYONE ELSE FIND ANY OF THIS A LITTLE, LITTLE, LITTLE...ODD...?
WELL OF COURSE WE DO, I MEAN THAT'S THE ENTIRE REASON WE'RE--
NO...NO, NOT THE TWO AGENTS, OR THEIR ORDERS...
THE NAMES...
LIKE, LIKE, LIKE UNLIKLISTAN...I'M SEARCHING MY MEMORY, BUT UNTIL RECENTLY I'D NEVER HEARD OF ANY SUCH PLACE ON EARTH...
HUH.
AND...AHHRRMM... KING AHUK-AHUK-HAREM? AND COME TO THAT, WHY WOULD ANYONE NAME A RADIOACTIVE ELEMENT SOMETHING LIKE UNSTABILIUM...?
HMMM.
DOESN'T IT ALL, ALL, ALL SOUND... MAYBE A LITTLE DUBIOUS...?
GOOD POINT, SENATOR.
LIKE--JUST AS A FOR INSTANCE--PROFESSOR DUBIOUS?

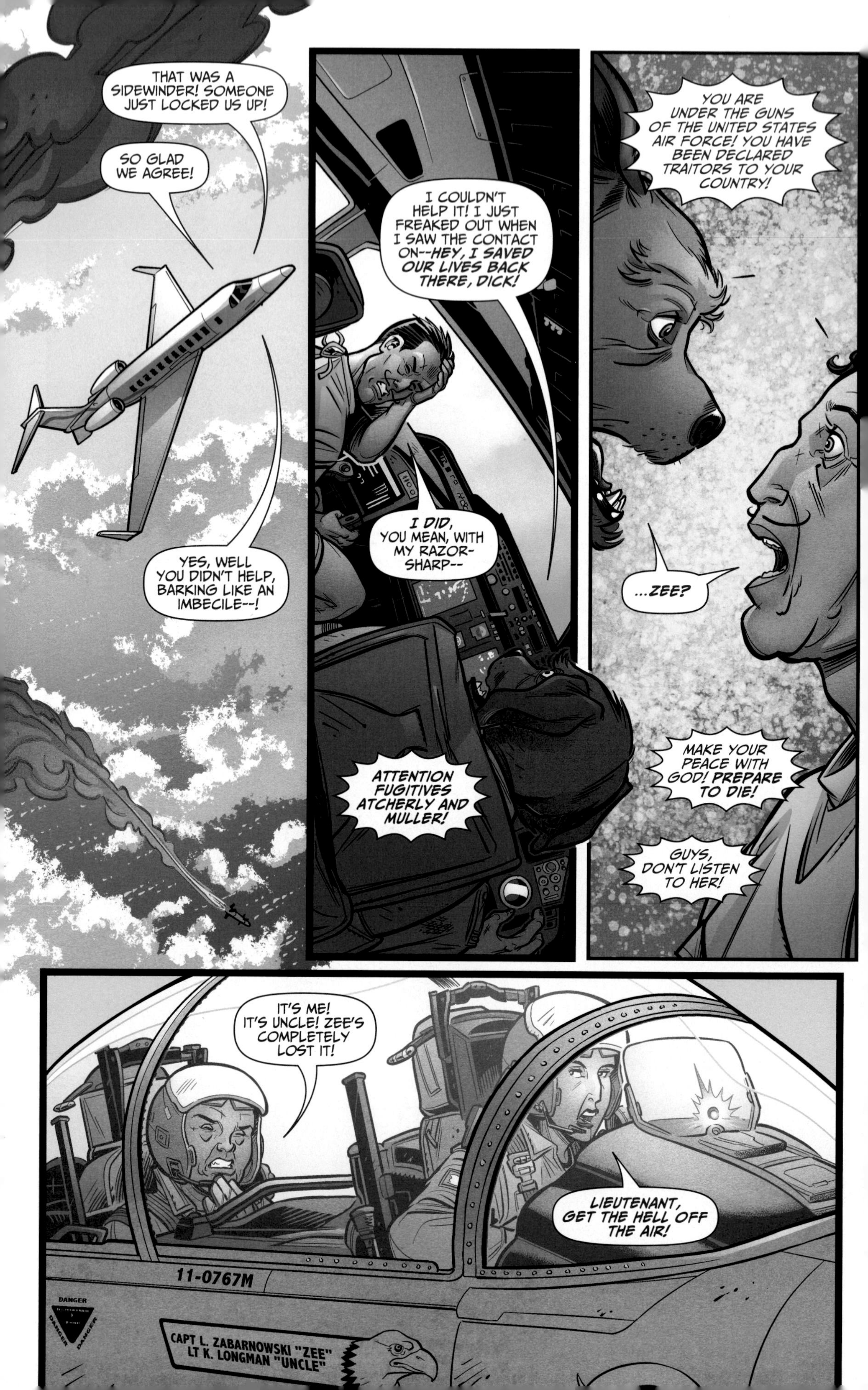
THAT WAS A SIDEWINDER! SOMEONE JUST LOCKED US UP!
SO GLAD WE AGREE!
YES, WELL YOU DIDN'T HELP, BARKING LIKE AN IMBECILE--!
I COULDN'T HELP IT! I JUST FREAKED OUT WHEN I SAW THE CONTACT ON--HEY, I SAVED OUR LIVES BACK THERE, DICK!
I DID, YOU MEAN, WITH MY RAZOR-SHARP--
ATTENTION FUGITIVES ATCHERLY AND MULLER!
YOU ARE UNDER THE GUNS OF THE UNITED STATES AIR FORCE! YOU HAVE BEEN DECLARED TRAITORS TO YOUR COUNTRY!
...ZEE?
MAKE YOUR PEACE WITH GOD! PREPARE TO DIE!
GUYS, DON'T LISTEN TO HER!
IT'S ME! IT'S UNCLE! ZEE'S COMPLETELY LOST IT!
LIEUTENANT, GET THE HELL OFF THE AIR!
11-0767M
DANGER
CAPT L. ZABARNOWSKI "ZEE"
LT K. LONGMAN "UNCLE"

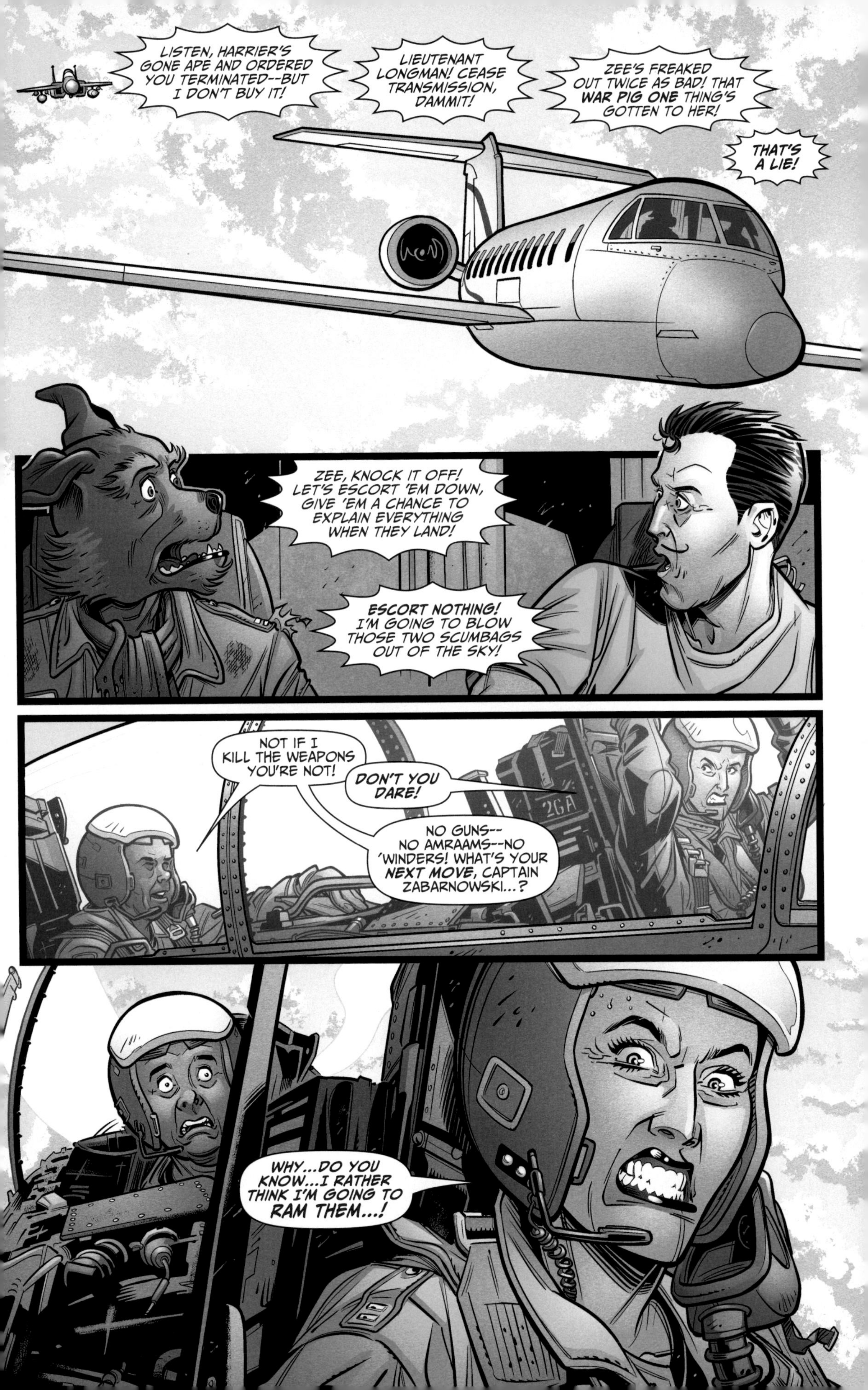
LISTEN, HARRIER'S GONE APE AND ORDERED YOU TERMINATED--BUT I DON'T BUY IT!
LIEUTENANT LONGMAN! CEASE TRANSMISSION, DAMMIT!
ZEE'S FREAKED OUT TWICE AS BAD! THAT WAR PIG ONE THING'S GOTTEN TO HER!
THAT'S A LIE!
ZEE, KNOCK IT OFF! LET'S ESCORT 'EM DOWN, GIVE 'EM A CHANCE TO EXPLAIN EVERYTHING WHEN THEY LAND!
ESCORT NOTHING! I'M GOING TO BLOW THOSE TWO SCUMBAGS OUT OF THE SKY!
NOT IF I KILL THE WEAPONS YOU'RE NOT!
DON'T YOU DARE!
NO GUNS-- NO AMRAAMS--NO 'WINDERS! WHAT'S YOUR NEXT MOVE, CAPTAIN ZABARNOWSKI...?
WHY...DO YOU KNOW...I RATHER THINK I'M GOING TO RAM THEM...!

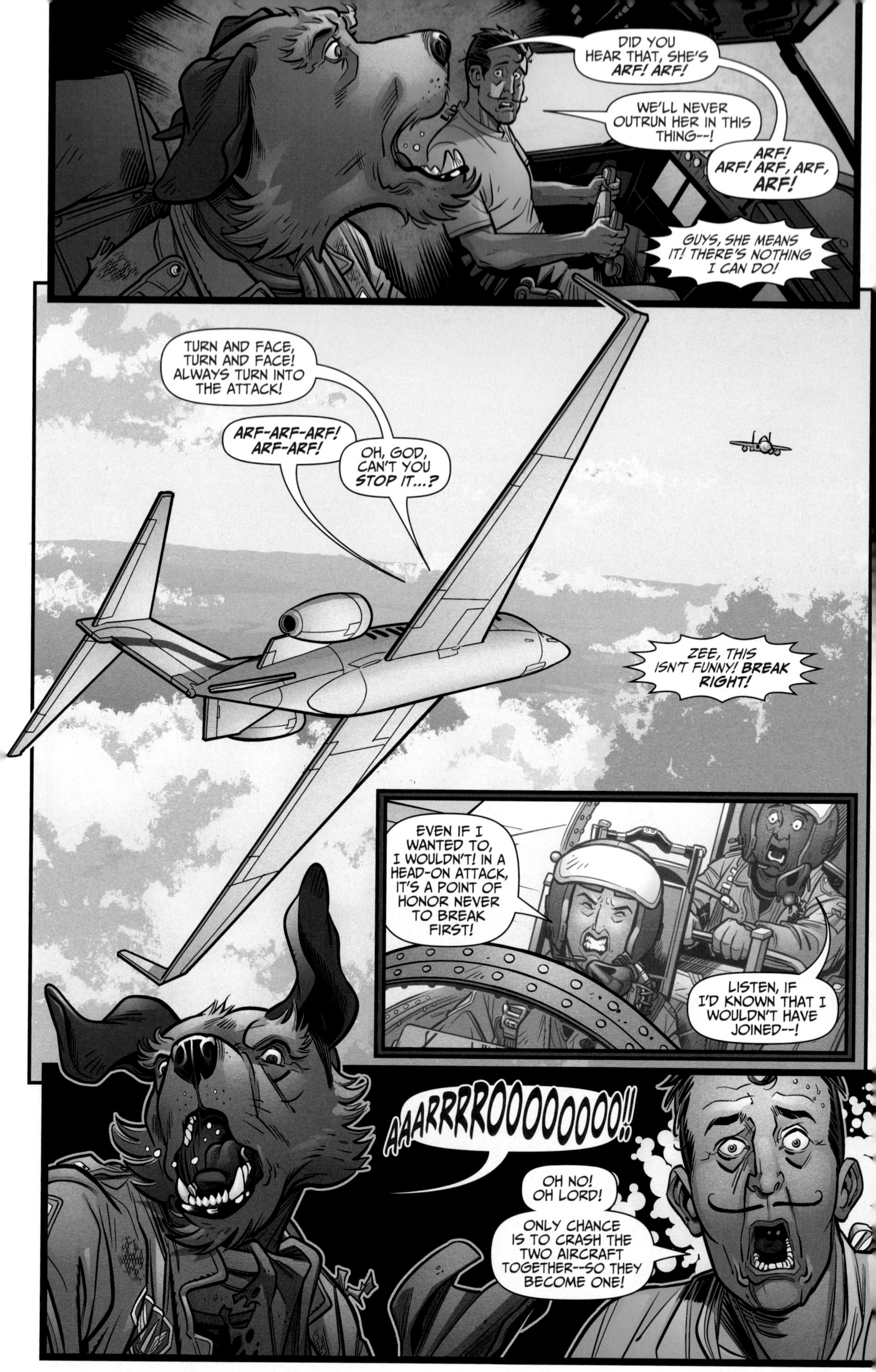

DID YOU HEAR THAT, SHE'S ARF! ARF!
WE'LL NEVER OUTRUN HER IN THIS THING--!
ARF! ARF! ARF, ARF, ARF!
GUYS, SHE MEANS IT! THERE'S NOTHING I CAN DO!
TURN AND FACE, TURN AND FACE! ALWAYS TURN INTO THE ATTACK!
ARF-ARF-ARF! ARF-ARF!
OH, GOD, CAN'T YOU STOP IT...?
ZEE, THIS ISN'T FUNNY! BREAK RIGHT!
EVEN IF I WANTED TO, I WOULDN'T! IN A HEAD-ON ATTACK, IT'S A POINT OF HONOR NEVER TO BREAK FIRST!
LISTEN, IF I'D KNOWN THAT I WOULDN'T HAVE JOINED--!
AAARRRROOOOOOOO!!
OH NO! OH LORD!
ONLY CHANCE IS TO CRASH THE TWO AIRCRAFT TOGETHER--SO THEY BECOME ONE!

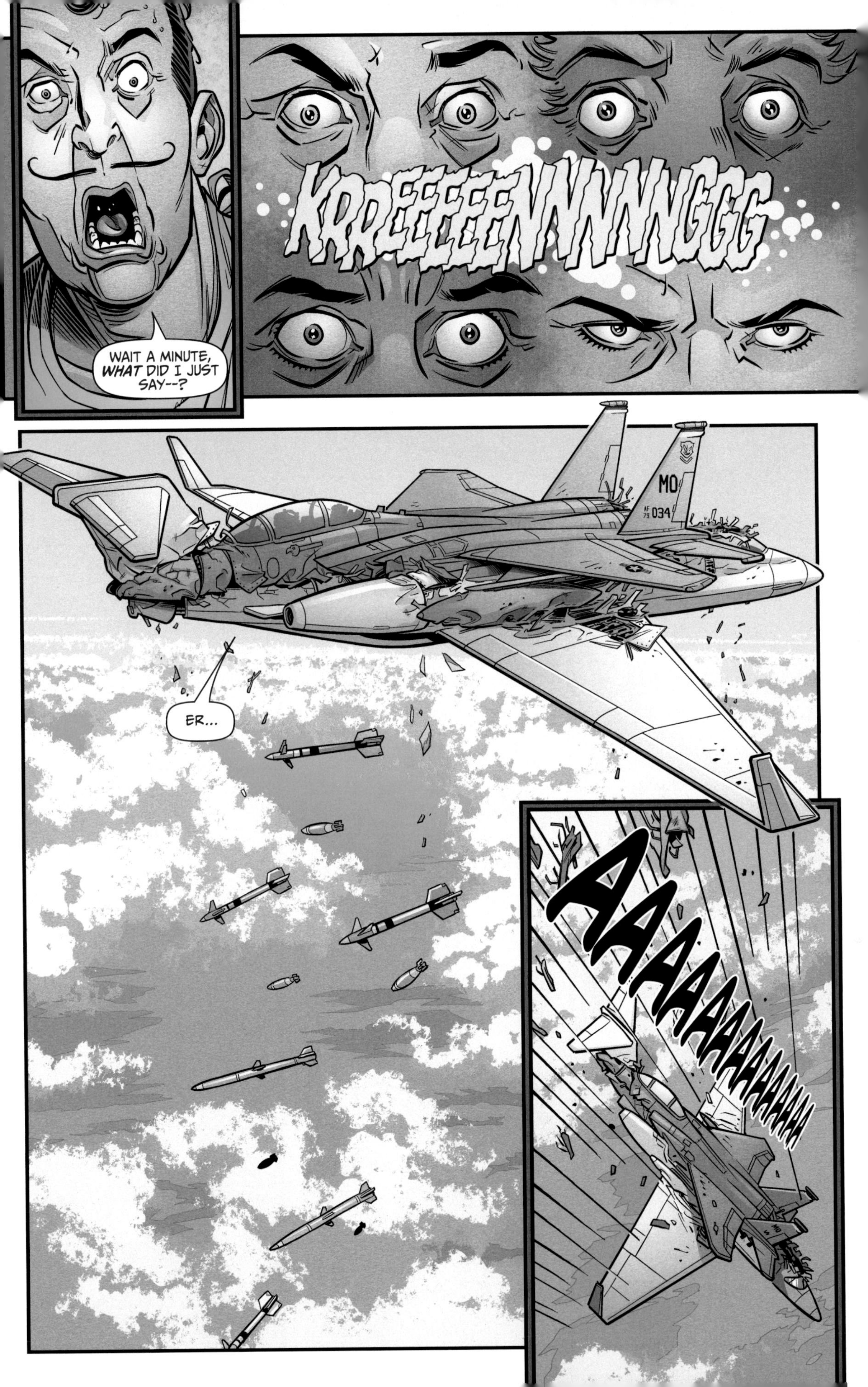
WAIT A MINUTE, WHAT DID I JUST SAY--?
KRREEEEENNNNNGGG
MO
034
ER...
AAAAAAAAAAAAAAAA

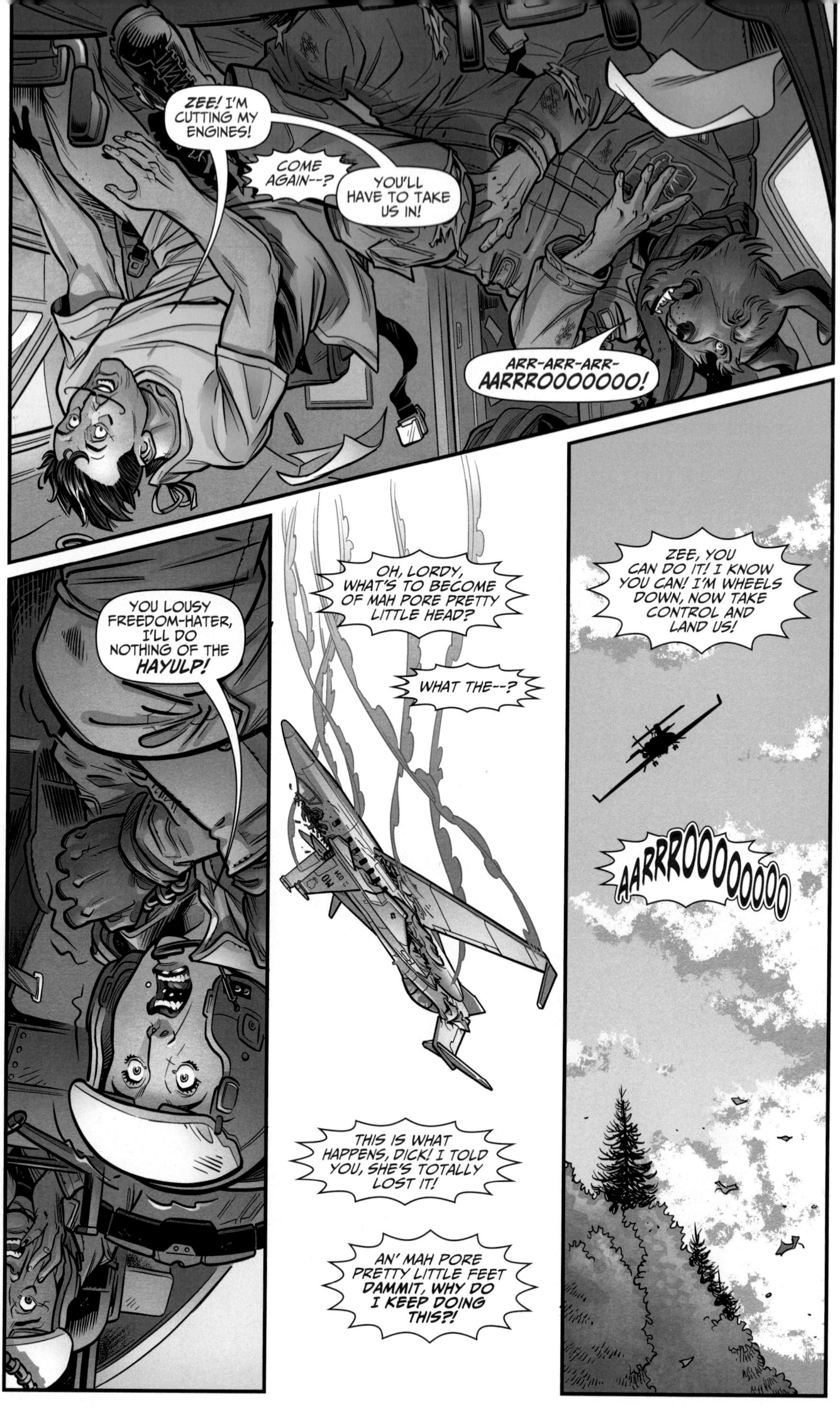
ZEE! I'M CUTTING MY ENGINES!
COME AGAIN--?
YOU'LL HAVE TO TAKE US IN!
ARR-ARR-ARR-AARRROOOOOOOO!
YOU LOUSY FREEDOM-HATER, I'LL DO NOTHING OF THE HAYULP!
OH, LORDY, WHAT'S TO BECOME OF MAH PORE PRETTY LITTLE HEAD?
WHAT THE--?
THIS IS WHAT HAPPENS, DICK! I TOLD YOU, SHE'S TOTALLY LOST IT!
AN' MAH PORE PRETTY LITTLE FEET DAMMIT, WHY DO I KEEP DOING THIS?!
ZEE, YOU CAN DO IT! I KNOW YOU CAN! I'M WHEELS DOWN, NOW TAKE CONTROL AND LAND US!
AARRROOOOOOOO

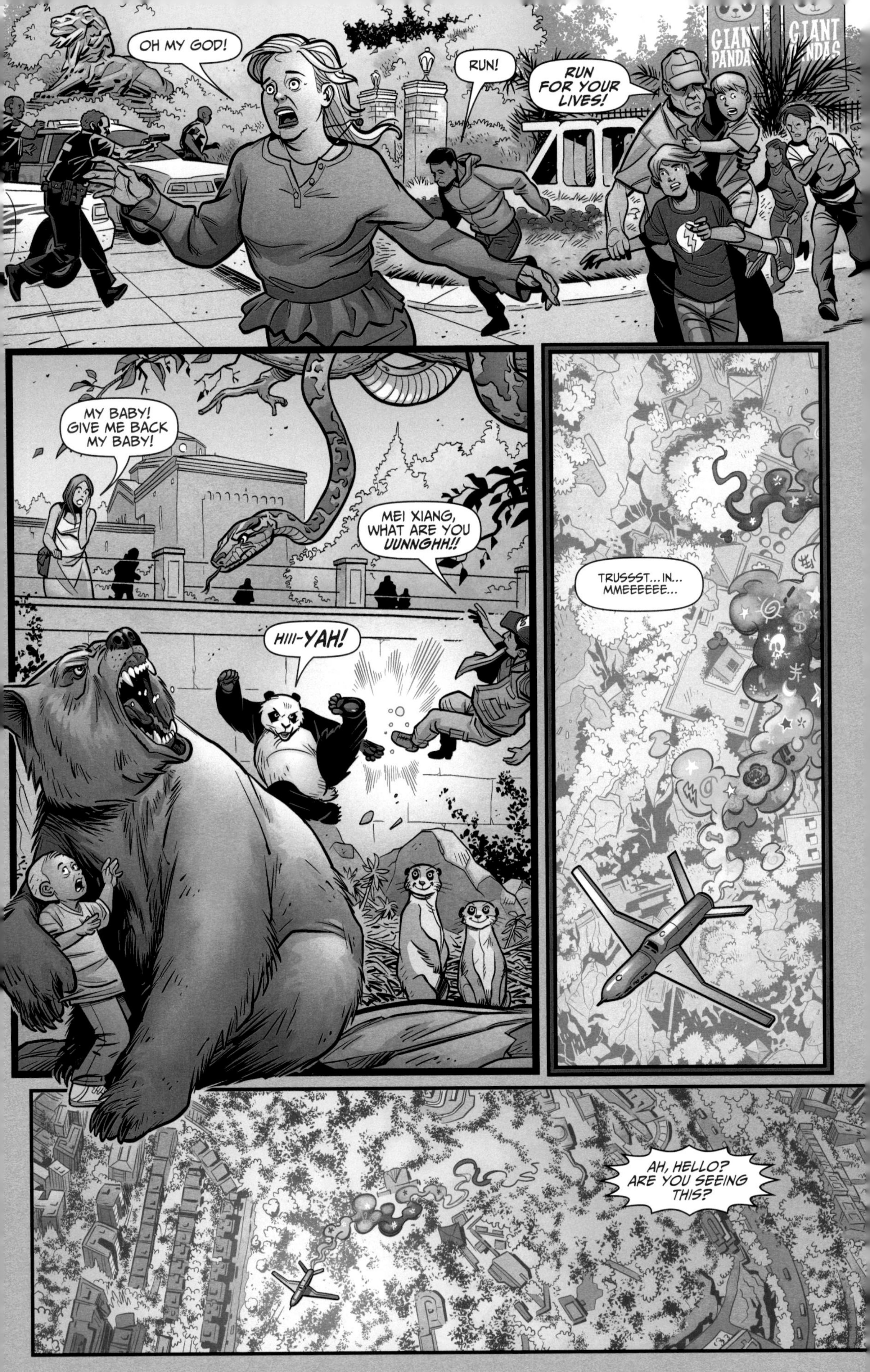
GIANT PANDAS
GIANT PANDAS
OH MY GOD!
RUN!
RUN FOR YOUR LIVES!
ZOO
MY BABY! GIVE ME BACK MY BABY!
MEI XIANG, WHAT ARE YOU UUNNGHH!!
HIII-YAH!
TRUSSST...IN... MMEEEEEE...
AH, HELLO? ARE YOU SEEING THIS?

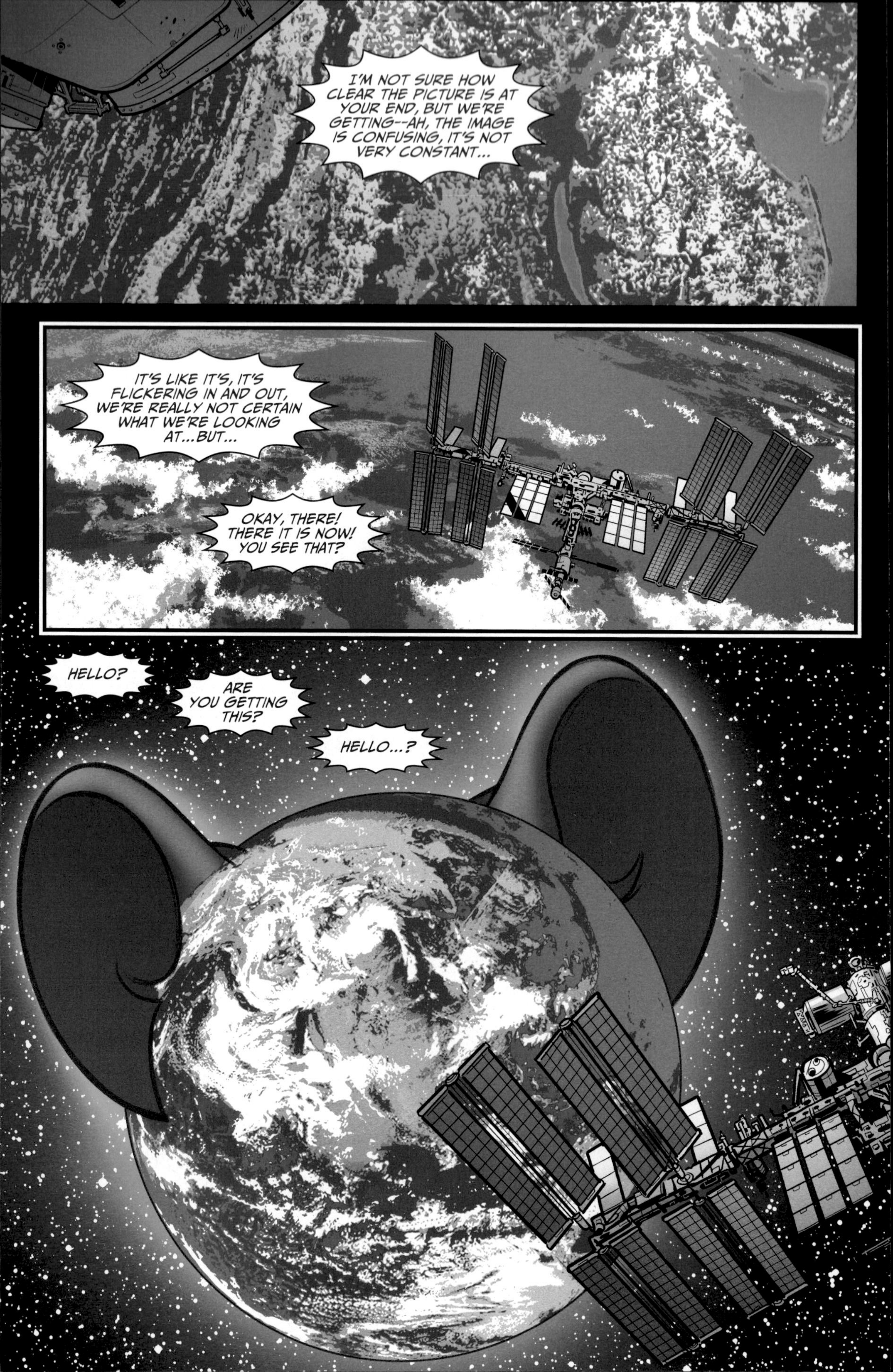
I'M NOT SURE HOW CLEAR THE PICTURE IS AT YOUR END, BUT WE'RE GETTING--AH, THE IMAGE IS CONFUSING, IT'S NOT VERY CONSTANT...
IT'S LIKE IT'S, IT'S FLICKERING IN AND OUT, WE'RE REALLY NOT CERTAIN WHAT WE'RE LOOKING AT...BUT...
OKAY, THERE! THERE IT IS NOW! YOU SEE THAT?
HELLO?
ARE YOU GETTING THIS?
HELLO...?

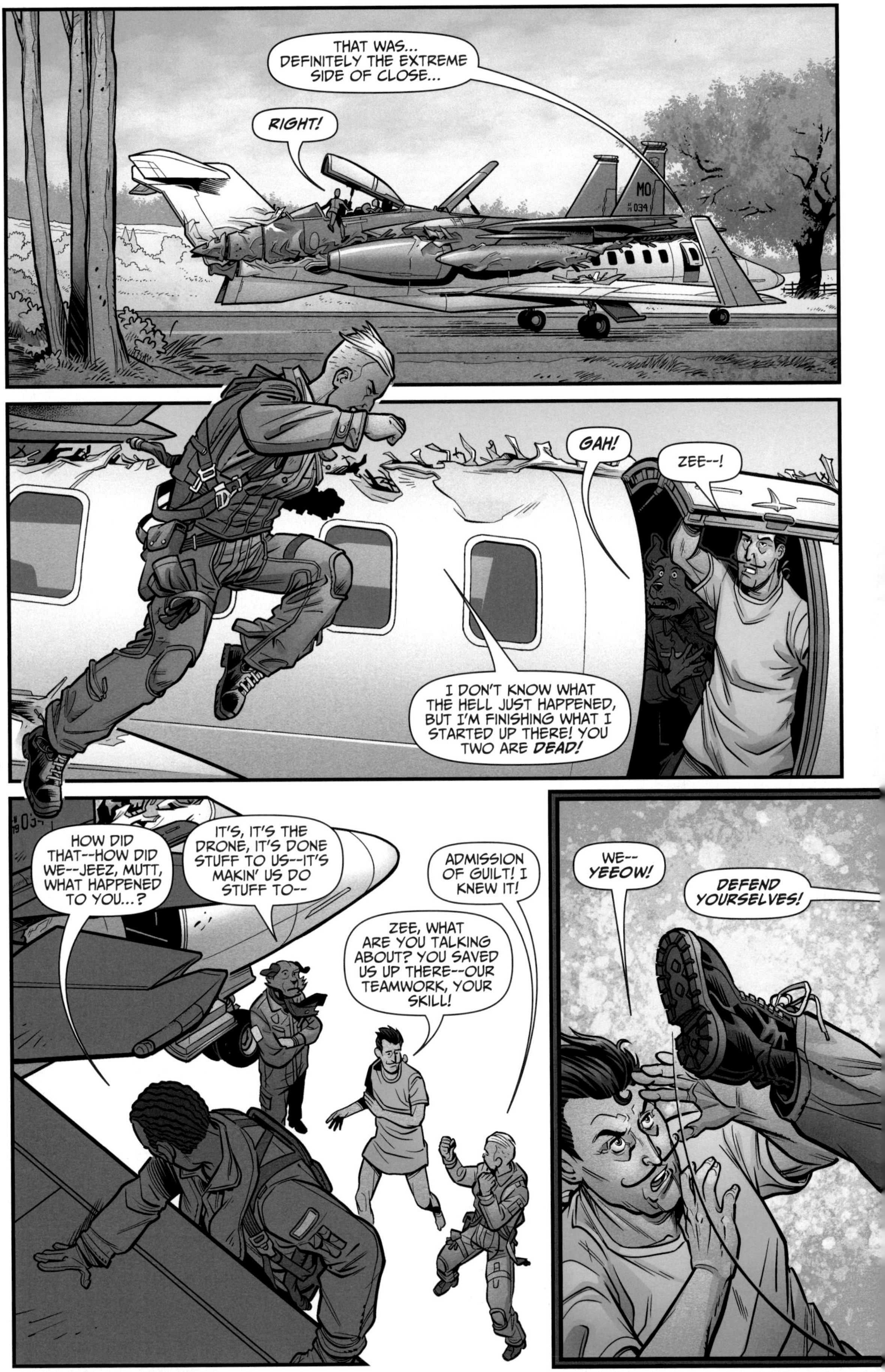
THAT WAS... DEFINITELY THE EXTREME SIDE OF CLOSE...
RIGHT!
MO
GAH!
ZEE--!
I DON'T KNOW WHAT THE HELL JUST HAPPENED, BUT I'M FINISHING WHAT I STARTED UP THERE! YOU TWO ARE DEAD!
HOW DID THAT--HOW DID WE--JEEZ, MUTT, WHAT HAPPENED TO YOU...?
IT'S, IT'S THE DRONE, IT'S DONE STUFF TO US--IT'S MAKIN' US DO STUFF TO--
ADMISSION OF GUILT! I KNEW IT!
ZEE, WHAT ARE YOU TALKING ABOUT? YOU SAVED US UP THERE--OUR TEAMWORK, YOUR SKILL!
WE-- YEEOW!
DEFEND YOURSELVES!

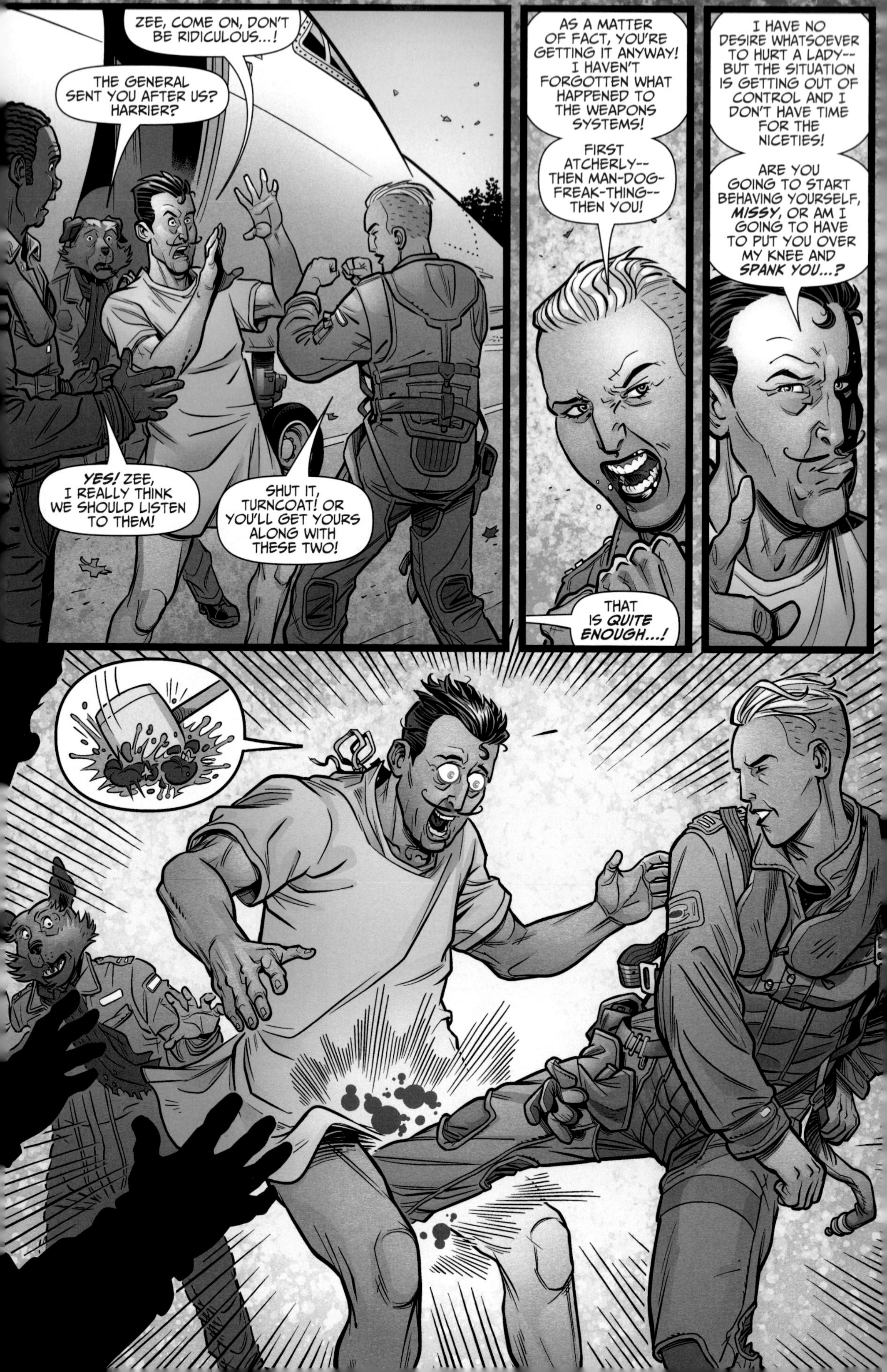

THE GENERAL SENT YOU AFTER US? HARRIER?
ZEE, COME ON, DON'T BE RIDICULOUS...!
YES! ZEE, I REALLY THINK WE SHOULD LISTEN TO THEM!
SHUT IT, TURNCOAT! OR YOU'LL GET YOURS ALONG WITH THESE TWO!
AS A MATTER OF FACT, YOU'RE GETTING IT ANYWAY! I HAVEN'T FORGOTTEN WHAT HAPPENED TO THE WEAPONS SYSTEMS!
FIRST ATCHERLY-- THEN MAN-DOG-FREAK-THING-- THEN YOU!
THAT IS QUITE ENOUGH...!
I HAVE NO DESIRE WHATSOEVER TO HURT A LADY-- BUT THE SITUATION IS GETTING OUT OF CONTROL AND I DON'T HAVE TIME FOR THE NICETIES!
ARE YOU GOING TO START BEHAVING YOURSELF, MISSY, OR AM I GOING TO HAVE TO PUT YOU OVER MY KNEE AND SPANK YOU...?

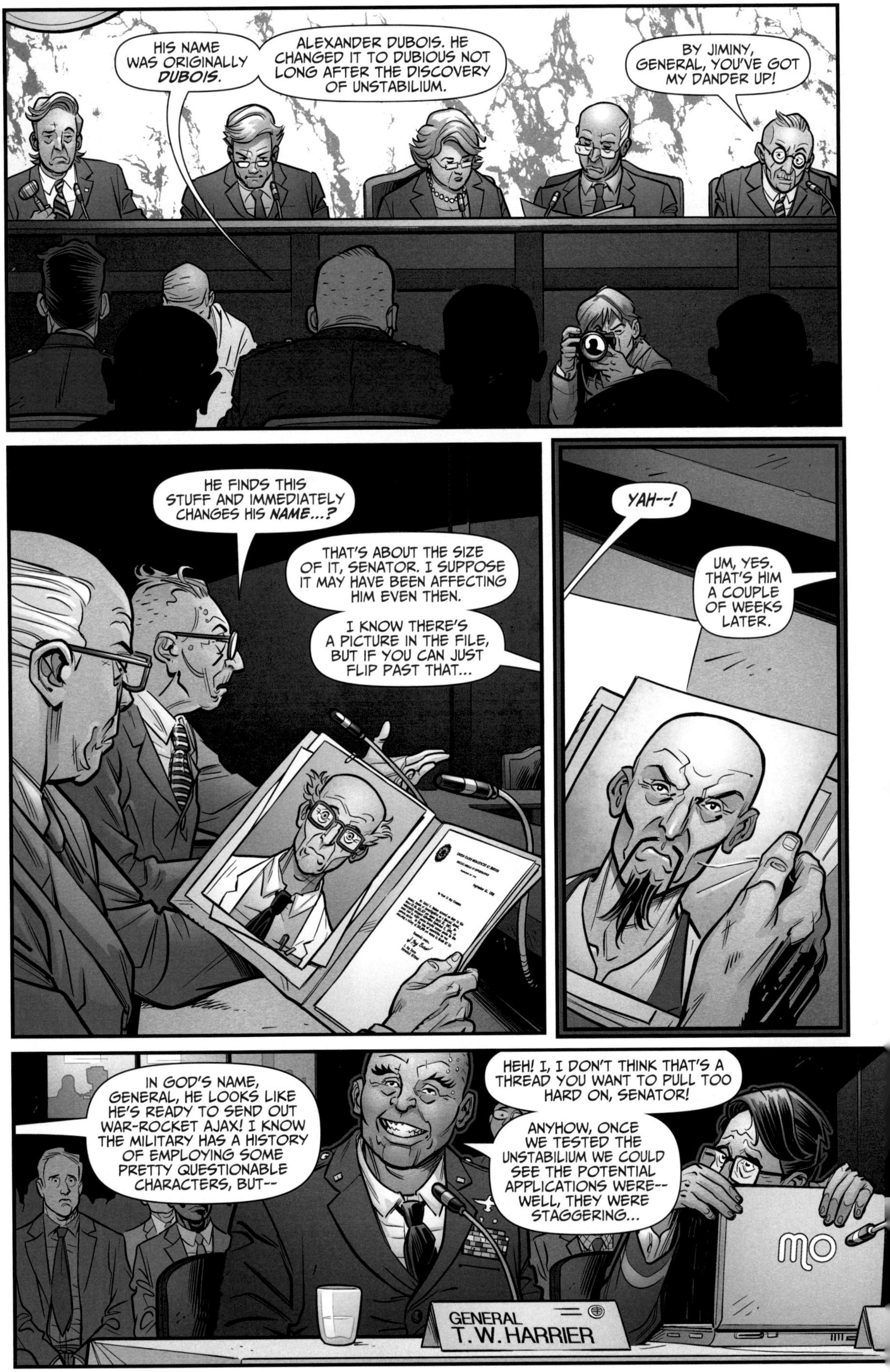
HIS NAME WAS ORIGINALLY *DUBOIS.*
ALEXANDER DUBOIS. HE CHANGED IT TO DUBIOUS NOT LONG AFTER THE DISCOVERY OF UNSTABILIUM.
BY JIMINY, GENERAL, YOU'VE GOT MY DANDER UP!
HE FINDS THIS STUFF AND IMMEDIATELY CHANGES HIS *NAME...?*
THAT'S ABOUT THE SIZE OF IT, SENATOR. I SUPPOSE IT MAY HAVE BEEN AFFECTING HIM EVEN THEN.
I KNOW THERE'S A PICTURE IN THE FILE, BUT IF YOU CAN JUST FLIP PAST THAT...
YAH--!
UM, YES. THAT'S HIM A COUPLE OF WEEKS LATER.
IN GOD'S NAME, GENERAL, HE LOOKS LIKE HE'S READY TO SEND OUT WAR-ROCKET AJAX! I KNOW THE MILITARY HAS A HISTORY OF EMPLOYING SOME PRETTY QUESTIONABLE CHARACTERS, BUT--
HEH! I, I DON'T THINK THAT'S A THREAD YOU WANT TO PULL TOO HARD ON, SENATOR!
ANYHOW, ONCE WE TESTED THE UNSTABILIUM WE COULD SEE THE POTENTIAL APPLICATIONS WERE-- WELL, THEY WERE STAGGERING...
GENERAL T.W. HARRIER
MO

I MEAN THE *SHEER POWER*--

YES, BUT WE KNOW WHAT HAPPENS AFTER THIS, GENERAL! THE UNSTABILIUM'S *UNSTABLE*-- THE SUBCOMMITTEE TOLD YOU TO GET LOST!

SO HOW DOES THE DAMN STUFF END UP IN A COUNTRY NO ONE'S EVER HEARD OF, RUN BY A KING WITH A NAME IT'S *IMPOSSIBLE TO BELIEVE...?*

I'M... JUST A LITTLE RELUCTANT TO...

HAVE YOU SEEN WHAT'S GOING ON OUTSIDE? *SPILL IT!*

WELL, WHILE I WAS TRYING TO SELL THE UNSTABILIUM TO THE ARMED FORCES SUBCOMMITTEE, THE PROFESSOR WAS WORKING ON REFINING IT. SO THE STABILITY ISSUES WOULD BE RESOLVED BEFORE THE DECISION WAS MADE.

EXCEPT... HE COULDN'T.

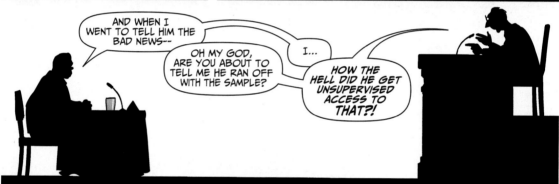

AND WHEN I WENT TO TELL HIM THE BAD NEWS--

OH MY GOD, ARE YOU ABOUT TO TELL ME HE RAN OFF WITH THE SAMPLE?

I...

HOW THE HELL DID HE GET UNSUPERVISED ACCESS TO THAT?!

ALL I CAN SAY IS IT--*ULP!* IT SEEMED LIKE A GOOD IDEA AT THE TIME.

IT...IT MAY HAVE HAD SOMETHING TO DO WITH MY OWN EXPOSURE TO THE UNSTABILIUM. I HAD NO PROBLEM WITH THE PROFESSOR LEAVING, UNTIL I STOPPED TO THINK ABOUT IT LATER ON--KIND OF LIKE WITH YOUR POINT ABOUT UNLIKLISTAN AND THE KING...

AND THEN IT DID SEEM... WELL...

DUBIOUS? BECAUSE I WAS GOING TO SAY *RIDICULOUS*, GENERAL.

I THINK WE LEFT DUBIOUS BEHIND A WHILE AGO.

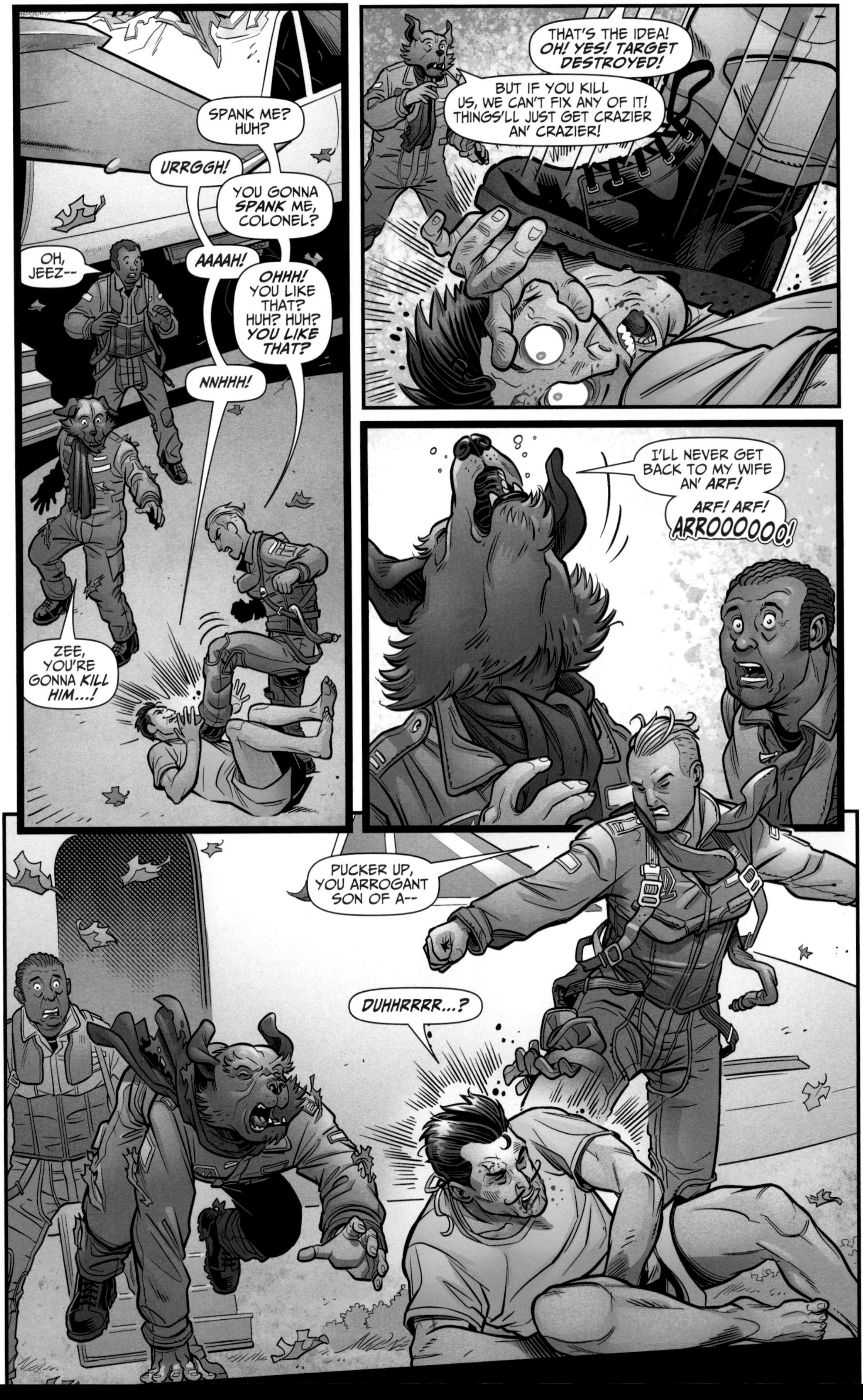
SPANK ME? HUH?
URRGGH!
YOU GONNA SPANK ME, COLONEL?
OH, JEEZ--
AAAAH!
OHHH! YOU LIKE THAT? HUH? HUH? YOU LIKE THAT?
NNHHH!
ZEE, YOU'RE GONNA KILL HIM...!
THAT'S THE IDEA! OH! YES! TARGET DESTROYED!
BUT IF YOU KILL US, WE CAN'T FIX ANY OF IT! THINGS'LL JUST GET CRAZIER AN' CRAZIER!
I'LL NEVER GET BACK TO MY WIFE AN' ARF!
ARF! ARF! ARROOOOOOO!
PUCKER UP, YOU ARROGANT SON OF A--
DUHHRRRR...?

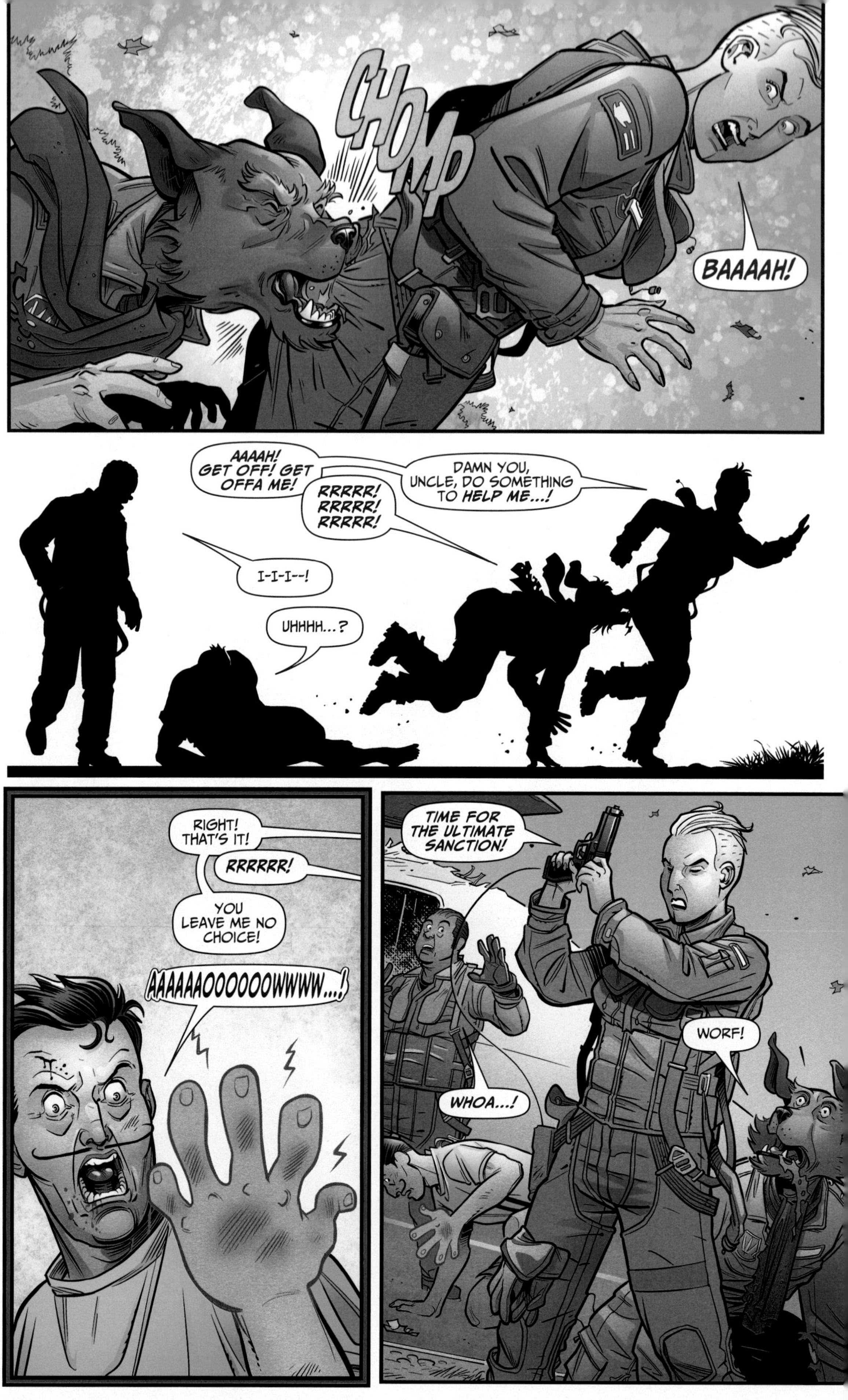
CHOMP
BAAAAH!
AAAAH! GET OFF! GET OFFA ME!
DAMN YOU, UNCLE, DO SOMETHING TO HELP ME...!
RRRRR! RRRRR! RRRRR!
I-I-I--!
UHHHH...?
RIGHT! THAT'S IT!
RRRRRR!
YOU LEAVE ME NO CHOICE!
AAAAAAOOOOOOWWWW...!
TIME FOR THE ULTIMATE SANCTION!
WORF!
WHOA...!

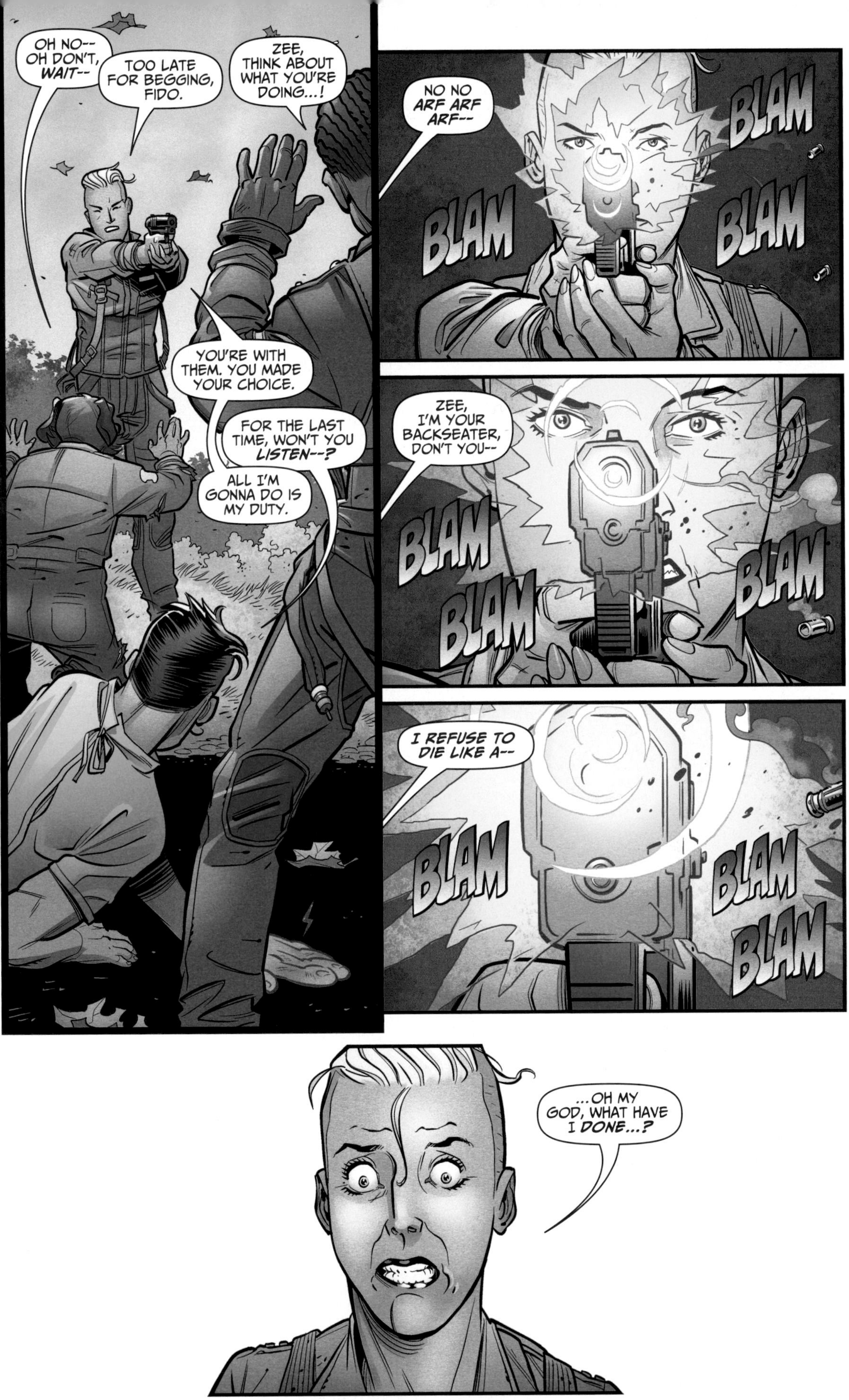

OH NO-- OH DON'T, *WAIT*--
TOO LATE FOR BEGGING, FIDO.
ZEE, THINK ABOUT WHAT YOU'RE DOING...!
YOU'RE WITH THEM. YOU MADE YOUR CHOICE.
FOR THE LAST TIME, WON'T YOU *LISTEN*--?
ALL I'M GONNA DO IS MY DUTY.
NO NO *ARF ARF ARF*--
BLAM
BLAM
BLAM
ZEE, I'M YOUR BACKSEATER, DON'T YOU--
BLAM
BLAM
BLAM
I REFUSE TO DIE LIKE A--
BLAM
BLAM
BLAM
...OH MY GOD, WHAT HAVE I *DONE*...?

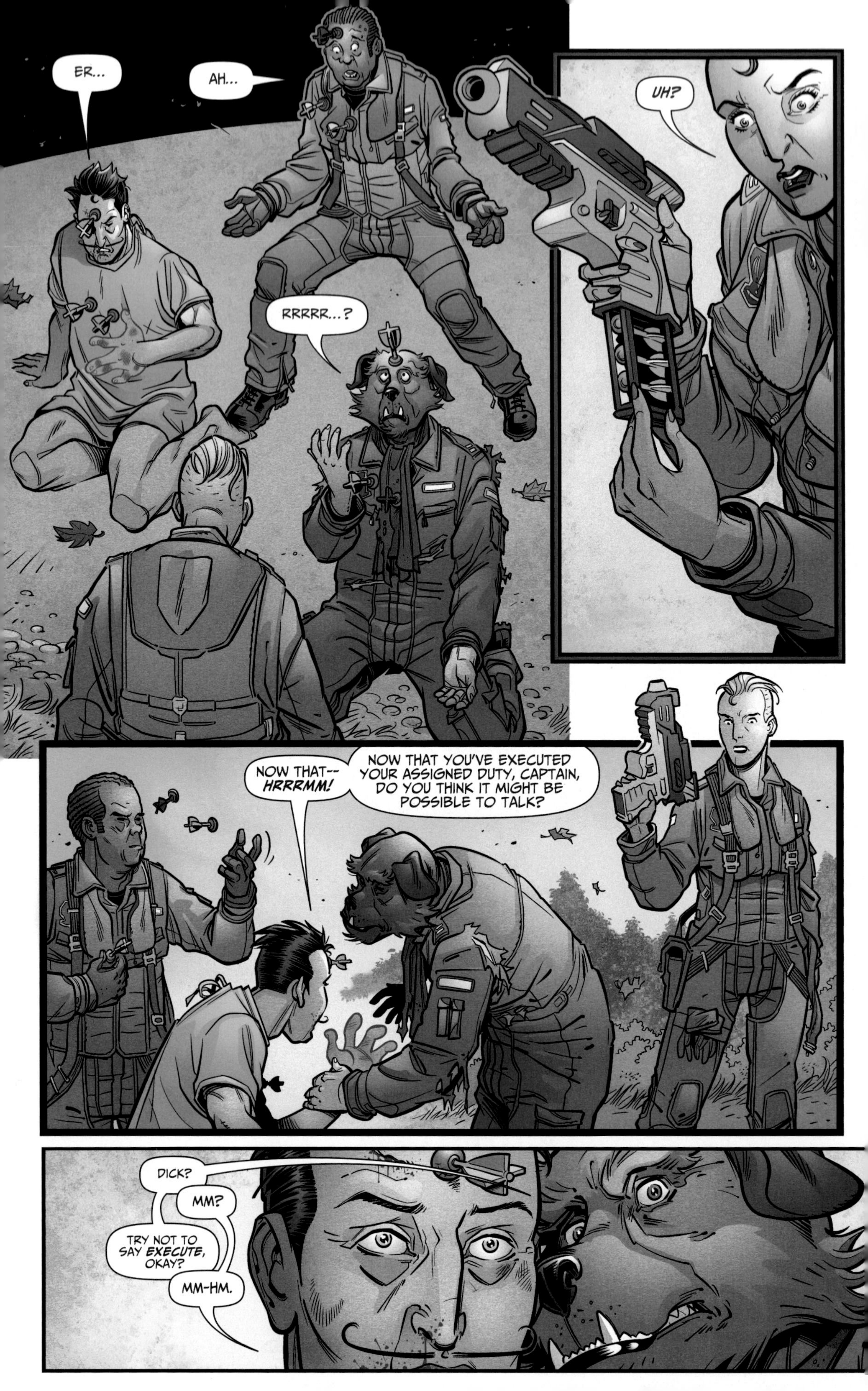
ER...
AH...
RRRRR...?
UH?
NOW THAT--
HRRRMM!
NOW THAT YOU'VE EXECUTED YOUR ASSIGNED DUTY, CAPTAIN, DO YOU THINK IT MIGHT BE POSSIBLE TO TALK?
DICK?
MM?
TRY NOT TO SAY *EXECUTE*, OKAY?
MM-HM.

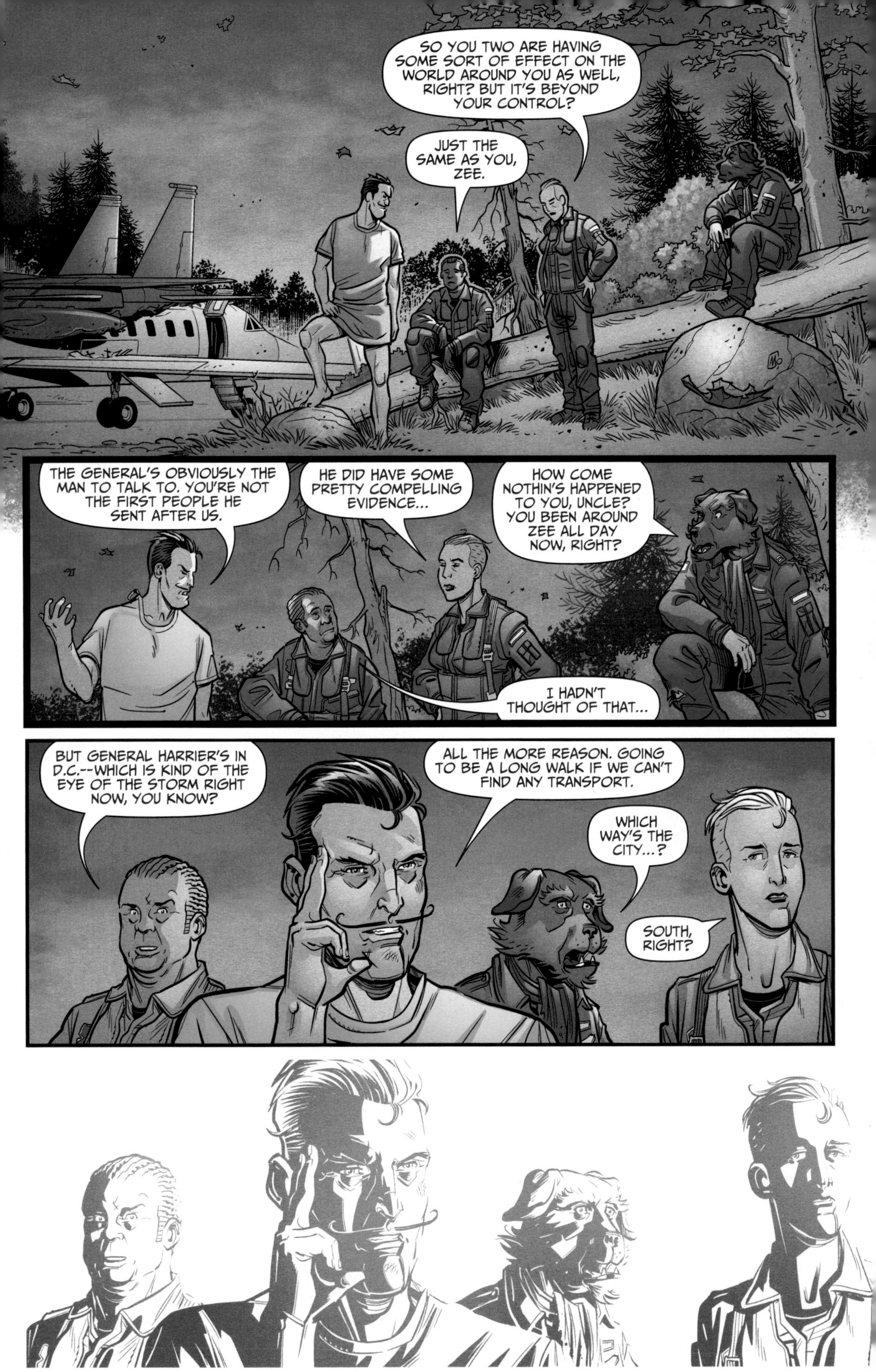
SO YOU TWO ARE HAVING SOME SORT OF EFFECT ON THE WORLD AROUND YOU AS WELL, RIGHT? BUT IT'S BEYOND YOUR CONTROL?
JUST THE SAME AS YOU, ZEE.
THE GENERAL'S OBVIOUSLY THE MAN TO TALK TO. YOU'RE NOT THE FIRST PEOPLE HE SENT AFTER US.
HE DID HAVE SOME PRETTY COMPELLING EVIDENCE...
HOW COME NOTHIN'S HAPPENED TO YOU, UNCLE? YOU BEEN AROUND ZEE ALL DAY NOW, RIGHT?
I HADN'T THOUGHT OF THAT...
BUT GENERAL HARRIER'S IN D.C.--WHICH IS KIND OF THE EYE OF THE STORM RIGHT NOW, YOU KNOW?
ALL THE MORE REASON. GOING TO BE A LONG WALK IF WE CAN'T FIND ANY TRANSPORT.
WHICH WAY'S THE CITY...?
SOUTH, RIGHT?

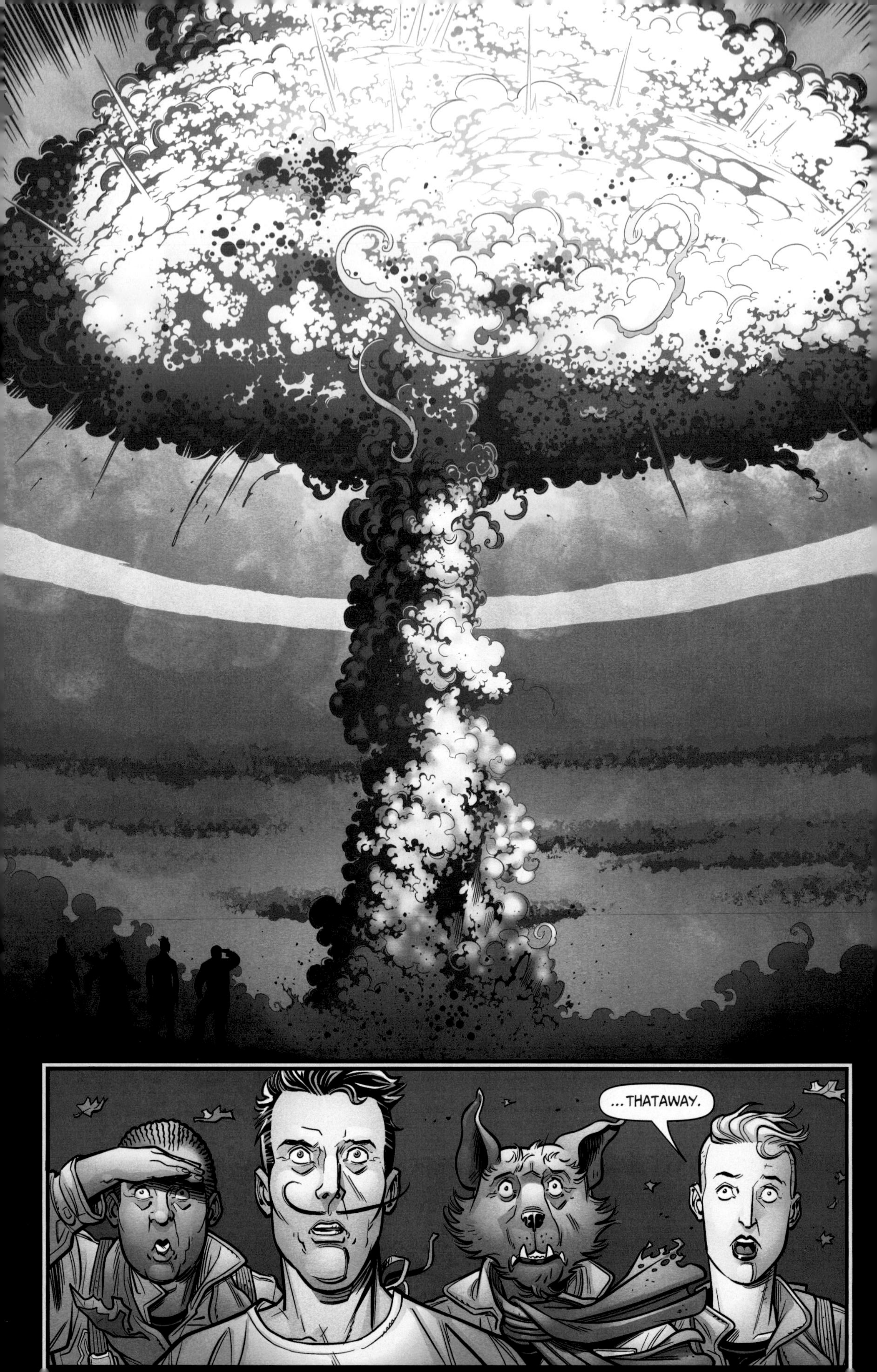
...THATAWAY.

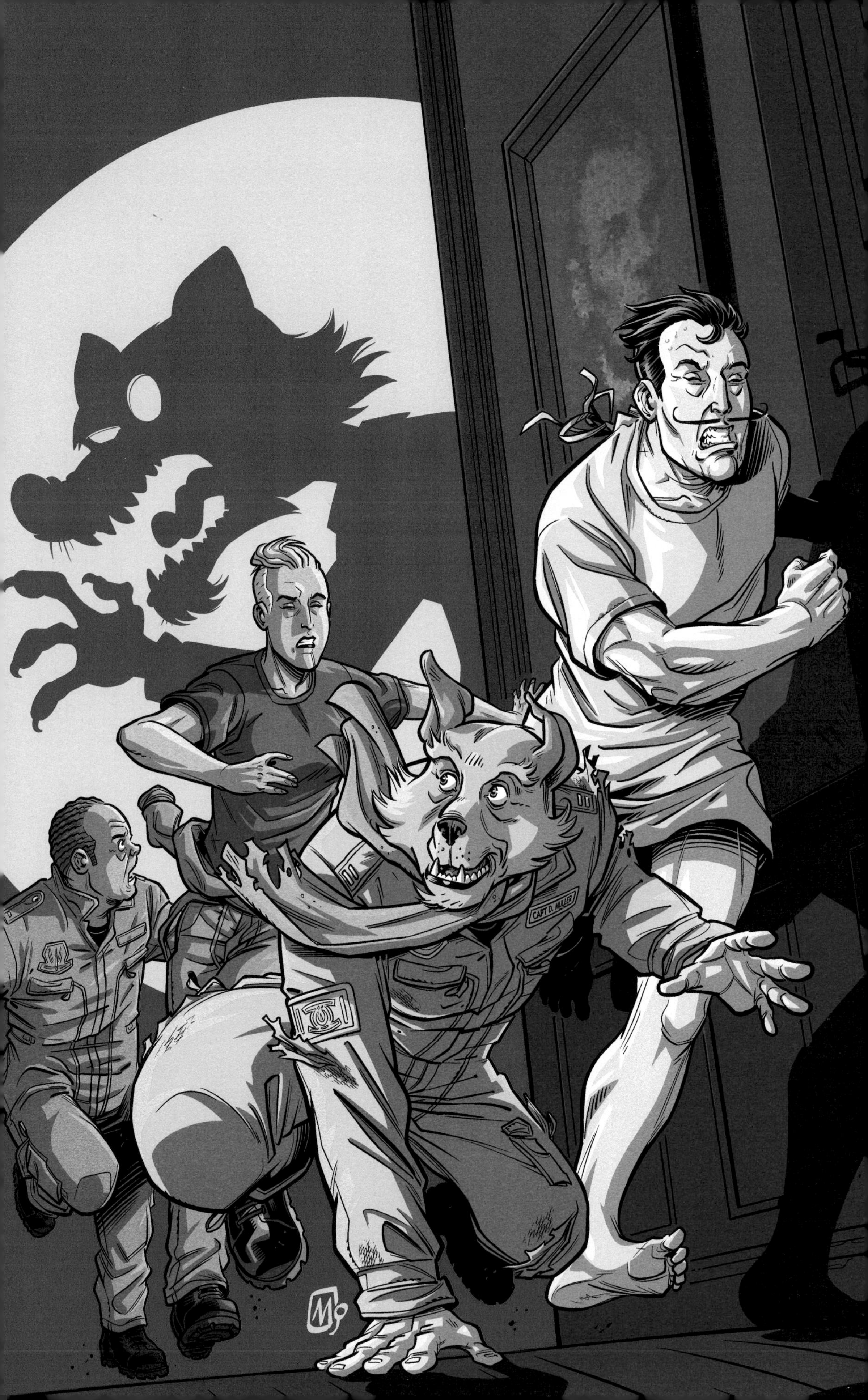
CAPT D. MULLER

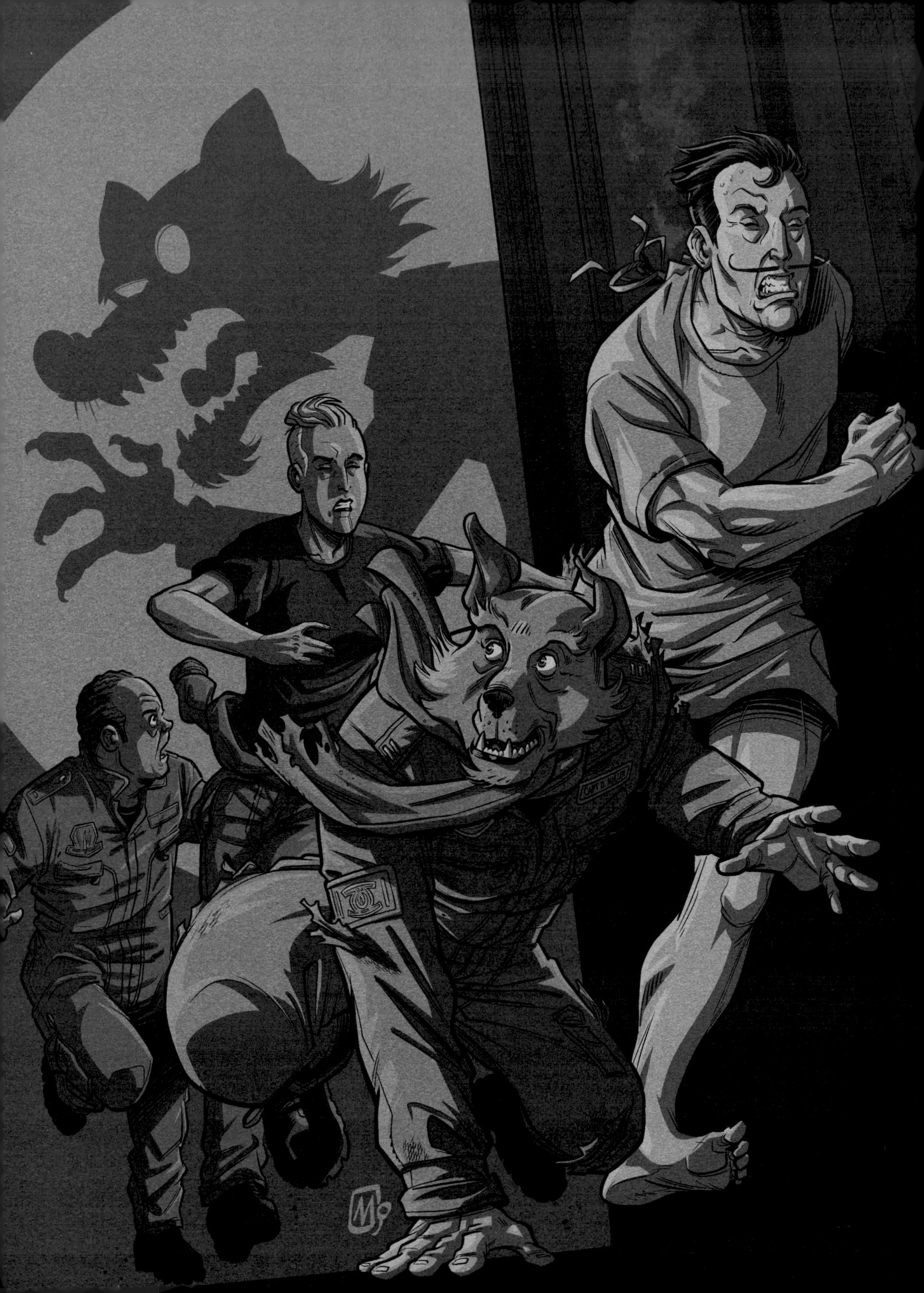

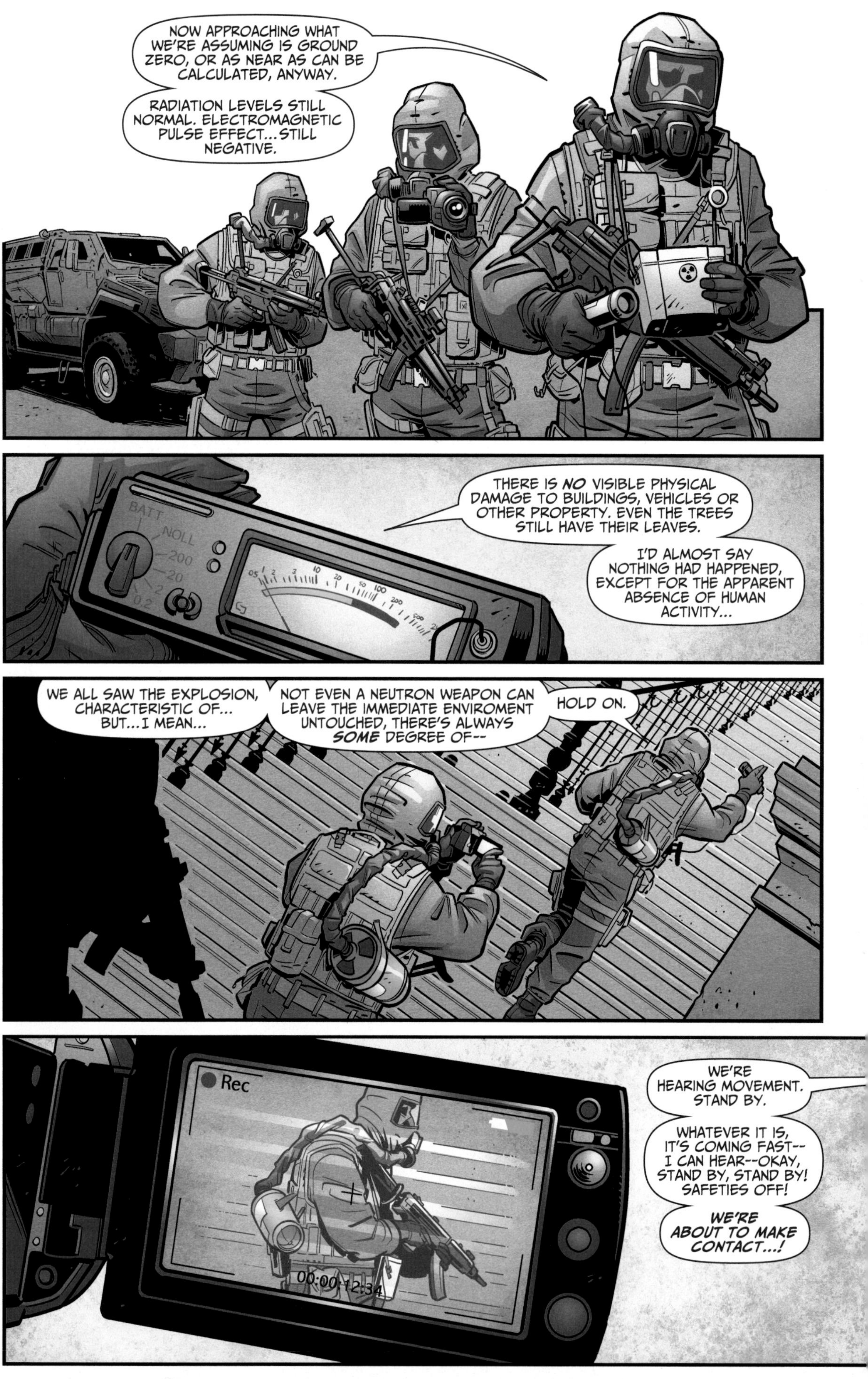
NOW APPROACHING WHAT WE'RE ASSUMING IS GROUND ZERO, OR AS NEAR AS CAN BE CALCULATED, ANYWAY.
RADIATION LEVELS STILL NORMAL. ELECTROMAGNETIC PULSE EFFECT...STILL NEGATIVE.
BATT
NOLL
200
20
2
0.2
THERE IS NO VISIBLE PHYSICAL DAMAGE TO BUILDINGS, VEHICLES OR OTHER PROPERTY. EVEN THE TREES STILL HAVE THEIR LEAVES.
I'D ALMOST SAY NOTHING HAD HAPPENED, EXCEPT FOR THE APPARENT ABSENCE OF HUMAN ACTIVITY...
WE ALL SAW THE EXPLOSION, CHARACTERISTIC OF... BUT...I MEAN...
NOT EVEN A NEUTRON WEAPON CAN LEAVE THE IMMEDIATE ENVIROMENT UNTOUCHED, THERE'S ALWAYS SOME DEGREE OF--
HOLD ON.
Rec
00:00:12:34
WE'RE HEARING MOVEMENT. STAND BY.
WHATEVER IT IS, IT'S COMING FAST-- I CAN HEAR--OKAY, STAND BY, STAND BY! SAFETIES OFF!
WE'RE ABOUT TO MAKE CONTACT...!

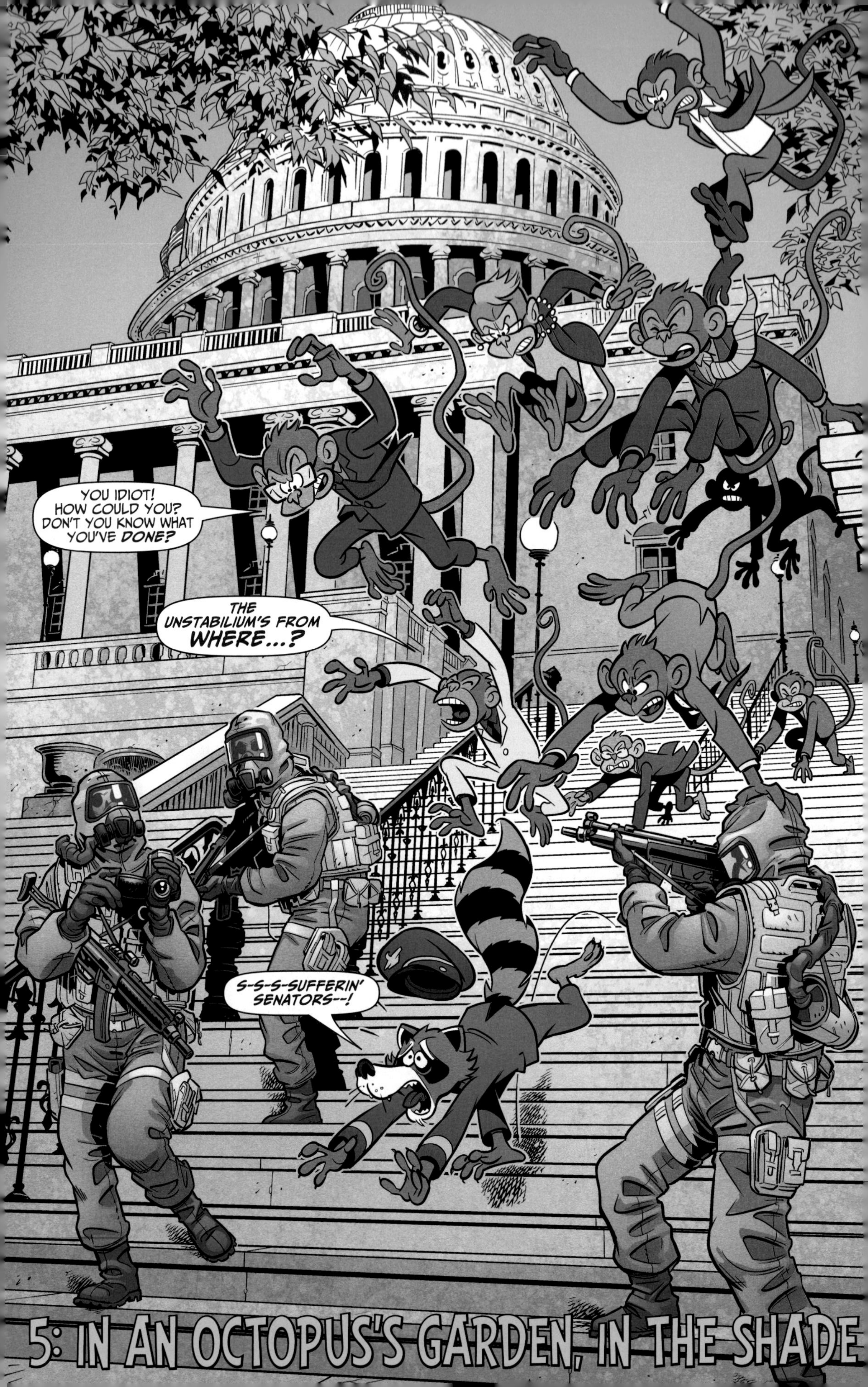
YOU IDIOT! HOW COULD YOU? DON'T YOU KNOW WHAT YOU'VE DONE?
THE UNSTABILIUM'S FROM WHERE...?
S-S-S-SUFFERIN' SENATORS--!

5: IN AN OCTOPUS'S GARDEN, IN THE SHADE

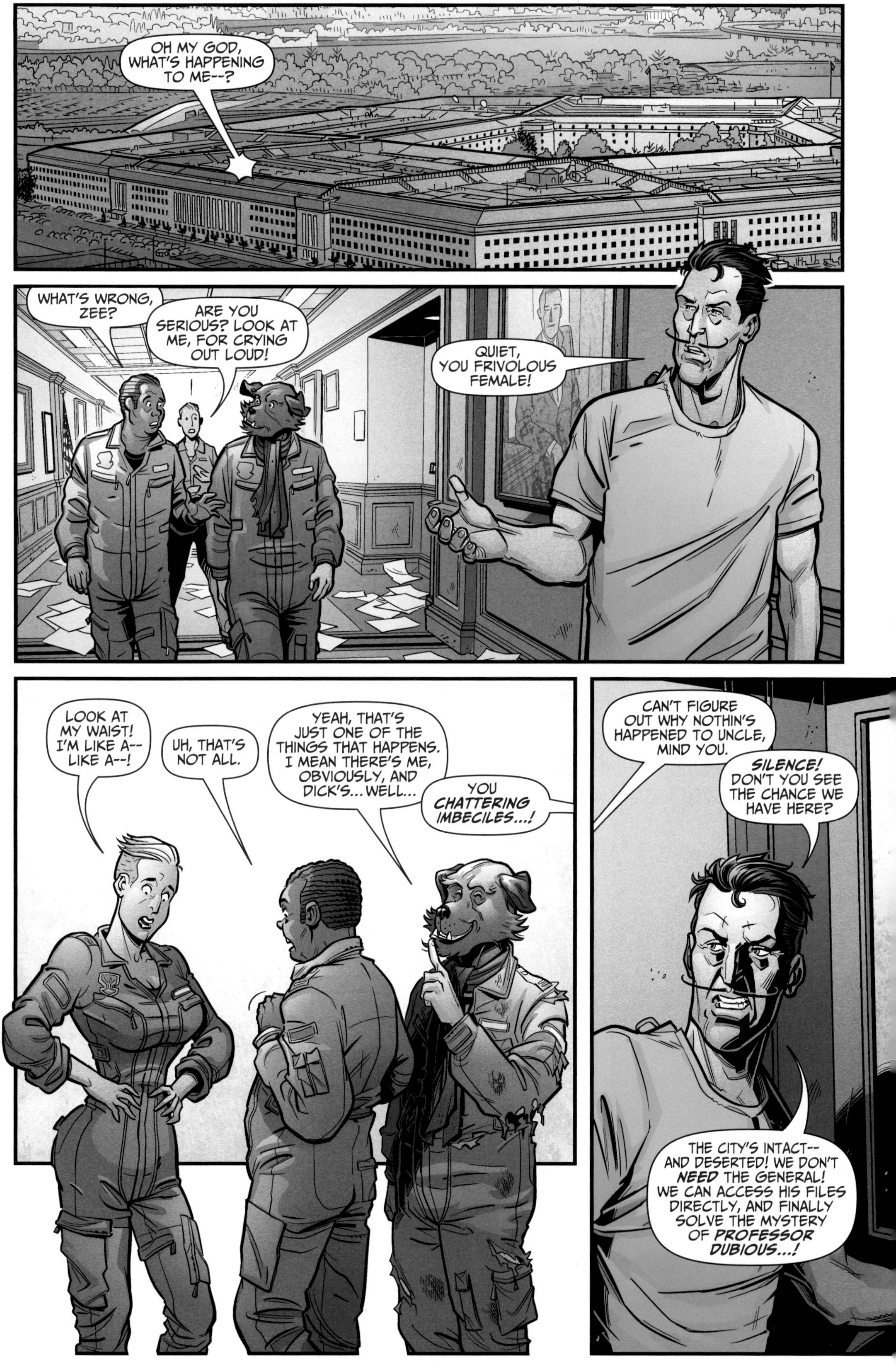
OH MY GOD, WHAT'S HAPPENING TO ME--?
WHAT'S WRONG, ZEE?
ARE YOU SERIOUS? LOOK AT ME, FOR CRYING OUT LOUD!
QUIET, YOU FRIVOLOUS FEMALE!
LOOK AT MY WAIST! I'M LIKE A-- LIKE A--!
UH, THAT'S NOT ALL.
YEAH, THAT'S JUST ONE OF THE THINGS THAT HAPPENS. I MEAN THERE'S ME, OBVIOUSLY, AND DICK'S...WELL...
YOU *CHATTERING IMBECILES...!*
CAN'T FIGURE OUT WHY NOTHIN'S HAPPENED TO UNCLE, MIND YOU.
SILENCE! DON'T YOU SEE THE CHANCE WE HAVE HERE?
THE CITY'S INTACT-- AND DESERTED! WE DON'T *NEED* THE GENERAL! WE CAN ACCESS HIS FILES DIRECTLY, AND FINALLY SOLVE THE MYSTERY OF *PROFESSOR DUBIOUS...!*

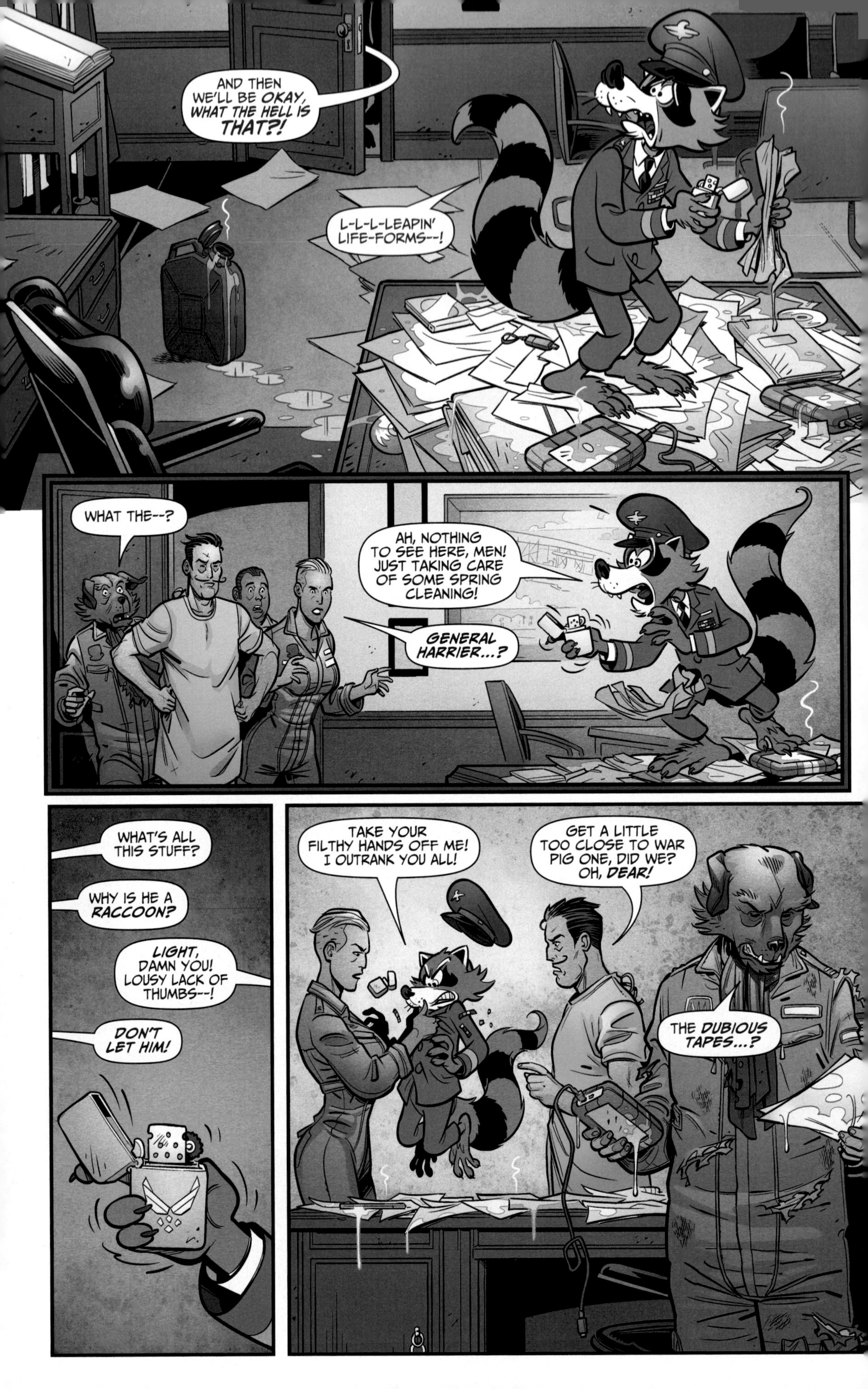
AND THEN WE'LL BE *OKAY*, WHAT THE HELL IS *THAT?!*
L-L-L-LEAPIN' LIFE-FORMS--!
WHAT THE--?
AH, NOTHING TO SEE HERE, MEN! JUST TAKING CARE OF SOME SPRING CLEANING!
GENERAL HARRIER...?
WHAT'S ALL THIS STUFF?
WHY IS HE A *RACCOON?*
LIGHT, DAMN YOU! LOUSY LACK OF THUMBS--!
DON'T LET HIM!
TAKE YOUR FILTHY HANDS OFF ME! I OUTRANK YOU ALL!
GET A LITTLE TOO CLOSE TO WAR PIG ONE, DID WE? OH, *DEAR!*
THE *DUBIOUS TAPES...?*

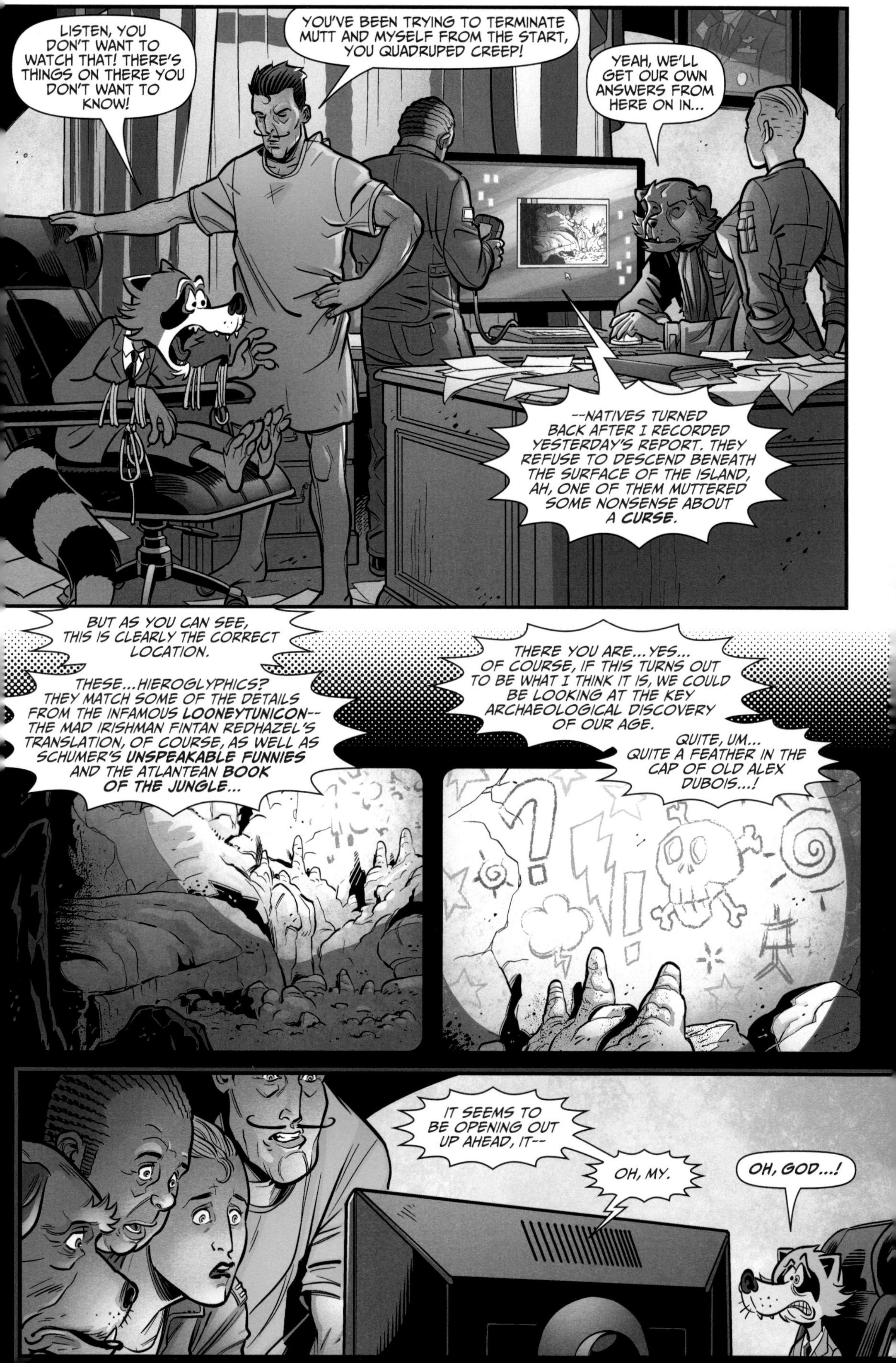
LISTEN, YOU DON'T WANT TO WATCH THAT! THERE'S THINGS ON THERE YOU DON'T WANT TO KNOW!
YOU'VE BEEN TRYING TO TERMINATE MUTT AND MYSELF FROM THE START, YOU QUADRUPED CREEP!
YEAH, WE'LL GET OUR OWN ANSWERS FROM HERE ON IN...
--NATIVES TURNED BACK AFTER I RECORDED YESTERDAY'S REPORT. THEY REFUSE TO DESCEND BENEATH THE SURFACE OF THE ISLAND, AH, ONE OF THEM MUTTERED SOME NONSENSE ABOUT A **CURSE**.
BUT AS YOU CAN SEE, THIS IS CLEARLY THE CORRECT LOCATION.
THESE...HIEROGLYPHICS? THEY MATCH SOME OF THE DETAILS FROM THE INFAMOUS **LOONEYTUNICON**-- THE MAD IRISHMAN FINTAN REDHAZEL'S TRANSLATION, OF COURSE, AS WELL AS SCHUMER'S **UNSPEAKABLE FUNNIES** AND THE ATLANTEAN **BOOK OF THE JUNGLE**...
THERE YOU ARE...YES... OF COURSE, IF THIS TURNS OUT TO BE WHAT I THINK IT IS, WE COULD BE LOOKING AT THE KEY ARCHAEOLOGICAL DISCOVERY OF OUR AGE.
QUITE, UM... QUITE A FEATHER IN THE CAP OF OLD ALEX DUBOIS...!
IT SEEMS TO BE OPENING OUT UP AHEAD, IT--
OH, MY.
OH, GOD...!

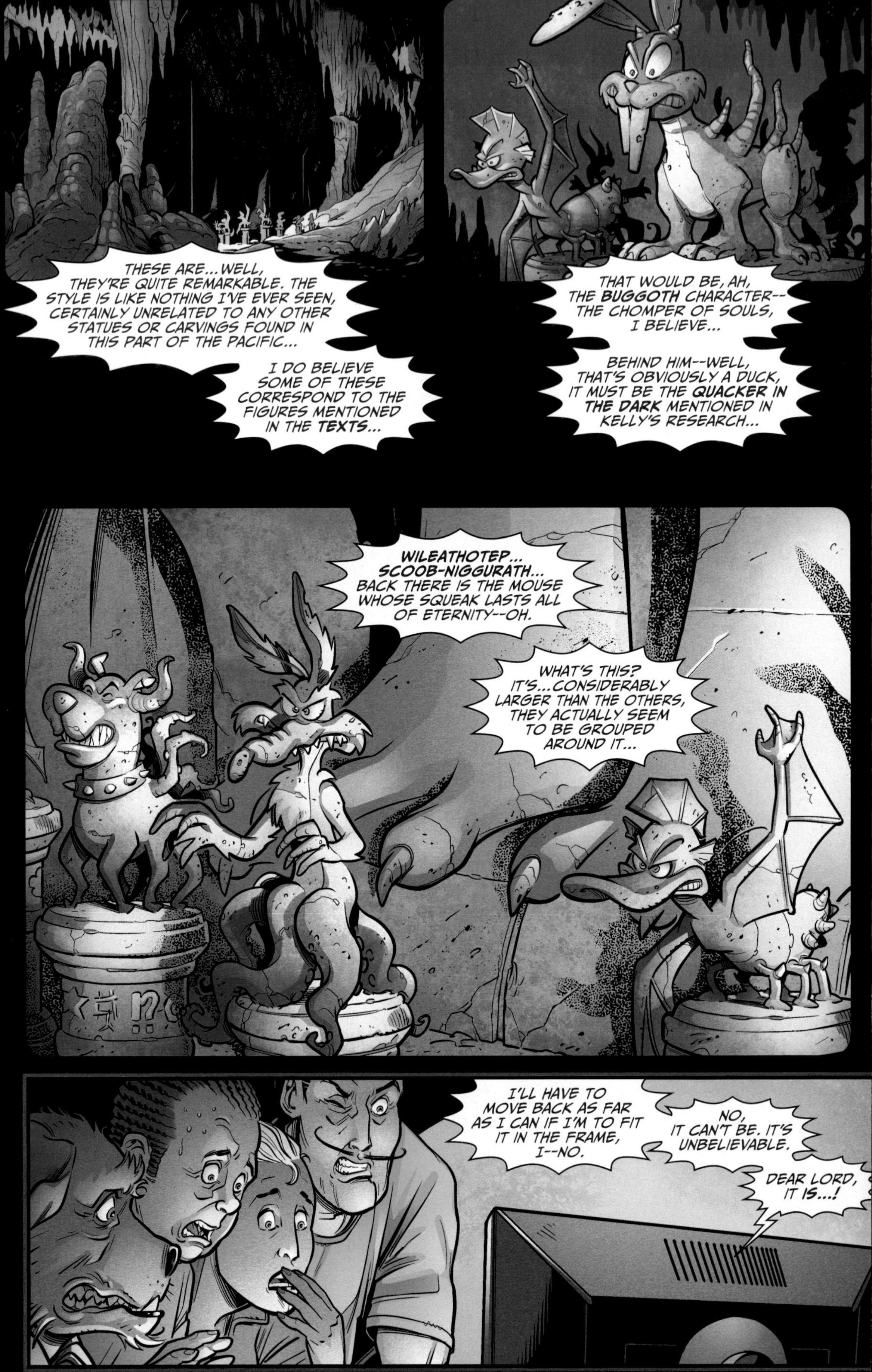
THESE ARE...WELL, THEY'RE QUITE REMARKABLE. THE STYLE IS LIKE NOTHING I'VE EVER SEEN, CERTAINLY UNRELATED TO ANY OTHER STATUES OR CARVINGS FOUND IN THIS PART OF THE PACIFIC...
I DO BELIEVE SOME OF THESE CORRESPOND TO THE FIGURES MENTIONED IN THE **TEXTS**...
THAT WOULD BE, AH, THE **BUGGOTH** CHARACTER-- THE CHOMPER OF SOULS, I BELIEVE...
BEHIND HIM--WELL, THAT'S OBVIOUSLY A DUCK, IT MUST BE THE **QUACKER IN THE DARK** MENTIONED IN KELLY'S RESEARCH...
WILEATHOTEP... SCOOB-NIGGURATH... BACK THERE IS THE MOUSE WHOSE SQUEAK LASTS ALL OF ETERNITY--OH.
WHAT'S THIS? IT'S...CONSIDERABLY LARGER THAN THE OTHERS, THEY ACTUALLY SEEM TO BE GROUPED AROUND IT...
I'LL HAVE TO MOVE BACK AS FAR AS I CAN IF I'M TO FIT IT IN THE FRAME, I--NO.
NO, IT CAN'T BE. IT'S UNBELIEVABLE.
DEAR LORD, IT **IS**...!

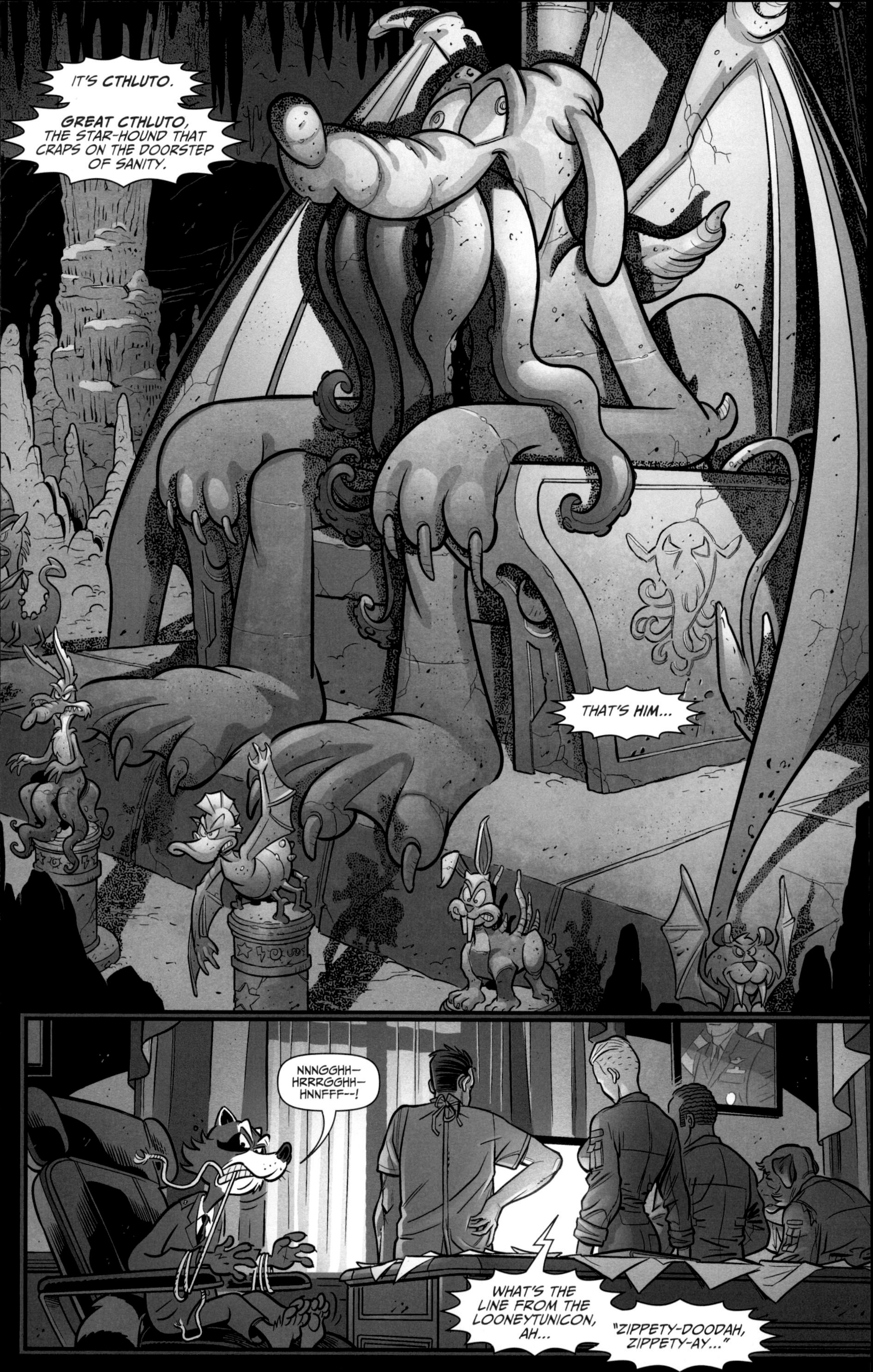
IT'S CTHLUTO.
GREAT CTHLUTO, THE STAR-HOUND THAT CRAPS ON THE DOORSTEP OF SANITY.
THAT'S HIM...
NNNGGHH-HRRRGGHH-HNNFFF--!
WHAT'S THE LINE FROM THE LOONEYTUNICON, AH...
"ZIPPETY-DOODAH, ZIPPETY-AY..."

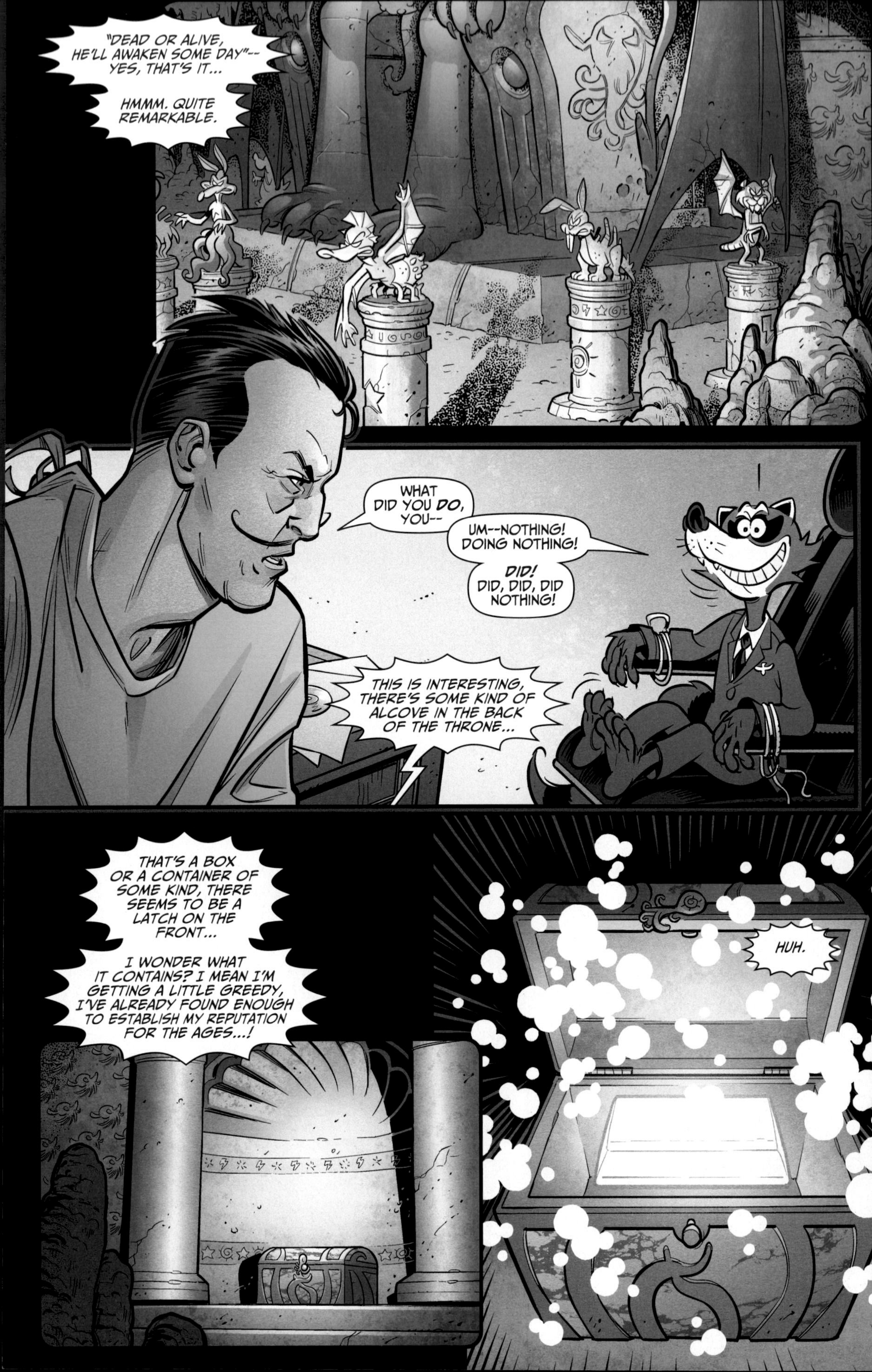
"DEAD OR ALIVE, HE'LL AWAKEN SOME DAY"-- YES, THAT'S IT...
HMMM. QUITE REMARKABLE.
WHAT DID YOU DO, YOU--
UM--NOTHING! DOING NOTHING!
DID! DID, DID, DID NOTHING!
THIS IS INTERESTING, THERE'S SOME KIND OF ALCOVE IN THE BACK OF THE THRONE...
THAT'S A BOX OR A CONTAINER OF SOME KIND, THERE SEEMS TO BE A LATCH ON THE FRONT...
I WONDER WHAT IT CONTAINS? I MEAN I'M GETTING A LITTLE GREEDY, I'VE ALREADY FOUND ENOUGH TO ESTABLISH MY REPUTATION FOR THE AGES...!
HUH.

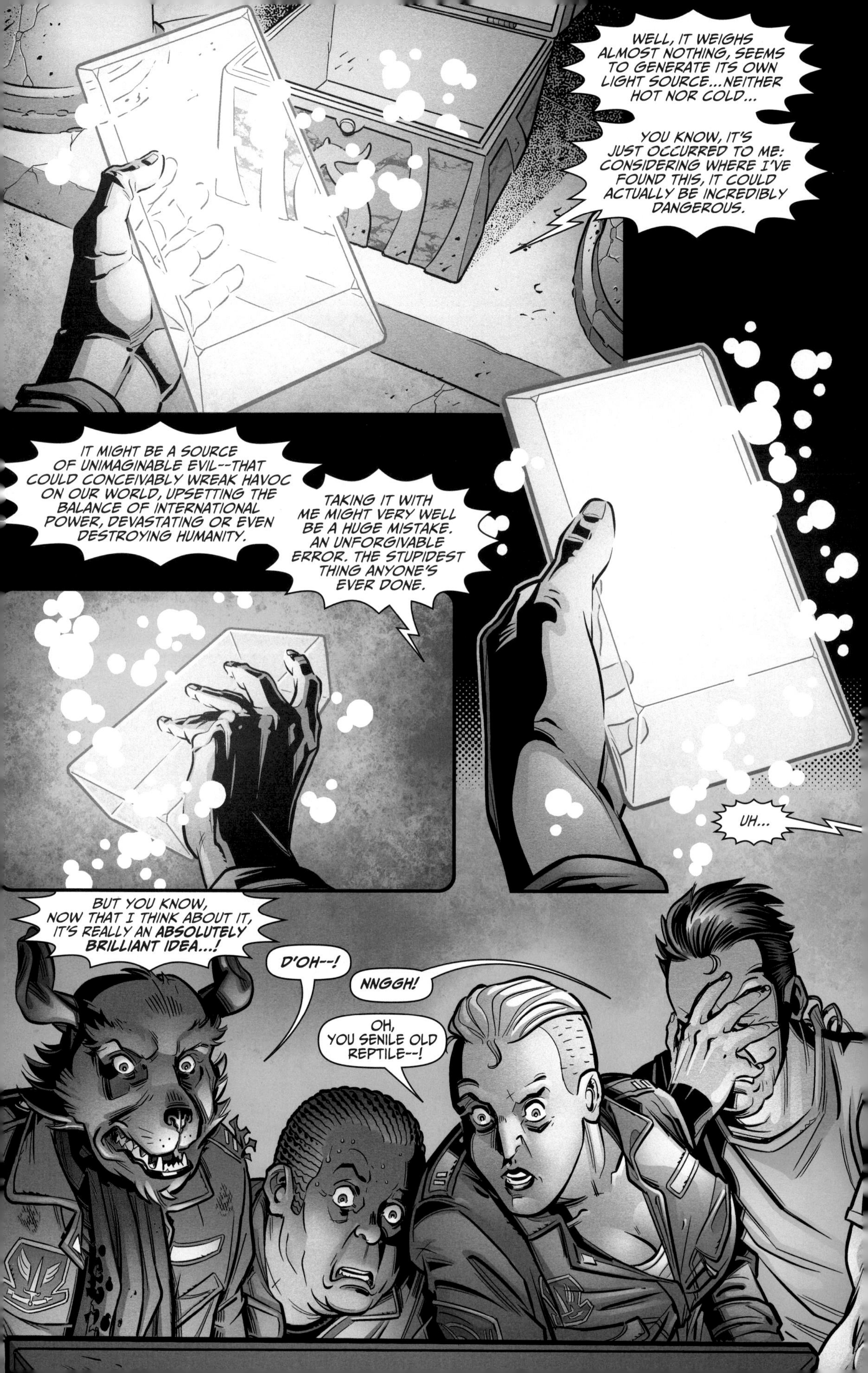
WELL, IT WEIGHS ALMOST NOTHING, SEEMS TO GENERATE ITS OWN LIGHT SOURCE...NEITHER HOT NOR COLD...
YOU KNOW, IT'S JUST OCCURRED TO ME: CONSIDERING WHERE I'VE FOUND THIS, IT COULD ACTUALLY BE INCREDIBLY DANGEROUS.
IT MIGHT BE A SOURCE OF UNIMAGINABLE EVIL--THAT COULD CONCEIVABLY WREAK HAVOC ON OUR WORLD, UPSETTING THE BALANCE OF INTERNATIONAL POWER, DEVASTATING OR EVEN DESTROYING HUMANITY.
TAKING IT WITH ME MIGHT VERY WELL BE A HUGE MISTAKE. AN UNFORGIVABLE ERROR. THE STUPIDEST THING ANYONE'S EVER DONE.
UH...
BUT YOU KNOW, NOW THAT I THINK ABOUT IT, IT'S REALLY AN ABSOLUTELY BRILLIANT IDEA...!
D'OH--!
NNGGH!
OH, YOU SENILE OLD REPTILE--!

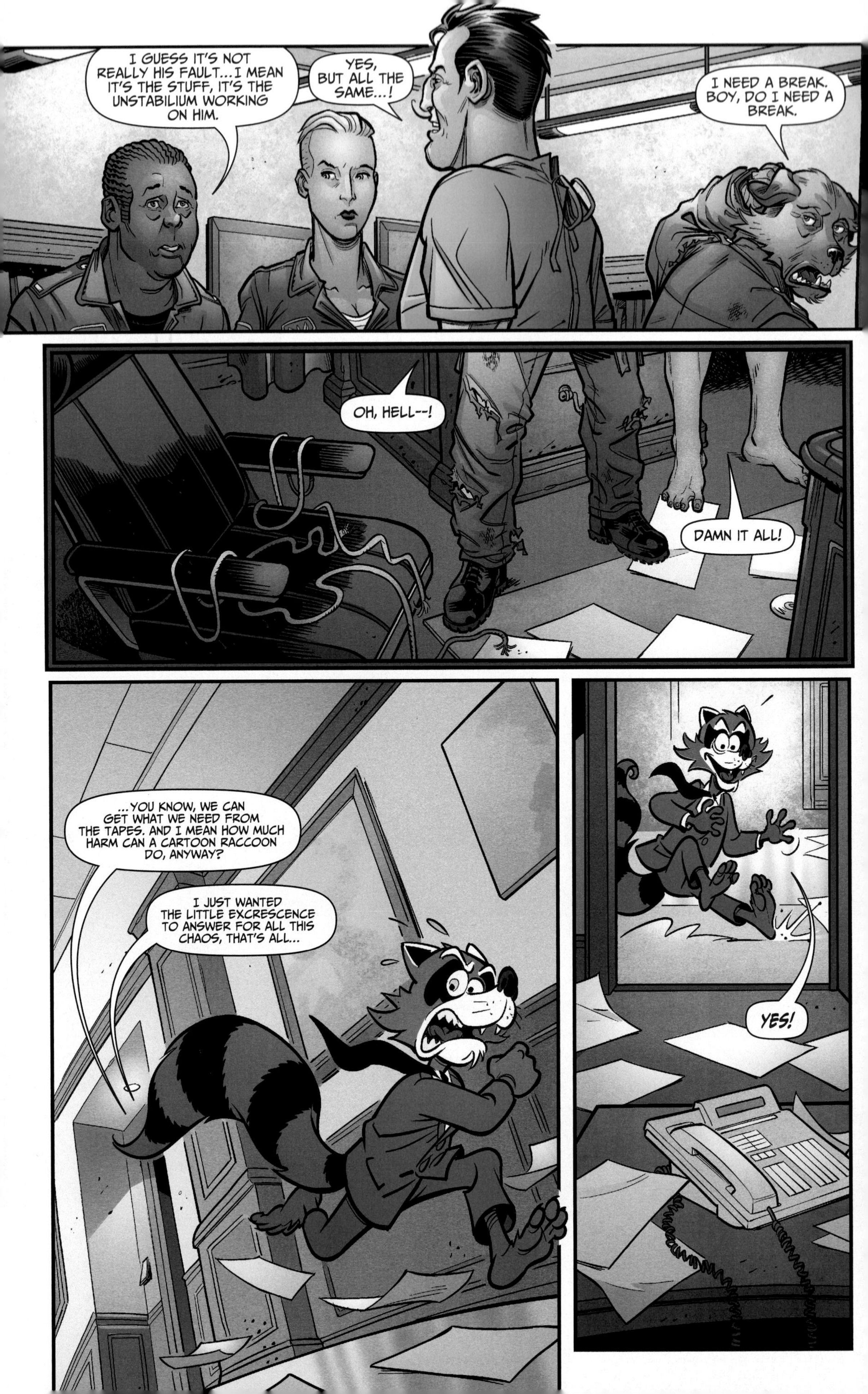
I GUESS IT'S NOT REALLY HIS FAULT...I MEAN IT'S THE STUFF, IT'S THE UNSTABILIUM WORKING ON HIM.
YES, BUT ALL THE SAME...!
I NEED A BREAK. BOY, DO I NEED A BREAK.
OH, HELL--!
DAMN IT ALL!
...YOU KNOW, WE CAN GET WHAT WE NEED FROM THE TAPES. AND I MEAN HOW MUCH HARM CAN A CARTOON RACCOON DO, ANYWAY?
I JUST WANTED THE LITTLE EXCRESCENCE TO ANSWER FOR ALL THIS CHAOS, THAT'S ALL...
YES!

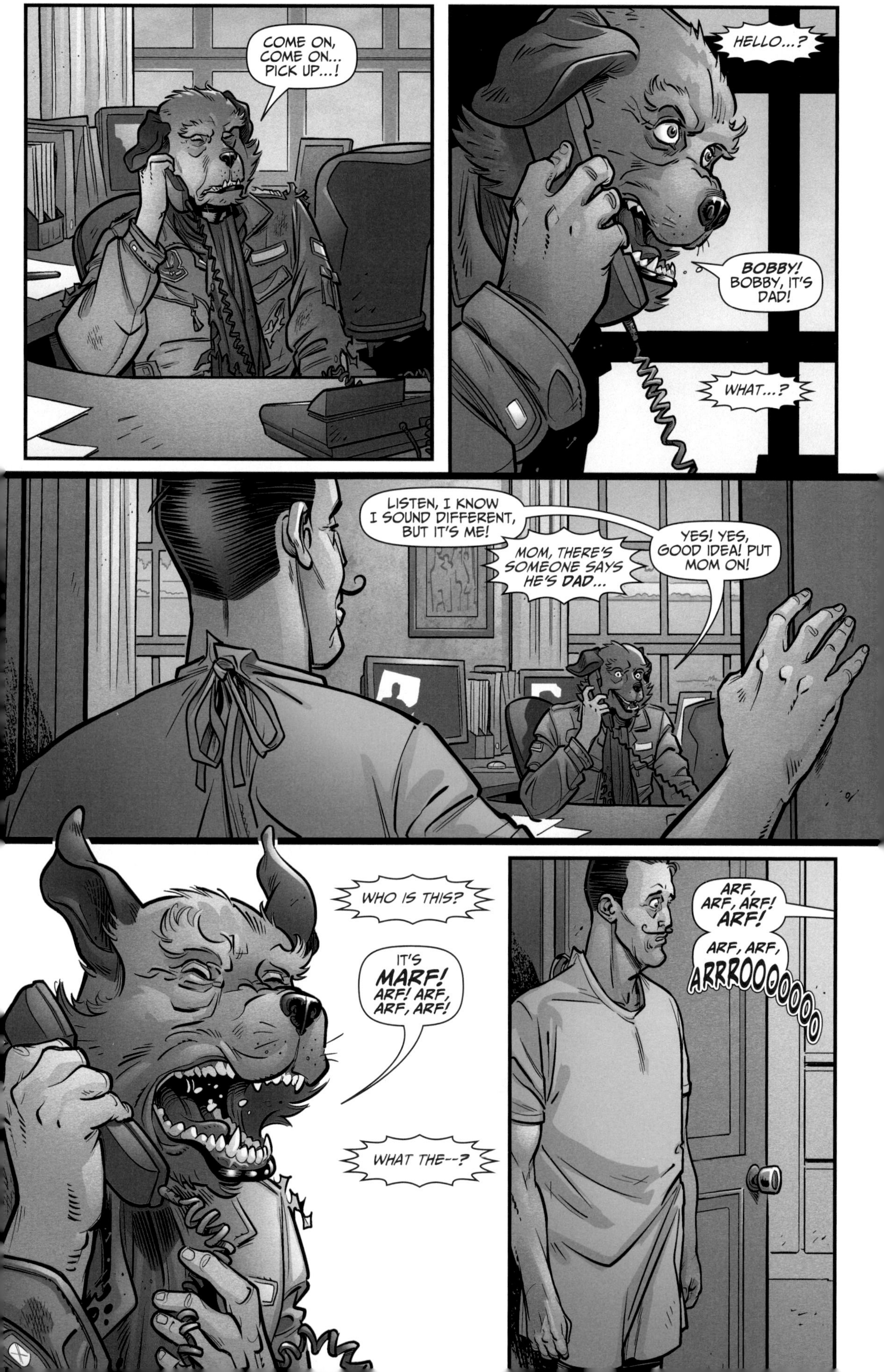
COME ON, COME ON... PICK UP...!
HELLO...?
BOBBY! BOBBY, IT'S DAD!
WHAT...?
LISTEN, I KNOW I SOUND DIFFERENT, BUT IT'S ME!
MOM, THERE'S SOMEONE SAYS HE'S DAD...
YES! YES, GOOD IDEA! PUT MOM ON!
WHO IS THIS?
IT'S MARF! ARF! ARF, ARF, ARF!
WHAT THE--?
ARF, ARF, ARF! ARF!
ARF, ARF, ARRROOOOOOOO

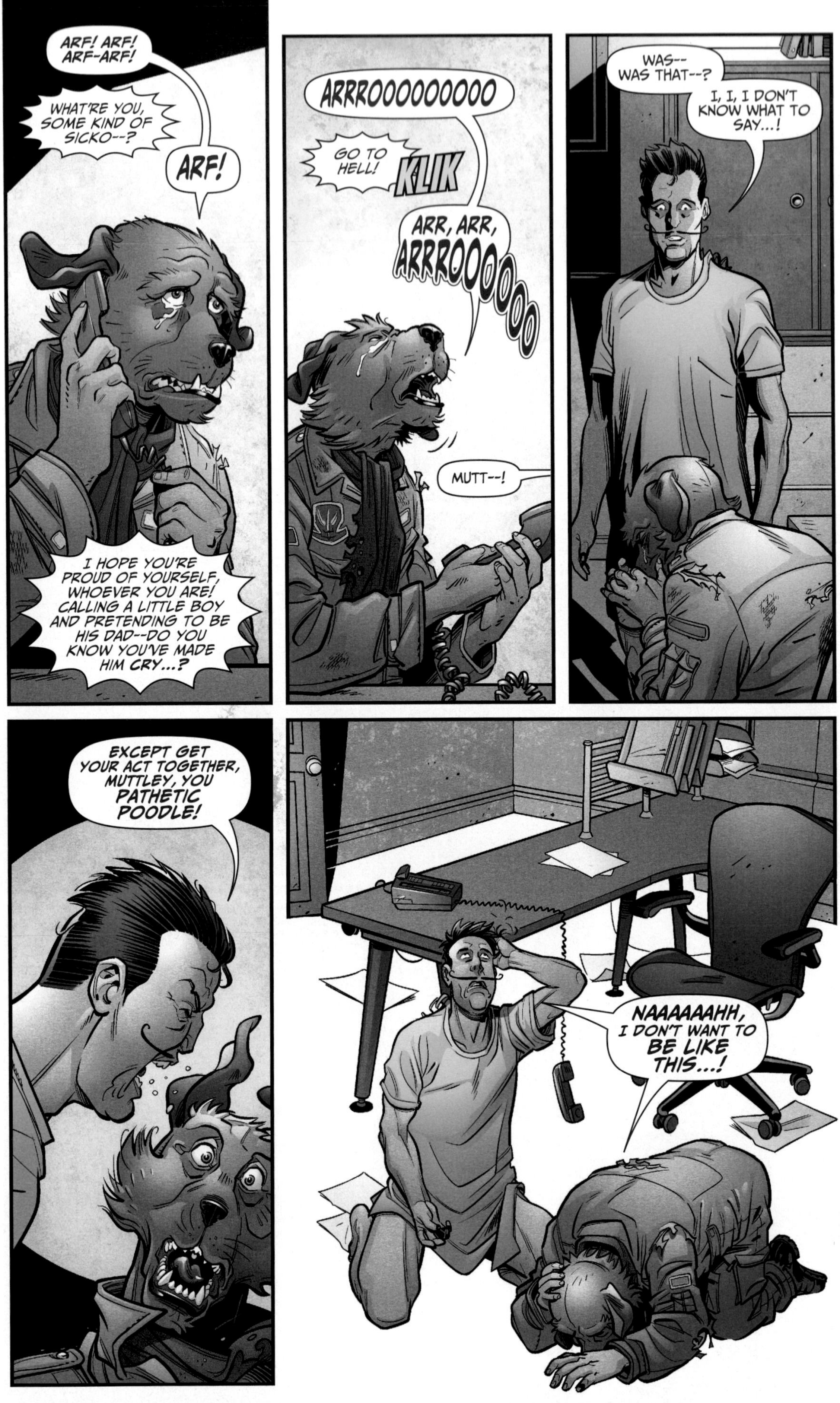
ARF! ARF! ARF-ARF!
WHAT'RE YOU, SOME KIND OF SICKO--?
ARF!
I HOPE YOU'RE PROUD OF YOURSELF, WHOEVER YOU ARE! CALLING A LITTLE BOY AND PRETENDING TO BE HIS DAD--DO YOU KNOW YOU'VE MADE HIM CRY...?
ARRROOOOOOOOO
GO TO HELL!
KLIK
ARR, ARR, ARRROOOOOO
MUTT--!
WAS-- WAS THAT--?
I, I, I DON'T KNOW WHAT TO SAY...!
EXCEPT GET YOUR ACT TOGETHER, MUTTLEY, YOU PATHETIC POODLE!
NAAAAAAHH, I DON'T WANT TO BE LIKE THIS...!

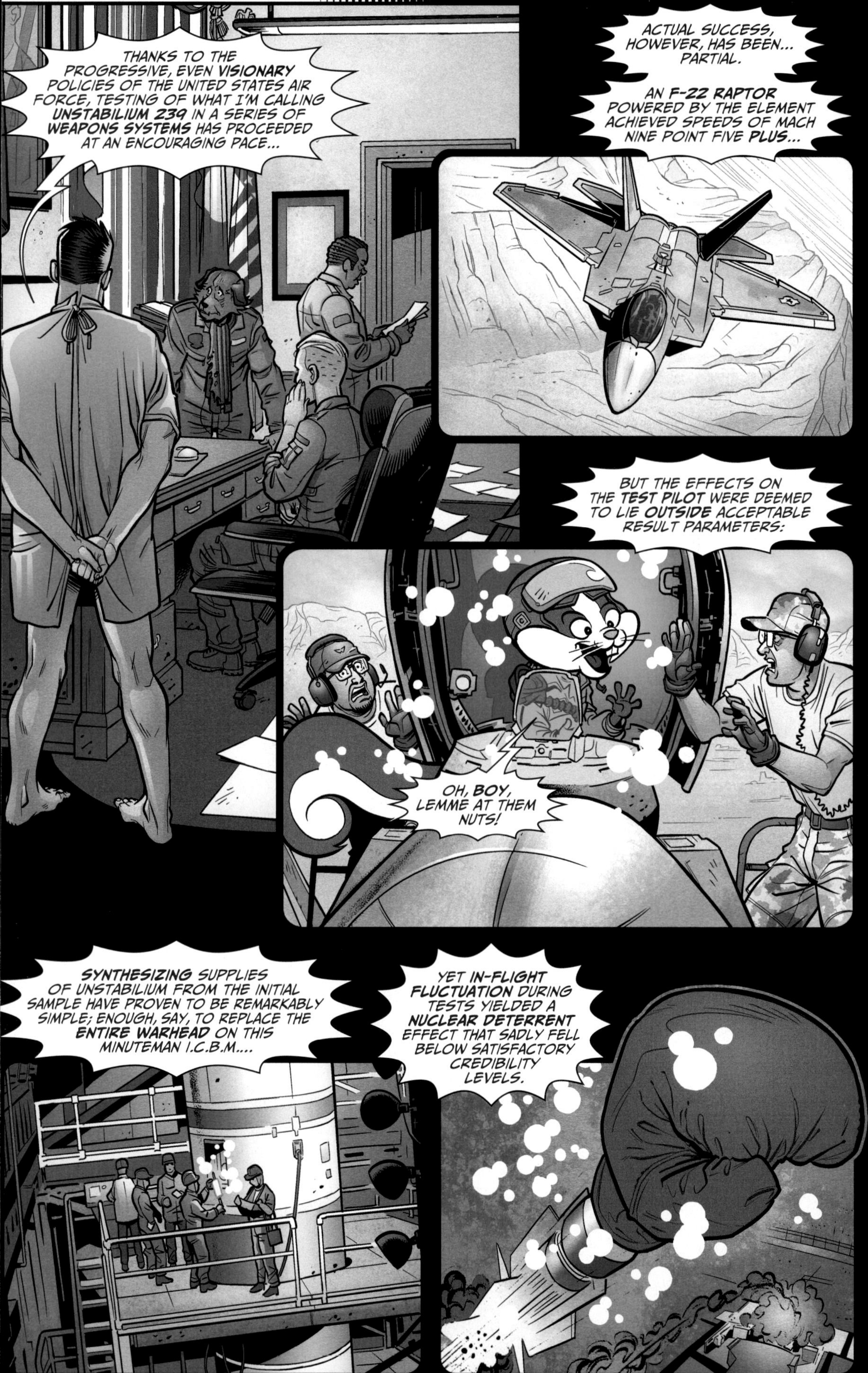
THANKS TO THE PROGRESSIVE, EVEN VISIONARY POLICIES OF THE UNITED STATES AIR FORCE, TESTING OF WHAT I'M CALLING UNSTABILIUM 239 IN A SERIES OF WEAPONS SYSTEMS HAS PROCEEDED AT AN ENCOURAGING PACE...
ACTUAL SUCCESS, HOWEVER, HAS BEEN... PARTIAL.
AN F-22 RAPTOR POWERED BY THE ELEMENT ACHIEVED SPEEDS OF MACH NINE POINT FIVE PLUS...
BUT THE EFFECTS ON THE TEST PILOT WERE DEEMED TO LIE OUTSIDE ACCEPTABLE RESULT PARAMETERS:
OH, BOY, LEMME AT THEM NUTS!
SYNTHESIZING SUPPLIES OF UNSTABILIUM FROM THE INITIAL SAMPLE HAVE PROVEN TO BE REMARKABLY SIMPLE; ENOUGH, SAY, TO REPLACE THE ENTIRE WARHEAD ON THIS MINUTEMAN I.C.B.M....
YET IN-FLIGHT FLUCTUATION DURING TESTS YIELDED A NUCLEAR DETERRENT EFFECT THAT SADLY FELL BELOW SATISFACTORY CREDIBILITY LEVELS.

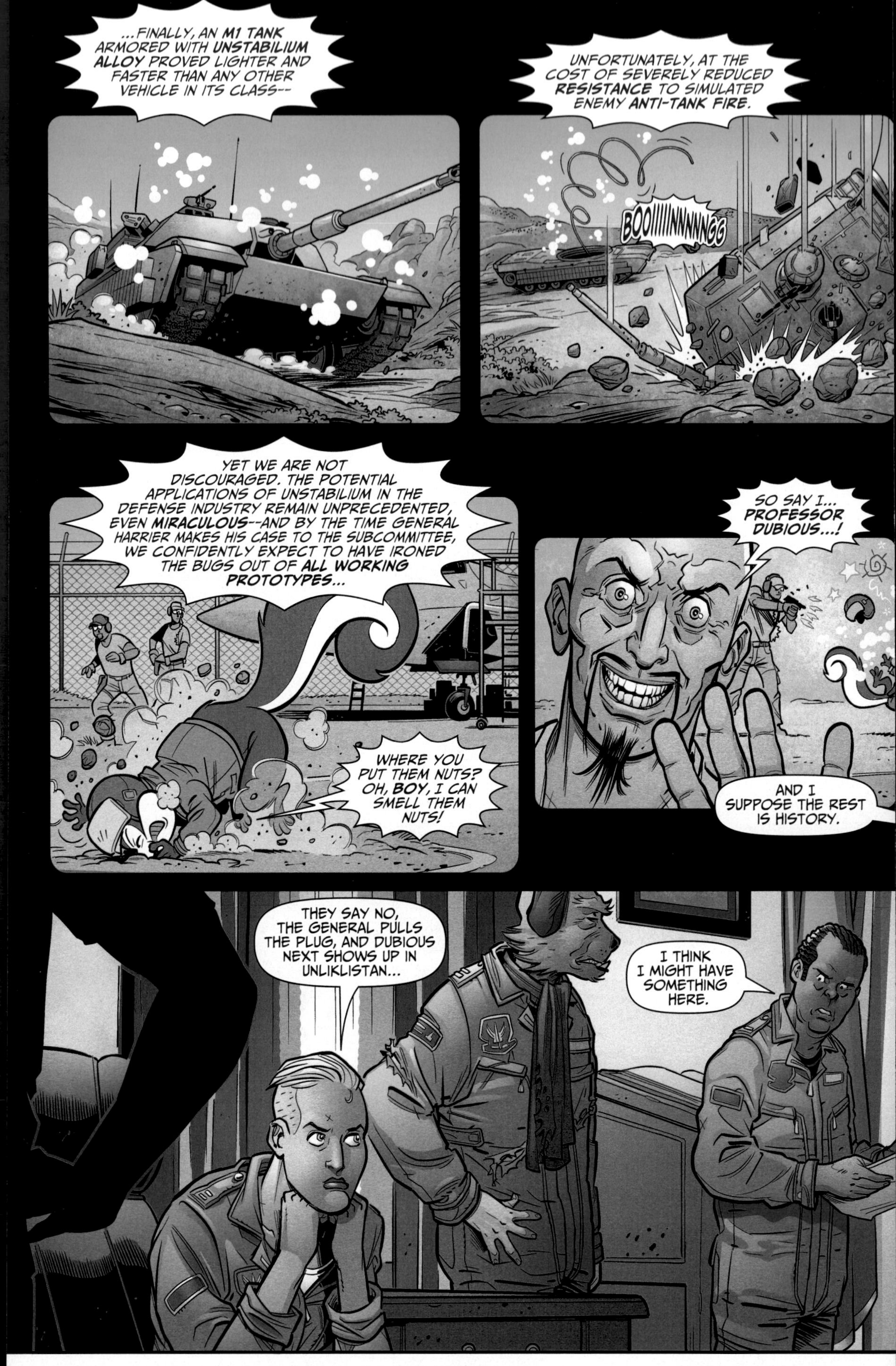

...FINALLY, AN M1 TANK ARMORED WITH UNSTABILIUM ALLOY PROVED LIGHTER AND FASTER THAN ANY OTHER VEHICLE IN ITS CLASS--
UNFORTUNATELY, AT THE COST OF SEVERELY REDUCED RESISTANCE TO SIMULATED ENEMY ANTI-TANK FIRE.
BOOIIIIINNNNNGG
YET WE ARE NOT DISCOURAGED. THE POTENTIAL APPLICATIONS OF UNSTABILIUM IN THE DEFENSE INDUSTRY REMAIN UNPRECEDENTED, EVEN MIRACULOUS--AND BY THE TIME GENERAL HARRIER MAKES HIS CASE TO THE SUBCOMMITTEE, WE CONFIDENTLY EXPECT TO HAVE IRONED THE BUGS OUT OF ALL WORKING PROTOTYPES...
WHERE YOU PUT THEM NUTS? OH, BOY, I CAN SMELL THEM NUTS!
SO SAY I... PROFESSOR DUBIOUS...!
AND I SUPPOSE THE REST IS HISTORY.
THEY SAY NO, THE GENERAL PULLS THE PLUG, AND DUBIOUS NEXT SHOWS UP IN UNLIKLISTAN...
I THINK I MIGHT HAVE SOMETHING HERE.

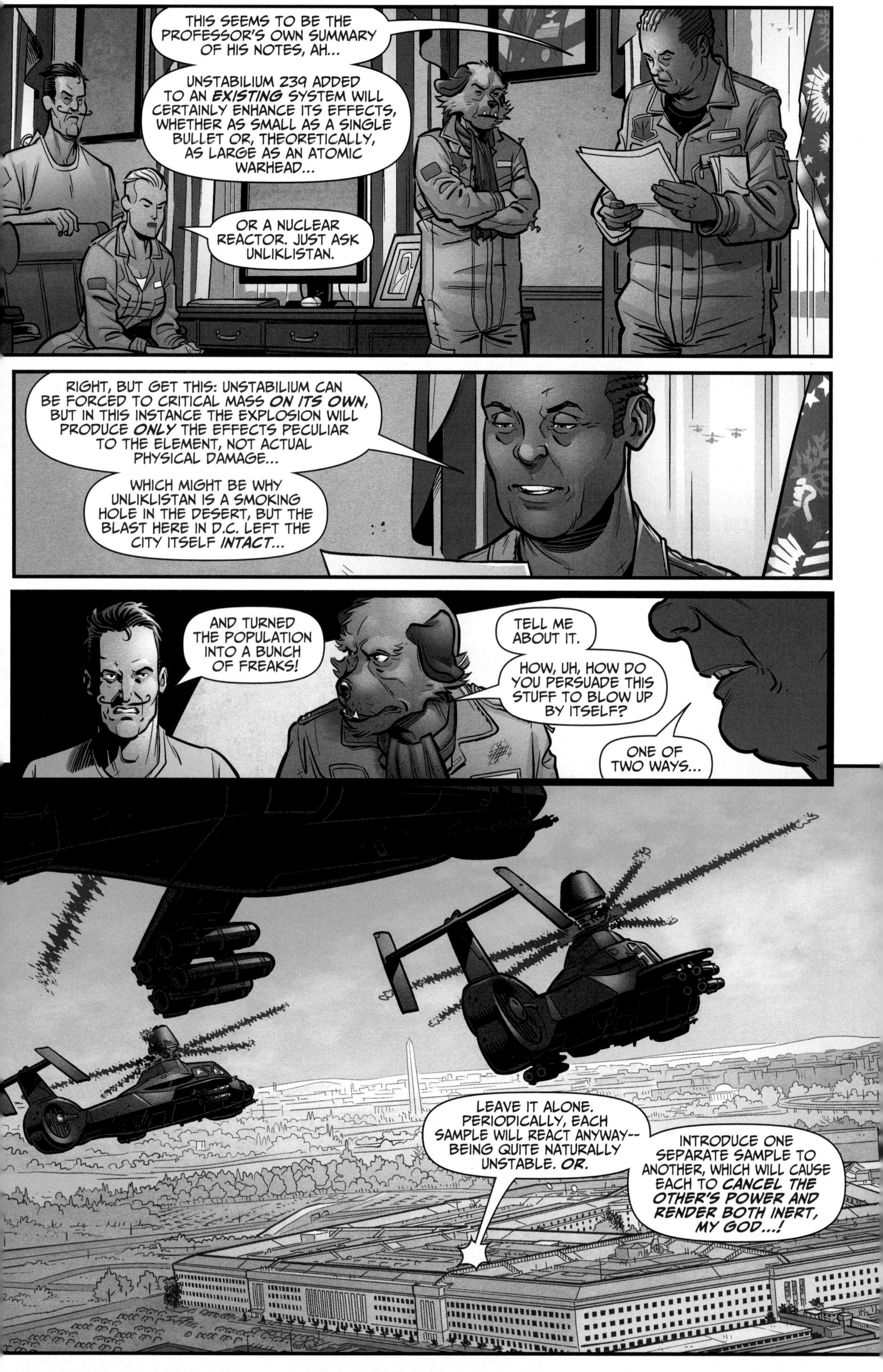
THIS SEEMS TO BE THE PROFESSOR'S OWN SUMMARY OF HIS NOTES, AH...
UNSTABILIUM 239 ADDED TO AN *EXISTING* SYSTEM WILL CERTAINLY ENHANCE ITS EFFECTS, WHETHER AS SMALL AS A SINGLE BULLET OR, THEORETICALLY, AS LARGE AS AN ATOMIC WARHEAD...
OR A NUCLEAR REACTOR. JUST ASK UNLIKLISTAN.
RIGHT, BUT GET THIS: UNSTABILIUM CAN BE FORCED TO CRITICAL MASS *ON ITS OWN*, BUT IN THIS INSTANCE THE EXPLOSION WILL PRODUCE *ONLY* THE EFFECTS PECULIAR TO THE ELEMENT, NOT ACTUAL PHYSICAL DAMAGE...
WHICH MIGHT BE WHY UNLIKLISTAN IS A SMOKING HOLE IN THE DESERT, BUT THE BLAST HERE IN D.C. LEFT THE CITY ITSELF *INTACT*...
AND TURNED THE POPULATION INTO A BUNCH OF FREAKS!
TELL ME ABOUT IT.
HOW, UH, HOW DO YOU PERSUADE THIS STUFF TO BLOW UP BY ITSELF?
ONE OF TWO WAYS...
LEAVE IT ALONE. PERIODICALLY, EACH SAMPLE WILL REACT ANYWAY-- BEING QUITE NATURALLY UNSTABLE. *OR.*
INTRODUCE ONE SEPARATE SAMPLE TO ANOTHER, WHICH WILL CAUSE EACH TO *CANCEL THE OTHER'S POWER AND RENDER BOTH INERT, MY GOD...!*

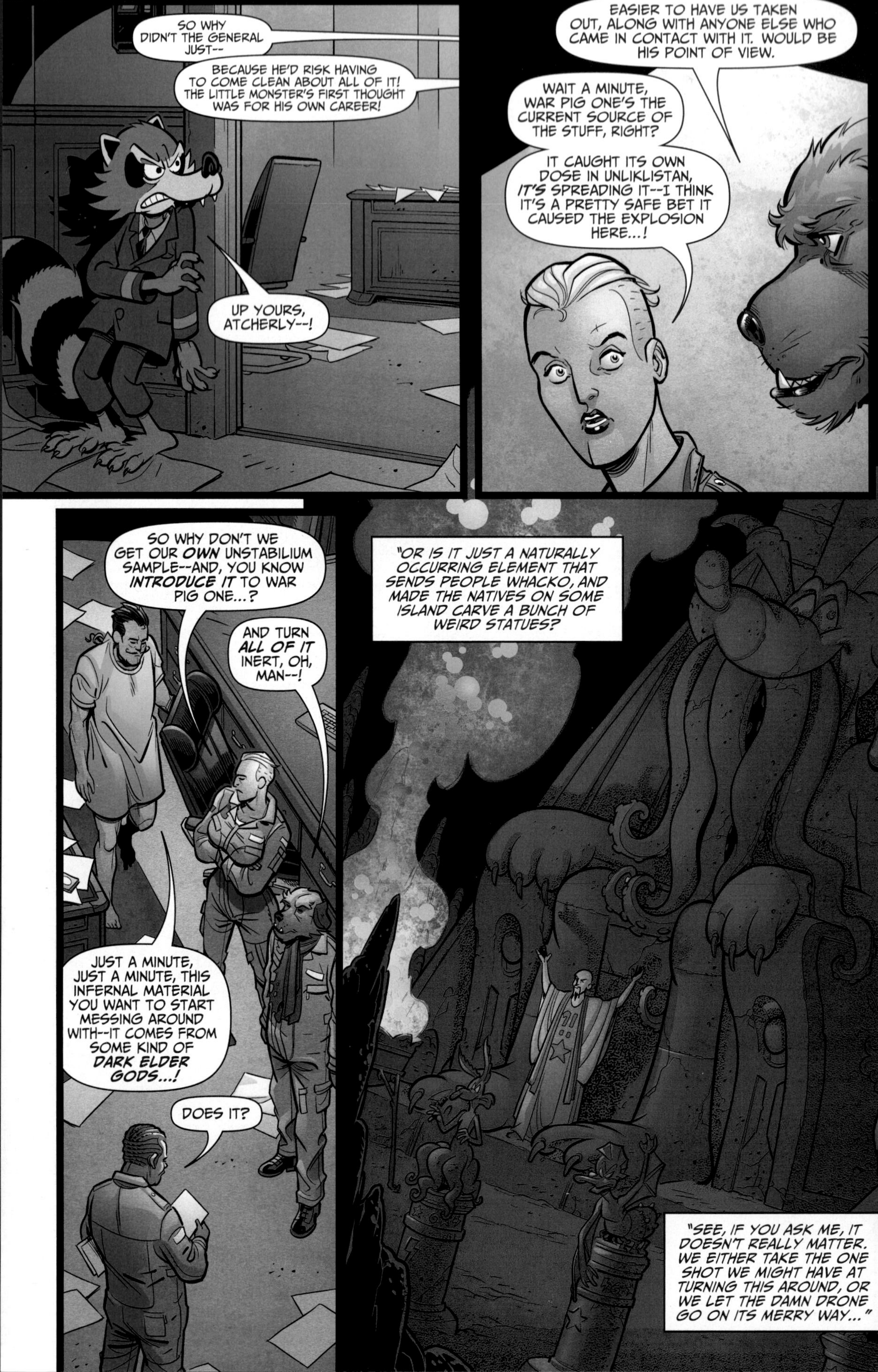
SO WHY DIDN'T THE GENERAL JUST--
BECAUSE HE'D RISK HAVING TO COME CLEAN ABOUT ALL OF IT! THE LITTLE MONSTER'S FIRST THOUGHT WAS FOR HIS OWN CAREER!
UP YOURS, ATCHERLY--!
EASIER TO HAVE US TAKEN OUT, ALONG WITH ANYONE ELSE WHO CAME IN CONTACT WITH IT. WOULD BE HIS POINT OF VIEW.
WAIT A MINUTE, WAR PIG ONE'S THE CURRENT SOURCE OF THE STUFF, RIGHT?
IT CAUGHT ITS OWN DOSE IN UNLIKLISTAN, *IT'S* SPREADING IT--I THINK IT'S A PRETTY SAFE BET IT CAUSED THE EXPLOSION HERE...!
SO WHY DON'T WE GET OUR *OWN* UNSTABILIUM SAMPLE--AND, YOU KNOW *INTRODUCE IT* TO WAR PIG ONE...?
AND TURN *ALL OF IT* INERT, OH, MAN--!
JUST A MINUTE, JUST A MINUTE, THIS INFERNAL MATERIAL YOU WANT TO START MESSING AROUND WITH--IT COMES FROM SOME KIND OF *DARK ELDER GODS...!*
DOES IT?
"OR IS IT JUST A NATURALLY OCCURRING ELEMENT THAT SENDS PEOPLE WHACKO, AND MADE THE NATIVES ON SOME ISLAND CARVE A BUNCH OF WEIRD STATUES?
"SEE, IF YOU ASK ME, IT DOESN'T REALLY MATTER. WE EITHER TAKE THE ONE SHOT WE MIGHT HAVE AT TURNING THIS AROUND, OR WE LET THE DAMN DRONE GO ON ITS MERRY WAY..."

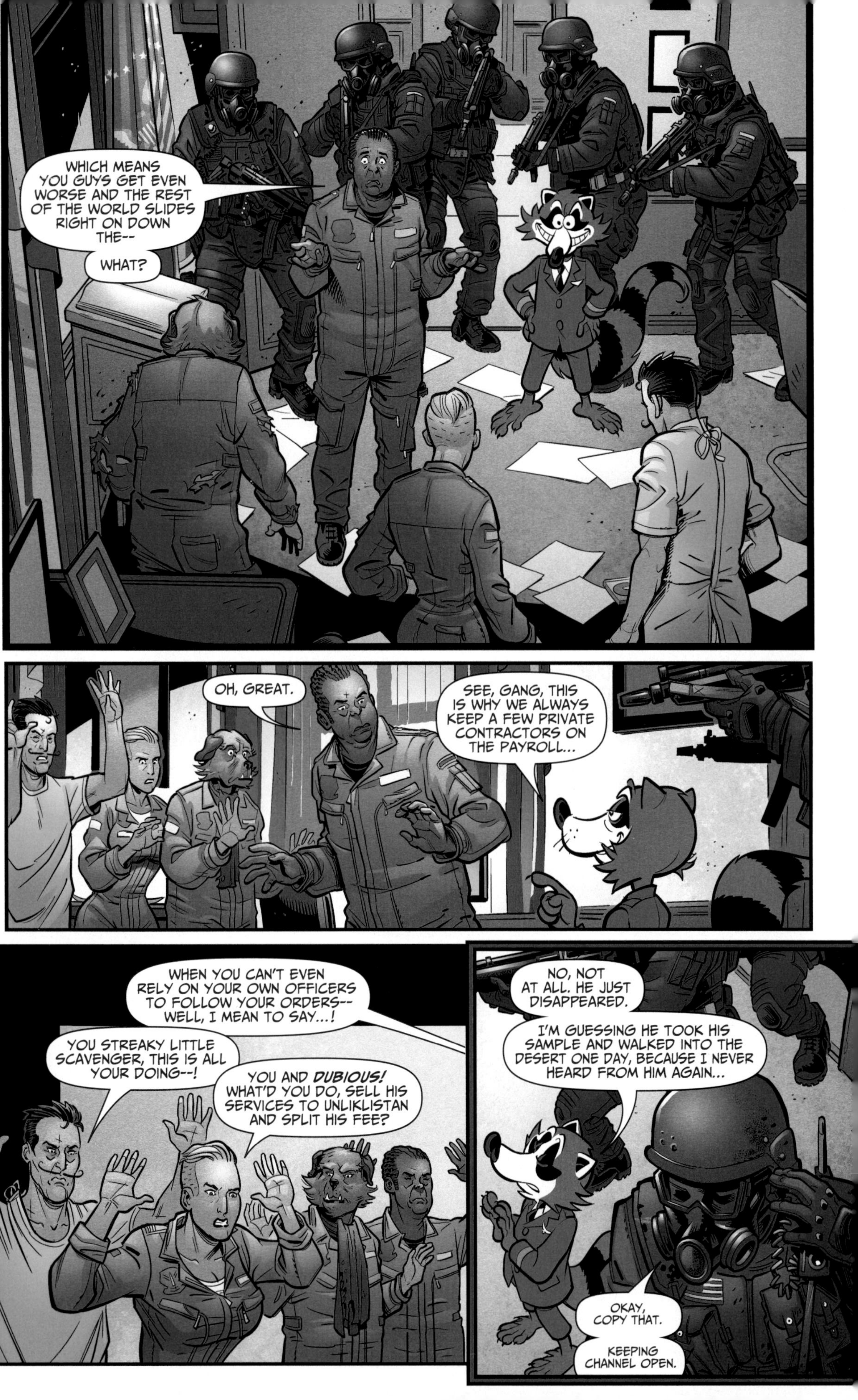
WHICH MEANS YOU GUYS GET EVEN WORSE AND THE REST OF THE WORLD SLIDES RIGHT ON DOWN THE--
WHAT?
OH, GREAT.
SEE, GANG, THIS IS WHY WE ALWAYS KEEP A FEW PRIVATE CONTRACTORS ON THE PAYROLL...
WHEN YOU CAN'T EVEN RELY ON YOUR OWN OFFICERS TO FOLLOW YOUR ORDERS-- WELL, I MEAN TO SAY...!
YOU STREAKY LITTLE SCAVENGER, THIS IS ALL YOUR DOING--!
YOU AND DUBIOUS! WHAT'D YOU DO, SELL HIS SERVICES TO UNLIKLISTAN AND SPLIT HIS FEE?
NO, NOT AT ALL. HE JUST DISAPPEARED.
I'M GUESSING HE TOOK HIS SAMPLE AND WALKED INTO THE DESERT ONE DAY, BECAUSE I NEVER HEARD FROM HIM AGAIN...
OKAY, COPY THAT.
KEEPING CHANNEL OPEN.

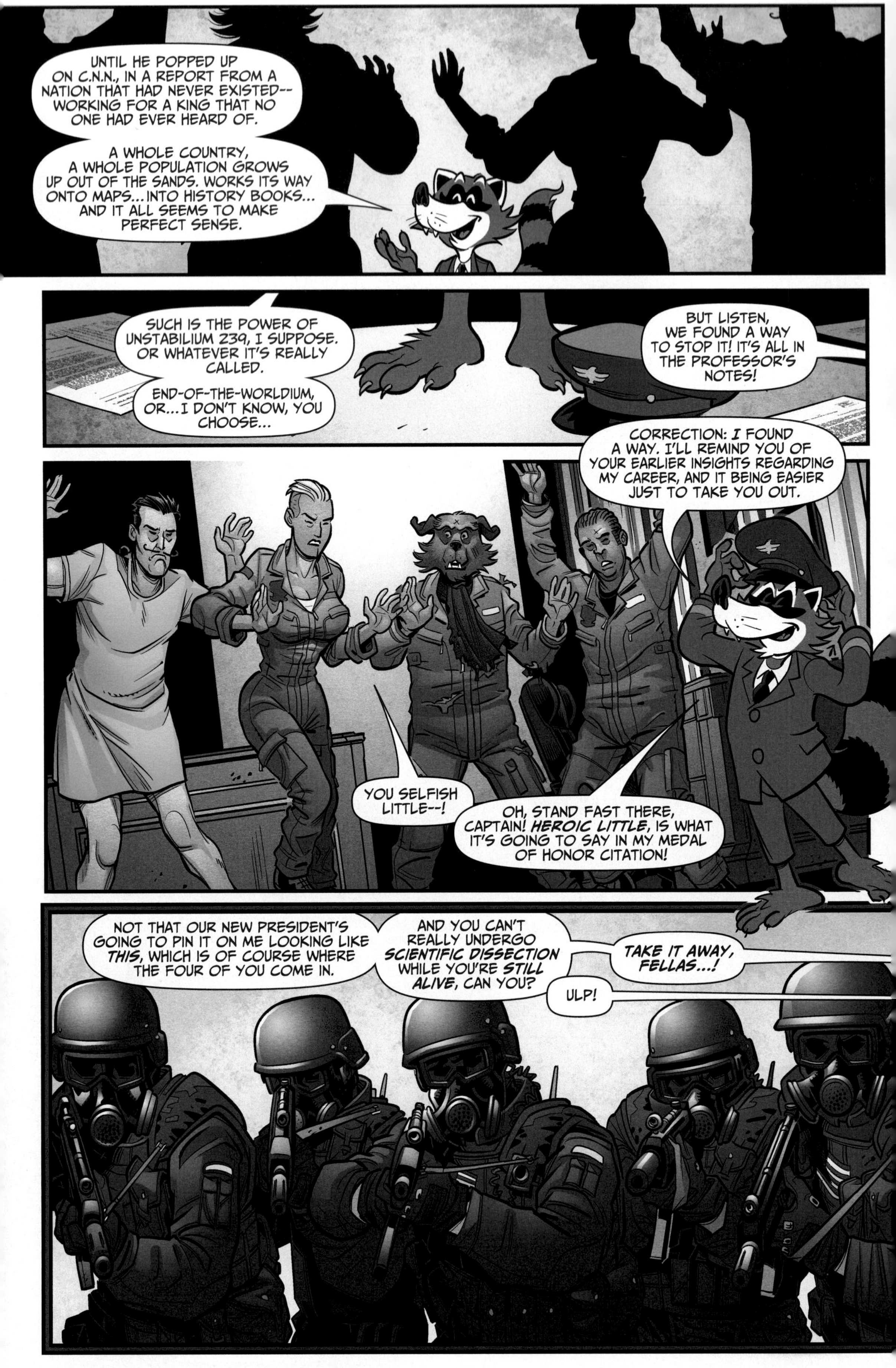
UNTIL HE POPPED UP ON C.N.N., IN A REPORT FROM A NATION THAT HAD NEVER EXISTED-- WORKING FOR A KING THAT NO ONE HAD EVER HEARD OF.
A WHOLE COUNTRY, A WHOLE POPULATION GROWS UP OUT OF THE SANDS. WORKS ITS WAY ONTO MAPS...INTO HISTORY BOOKS... AND IT ALL SEEMS TO MAKE PERFECT SENSE.
SUCH IS THE POWER OF UNSTABILIUM 239, I SUPPOSE. OR WHATEVER IT'S REALLY CALLED.
END-OF-THE-WORLDIUM, OR...I DON'T KNOW, YOU CHOOSE...
BUT LISTEN, WE FOUND A WAY TO STOP IT! IT'S ALL IN THE PROFESSOR'S NOTES!
CORRECTION: *I* FOUND A WAY. I'LL REMIND YOU OF YOUR EARLIER INSIGHTS REGARDING MY CAREER, AND IT BEING EASIER JUST TO TAKE YOU OUT.
YOU SELFISH LITTLE--!
OH, STAND FAST THERE, CAPTAIN! ***HEROIC LITTLE***, IS WHAT IT'S GOING TO SAY IN MY MEDAL OF HONOR CITATION!
NOT THAT OUR NEW PRESIDENT'S GOING TO PIN IT ON ME LOOKING LIKE *THIS*, WHICH IS OF COURSE WHERE THE FOUR OF YOU COME IN.
AND YOU CAN'T REALLY UNDERGO ***SCIENTIFIC DISSECTION*** WHILE YOU'RE *STILL ALIVE*, CAN YOU?
TAKE IT AWAY, FELLAS...!
ULP!

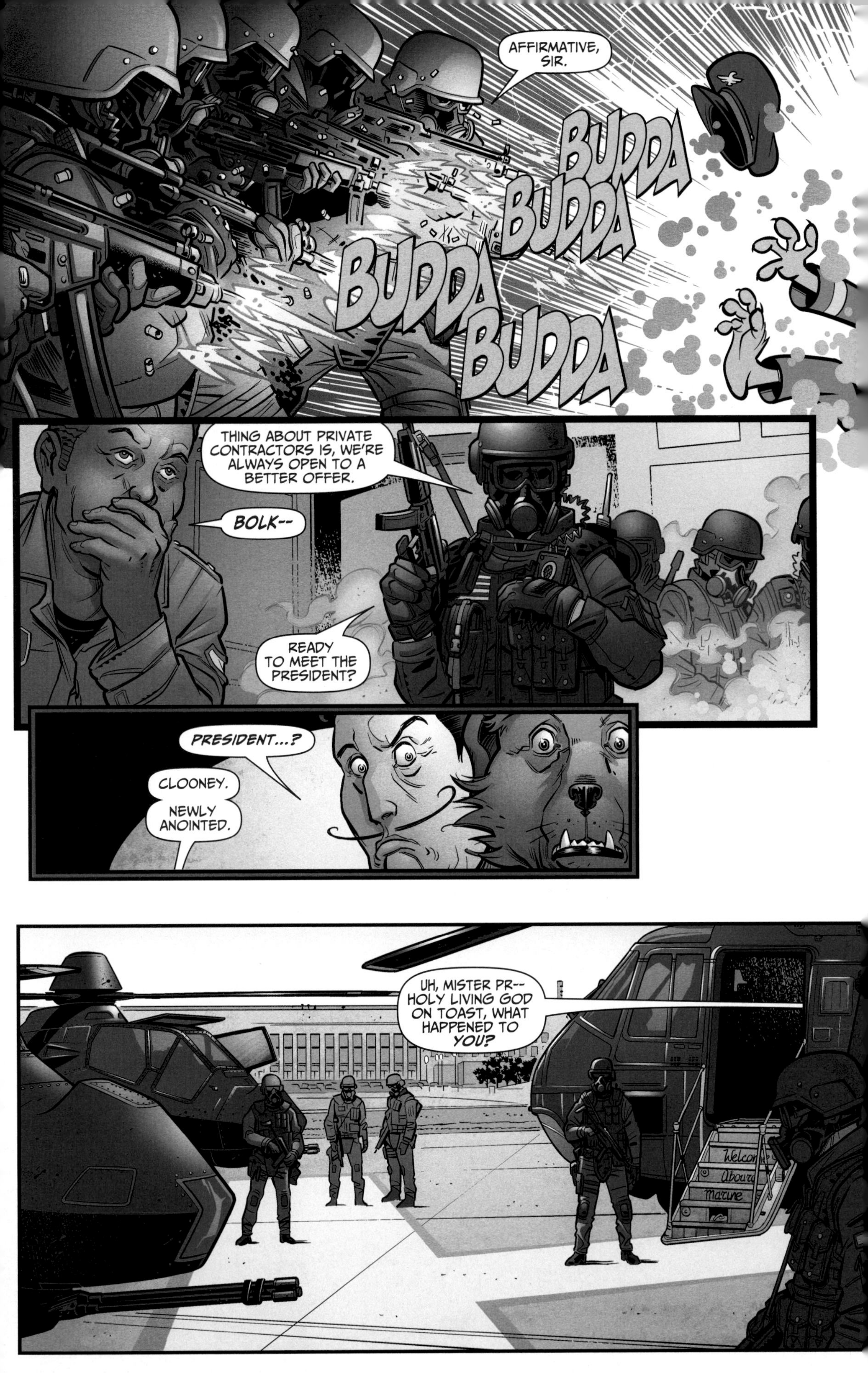
AFFIRMATIVE, SIR.
BUDDA BUDDA BUDDA BUDDA
THING ABOUT PRIVATE CONTRACTORS IS, WE'RE ALWAYS OPEN TO A BETTER OFFER.
BOLK--
READY TO MEET THE PRESIDENT?
PRESIDENT...?
CLOONEY.
NEWLY ANOINTED.
UH, MISTER PR-- HOLY LIVING GOD ON TOAST, WHAT HAPPENED TO YOU?
Marine

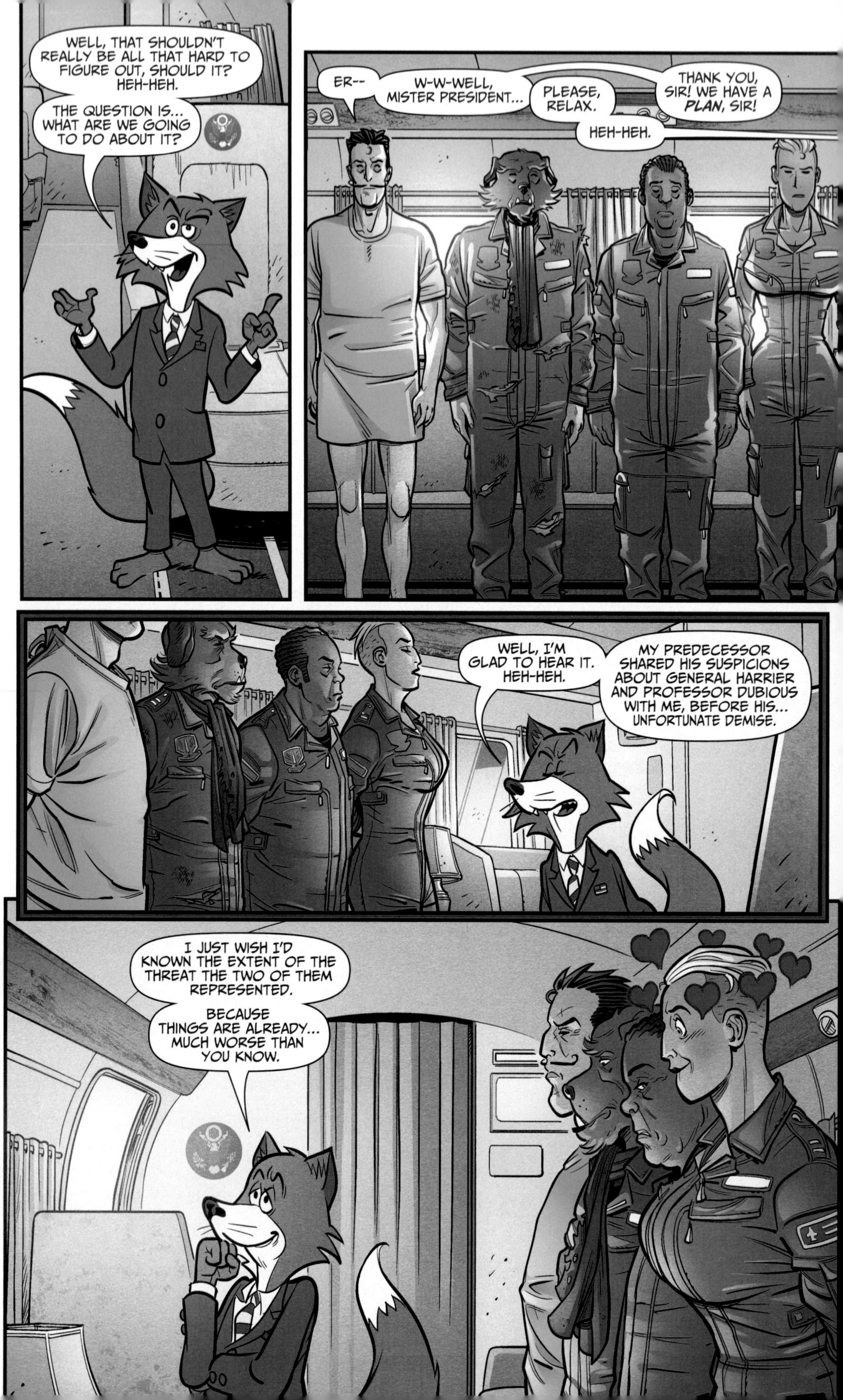
WELL, THAT SHOULDN'T REALLY BE ALL THAT HARD TO FIGURE OUT, SHOULD IT? HEH-HEH.
THE QUESTION IS... WHAT ARE WE GOING TO DO ABOUT IT?
ER--
W-W-WELL, MISTER PRESIDENT...
PLEASE, RELAX.
HEH-HEH.
THANK YOU, SIR! WE HAVE A *PLAN*, SIR!
WELL, I'M GLAD TO HEAR IT. HEH-HEH.
MY PREDECESSOR SHARED HIS SUSPICIONS ABOUT GENERAL HARRIER AND PROFESSOR DUBIOUS WITH ME, BEFORE HIS... UNFORTUNATE DEMISE.
I JUST WISH I'D KNOWN THE EXTENT OF THE THREAT THE TWO OF THEM REPRESENTED.
BECAUSE THINGS ARE ALREADY... MUCH WORSE THAN YOU KNOW.

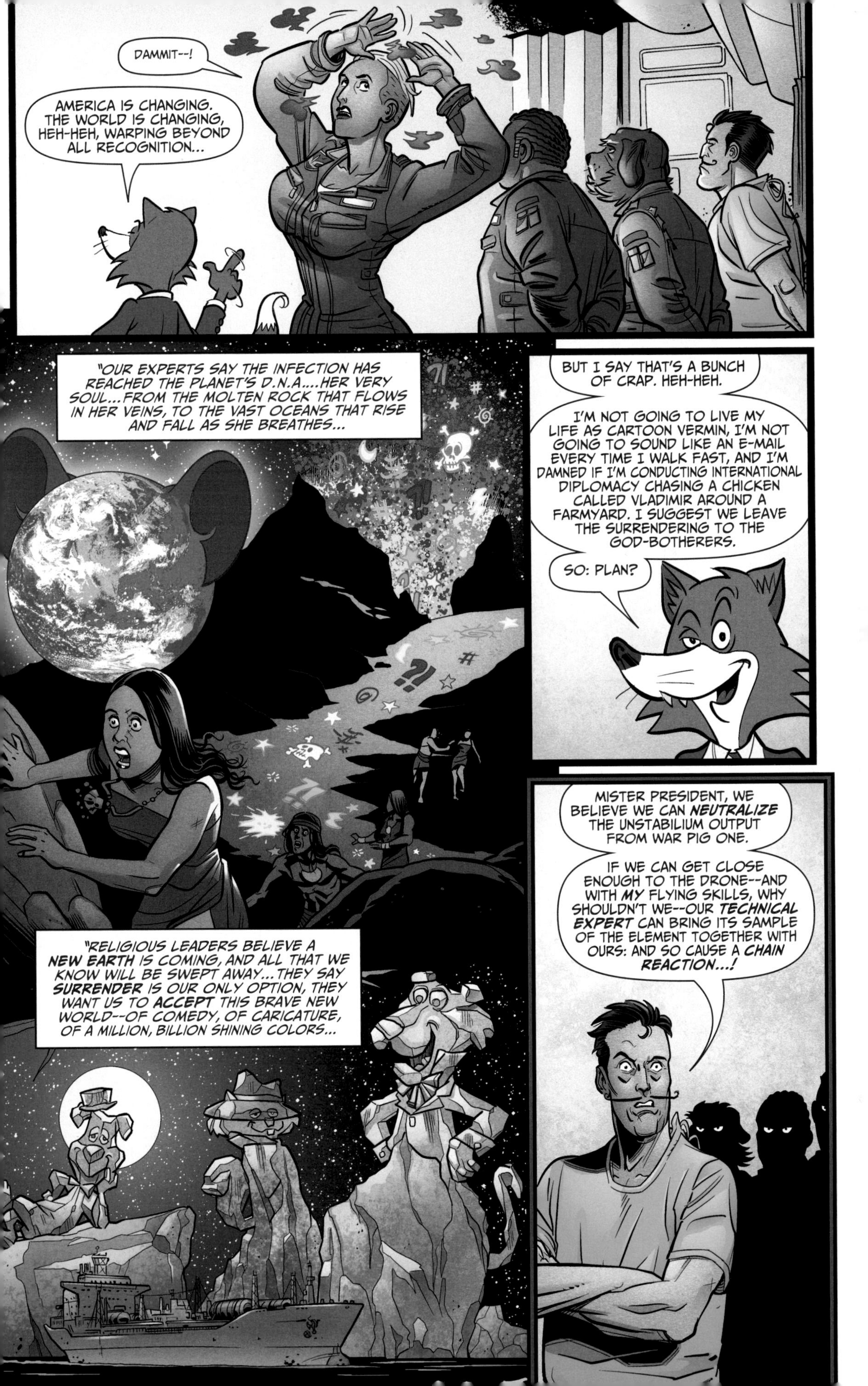
DAMMIT--!
AMERICA IS CHANGING. THE WORLD IS CHANGING, HEH-HEH, WARPING BEYOND ALL RECOGNITION...
"OUR EXPERTS SAY THE INFECTION HAS REACHED THE PLANET'S D.N.A....HER VERY SOUL...FROM THE MOLTEN ROCK THAT FLOWS IN HER VEINS, TO THE VAST OCEANS THAT RISE AND FALL AS SHE BREATHES...
BUT I SAY THAT'S A BUNCH OF CRAP. HEH-HEH.
I'M NOT GOING TO LIVE MY LIFE AS CARTOON VERMIN, I'M NOT GOING TO SOUND LIKE AN E-MAIL EVERY TIME I WALK FAST, AND I'M DAMNED IF I'M CONDUCTING INTERNATIONAL DIPLOMACY CHASING A CHICKEN CALLED VLADIMIR AROUND A FARMYARD. I SUGGEST WE LEAVE THE SURRENDERING TO THE GOD-BOTHERERS.
SO: PLAN?
"RELIGIOUS LEADERS BELIEVE A NEW EARTH IS COMING, AND ALL THAT WE KNOW WILL BE SWEPT AWAY...THEY SAY SURRENDER IS OUR ONLY OPTION, THEY WANT US TO ACCEPT THIS BRAVE NEW WORLD--OF COMEDY, OF CARICATURE, OF A MILLION, BILLION SHINING COLORS...
MISTER PRESIDENT, WE BELIEVE WE CAN NEUTRALIZE THE UNSTABILIUM OUTPUT FROM WAR PIG ONE.
IF WE CAN GET CLOSE ENOUGH TO THE DRONE--AND WITH MY FLYING SKILLS, WHY SHOULDN'T WE--OUR TECHNICAL EXPERT CAN BRING ITS SAMPLE OF THE ELEMENT TOGETHER WITH OURS: AND SO CAUSE A CHAIN REACTION...!

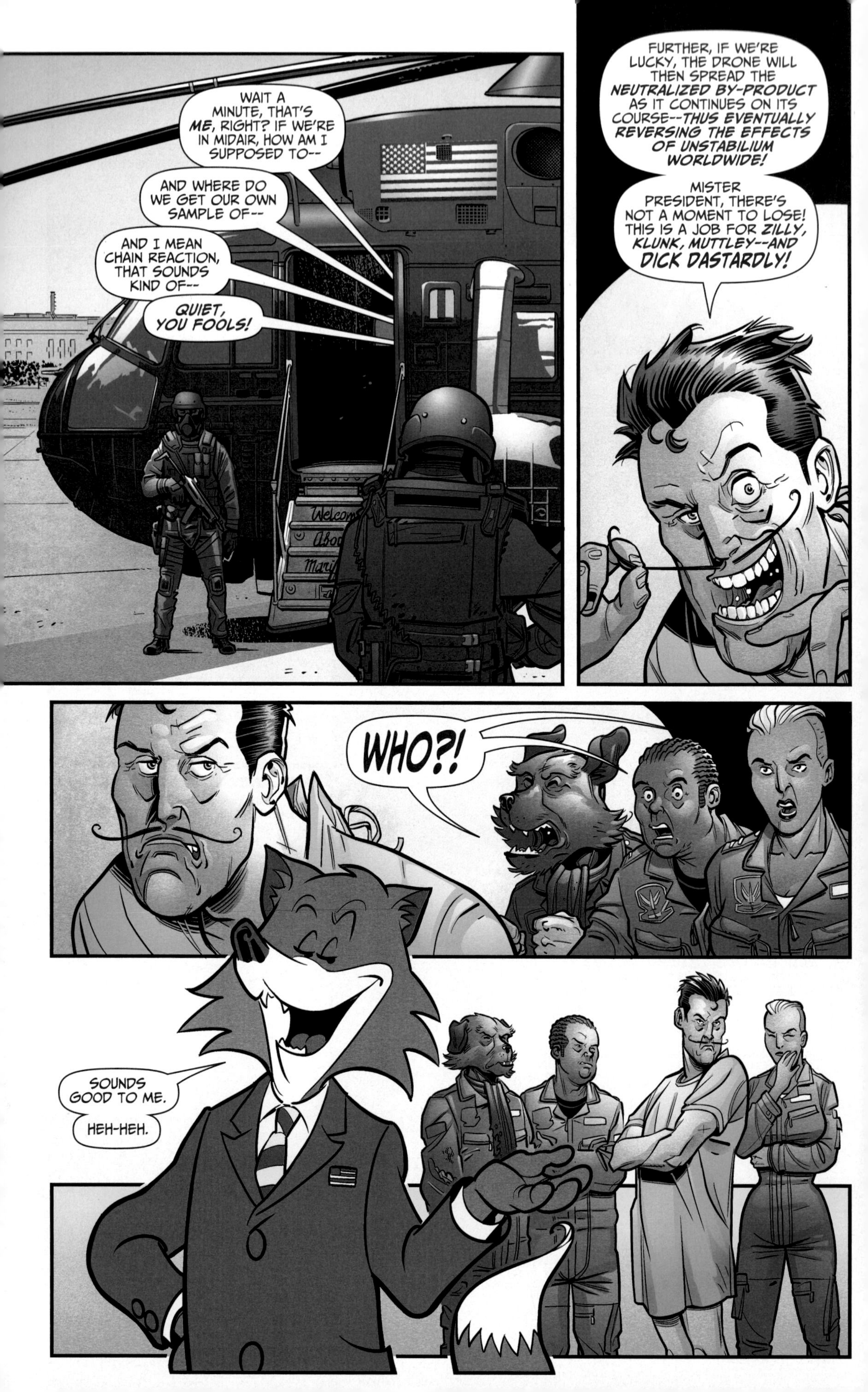
WAIT A MINUTE, THAT'S *ME*, RIGHT? IF WE'RE IN MIDAIR, HOW AM I SUPPOSED TO--
AND WHERE DO WE GET OUR OWN SAMPLE OF--
AND I MEAN CHAIN REACTION, THAT SOUNDS KIND OF--
QUIET, YOU FOOLS!
FURTHER, IF WE'RE LUCKY, THE DRONE WILL THEN SPREAD THE ***NEUTRALIZED BY-PRODUCT*** AS IT CONTINUES ON ITS COURSE--***THUS EVENTUALLY REVERSING THE EFFECTS OF UNSTABILIUM WORLDWIDE!***
MISTER PRESIDENT, THERE'S NOT A MOMENT TO LOSE! THIS IS A JOB FOR ***ZILLY, KLUNK, MUTTLEY***--AND ***DICK DASTARDLY!***
WHO?!
SOUNDS GOOD TO ME.
HEH-HEH.

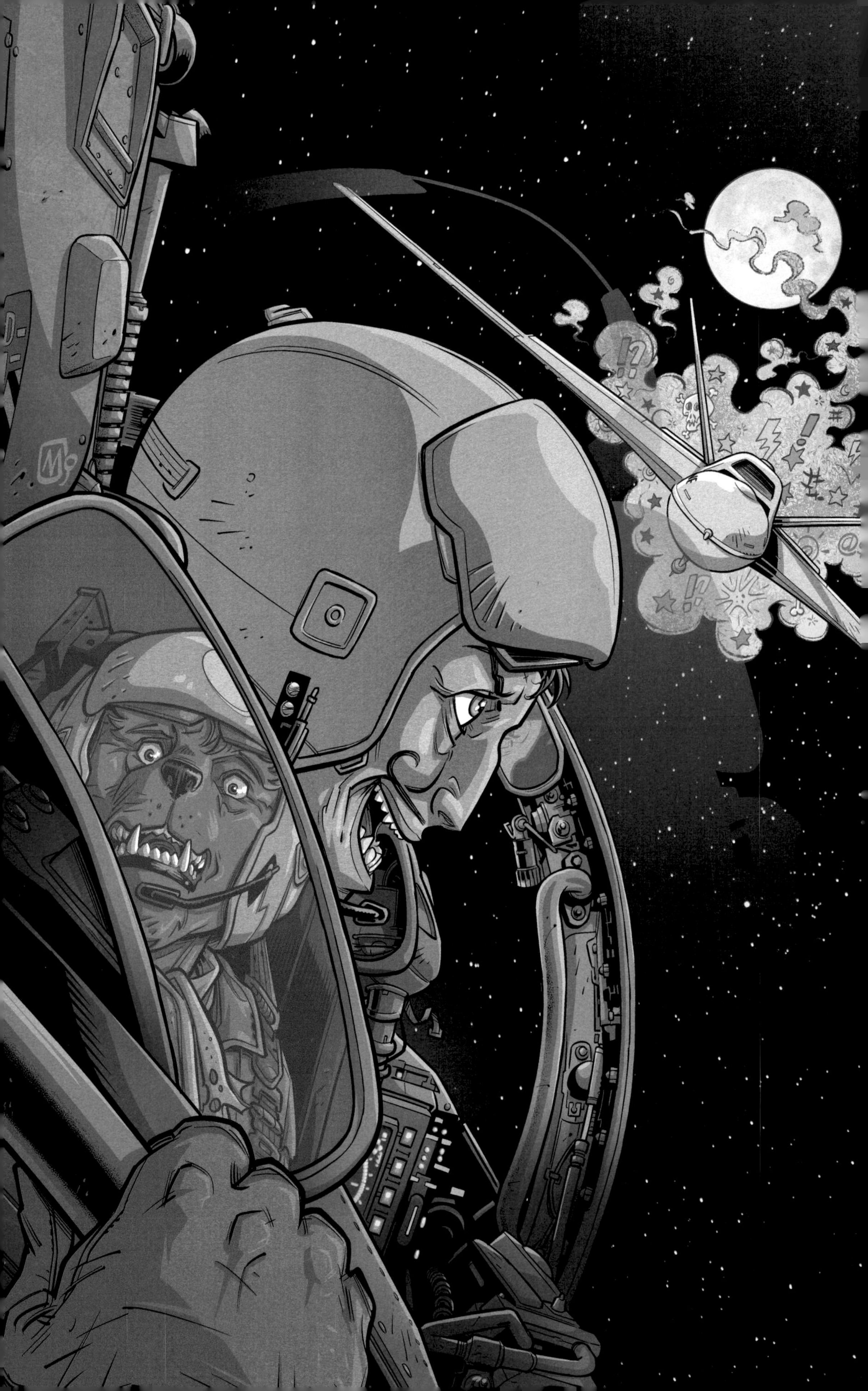

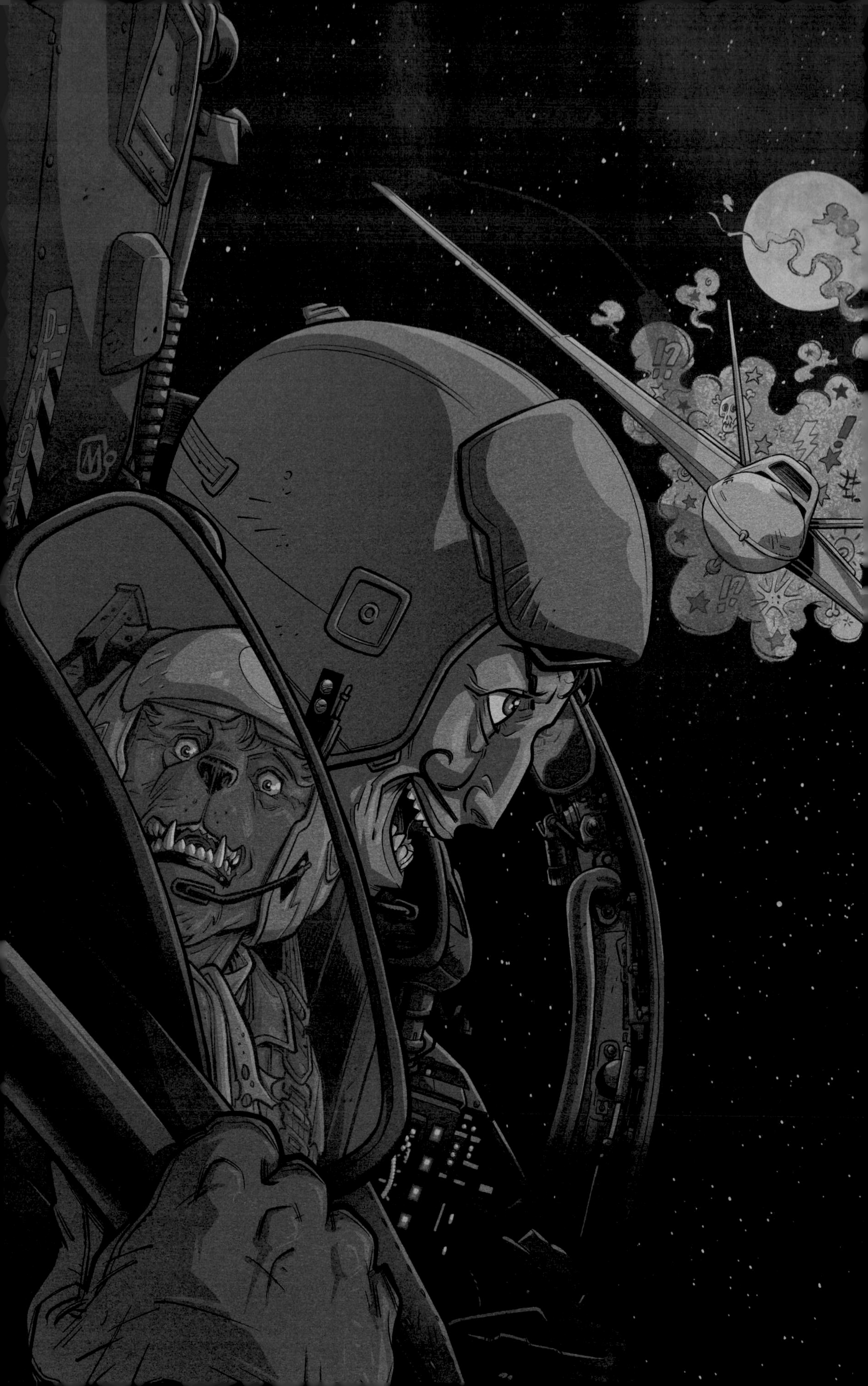
D-DANGER

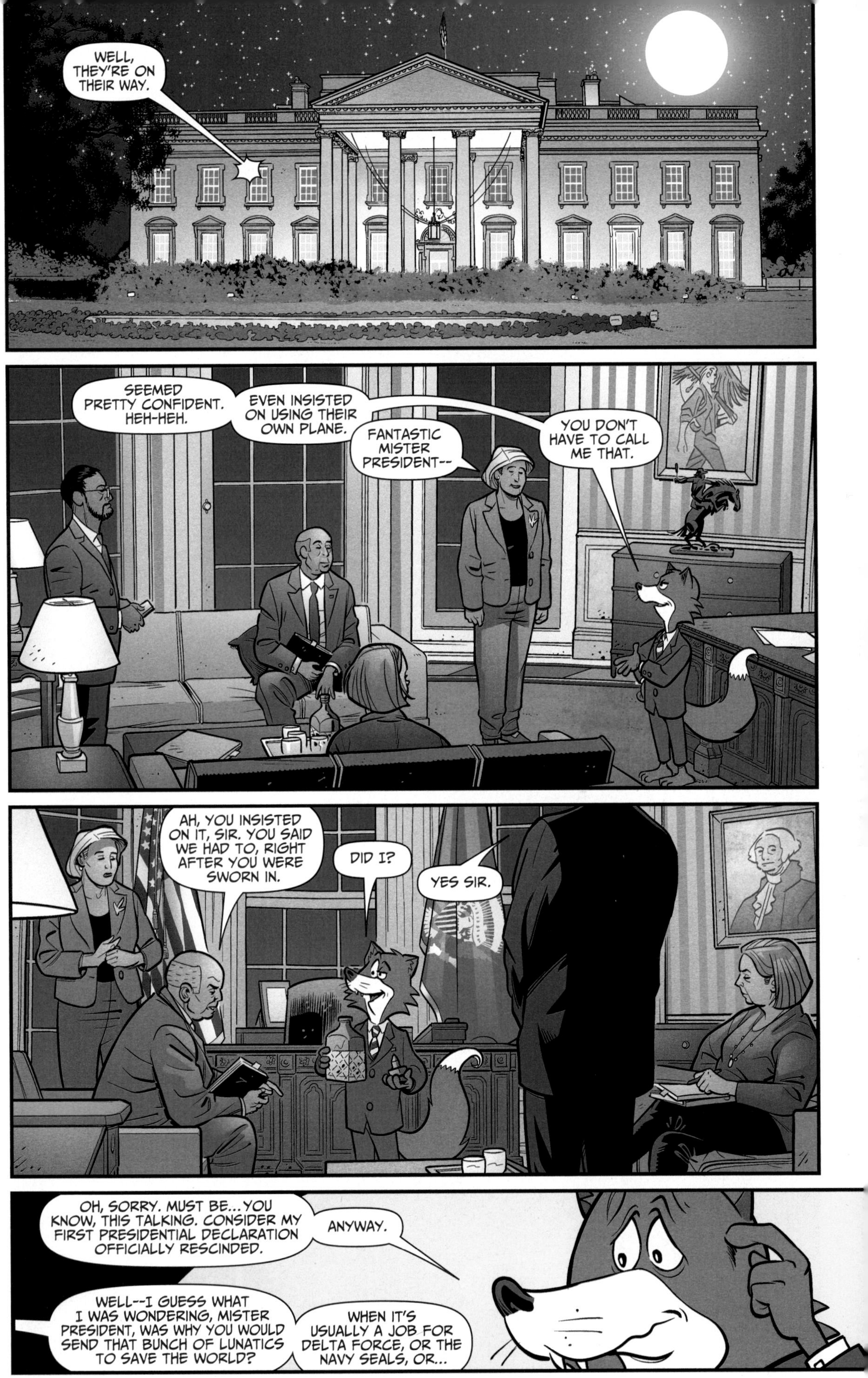
WELL, THEY'RE ON THEIR WAY.
SEEMED PRETTY CONFIDENT. HEH-HEH.
EVEN INSISTED ON USING THEIR OWN PLANE.
FANTASTIC MISTER PRESIDENT--
YOU DON'T HAVE TO CALL ME THAT.
AH, YOU INSISTED ON IT, SIR. YOU SAID WE HAD TO, RIGHT AFTER YOU WERE SWORN IN.
DID I?
YES SIR.
OH, SORRY. MUST BE... YOU KNOW, THIS TALKING. CONSIDER MY FIRST PRESIDENTIAL DECLARATION OFFICIALLY RESCINDED.
ANYWAY.
WELL--I GUESS WHAT I WAS WONDERING, MISTER PRESIDENT, WAS WHY YOU WOULD SEND THAT BUNCH OF LUNATICS TO SAVE THE WORLD?
WHEN IT'S USUALLY A JOB FOR DELTA FORCE, OR THE NAVY SEALS, OR...

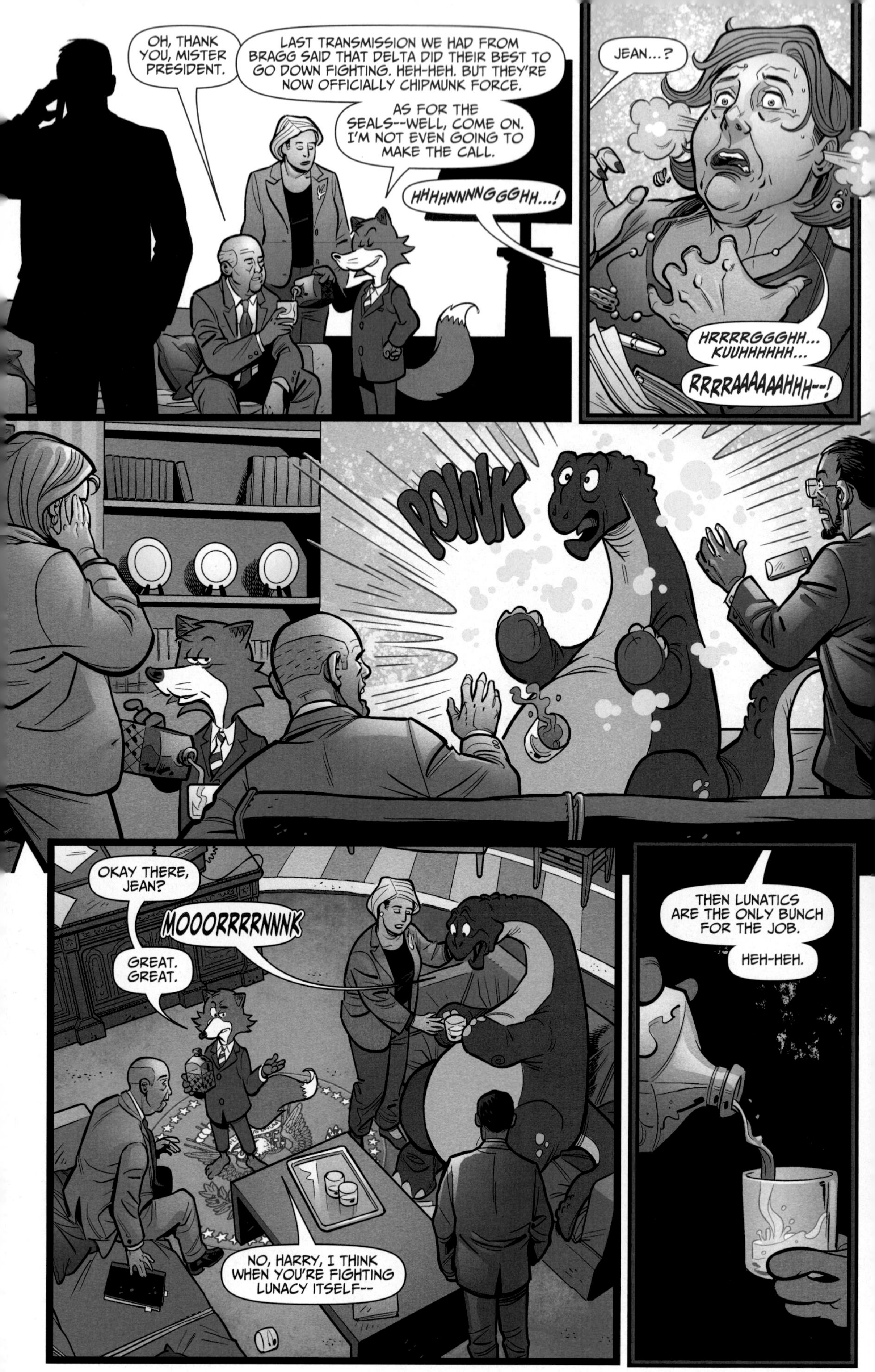
OH, THANK YOU, MISTER PRESIDENT.
LAST TRANSMISSION WE HAD FROM BRAGG SAID THAT DELTA DID THEIR BEST TO GO DOWN FIGHTING. HEH-HEH. BUT THEY'RE NOW OFFICIALLY CHIPMUNK FORCE.
AS FOR THE SEALS--WELL, COME ON. I'M NOT EVEN GOING TO MAKE THE CALL.
HHHHNNNNGGGHH...!
JEAN...?
HRRRRGGGHH... KUUHHHHHHH...
RRRRAAAAAAHHH--!
POINK
OKAY THERE, JEAN?
MOOORRRRNNNK
GREAT. GREAT.
NO, HARRY, I THINK WHEN YOU'RE FIGHTING LUNACY ITSELF--
THEN LUNATICS ARE THE ONLY BUNCH FOR THE JOB.
HEH-HEH.

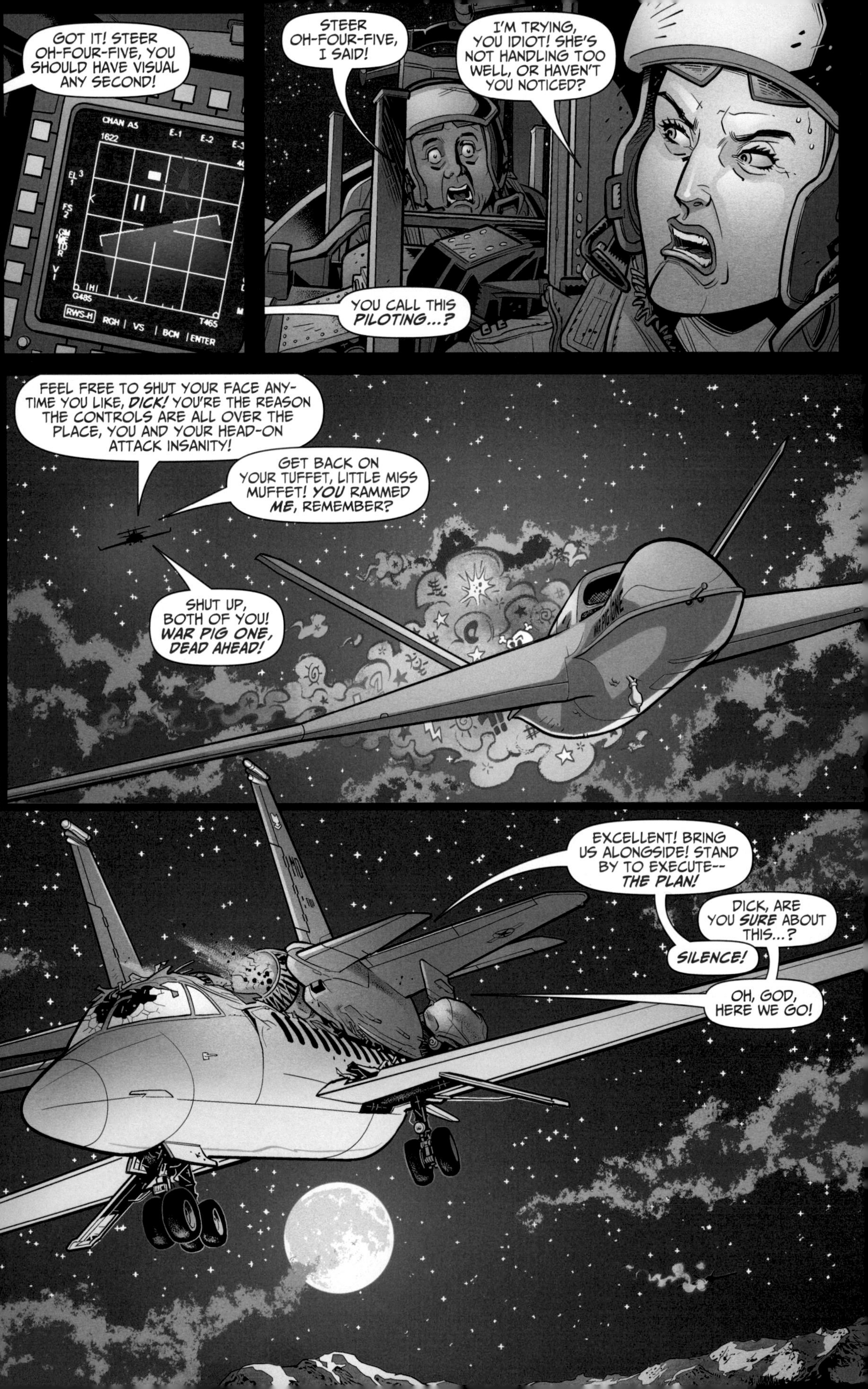
GOT IT! STEER OH-FOUR-FIVE, YOU SHOULD HAVE VISUAL ANY SECOND!
STEER OH-FOUR-FIVE, I SAID!
I'M TRYING, YOU IDIOT! SHE'S NOT HANDLING TOO WELL, OR HAVEN'T YOU NOTICED?
YOU CALL THIS *PILOTING...?*
FEEL FREE TO SHUT YOUR FACE ANY-TIME YOU LIKE, ***DICK!*** YOU'RE THE REASON THE CONTROLS ARE ALL OVER THE PLACE, YOU AND YOUR HEAD-ON ATTACK INSANITY!
GET BACK ON YOUR TUFFET, LITTLE MISS MUFFET! ***YOU*** RAMMED ***ME***, REMEMBER?
SHUT UP, BOTH OF YOU! ***WAR PIG ONE, DEAD AHEAD!***
EXCELLENT! BRING US ALONGSIDE! STAND BY TO EXECUTE-- ***THE PLAN!***
DICK, ARE YOU ***SURE*** ABOUT THIS...?
SILENCE!
OH, GOD, HERE WE GO!

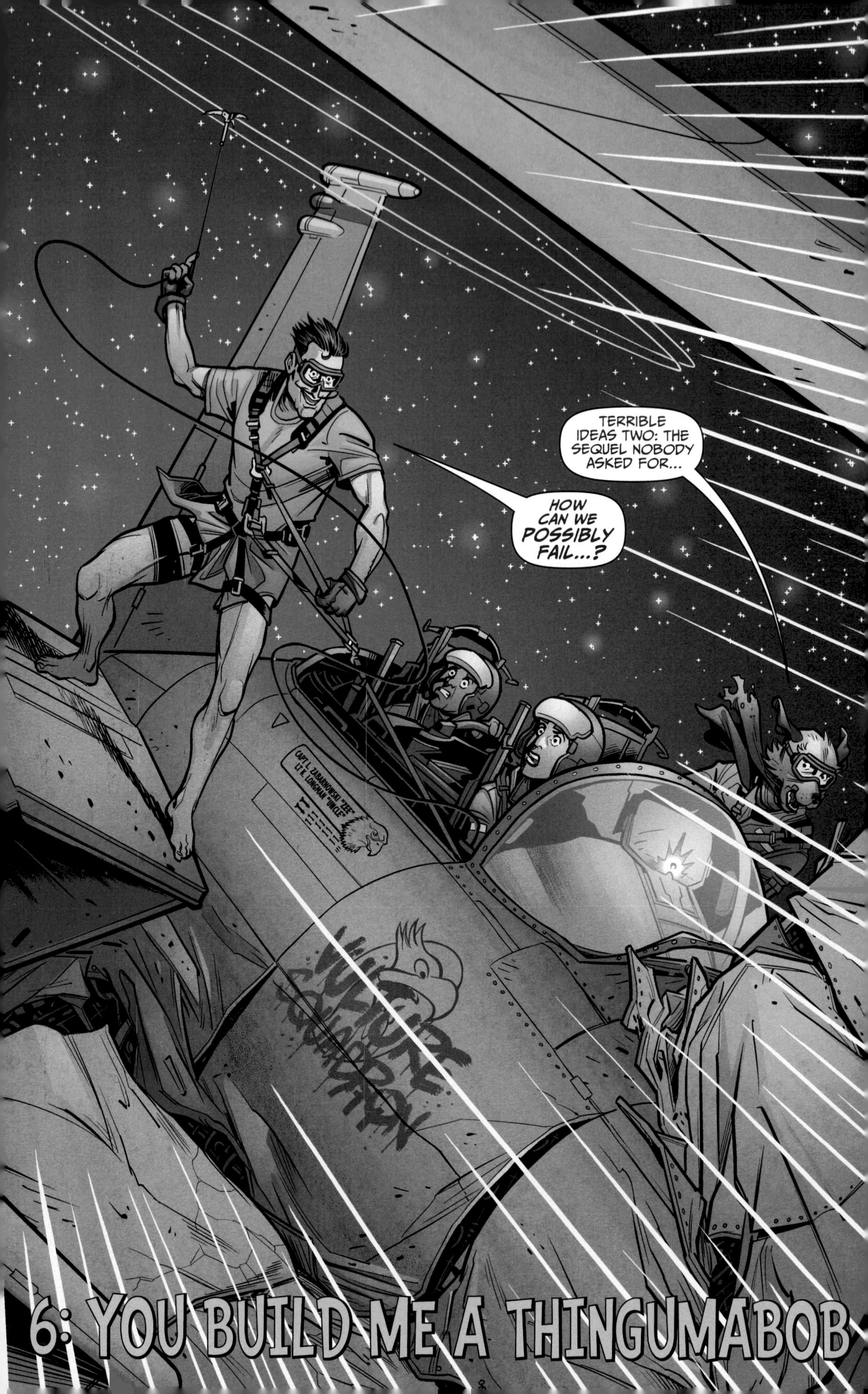
CAPT L. ZABARNOWSKI "ZEE"
LT K. LONGMAN "UNCLE"
TERRIBLE IDEAS TWO: THE SEQUEL NOBODY ASKED FOR...
HOW CAN WE POSSIBLY FAIL...?
6: YOU BUILD ME A THINGUMABOB

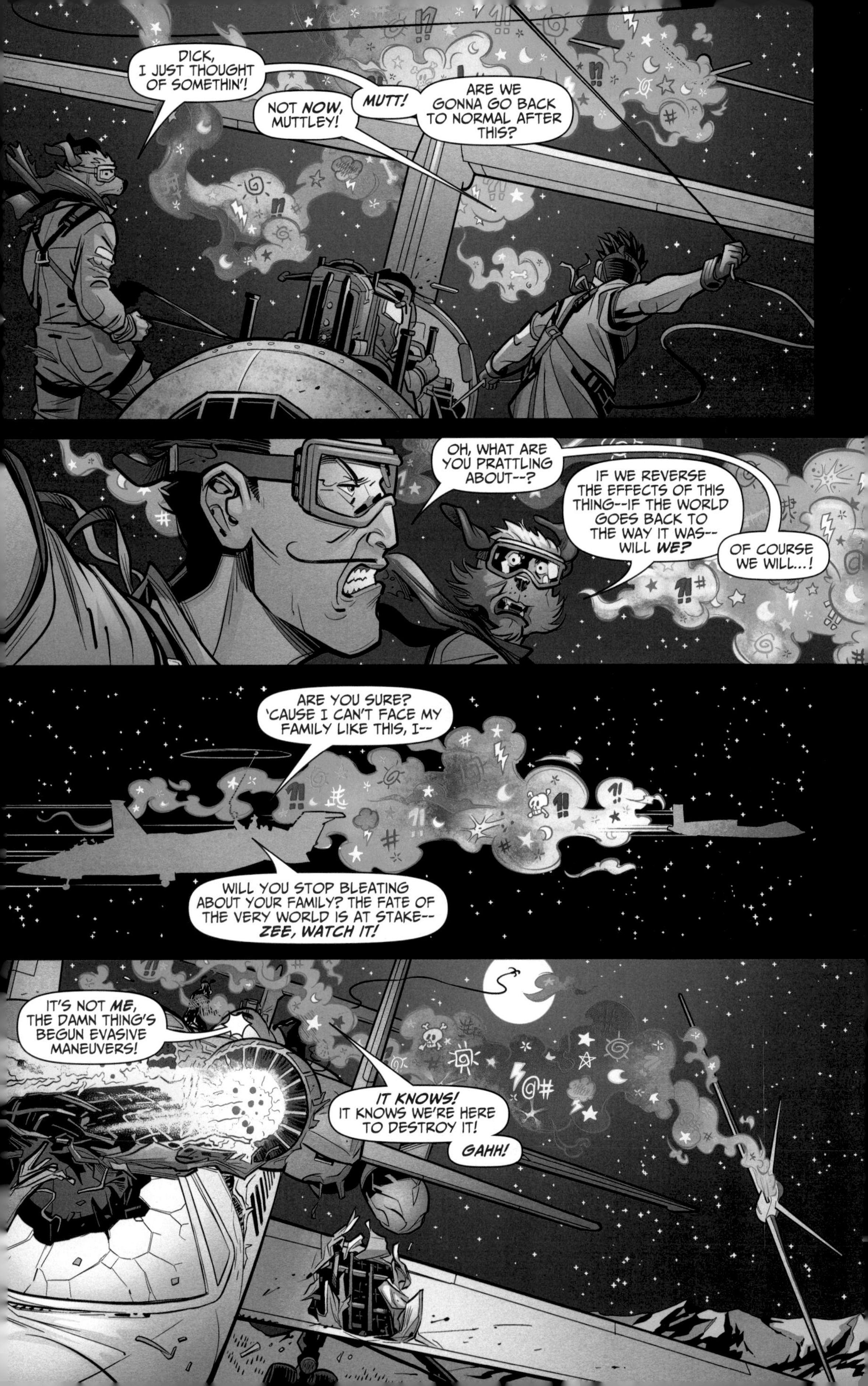
DICK, I JUST THOUGHT OF SOMETHIN'!
NOT NOW, MUTTLEY!
MUTT!
ARE WE GONNA GO BACK TO NORMAL AFTER THIS?
OH, WHAT ARE YOU PRATTLING ABOUT--?
IF WE REVERSE THE EFFECTS OF THIS THING--IF THE WORLD GOES BACK TO THE WAY IT WAS--WILL WE?
OF COURSE WE WILL...!
ARE YOU SURE? 'CAUSE I CAN'T FACE MY FAMILY LIKE THIS, I--
WILL YOU STOP BLEATING ABOUT YOUR FAMILY? THE FATE OF THE VERY WORLD IS AT STAKE-- ZEE, WATCH IT!
IT'S NOT ME, THE DAMN THING'S BEGUN EVASIVE MANEUVERS!
IT KNOWS! IT KNOWS WE'RE HERE TO DESTROY IT!
GAHH!

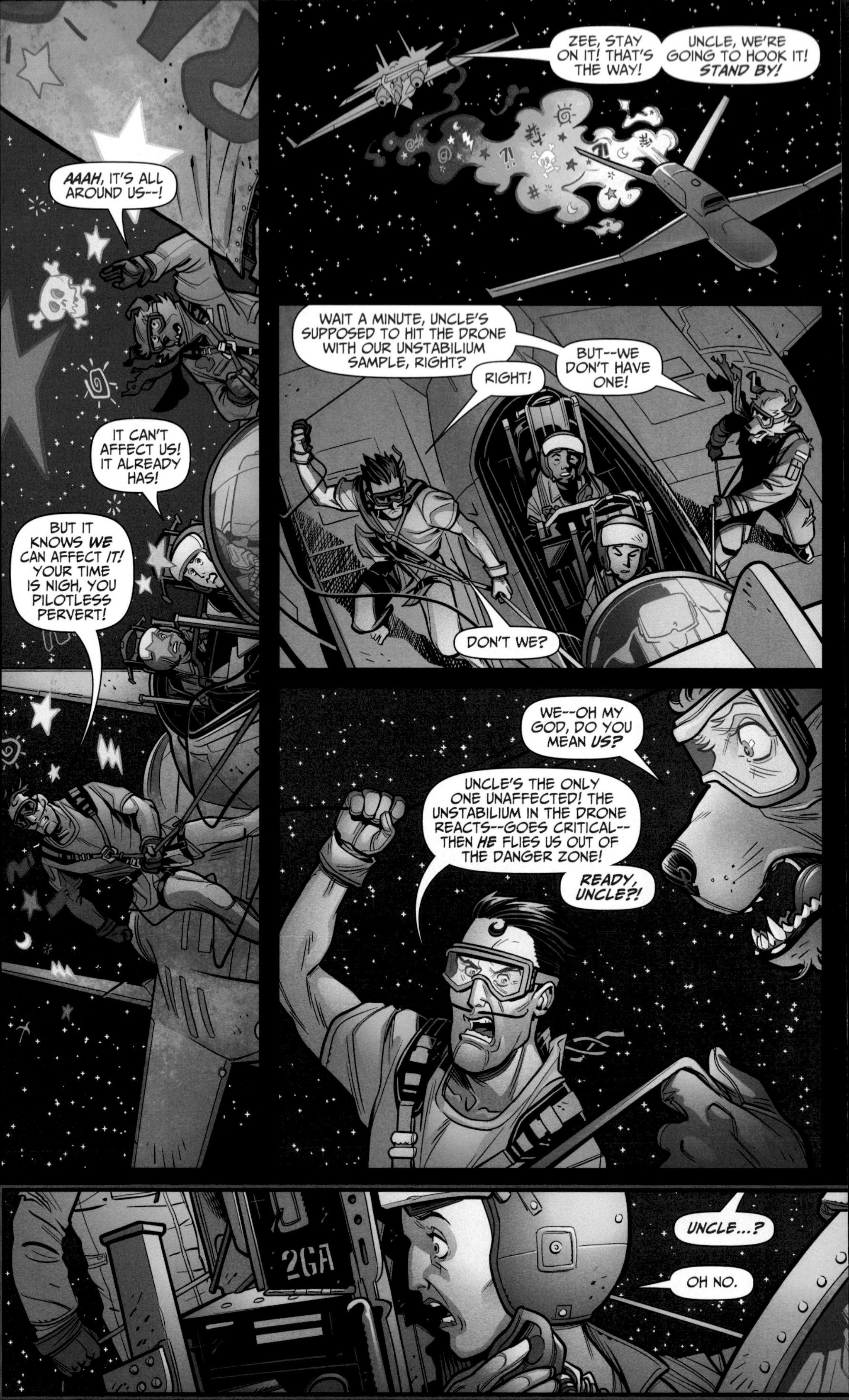
AAAH, IT'S ALL AROUND US--!
IT CAN'T AFFECT US! IT ALREADY HAS!
BUT IT KNOWS WE CAN AFFECT IT! YOUR TIME IS NIGH, YOU PILOTLESS PERVERT!
ZEE, STAY ON IT! THAT'S THE WAY!
UNCLE, WE'RE GOING TO HOOK IT! STAND BY!
WAIT A MINUTE, UNCLE'S SUPPOSED TO HIT THE DRONE WITH OUR UNSTABILIUM SAMPLE, RIGHT?
RIGHT!
BUT--WE DON'T HAVE ONE!
DON'T WE?
WE--OH MY GOD, DO YOU MEAN US?
UNCLE'S THE ONLY ONE UNAFFECTED! THE UNSTABILIUM IN THE DRONE REACTS--GOES CRITICAL--THEN HE FLIES US OUT OF THE DANGER ZONE!
READY, UNCLE?!
2GA
UNCLE...?
OH NO.

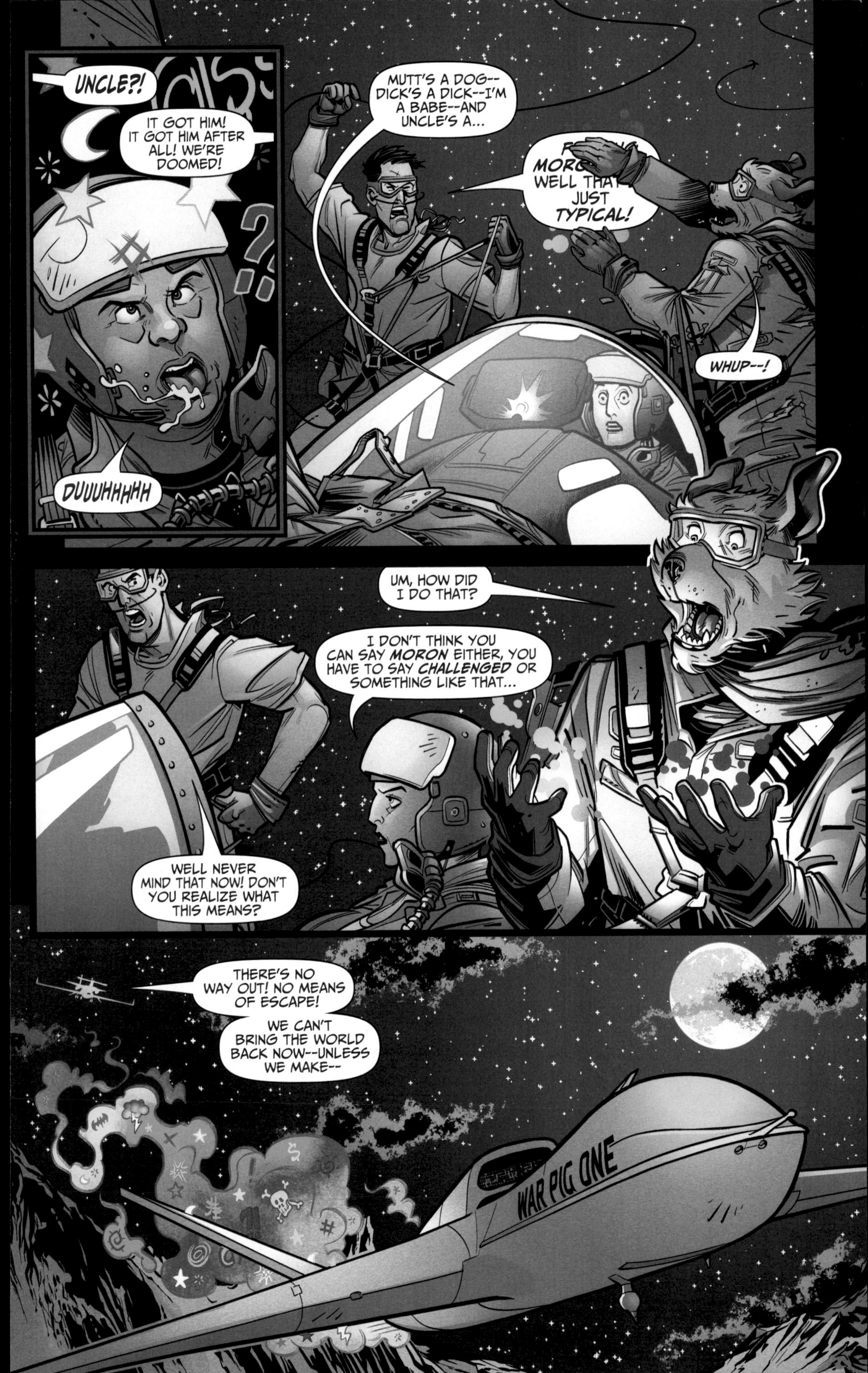
UNCLE?!
IT GOT HIM! IT GOT HIM AFTER ALL! WE'RE DOOMED!
DUUUHHHHH
MUTT'S A DOG--DICK'S A DICK--I'M A BABE--AND UNCLE'S A...
MORO WELL THAT JUST TYPICAL!
WHUP--!
UM, HOW DID I DO THAT?
I DON'T THINK YOU CAN SAY MORON EITHER, YOU HAVE TO SAY CHALLENGED OR SOMETHING LIKE THAT...
WELL NEVER MIND THAT NOW! DON'T YOU REALIZE WHAT THIS MEANS?
THERE'S NO WAY OUT! NO MEANS OF ESCAPE!
WE CAN'T BRING THE WORLD BACK NOW--UNLESS WE MAKE--
WAR PIG ONE

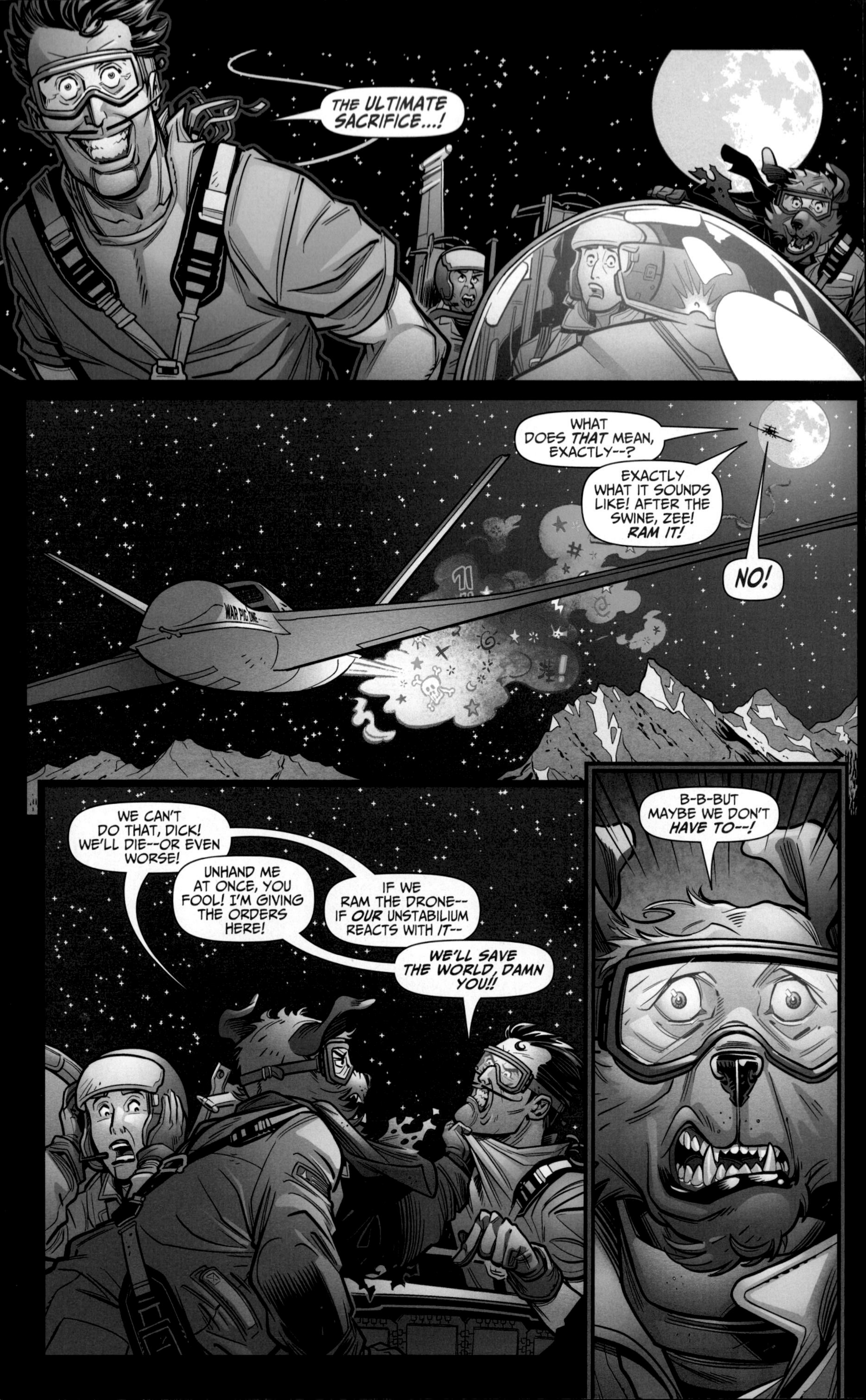
THE ULTIMATE SACRIFICE...!
WHAT DOES THAT MEAN, EXACTLY--?
EXACTLY WHAT IT SOUNDS LIKE! AFTER THE SWINE, ZEE! RAM IT!
NO!
WAR PIG ONE
WE CAN'T DO THAT, DICK! WE'LL DIE--OR EVEN WORSE!
UNHAND ME AT ONCE, YOU FOOL! I'M GIVING THE ORDERS HERE!
IF WE RAM THE DRONE-- IF OUR UNSTABILIUM REACTS WITH IT--
WE'LL SAVE THE WORLD, DAMN YOU!!
B-B-BUT MAYBE WE DON'T HAVE TO--!

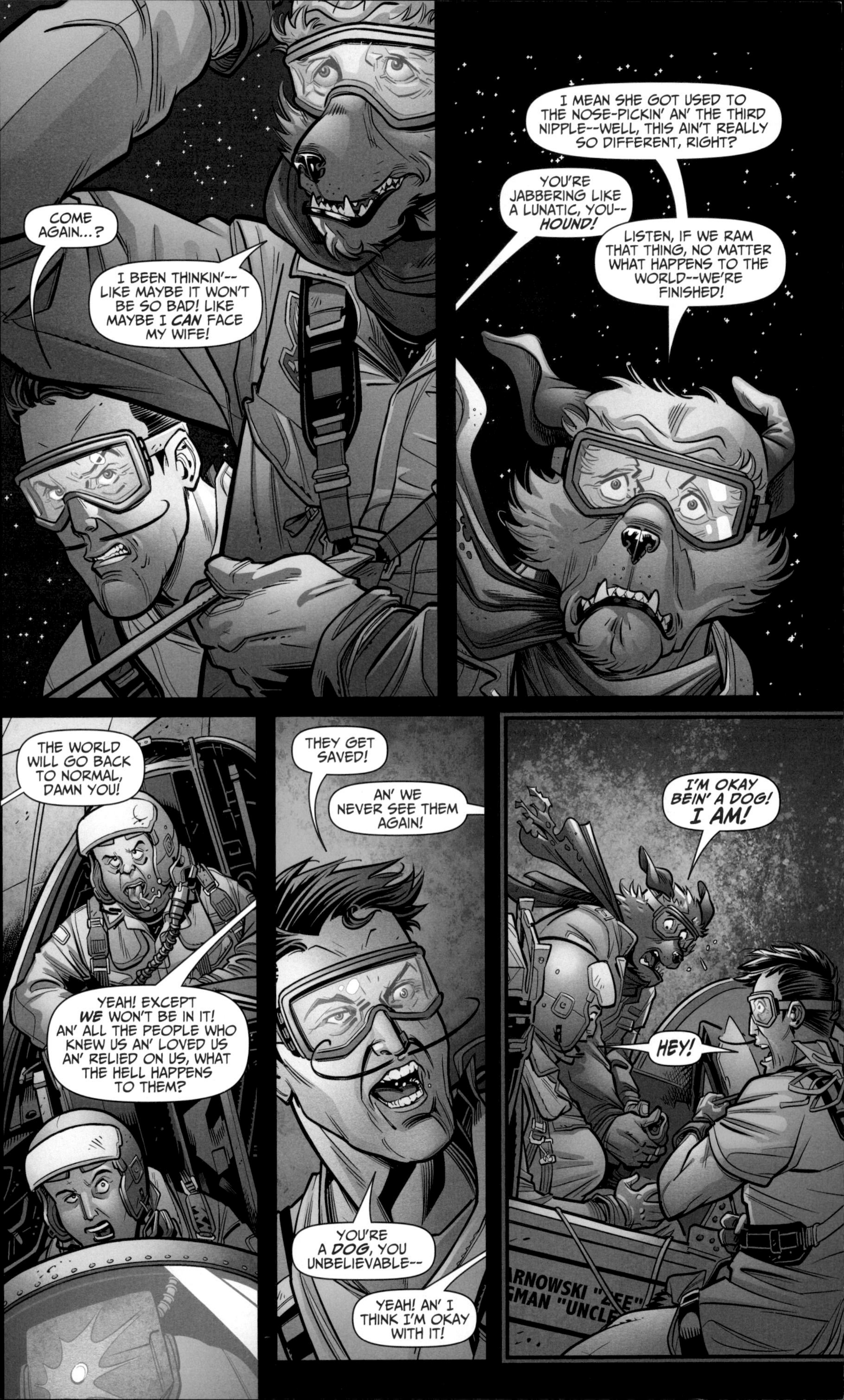
COME AGAIN...?
I BEEN THINKIN'-- LIKE MAYBE IT WON'T BE SO BAD! LIKE MAYBE I *CAN* FACE MY WIFE!
I MEAN SHE GOT USED TO THE NOSE-PICKIN' AN' THE THIRD NIPPLE--WELL, THIS AIN'T REALLY SO DIFFERENT, RIGHT?
YOU'RE JABBERING LIKE A LUNATIC, YOU-- ***HOUND!***
LISTEN, IF WE RAM THAT THING, NO MATTER WHAT HAPPENS TO THE WORLD--WE'RE FINISHED!
THE WORLD WILL GO BACK TO NORMAL, DAMN YOU!
YEAH! EXCEPT ***WE*** WON'T BE IN IT! AN' ALL THE PEOPLE WHO KNEW US AN' LOVED US AN' RELIED ON US, WHAT THE HELL HAPPENS TO THEM?
THEY GET SAVED!
AN' WE NEVER SEE THEM AGAIN!
YOU'RE A ***DOG***, YOU UNBELIEVABLE--
YEAH! AN' I THINK I'M OKAY WITH IT!
I'M OKAY BEIN' A DOG! ***I AM!***
HEY!

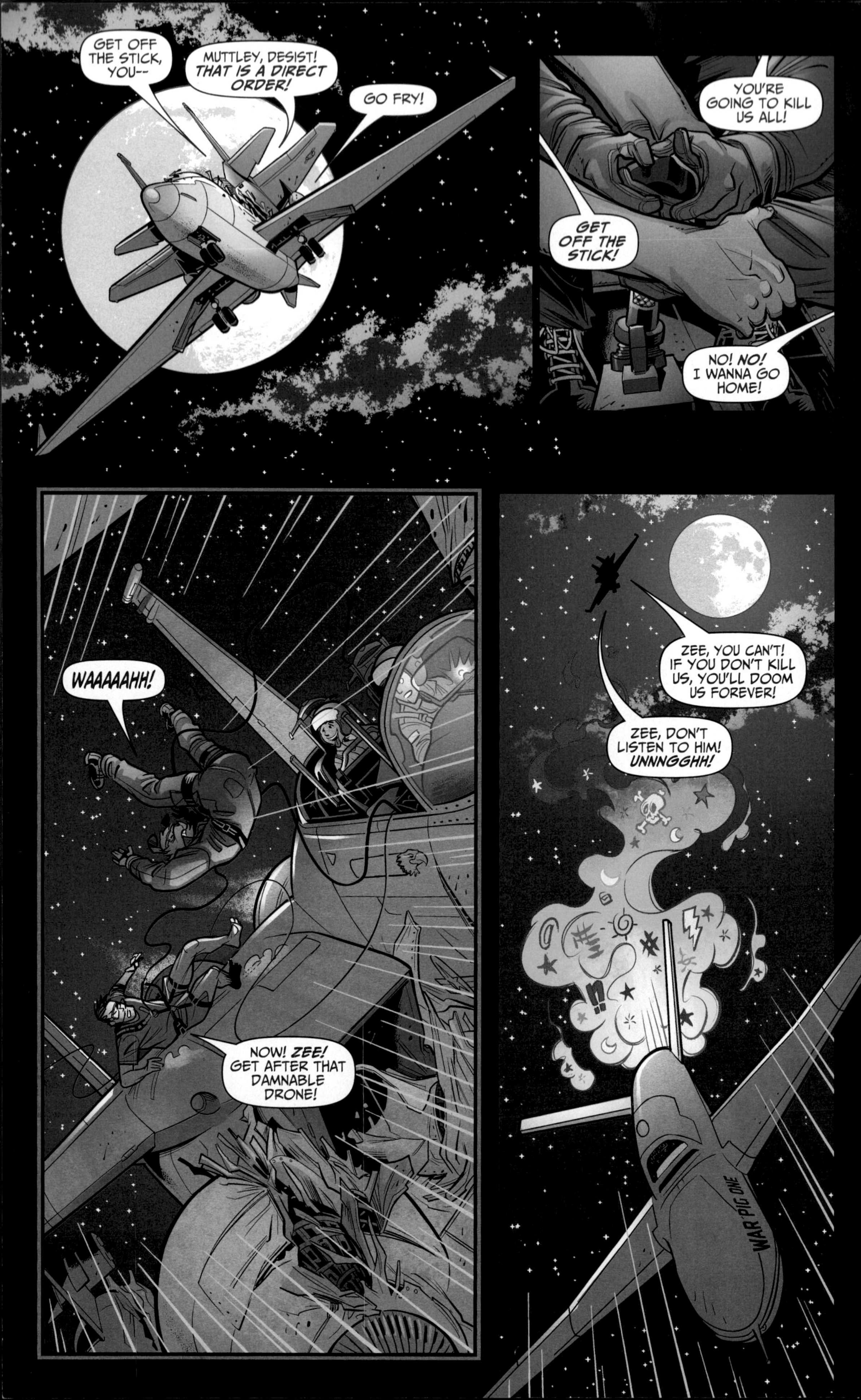
GET OFF THE STICK, YOU--
MUTTLEY, DESIST! THAT IS A DIRECT ORDER!
GO FRY!
YOU'RE GOING TO KILL US ALL!
GET OFF THE STICK!
NO! NO! I WANNA GO HOME!
WAAAAAHH!
NOW! ZEE! GET AFTER THAT DAMNABLE DRONE!
ZEE, YOU CAN'T! IF YOU DON'T KILL US, YOU'LL DOOM US FOREVER!
ZEE, DON'T LISTEN TO HIM! UNNNGGHH!
WAR PIG ONE

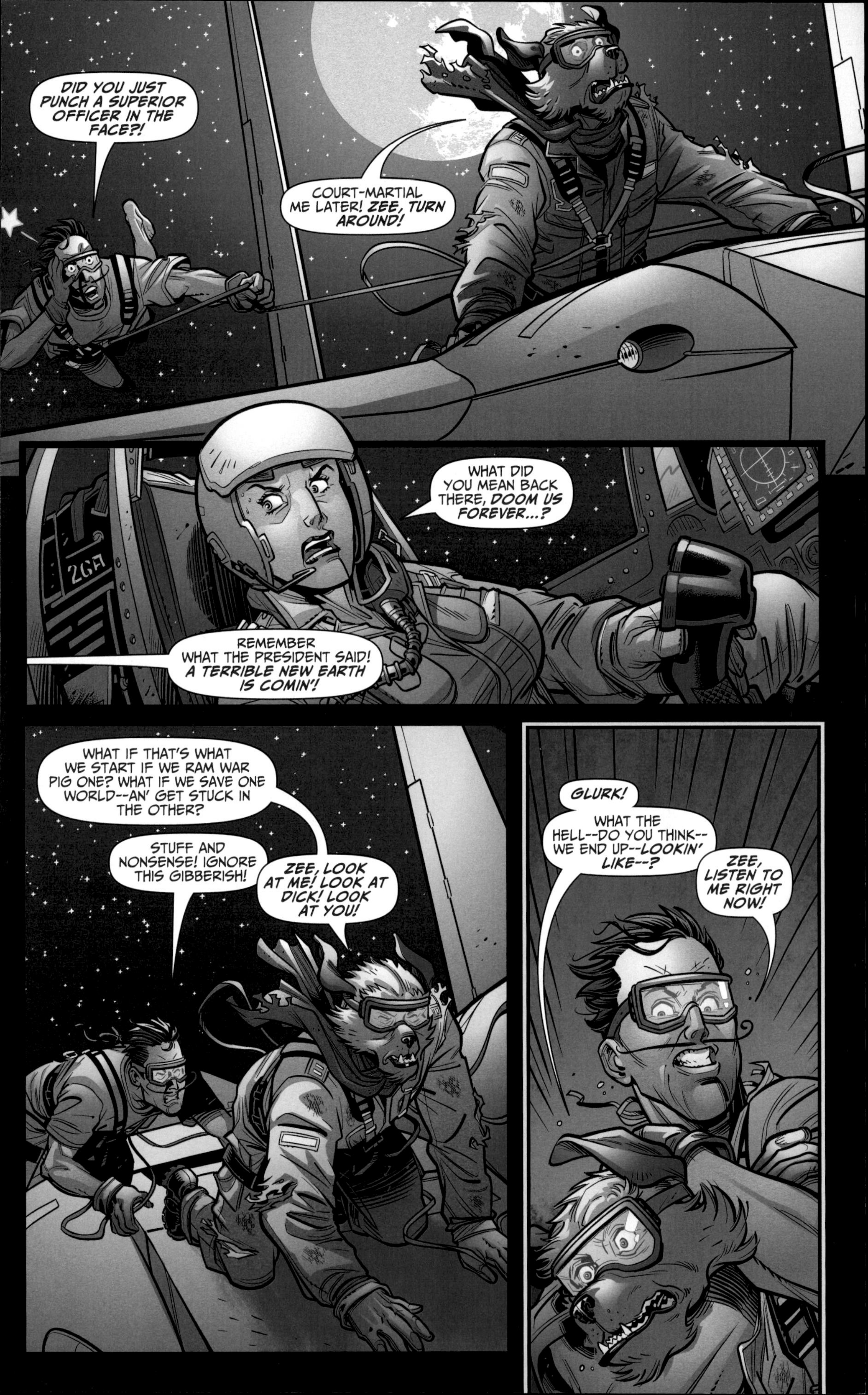
DID YOU JUST PUNCH A SUPERIOR OFFICER IN THE FACE?!
COURT-MARTIAL ME LATER! ZEE, TURN AROUND!
WHAT DID YOU MEAN BACK THERE, DOOM US FOREVER...?
REMEMBER WHAT THE PRESIDENT SAID! A TERRIBLE NEW EARTH IS COMIN'!
WHAT IF THAT'S WHAT WE START IF WE RAM WAR PIG ONE? WHAT IF WE SAVE ONE WORLD--AN' GET STUCK IN THE OTHER?
STUFF AND NONSENSE! IGNORE THIS GIBBERISH!
ZEE, LOOK AT ME! LOOK AT DICK! LOOK AT YOU!
GLURK!
WHAT THE HELL--DO YOU THINK--WE END UP--LOOKIN' LIKE--?
ZEE, LISTEN TO ME RIGHT NOW!

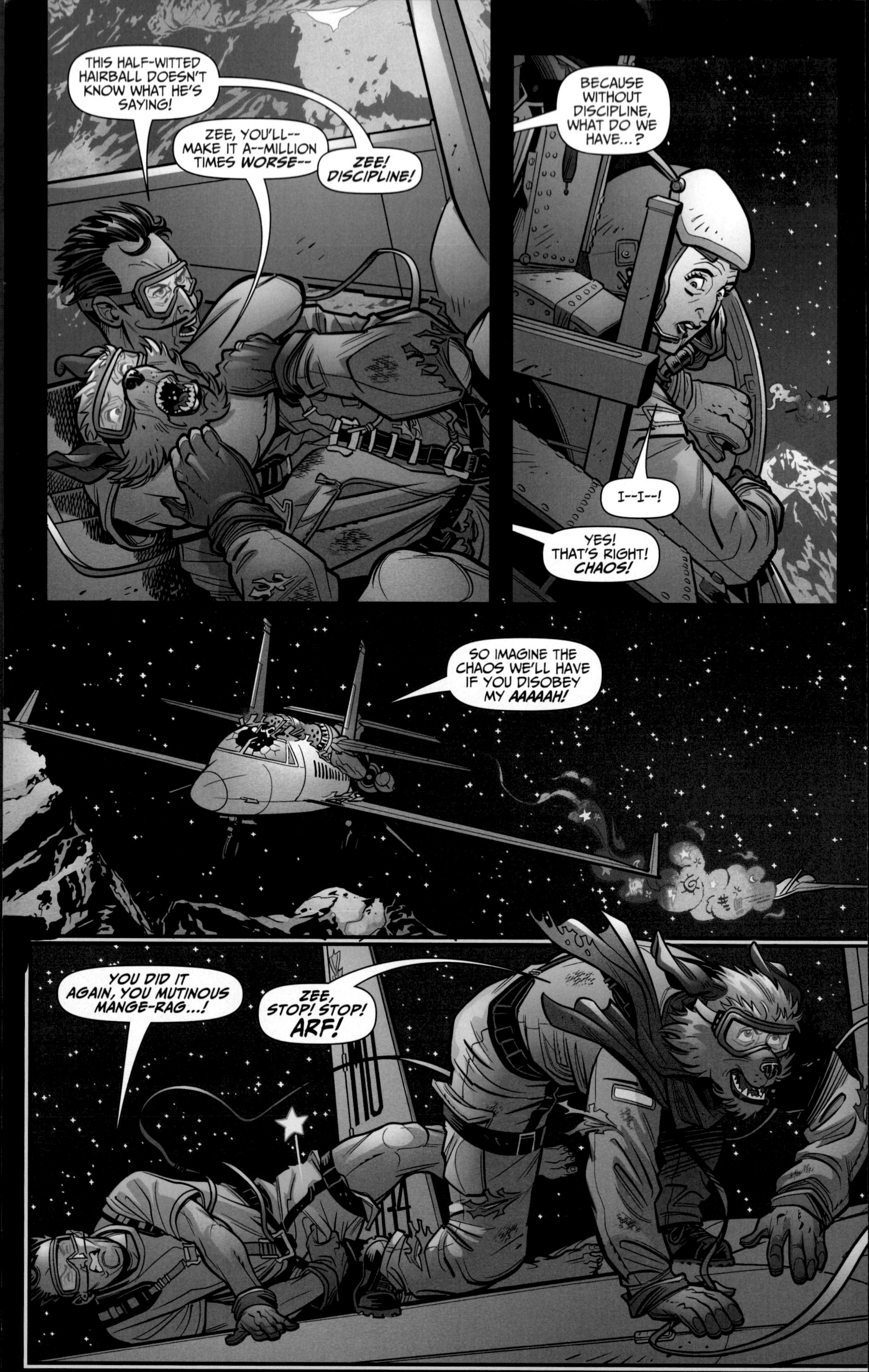
THIS HALF-WITTED HAIRBALL DOESN'T KNOW WHAT HE'S SAYING!
ZEE, YOU'LL-- MAKE IT A--MILLION TIMES *WORSE*--
ZEE! DISCIPLINE!
BECAUSE WITHOUT DISCIPLINE, WHAT DO WE HAVE...?
I--I--!
YES! THAT'S RIGHT! *CHAOS!*
SO IMAGINE THE CHAOS WE'LL HAVE IF YOU DISOBEY MY *AAAAAH!*
YOU DID IT AGAIN, YOU MUTINOUS MANGE-RAG...!
ZEE, STOP! STOP! ARF!

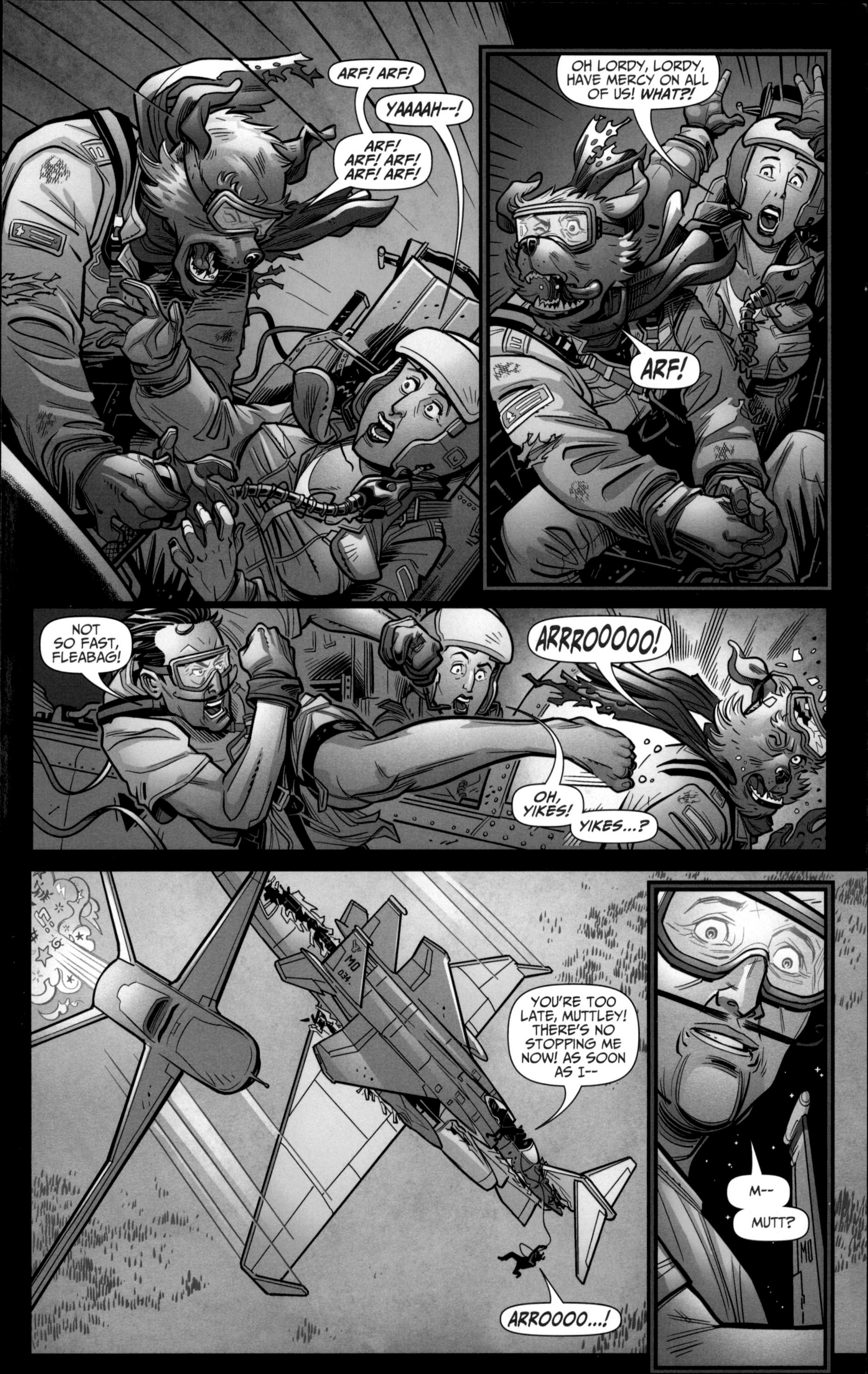
ARF! ARF!
YAAAAH--!
ARF! ARF! ARF! ARF! ARF!
OH LORDY, LORDY, HAVE MERCY ON ALL OF US! WHAT?!
ARF!
NOT SO FAST, FLEABAG!
ARRROOOOO!
OH, YIKES!
YIKES...?
YOU'RE TOO LATE, MUTTLEY! THERE'S NO STOPPING ME NOW! AS SOON AS I--
ARROOOO...!
M--
MUTT?

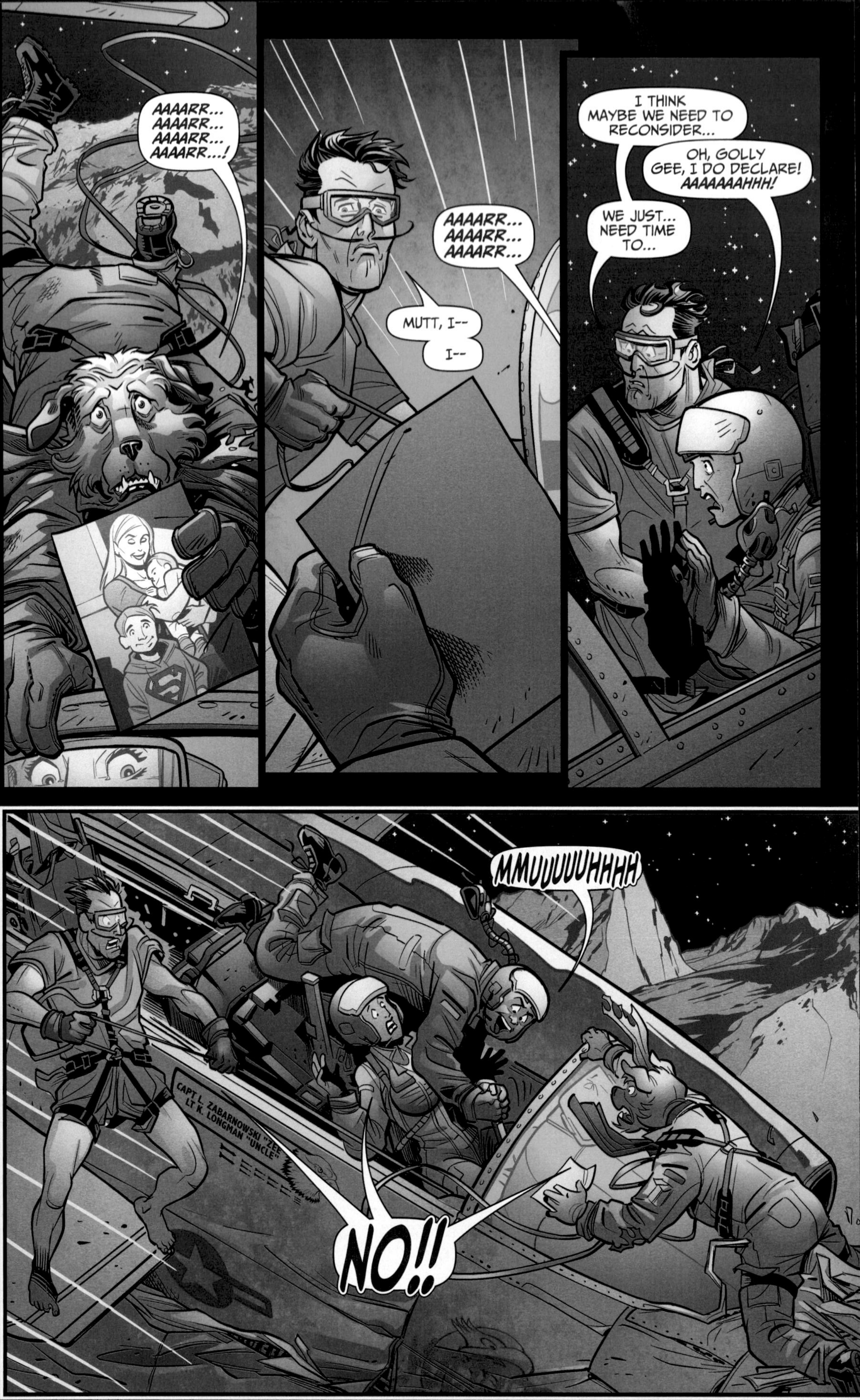
AAAARR...
AAAARR...
AAAARR...
AAAARR...!
AAAARR...
AAAARR...
AAAARR...
MUTT, I--
I--
I THINK MAYBE WE NEED TO RECONSIDER...
OH, GOLLY GEE, I DO DECLARE! AAAAAAAHHH!
WE JUST... NEED TIME TO...
MMUUUUUHHHH
CAPT L. ZABARNOWSKI "ZEE"
LT K. LONGMAN "UNCLE"
NO!!

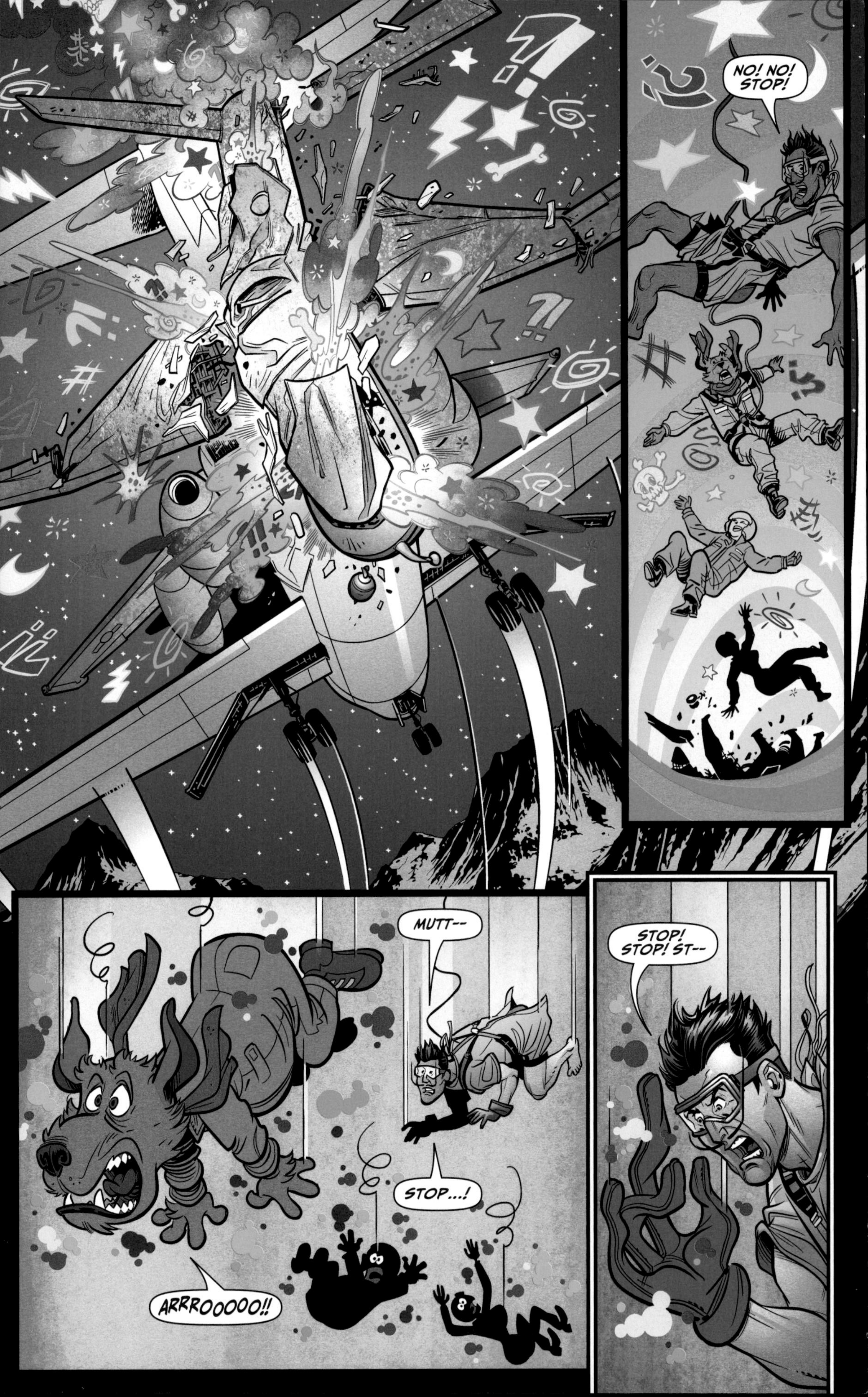
NO! NO! STOP!
MUTT--
STOP...!
ARRROOOOO!!
STOP! STOP! ST--

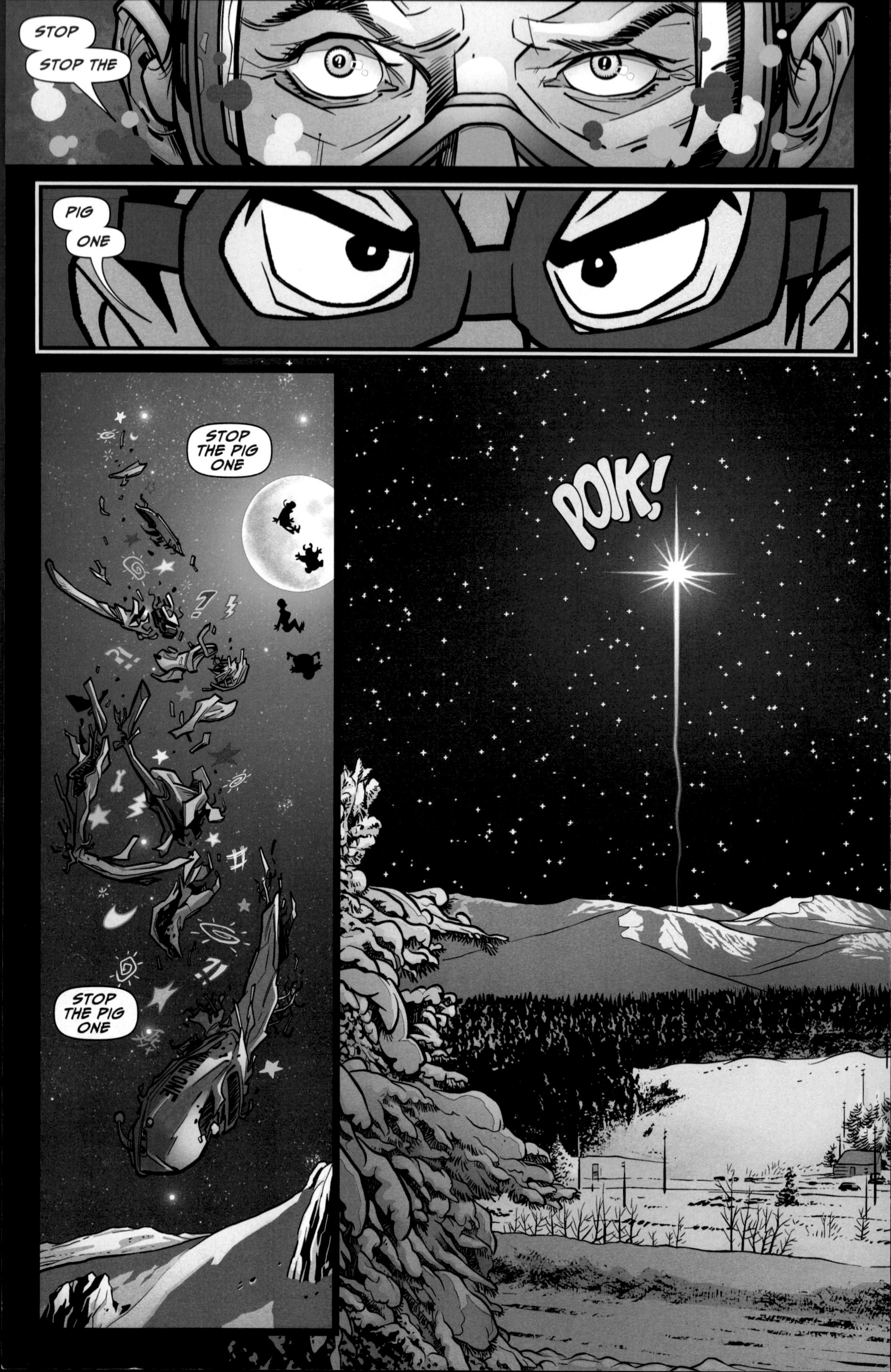
STOP
STOP THE
PIG
ONE
STOP THE PIG ONE
STOP THE PIG ONE
POIK!

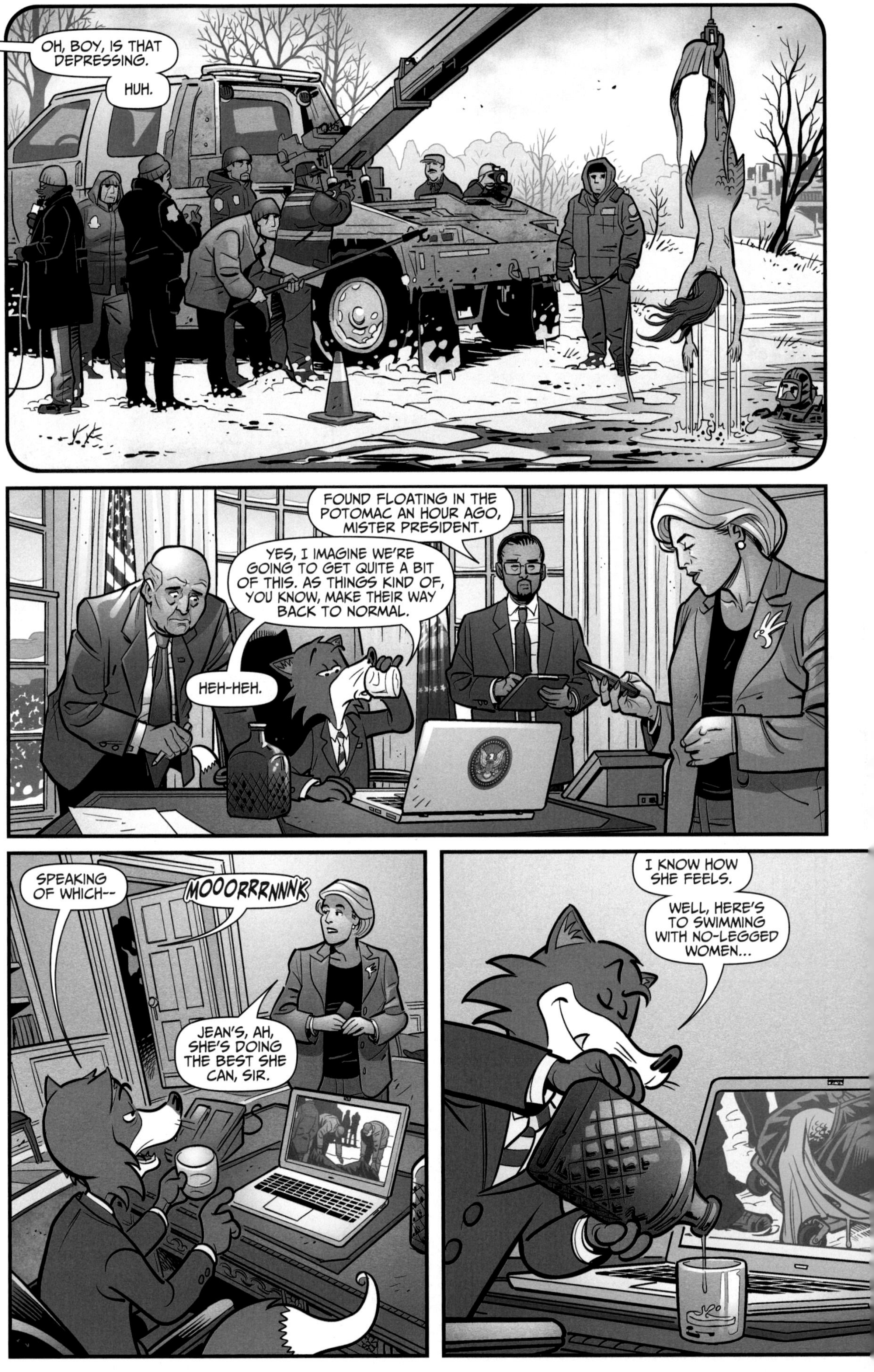

OH, BOY, IS THAT DEPRESSING.
HUH.
FOUND FLOATING IN THE POTOMAC AN HOUR AGO, MISTER PRESIDENT.
YES, I IMAGINE WE'RE GOING TO GET QUITE A BIT OF THIS. AS THINGS KIND OF, YOU KNOW, MAKE THEIR WAY BACK TO NORMAL.
HEH-HEH.
SPEAKING OF WHICH--
MOOORRRNNNK
JEAN'S, AH, SHE'S DOING THE BEST SHE CAN, SIR.
I KNOW HOW SHE FEELS.
WELL, HERE'S TO SWIMMING WITH NO-LEGGED WOMEN...

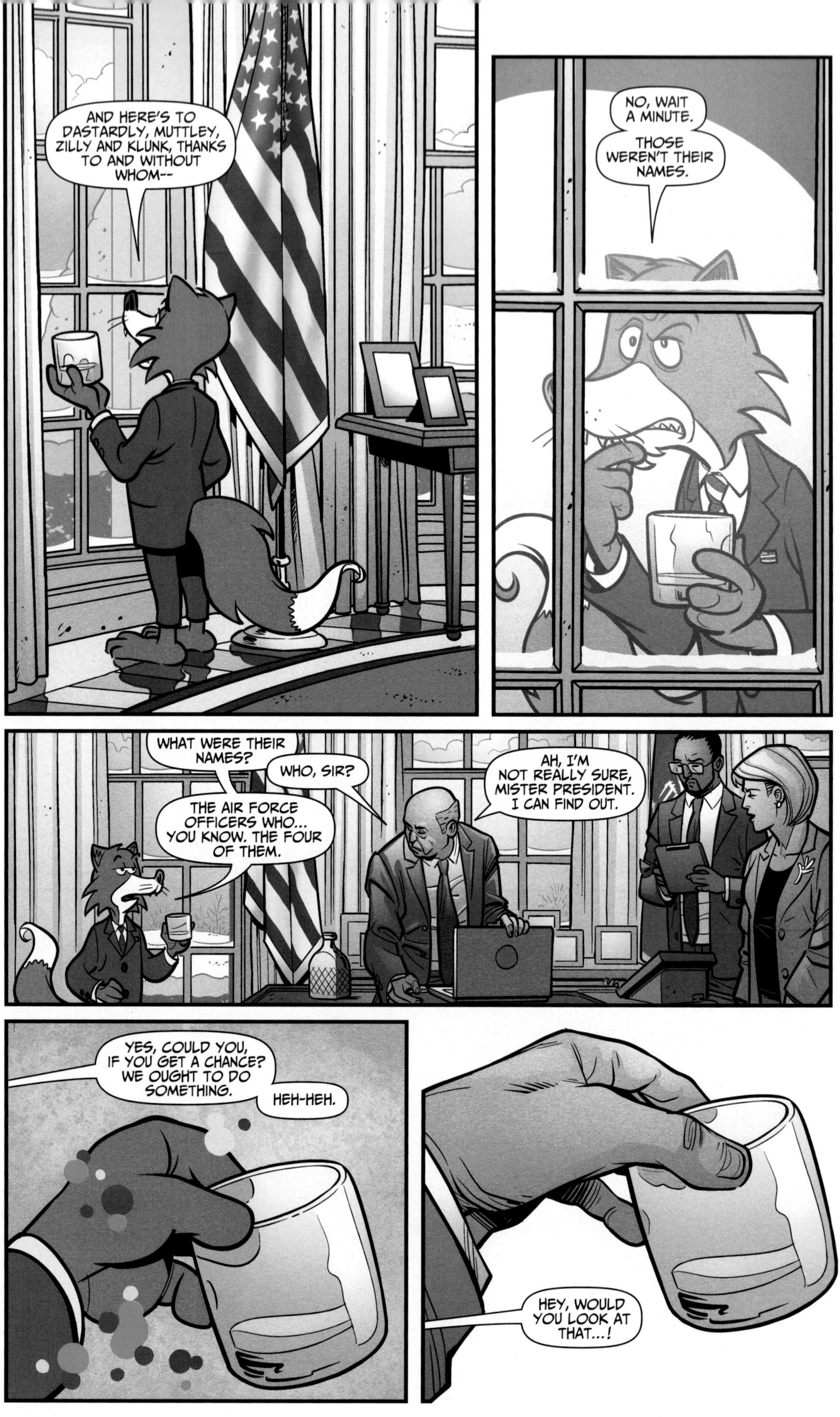
AND HERE'S TO DASTARDLY, MUTTLEY, ZILLY AND KLUNK, THANKS TO AND WITHOUT WHOM--
NO, WAIT A MINUTE.
THOSE WEREN'T THEIR NAMES.
WHAT WERE THEIR NAMES?
WHO, SIR?
THE AIR FORCE OFFICERS WHO... YOU KNOW. THE FOUR OF THEM.
AH, I'M NOT REALLY SURE, MISTER PRESIDENT. I CAN FIND OUT.
YES, COULD YOU, IF YOU GET A CHANCE? WE OUGHT TO DO SOMETHING.
HEH-HEH.
HEY, WOULD YOU LOOK AT THAT...!

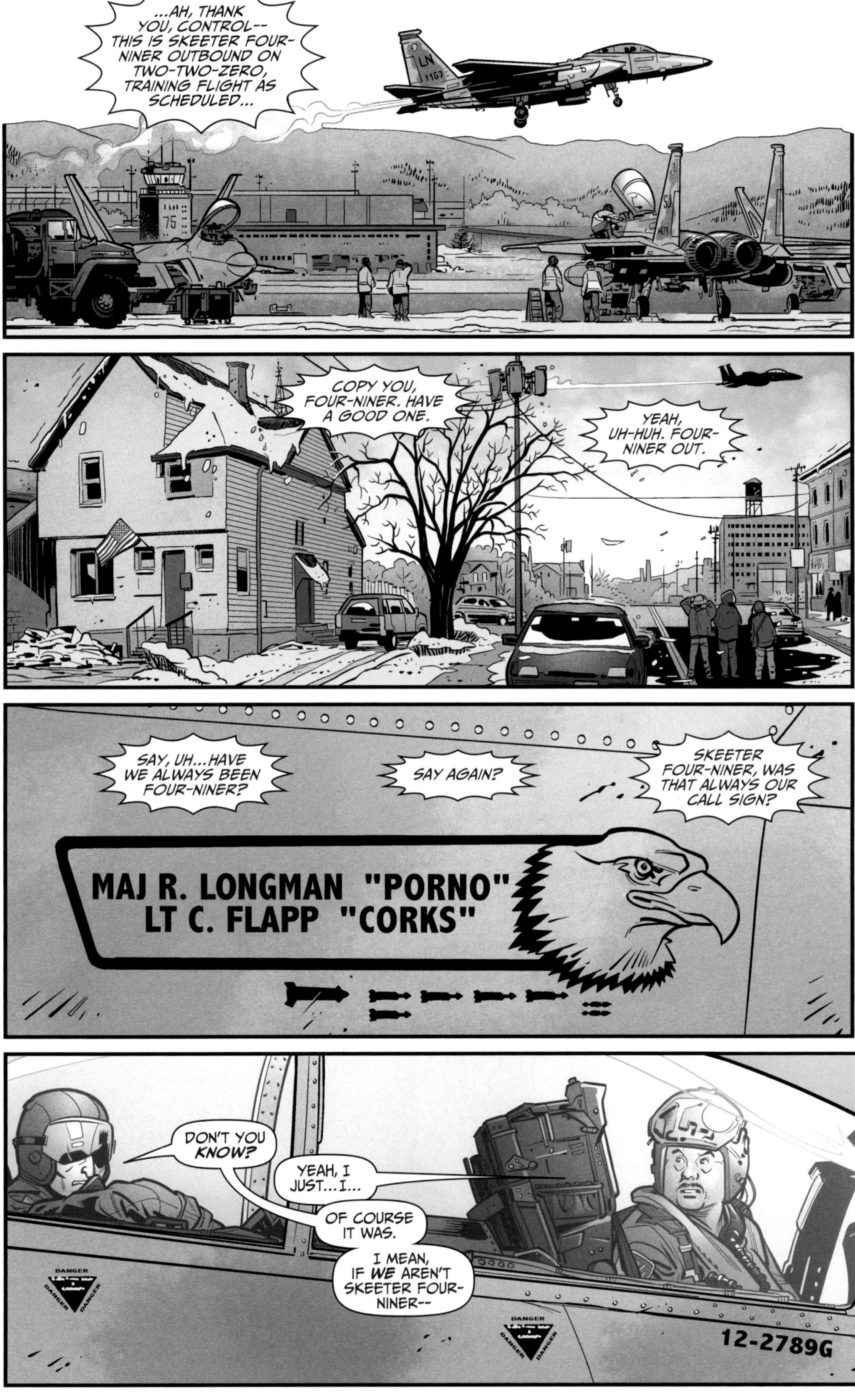
...AH, THANK YOU, CONTROL-- THIS IS SKEETER FOUR-NINER OUTBOUND ON TWO-TWO-ZERO, TRAINING FLIGHT AS SCHEDULED...
LN
75
COPY YOU, FOUR-NINER. HAVE A GOOD ONE.
YEAH, UH-HUH. FOUR-NINER OUT.
SAY, UH...HAVE WE ALWAYS BEEN FOUR-NINER?
SAY AGAIN?
SKEETER FOUR-NINER, WAS THAT ALWAYS OUR CALL SIGN?
MAJ R. LONGMAN "PORNO"
LT C. FLAPP "CORKS"
DON'T YOU KNOW?
YEAH, I JUST...I...
OF COURSE IT WAS.
I MEAN, IF WE AREN'T SKEETER FOUR-NINER--
DANGER
12-2789G

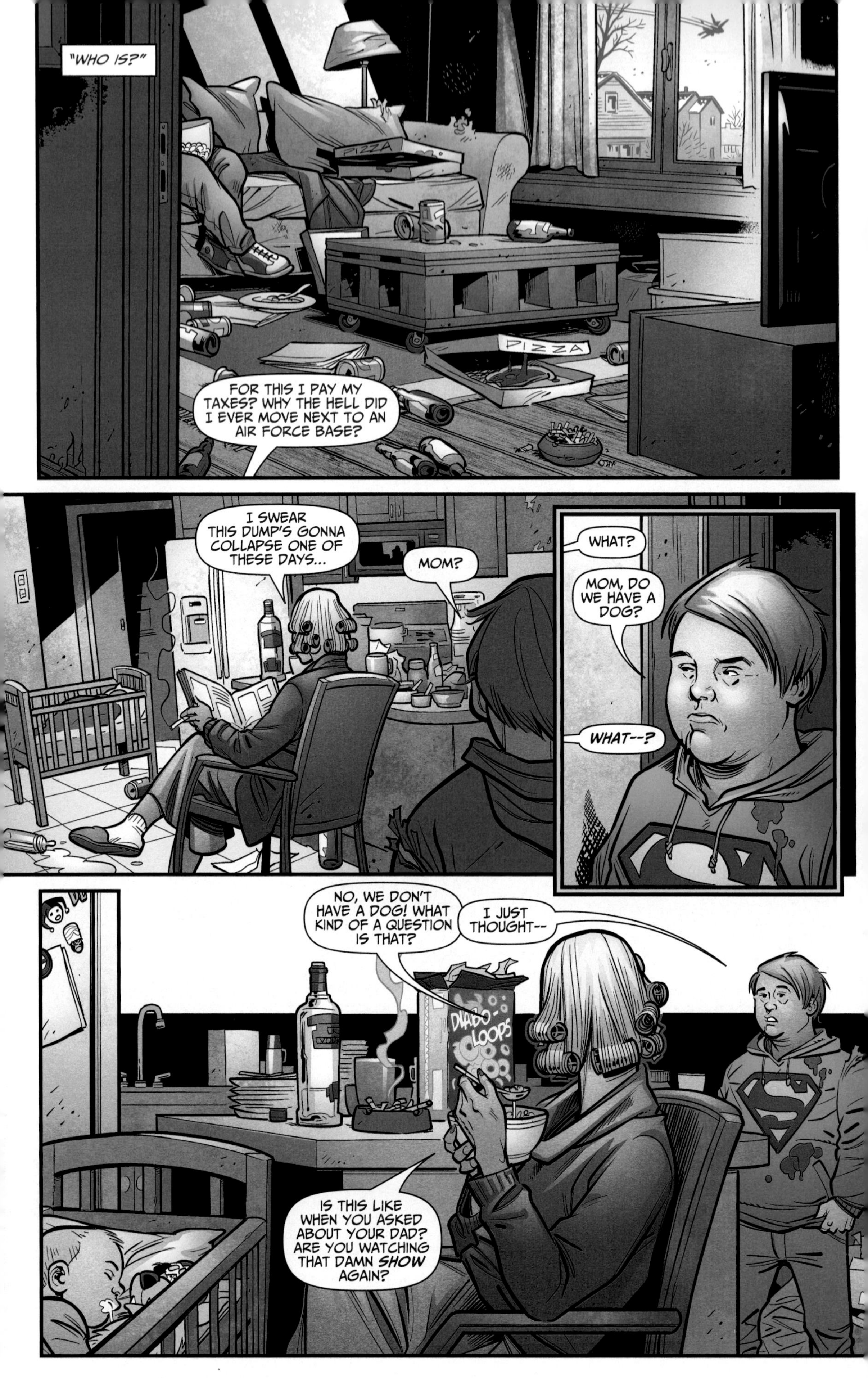
"WHO IS?"
PIZZA
PIZZA
FOR THIS I PAY MY TAXES? WHY THE HELL DID I EVER MOVE NEXT TO AN AIR FORCE BASE?
I SWEAR THIS DUMP'S GONNA COLLAPSE ONE OF THESE DAYS...
MOM?
WHAT?
MOM, DO WE HAVE A DOG?
WHAT--?
NO, WE DON'T HAVE A DOG! WHAT KIND OF A QUESTION IS THAT?
I JUST THOUGHT--
DIABO-LOOPS
IS THIS LIKE WHEN YOU ASKED ABOUT YOUR DAD? ARE YOU WATCHING THAT DAMN *SHOW* AGAIN?

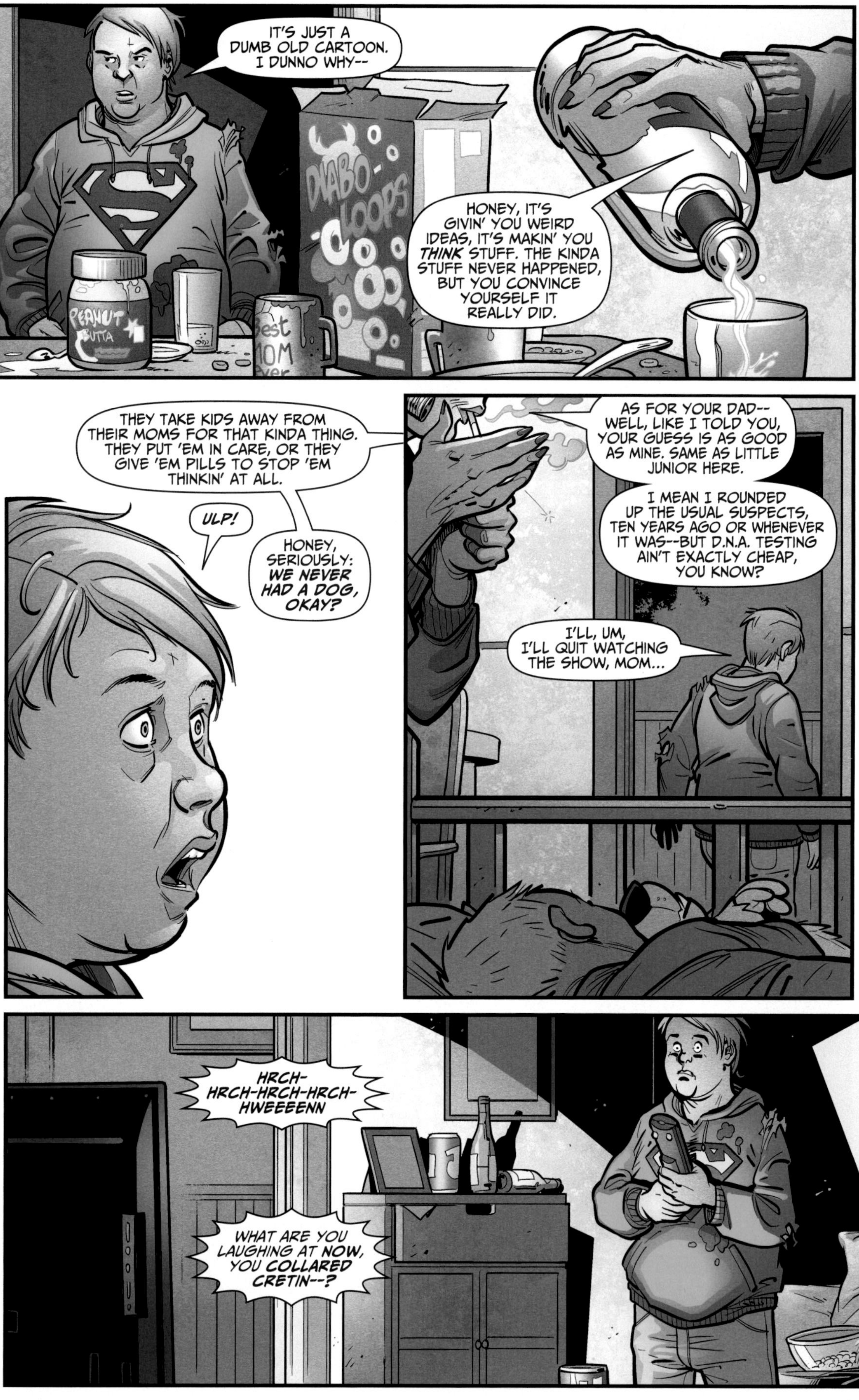

IT'S JUST A DUMB OLD CARTOON. I DUNNO WHY--
DIABO-LOOPS
HONEY, IT'S GIVIN' YOU WEIRD IDEAS, IT'S MAKIN' YOU *THINK* STUFF. THE KINDA STUFF NEVER HAPPENED, BUT YOU CONVINCE YOURSELF IT REALLY DID.
PEANUT BUTTA
Best MOM Ever
THEY TAKE KIDS AWAY FROM THEIR MOMS FOR THAT KINDA THING. THEY PUT 'EM IN CARE, OR THEY GIVE 'EM PILLS TO STOP 'EM THINKIN' AT ALL.
ULP!
HONEY, SERIOUSLY: ***WE NEVER HAD A DOG, OKAY?***
AS FOR YOUR DAD-- WELL, LIKE I TOLD YOU, YOUR GUESS IS AS GOOD AS MINE. SAME AS LITTLE JUNIOR HERE.
I MEAN I ROUNDED UP THE USUAL SUSPECTS, TEN YEARS AGO OR WHENEVER IT WAS--BUT D.N.A. TESTING AIN'T EXACTLY CHEAP, YOU KNOW?
I'LL, UM, I'LL QUIT WATCHING THE SHOW, MOM...
HRCH-HRCH-HRCH-HRCH-HWEEEENN
*WHAT ARE YOU LAUGHING AT **NOW**, YOU **COLLARED CRETIN**--?*

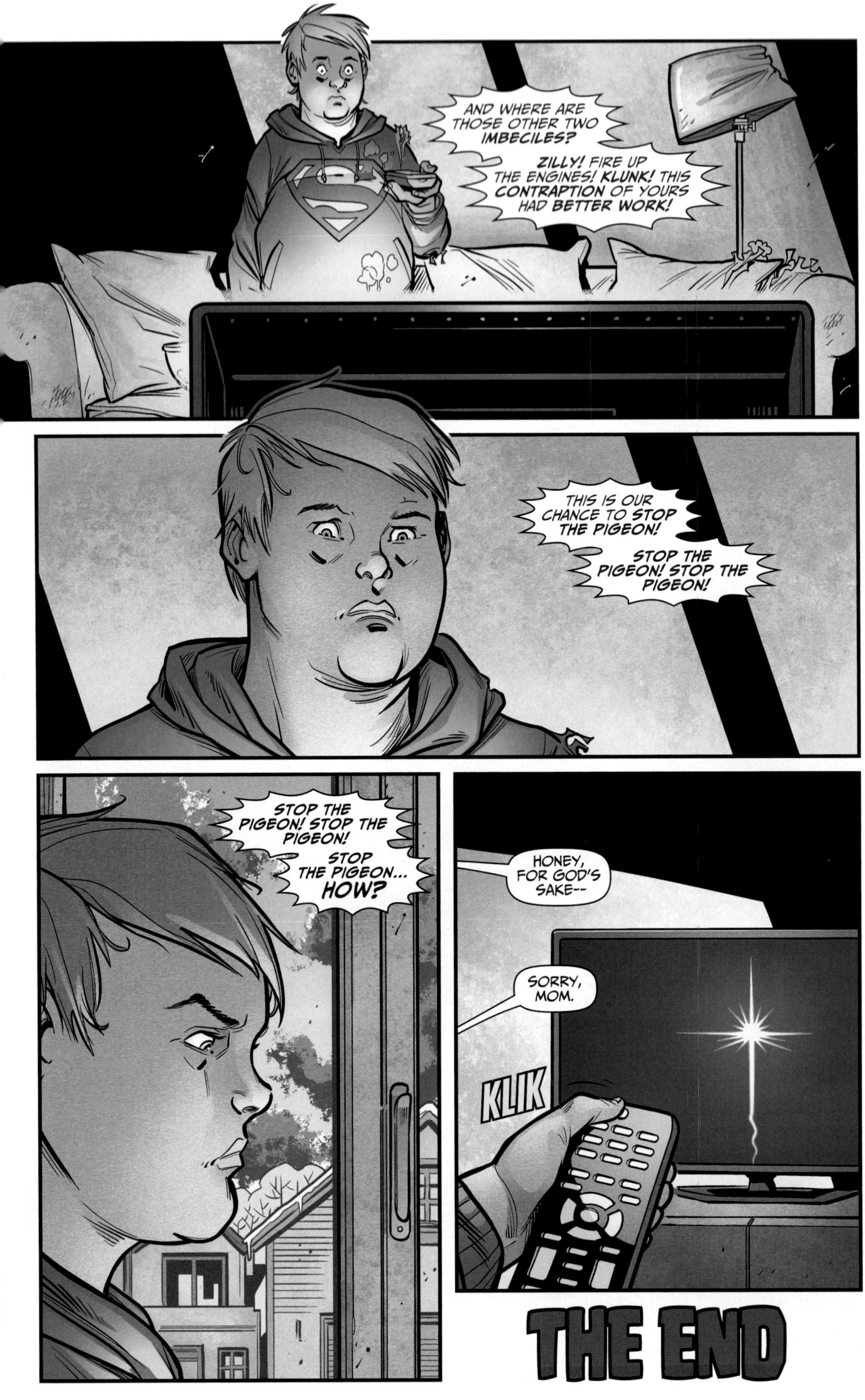
AND WHERE ARE THOSE OTHER TWO IMBECILES?
ZILLY! FIRE UP THE ENGINES! KLUNK! THIS CONTRAPTION OF YOURS HAD BETTER WORK!
THIS IS OUR CHANCE TO STOP THE PIGEON!
STOP THE PIGEON! STOP THE PIGEON!
STOP THE PIGEON! STOP THE PIGEON!
STOP THE PIGEON... HOW?
HONEY, FOR GOD'S SAKE--
SORRY, MOM.
KLIK
THE END

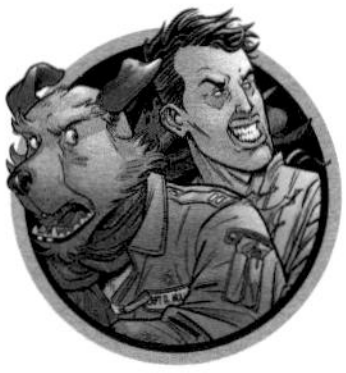

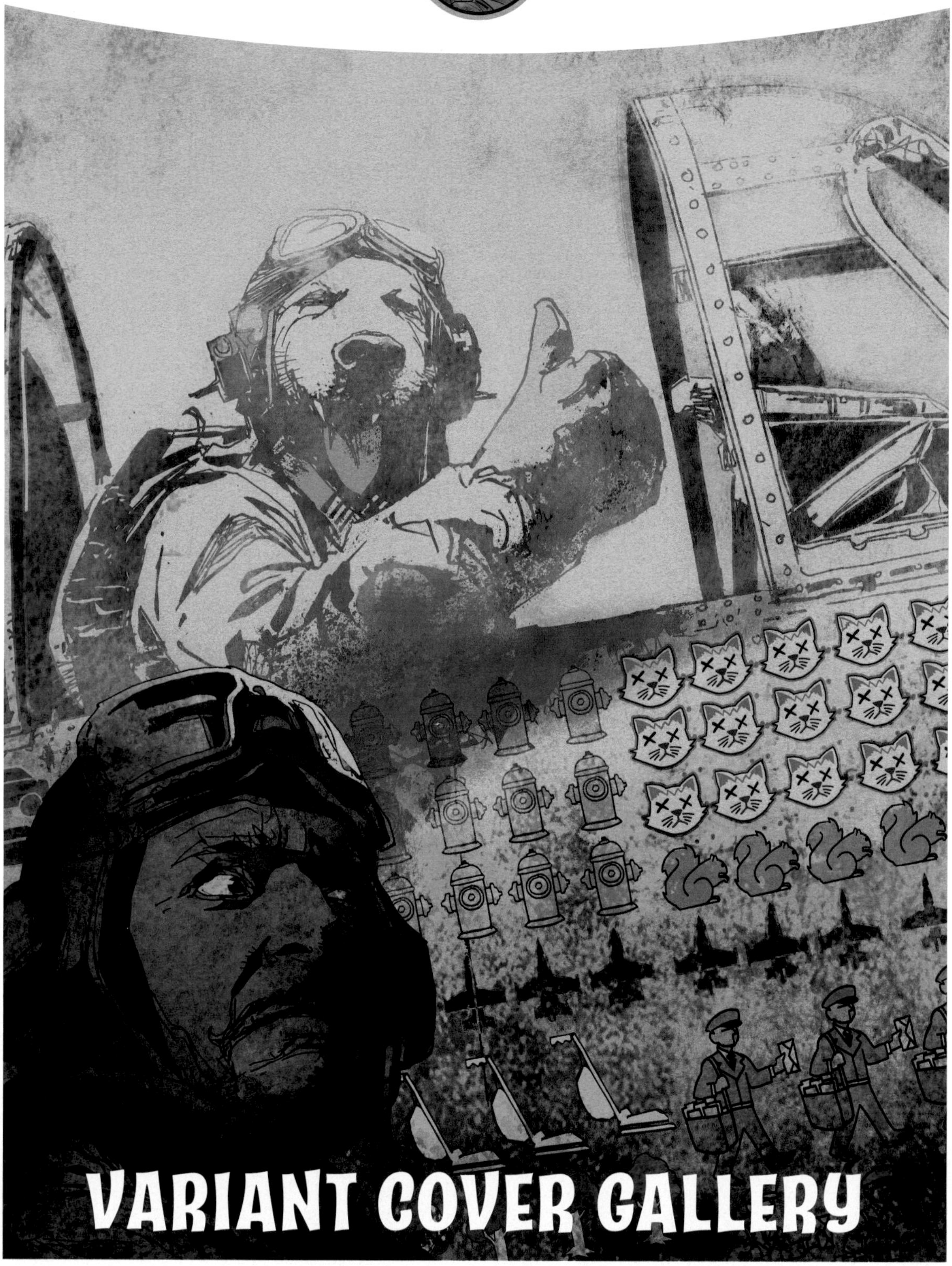

VARIANT COVER GALLERY

Variant cover art for issue #1 by LIAM SHARP

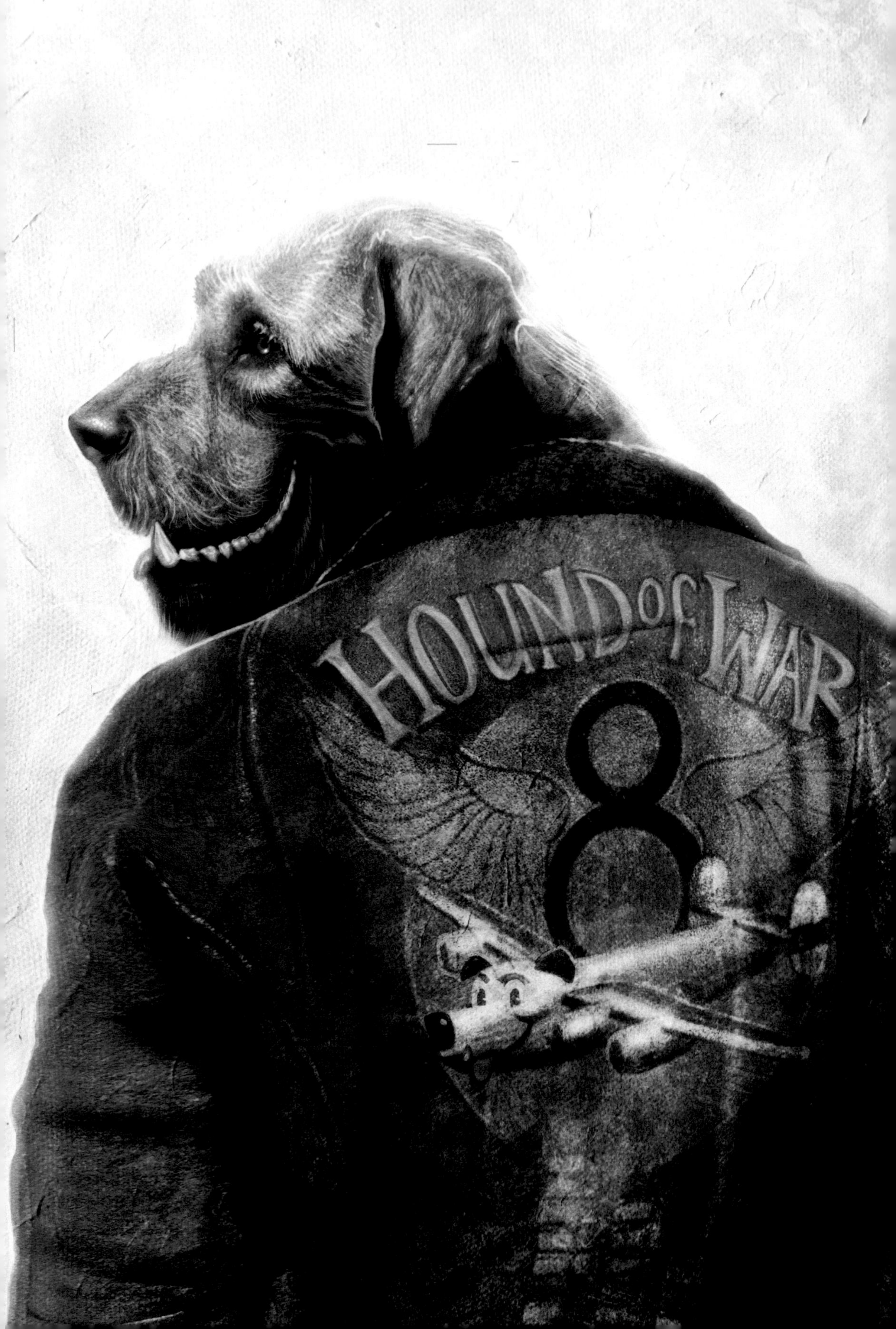
HOUND of WAR
8

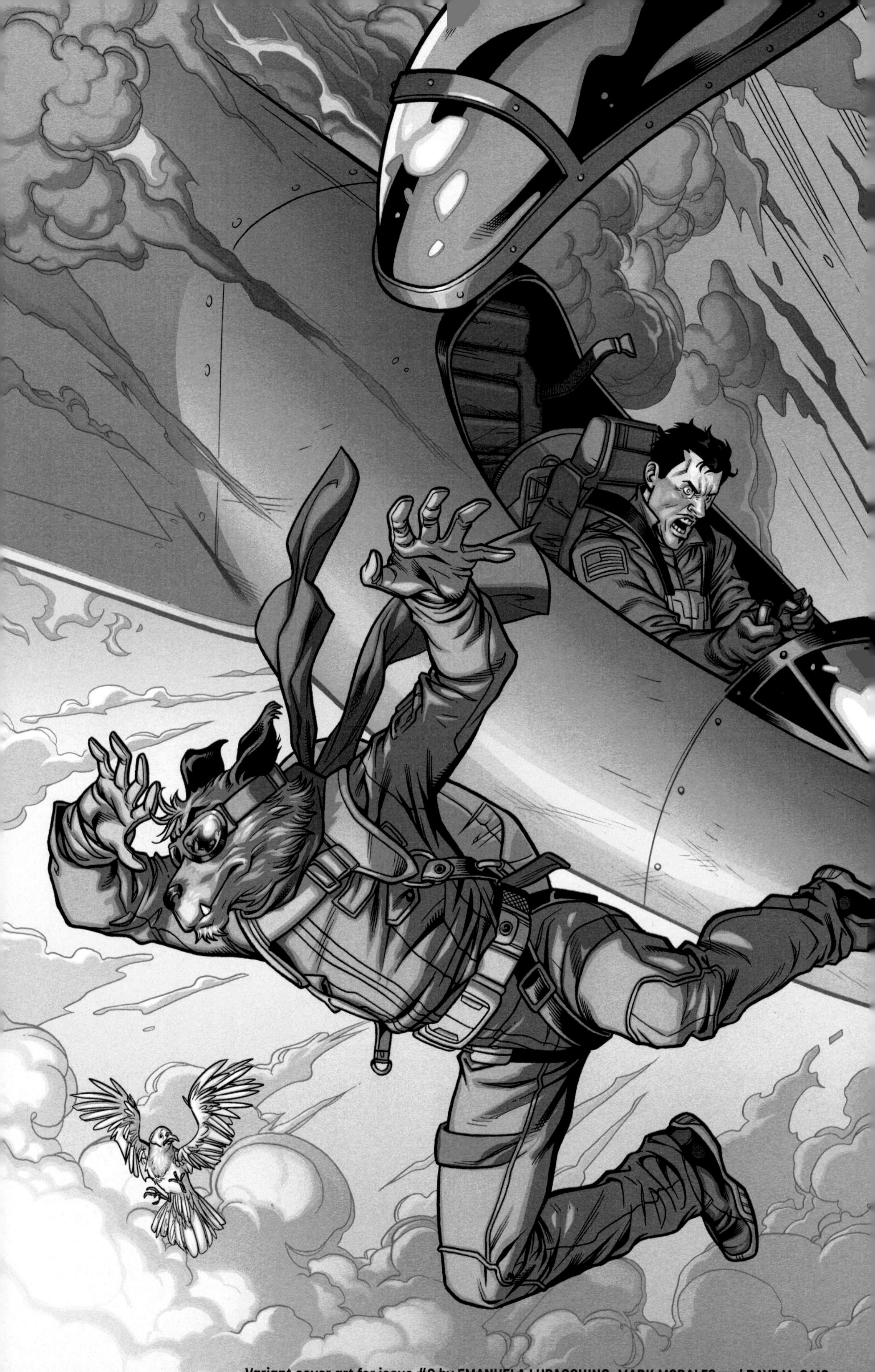

Variant cover art for issue #2 by EMANUELA LUPACCHINO, MARK MORALES and DAVE McCAIG

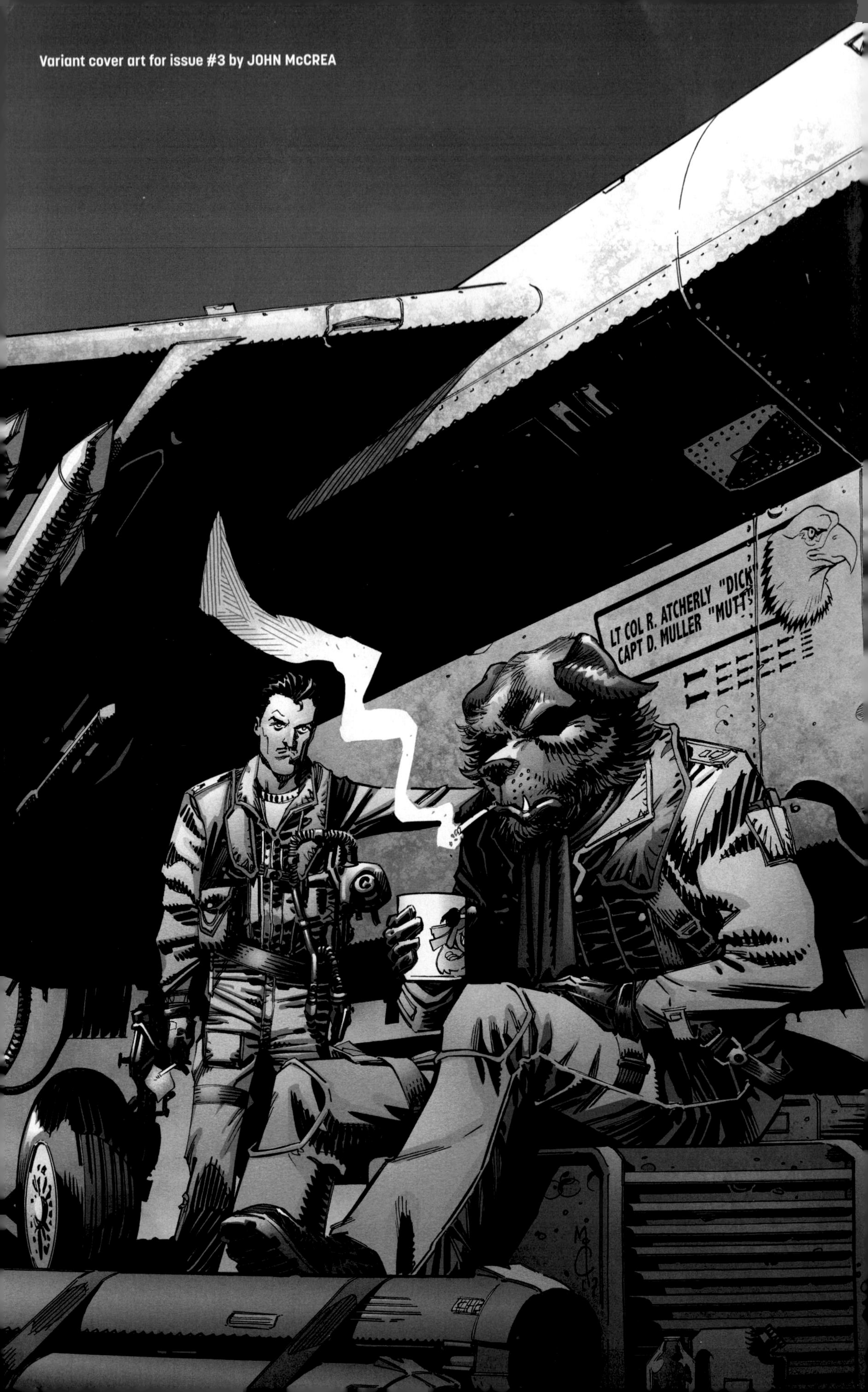
LT COL R. ATCHERLY "DICK"
CAPT D. MULLER "MUTT"

Variant cover art for issue #3 by JOHN McCREA

Variant cover art for issue #4 by STEVE PUGH

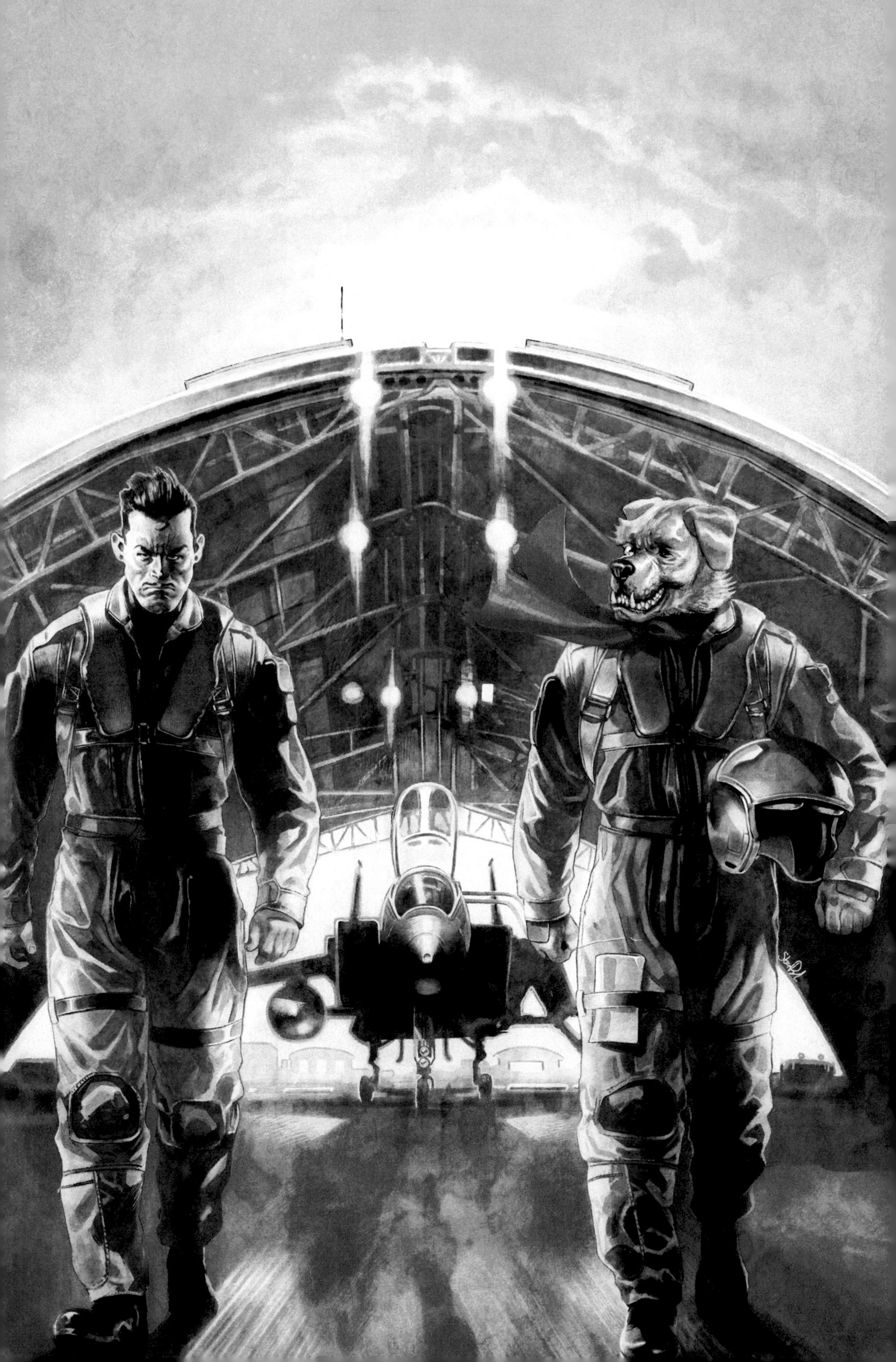

Variant cover art for issue #5 by HOWARD CHAYKIN and WIL QUINTANA

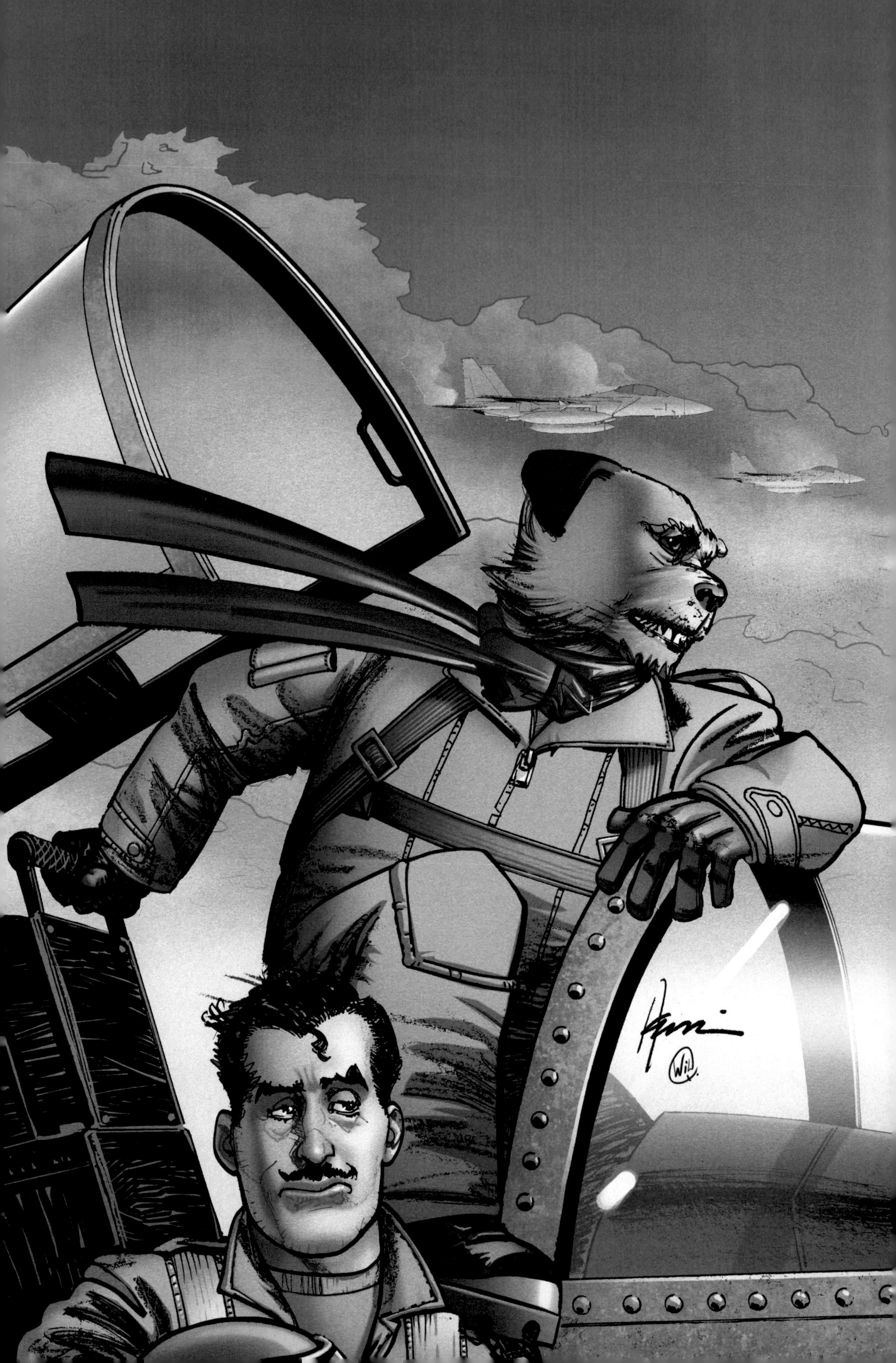

Variant cover art for issue #6 by BILL SIENKIEWICZ

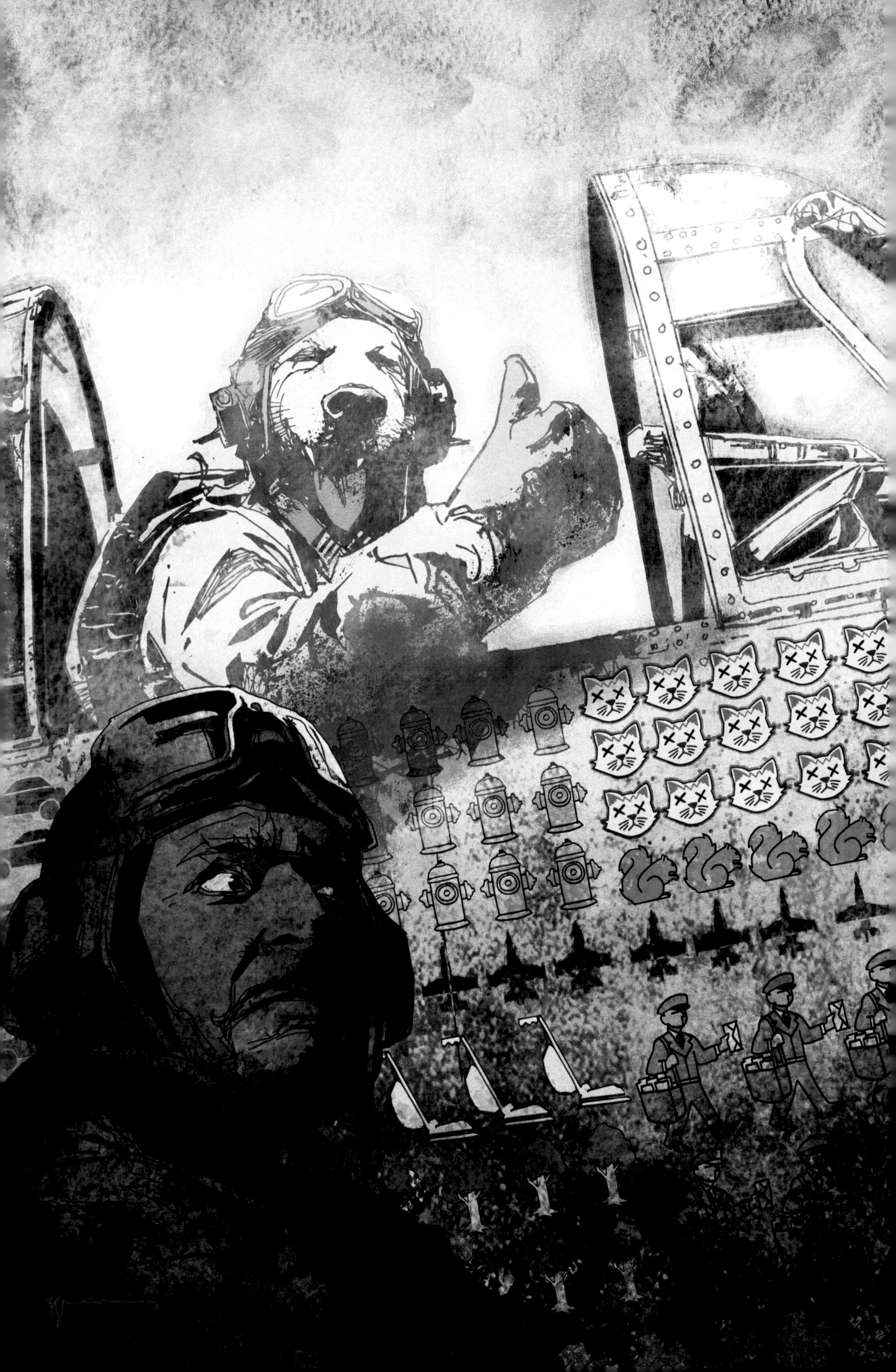

DRAW THAT PIGEON!
Character designs and sketches by MAURICET

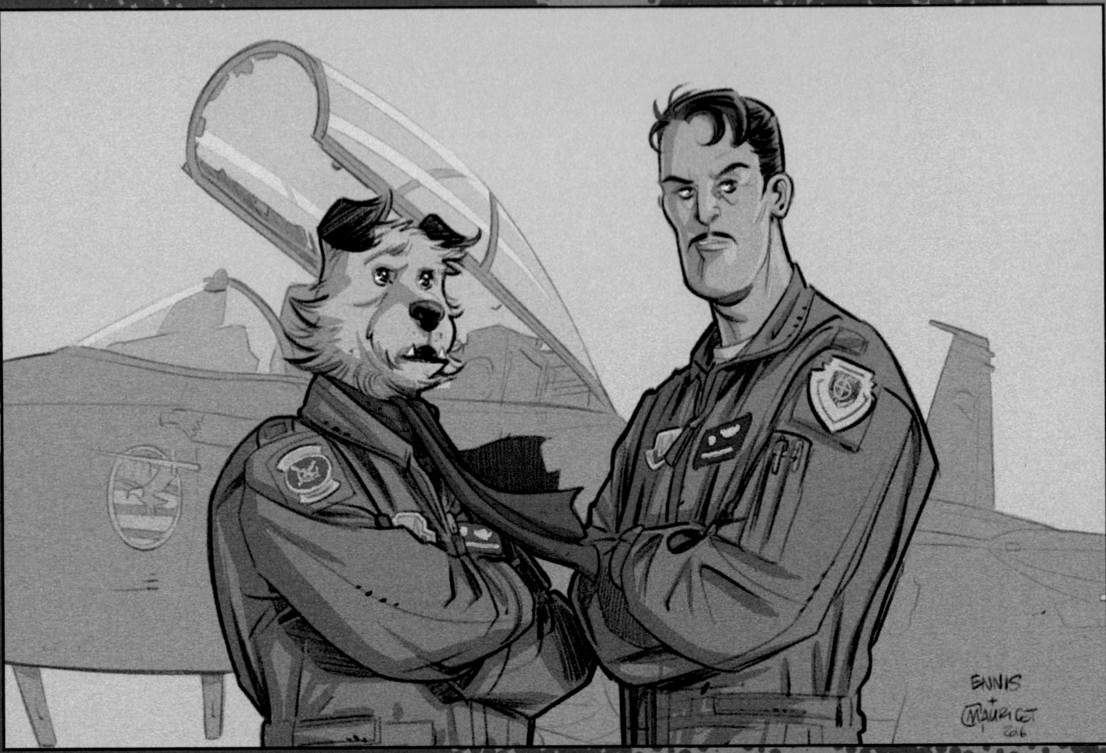
ENNIS
+
MAURICET
2016

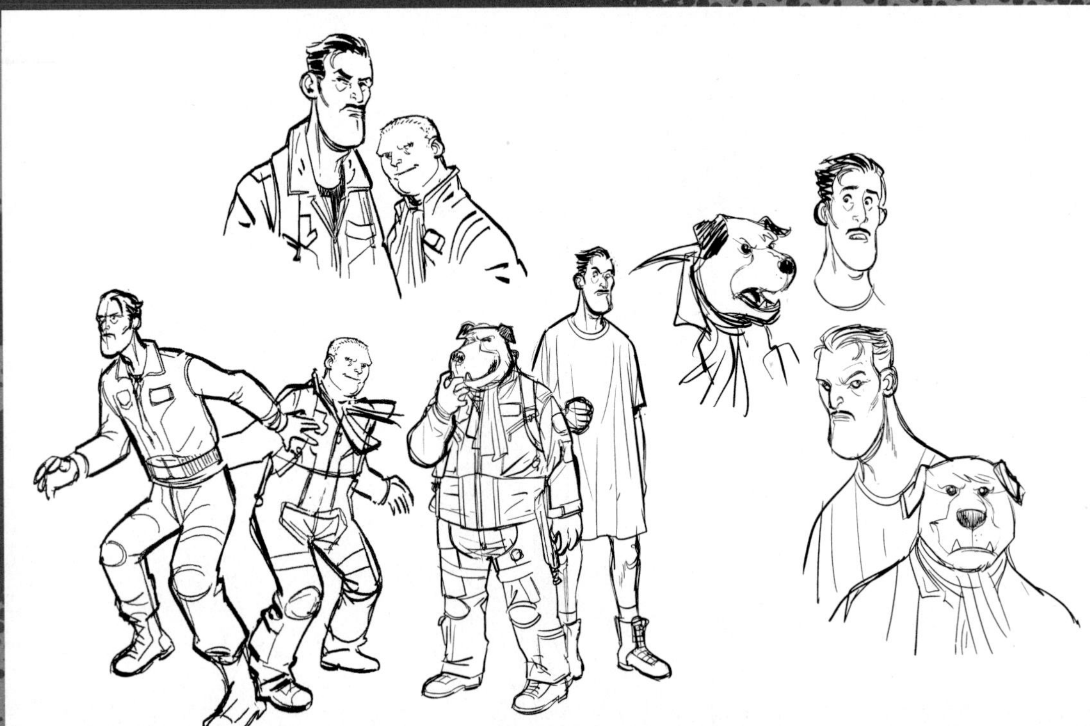

DASTARDLY & MUTTLEY #3

I'LL BE GONE WHEN THE MORNING COMES.

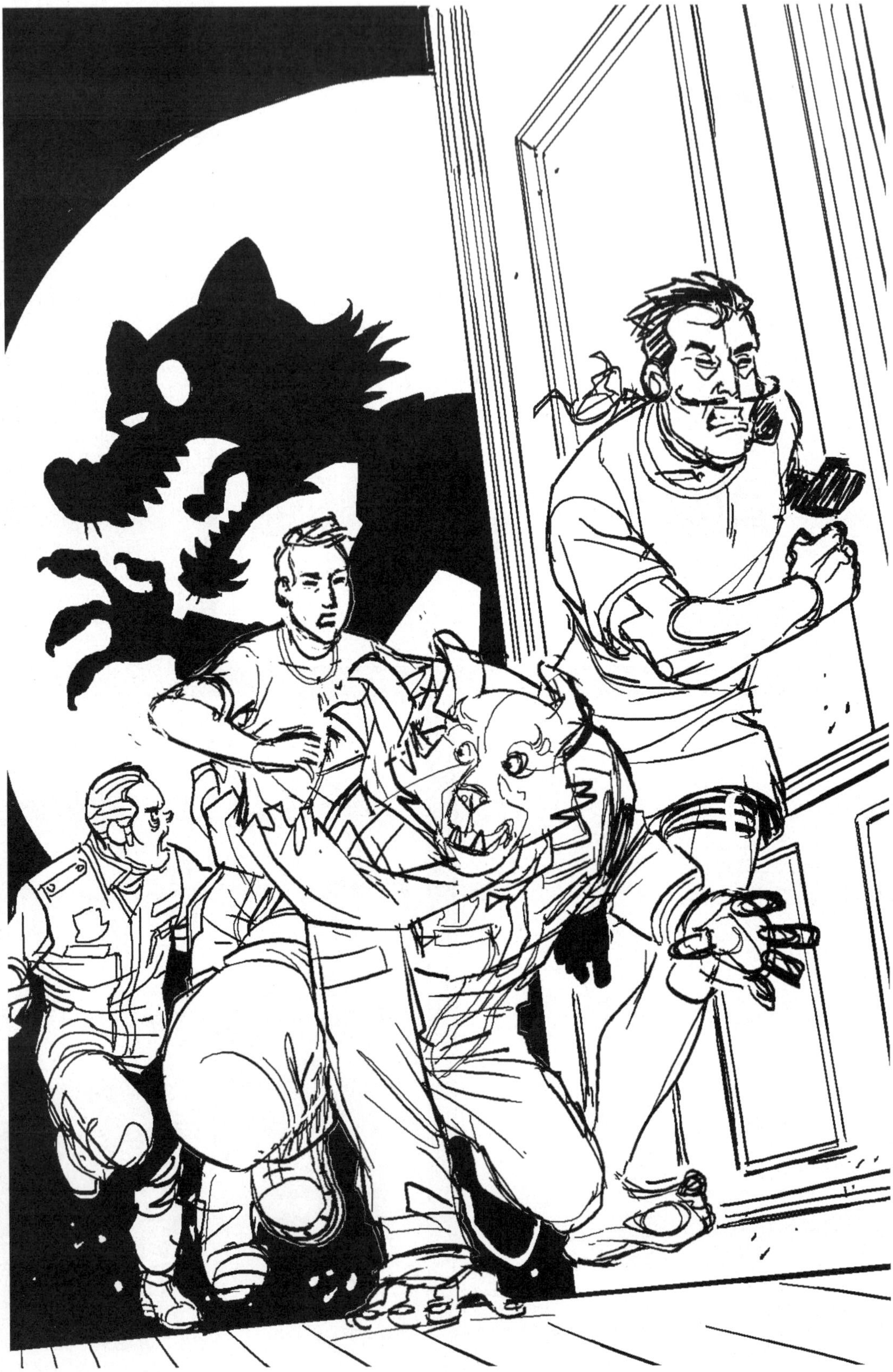

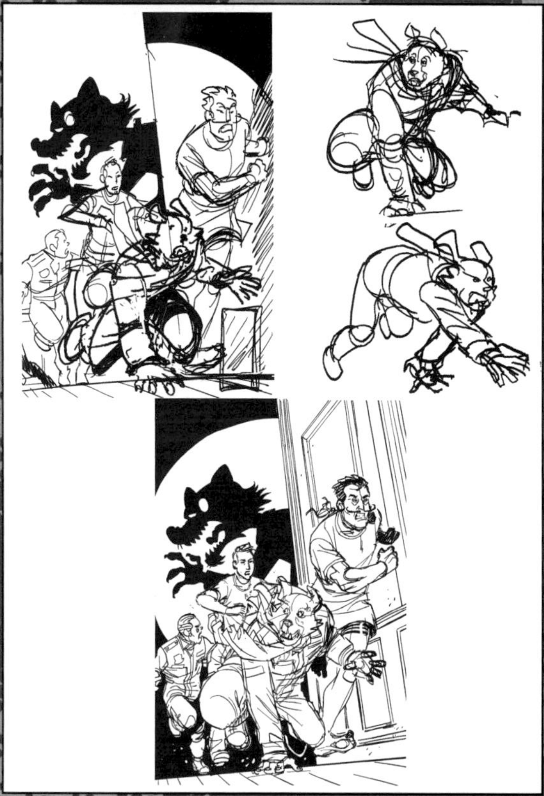

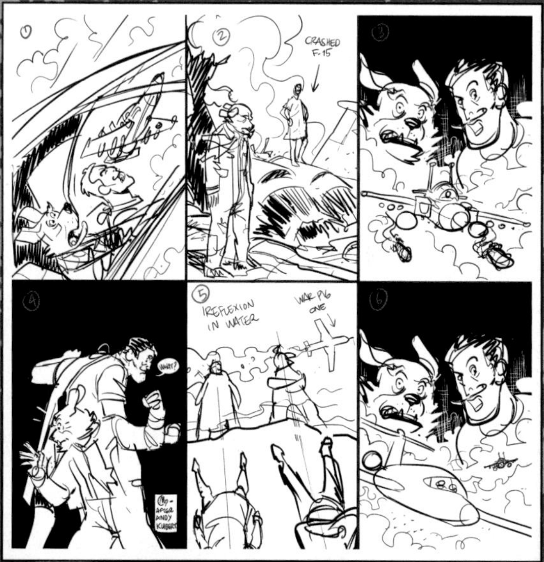
1
2
CRASHED F-15
3
4
WHAT?
AFTER ANDY KUBERT
5
IREFLEXION IN WATER
WAR PIG ONE
6

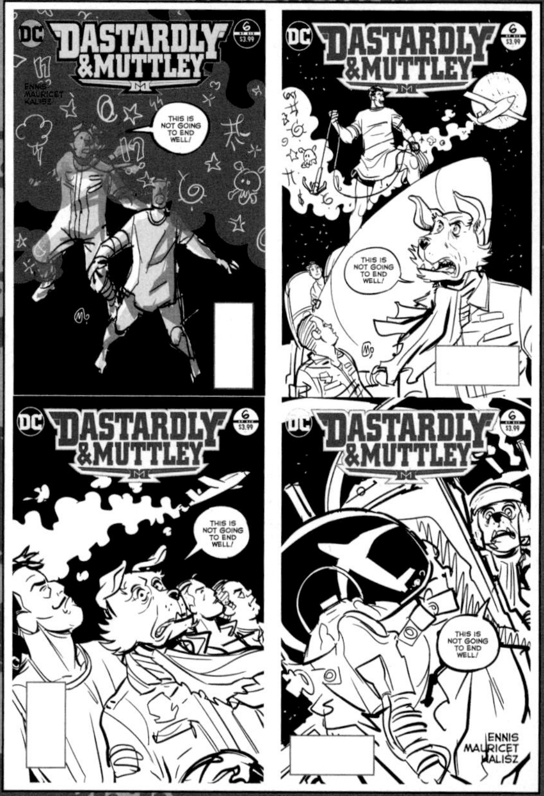
DC
DASTARDLY & MUTTLEY
6
$3.99
ENNIS MAURICET KALISZ
THIS IS NOT GOING TO END WELL!
DC
DASTARDLY & MUTTLEY
6
$3.99
THIS IS NOT GOING TO END WELL!
DC
DASTARDLY & MUTTLEY
6
$3.99
THIS IS NOT GOING TO END WELL!
DC
DASTARDLY & MUTTLEY
6
$3.99
THIS IS NOT GOING TO END WELL!
ENNIS MAURICET KALISZ

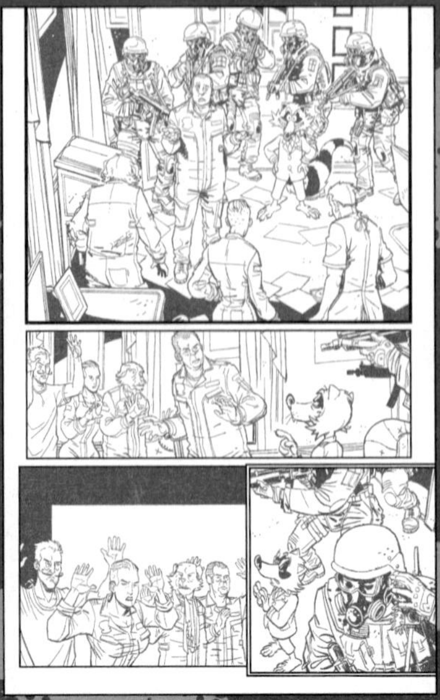

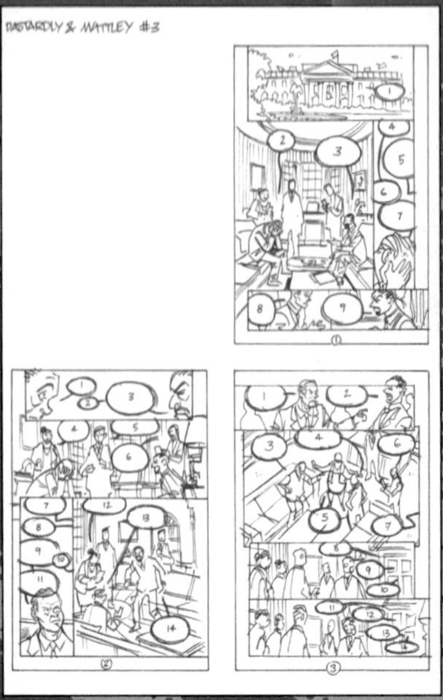
DASTARDLY & MUTTLEY #3

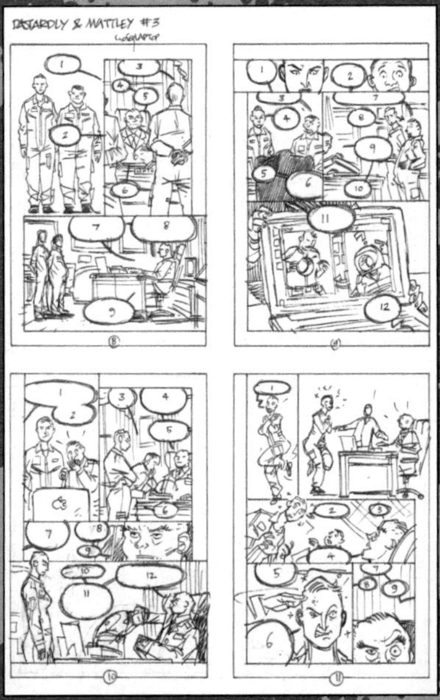
DASTARDLY & MUTTLEY #3

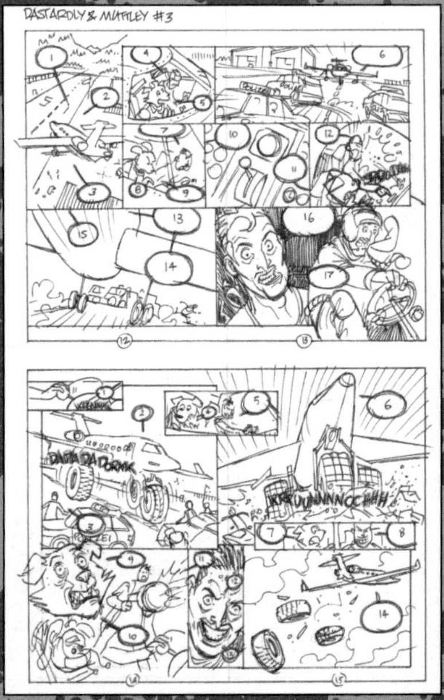
DASTARDLY & MUTTLEY #3

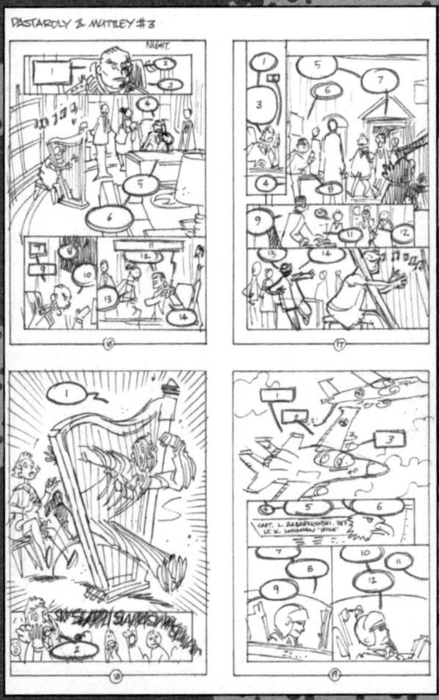
DASTARDLY & MUTTLEY #3
NIGHT

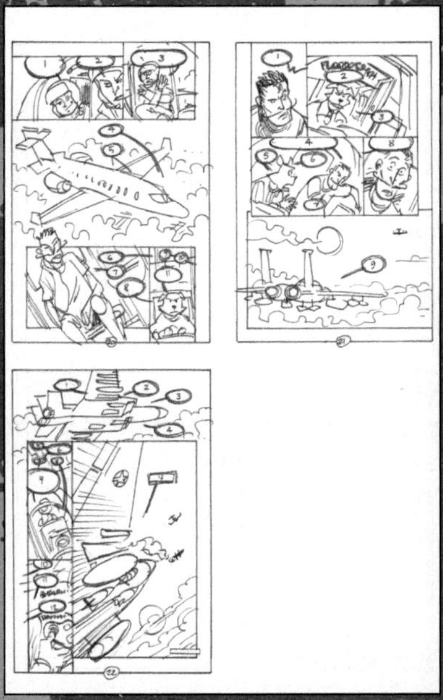